French Caricature
and the
French Revolution, 1789–1799

French Caricature
and the
French Revolution, 1789–1799

Grunwald Center for the Graphic Arts
Wight Art Gallery
University of California, Los Angeles

Published in conjunction with an exhibition co-organized by the University of California, Los Angeles,
and the Bibliothèque nationale de France, Paris, as part of 1789–1989,
The French Revolution: A UCLA Bicentennial Program

Major support for the catalogue and exhibition has been provided
by the National Endowment for the Humanities.

The catalogue has been published with the assistance of
the Getty Grant Program.

Printed in the United States.

This catalogue has been published in conjunction with the exhibition *Politics and Polemics: French Caricature and the French Revolution, 1789-1799*. A French edition of the catalogue, entitled *Politique et polémique: La Caricature française et la Révolution, 1789-1799*, has also been published by the Grunwald Center for the Graphic Arts, Wight Art Gallery, University of California, Los Angeles. Exhibition schedule: Wight Art Gallery, University of California, Los Angeles, 1 November–18 December 1988; The Grey Art Gallery and Study Center, New York University, 15 January–20 February 1989; Bibliothèque nationale de France, Paris, 15 March–30 April 1989; Musée de la Révolution française, Vizille, 1 June–20 July 1989.

Albert Boime's essay originally appeared in *Arts Magazine* 62, no. 6 (February 1988), and it is published here in a slightly different form with permission of the editors of that journal. Klaus Herding's essay was previously published in 1988 as "Visuelle Zeichensysteme in der Graphik der Französischen Revolution," in *Die Französische Revolution als Bruch des gesellschaftlichen Bewusstseins: Vorlagen und Diskussionen der internationalen Arbeitstagung am Zentrum für interdisziplinäre Forschung der Universität der Bielefeld, 28. Mai–1. Juni 1985.* It appears here in English for the first time and has been published with the permission of R. Oldenbourg Verlag, Munich.

Library of Congress Cataloging-in-Publication Data

French Caricature and the French Revolution, 1789-1799.
     p.   cm.
     "Published in conjunction with an exhibition co-organized by the University of California, Los Angeles, and the Bibliothèque nationale de France as part of *1789-1989*, The French Revolution: A UCLA Bicentennial Program."
     Bibliography: p.
     ISBN 0-943739-06-3. ISBN 0-943739-05-5 (pbk.)
     1. France — History — Revolution, 1789-1799 — Caricatures and cartoons — Exhibitions. 2. French wit and humor, Pictorial — Exhibitions. 3. France — History — Revolution, 1789-1799 — Art and the revolution — Exhibitions. I. Grunwald Center for the Graphic Arts. II. University of California, Los Angeles. III. France. Bibliothèque nationale.
     DC149.5.F75 1988
     944.04 — dc19   88-16559
                                  CIP

ISBN 0-943739-05-5 [paper]
     0-943739-06-3 [cloth]

Distributed by the University of Chicago Press, Chicago 60637

Cover: Anonymous French. *Louis seize (Louis XVI)*, 1792, after Joseph Boze. (Cat. no. 65).

Back Cover: Philibert-Louis Debucourt (French, 1755-1832). *La Paix/ à Bonaparte pacificateur/dix huit brumaire (Peace/to Bonaparte the Peacemaker/Eighteenth of Brumaire)*, 1801. (Cat. no. 187).

Designers	Thomas Hartman, Robin Weisz
Editor	Lynne Hockman
Production Coordinator	Judy Hale
Printing	Alan Lithograph
Typesetting	Central Typesetting Company

Produced by UCLA Publication Services Department

Contents

Forewords

Long overshadowed by rival British caricature and by the art of Daumier and other later artists, French political caricature of the revolutionary era is little known outside France. Yet it should obviously claim our intellectual attention, and much of it may still have a claim upon our emotions. Often grotesque, as in the British mode, this caricature is also uniquely disturbing and eerie. Perhaps this is so because it emerged day by day from the shattering Parisian clash of revolutionary joy and revolutionary violence.

During the 1790s political caricature, whether funny or vicious, was constantly exploited by the various factions pitted against each other. All kinds of prints could be purchased at printshops on the rue Saint-Jacques, among the porticoes of the Palais-Royal, or from street hawkers. Unlike patriotic and religious allegories or formal portraits, caricatures were obviously purchased for their topicality and bite. They snapped at both the humble and the highly placed; their targets were well defined, though their technique was often naive and crude. Yet much of what is rough-hewn and even clumsy in this art bears the mark, not simply of haste, but of historical shock. Surely this, if anything, links us to those anonymous French citizens who, for a penny or two, purchased these images. For taken together, they suggest what was then and still is a common apprehension of history as something grotesquely grand and frighteningly jumbled, running at fatal speed.

Whatever we may feel and however we may judge these images, the experience of looking at them has been made possible at UCLA by the unfailing support that former Executive Vice-Chancellor William D. Schaefer and Chancellor Charles E. Young have given our work. We have also been fortunate to find in Paris, not only all the prints here presented, but also the charm and efficiency of Madame Laure Beaumont-Maillet, Director of the Cabinet des estampes at the Bibliothèque nationale. Her kindness and sense of humor have made our collaboration a constant pleasure. Our desire to present popular images of the Revolution has been shaped by the clear ideas of many American and European colleagues, but these ideas would not have been refined into reality

without the guiding intelligence of Professor James Cuno, our curator. It is he who has given these images of the French Revolution, now two hundred years later, another public life.

To the University of California, Los Angeles, to the Bibliothèque nationale de France, and to the National Endowment for the Humanities, we express our deepest appreciation for encouragement, advice, and financial support. To all visitors, in America and in France, we extend our wish that you may have as much pleasure in viewing this exhibition as we had in organizing it.

Robert M. Maniquis
Director
1789–1989, The French Revolution: A UCLA Bicentennial Program

---

The exhibition that we are presenting on revolutionary caricature begins, as it should, well before the significant "episode" of 1789. At the beginning of the exhibition, the condemnation or the expulsion of the Society of Jesus, which began as early as the 1760s, is evoked. This unusual action, accomplished by the Parlement with the more or less forced approval of the monarchy, undoubtedly represents the first indication of anti-clericalism in the political and social life of the nation, even if those responsible for the decision in question had not initially conceived it in this spirit.

Representations of the fight for independence in North America, which chronologically followed this "anti-Jesuit" iconography, reflect one of the most successful and, at the same time "dangerous," acts of Louis XVI's reign. There was, as a result of this policy, an opening up toward social and human progress as represented by the Revolution across the Atlantic; but the monarchy also incurred considerable debt with dire, if not almost fatal, financial consequences. These events prepared, for better or for worse, the decisive year at the end of which the Old Regime would disappear.

Some of the engravings shown in the exhibition compel the viewer to reenter the now familiar world of the three functions defined by Georges Dumézil: religion, war, and production or economic "fecundity." In a still Bourbon France, the classes corresponding to these "rules" were the clergy, the nobility, and the Third Estate. As one caricature indicates (cat. no. 27), this last group often expressed itself virulently: "It was about time I woke up because the oppression of my shackles gave me terrible nightmares," cries a commoner under the frightened eyes of a priest and of a nobleman who observe him at the very moment when his chains are about to break.

A little later, the aristocratic Hydra—under the aegis of the Bastille, which is destined to be destroyed—refers to the general diabolization of the nobility (cat. nos. 25, 26). As a result of this process, a great number of persons of modest origin perished on the scaffold, people to whom, rightly or wrongly, aristocratic opinions were attributed, though not a single drop of blue blood flowed in their veins.

A surprising engraving, *A bas les impiots* (cat. no. 35), could well, almost to the last detail, illustrate a scene of the seventeenth century: for it is well-known to what extent anti-fiscal revolts were typical of the reigns of Louis XIII and Louis XIV, far more so than that of the unfortunate Louis XVI.

Since we refer here to the classical era, we should add that Molière's medicine is not far removed from the preoccupations of our artists: enemas, if not bloodletting, flourished almost everywhere, primarily directed at the posteriors of ecclesiastics, some of whom, so we are told, had committed the sin of rejecting the new ideas; they therefore had to be forced to comply.

In my role as a historian specializing in the Old Regime, I find myself in a state of communion and familiarity with the caricatures that illustrate the agony of an old system. In contrast, the revolutionary decade is not as closely related to my own research activities. Shall I admit that, in our fortunate era when the death penalty has been abolished, the image of the hand that held Louis Capet's dripping head up to the mob (cat. no. 90) does not evoke for me the most attractive aspect of the admirable drama of the ten years from 1789 to 1799?

The agonistic theme of the freedom of the press, of course, arouses altogether positive feelings, even if, as is well known, the expression and publication of the most diverse opinions would only be fully realized in the newspapers of the ultraliberal Third Republic.

Permit me to conclude on a note of outright affection and to express my predilection for Charlotte Corday, who is amiably illustrated here. The heroine from Caen showed herself to be at once in favor of liberties (she professed Girondist opinions) and against the Terror (she thought, not without malicious exaggeration, that it was her duty to annihilate Marat, whom she abhorred). But here, needless to say, I have gone beyond the limits of the remarks permissible to a professional scholar. One should not choose sides but describe the facts, better yet, construct models of them. I am persuaded that both this beautiful collection of caricatures and the forthcoming exhibition of revolutionary treasures belonging to the Bibliothèque nationale, will permit many writers, intellectuals, and cultured persons, as well as historians, to bring to the Revolution the enlightened and objective judgment that it deserves from a distance of two centuries. Whatever it may be, this judgment will have to respect the diversity of attitudes and political, ideological, and philosophical positions that characterize the open pluralism of the end of our century.

Emmanuel Le Roy Ladurie
Professor of the Collège de France
General Administrator of the Bibliothèque nationale de France

———————

It is with great pleasure and pride that we present the exhibition *Politics and Polemics: French Caricature and the French Revolution, 1789–1799*, organized at the Wight Art Gallery by the Grunwald Center for the Graphic Arts in celebration of the Bicentennial of the French Revolution.

It was over three years ago that Professor Robert Maniquis of the UCLA English Department came to the gallery with the idea of organizing an exhibition to celebrate the Bicentennial. As a professor of literature, he was interested in gathering images that would help to illuminate the political, cultural, and social climate of late eighteenth-century France. Very early in the process of organizing the exhibition, we were fortunate to obtain the commitment of James Cuno, initially as a guest curator and later as Director of the Grunwald Center for the Graphic Arts.

An interdisciplinary project of this sort, which brings together scholars from many fields of cultural studies, gives meaning and strength to the artistic and educational mission of a university art museum. It is the result of more than two years of planning by Director James Cuno and Curator Cynthia Burlingham of the Grunwald Center. They and the authors of the exhibition catalogue are to be praised for bringing to light both the artistic and art historical significance of French caricature of this period, a study long overdue.

As a central part of *1789 – 1989, The French Revolution: A UCLA Bicentennial Program*, the exhibition has been substantially funded by the university, and we are extremely grateful to Chancellor Charles E. Young for his support. Finally, I must personally thank the directors of the institutions with whom we are sharing this exhibition: Thomas W. Sokolowski of the Grey Art Gallery and Study Center, New York University, Emmanuel Le Roy Ladurie of the Bibliothèque nationale, and Philippe Bordes of the Musée de la Révolution française. Their support of the exhibition and the many contributions made by their respective staffs have been crucial to the success of this project.

Edith A. Tonelli
Director
Wight Art Gallery, UCLA

———————

The Grey Art Gallery and Study Center is proud to host the exhibition *Politics and Polemics: French Caricature and the French Revolution, 1789–1799.* This exhibition will be a highlight of the one and a half year commemoration of the French Revolution held at New York University. *The French Revolution and Its Modern Legacy: A Bicentennial Reappraisal* will include scholarly symposia, lectures, films, radio broadcasts, art exhibitions, and related courses. The program is designed to illuminate the Revolution as it unfolded and to show how profoundly this seminal event has influenced every dimension of human activity in modern times.

Considering the political climate of the late 1980s, as well as the bitterly ironic art that has been created to critique it, an exhibition devoted to eighteenth-century caricature can effectively aid in drawing needed parallels between our own time and the past. As the exhibition and the accompanying catalogue decisively prove, the art of social concern is not limited to reporting the effects of political upheaval; it can also serve as a catalyst to bring about change.

The events of 1789 gain larger importance when viewed as a template for the numerous revolutionary outbursts that followed, not only within the period of the Enlightenment, but in 1830, 1848, 1870, and 1968 as well. The art of revolutionary France proved that formal aesthetics and visual iconography could enter quite ably into the political and social debates, and the fact that these caricatures still retain their sting is evidence of their power.

We are extremely grateful to the Swann Foundation for Caricature and Cartoon for its generous support of the exhibition at the Grey Art Gallery and Study Center.

Thomas W. Sokolowski
Director
The Grey Art Gallery and Study Center
New York University

———————

The Musée de la Révolution française, a young institution located in a historic castle at the foot of the Alps and created on the occasion of the Bicentennial, is very proud to be among the hosts of a project whose authority rests on a thorough program of historical inquiry and on a judicious choice of prints drawn from the many thousand available in the French national collection. After two centuries, the caricatures of the Revolution are once again being taken seriously. Perhaps more vividly than any other visual trace of this intensely active period, these prints capture the extraordinary energy unleashed to change the course of history. Usually viewed as marginalia to the more imposing forms of artistic production, these compositions, fueled by political conviction and formal invention, fully merit the closer scrutiny that they are given here.

Taking his cue from the social historian, the art historian notes the varied and irreconcilable array of stylistic options and creative tools that can characterize a single period. There is no need to lament the possible menace this open attitude might represent to the more usual and conventional preoccupations with high art. A keen awareness of the complexity and vitality of popular expression and of the pressure it exerted on political and aesthetic consciousness of the revolutionary years is surely necessary for a better understanding of the emergent conceptions of modern art, which by comparison seem to have restrained both invention and audience. Happily, a revealing enterprise such as the present exhibition confirms our faith in the future of a museum whose ambition is not only to collect, preserve, and exhibit prime examples of the visual creations of the Revolution but to reinscribe a decisive decade of artistic production, mostly "deleted" from the history of art, within the mainstream of a neat succession of periods and styles—even if this means disrupting the steady course of the familiar flow.

Philippe Bordes
Director
Musée de la Révolution française, Vizille

Acknowledgments

During the French Revolution, printed images formed a highly polemical visual discourse intent on establishing the bases for a new social and political consensus. It is for this reason that we have chosen to commemorate the Bicentennial of the French Revolution with an exhibition of prints produced in France during this vital period. In so doing, we have been privileged to draw upon the incomparably rich collections of historical and satirical prints in the Cabinet des estampes of the Bibliothèque nationale. Nowhere else can one examine in such breadth and depth the competing ambitions of the many political and social factions that contributed to the emerging self-image of revolutionary France.

Numerous individuals, in addition to our authors, have contributed significantly to this publication and to the exhibition, and they should be acknowledged here. First and foremost, Robert Maniquis, Director, *1789–1989, The French Revolution, A* UCLA *Bicentennial Program*, has been involved with the organization of the exhibition since its very inception. It was he who first contacted the Bibliothèque nationale and secured for UCLA the right to draw upon its extraordinary holdings of revolutionary caricatures and historical prints, and he has continued to work closely with us in making the final arrangements for the exhibition. Laure Beaumont-Maillet, Director, Cabinet des estampes, Bibliothèque nationale, has extended every courtesy in supporting the exhibition. She has always been available with her time, her advice, and her thorough knowledge of the collections under her charge. We are extremely grateful to her and to Robert Maniquis for their considerable efforts on our behalf. We also wish to acknowledge Andrée Pouderoux of the Service des expositions extérieures, who assisted with every aspect of the organization of the loans.

Two generous grants from the National Endowment for the Humanities permitted us to proceed with the planning and implementation of the exhibition. The first—written under the direction of Edith A. Tonelli, Director, Wight Art Gallery, with the assistance of Katherine Hart, former Assistant Curator, and Carol Heepke, former Director of Education and Community Development, Wight Art Gallery—brought us together at Columbia University for a planning meeting with Carl Woodring of that university, Linda Nochlin of the Graduate Center of the City University of New York, Ronald Paulson of the Johns Hopkins University, and Claude Langlois of the Université de Rouen. The results of that meeting were later refined in a discussion with Lynn Hunt of the University of Pennsylvania. The second National Endowment for the Humanities grant was written with the assistance of Karen Chorpening, Administrative Assistant, and Thomas Hartman, Director of Design and Facilities, at the Wight Art Gallery. Their role in preparing the grant application was critical, as was the participation of Connie Whitley and Fernando Acosta of UCLA's Office of Contract and Grant Administration. Patricia Capps, Administrative Manager, and Cindi Dale, Director of Education and Community Development, at the Wight Art Gallery, have also been essential to the success of the exhibition, and we wish to thank them very much for their efforts, as always.

Additional support for the exhibition has been granted by the Swann Foundation for Caricature and Cartoon, and we would like to thank Alan M. Fern and Henry J. Goldschmidt, trustees of the Foundation, for their full support. Arlette Crandall, College of Fine Arts, UCLA, who is the Executive Director of the Southern Californian Committee on the French Revolution, has provided much advice and numerous contacts, and we are deeply indebted to her. She introduced us to Bernard Miyet, Consul General of France in Los Angeles, who has given much time and advice and facilitated many of the last minute details of the exhibition and its accompanying symposia. Alexandre Tolstoi, Cultural Attaché of the French Cultural Services in Los Angeles, and Dr. Ruzena Berler, President of the Alliance Française of Beverly Hills, have also been very generous in their support of the exhibition, as has Air France, which provided essential transportation to Los Angeles of our European authors and symposia participants.

Our research in Europe was assisted by Françoise Juestaz and François Fossier, curators in the Cabinet des estampes of the Bibliothèque nationale, and their able staff; Michel Melot and

Christian Derouet of the Centre Georges Pompidou; Henri Zerner of Harvard University; Claude Langlois of the Université de Rouen; Werner Hofmann of the Hamburger Kunsthalle; Patricia Rubin of the Courtauld Institute; Charles Robertson of the Oxford Polytechnic; and the staff of the Print Room of the British Museum. We thank them very much for their many valuable contributions. They made the long and often lonely hours of library research warm and enjoyable, even possible.

The catalogue is the result of significant contributions by many colleagues and friends. Robert Darnton of Princeton University, Robert Rosenblum of the Institute of Fine Arts, New York University, Thomas Crow of the University of Michigan, John O'Brian of the University of British Columbia, Deborah Marrow of the J. Paul Getty Trust, and Penny Kaiserlian, Karen Wilson, and Emily Young of the University of Chicago Press all provided much-needed and timely assistance throughout its preparation. Lisa Harries of the Universität Hamburg translated Klaus Herding's essay from the original German. The translations of the essays by Michel Melot and Claude Langlois into English and the translation of the entire English catalogue to produce the French edition are the work of Monique Roy and Eric Gans of Moneric Translations, Los Angeles. We thank Monique and Eric for their invaluable advice, perceptive translations, and cool and conscientious work under the fire of fast-approaching press deadlines.

The catalogue was designed and its production supervised by Thomas Hartman of the Wight Art Gallery and Robin Weisz and Judy Hale of UCLA Publications Services. Its appearance is entirely the result of their good judgment and considerable skills; they made the difficult task of creating a book appear easy. Jennifer Gordon, Kay Rough, Rebecca Cramer, and Julie Deichmann of the Grunwald Center contributed critical research and countless clerical skills to the catalogue. They, along with Susan Melton and Maureen McGee of the Grunwald Center—who respectively organized the travel of the exhibition and the care of its objects—and Barbara Sabatine, UCLA Art Council Graduate Curatorial Fellow, made the exhibition and catalogue a truly cooperative venture. Their good humor has been essential to its success.

In the end, however, two people deserve special recognition. Lynne Hockman has edited the catalogue with extraordinary care and precision. Her forceful queries, infallible memory, and clear sense of literary style have made its text a probing and ele-

gant study, while her patience and good humor have made the task of preparing it a much-valued experience. And Cynthia Burlingham, Curator of the Grunwald Center, has, as with every project on which we have worked together, given fully of her time, talents, and friendship. She has managed every aspect of the production of this catalogue with tremendous skill and dedication, and I owe her a great debt of gratitude. No one has given more to this catalogue than Cindy or Lynne.

Finally, I acknowledge Sarah, Claire, and Kate, who have sacrificed much for the success of this project. Their support has been constant and sustaining.

James Cuno
Director
Grunwald Center for the Graphic Arts, UCLA

Introduction

The historian of the French Revolution . . . must produce more than proof of competence. He must show his colours. He must state from the outset where he comes from, what he thinks and what he is looking for; what he writes about the French Revolution is assigned a meaning and label even before he starts working: the writing is taken as his *opinion*, a form of judgement that is not required when dealing with the Merovingians but indispensable when it comes to treating 1789 or 1793. As soon as the historian states that opinion, the matter is settled; he is labelled a royalist, a liberal or a Jacobin. Once he has given the password his history has a specific meaning, a determined place and a claim to legitimacy.

— François Furet

To write on the polemics and politics of the French Revolution is to throw oneself into a polemical discourse that is itself highly charged with political implications. François Furet's observation, in the form of a lament, quoted above, appears at the beginning of his own position paper on the state of this discourse.[1] His, as he notes at the outset, is "a brief against the communist historians of the French Revolution," by which he means the school of French revolutionary historical studies dominant since 1886 and recently represented by the work of Georges Lefebvre and Albert Soboul.[2] The orthodox tradition, as it is called, maintained that class antagonisms led to a radical break in the order of French society and the founding of a new era marked by the rise of the bourgeoisie and capitalist enterprise. This view was vigorously challenged in 1964 by Alfred Cobban of the University of London, who claimed that "the orthodox theory of the Revolution has now assumed some of the characteristics of a religious belief."[3] He argued against a reading of the Revolution as a radical, social, and economic watershed in French history and claimed rather that those who emerged from the revolutionary period with money, status, or property, for the most part had possessed it before 1789.

At issue for Cobban and other English and American scholars was the whole notion of the Revolution as a bourgeois revolution; they even questioned the extent to which there was any real social conflict between the bourgeoisie and the aristocracy before 1789.[4] Such arguments have resulted in passionate and rigorous defenses of the orthodox tradition by the French historians Claude Mazauric and Jacques Godechot,[5] making the debate seem an entirely Anglo-French affair with English and American historians cast in the role of conservative revisionists. However, a recent conference in Chicago suggests that the most influential revisionist work to date is not that of an American or Englishman, but of a Frenchman: François Furet has successfully taken the debate from the issue of social versus political history to one centered on intellectual history, specifically the persuasive ideas on equality proposed by Rousseau.[6]

The effect of such highly charged debates among scholars of the French Revolution is to make the writing of its history indeed a very polemical affair.[7] Some scholars have taken ironic stances to distance themselves and their work from the heat of the battle. Richard Cobb, the Oxford don and historian of the period, went so far as to argue in 1981 that the French Revolution should never have happened, possibly never did happen, and in any case had no effect one way or the other on most people's lives.[8] Our project, *French Caricature and the French Revolution, 1789–1799*, assumes no such distancing posture; it seeks, however, to turn from the polemics of historical writing about the French Revolution to the polemics of the Revolution itself, the numerous attempts to alter and, in some cases, to remake the political and social structures of French life.[9]

We have chosen to define the revolutionary period as 1789–1799, beginning with the destruction of the Bastille and continuing to 18 brumaire and the Consulate of Napoleon. This in itself is a problematic act, for the chronological parameters of the Revolution can justifiably extend from 1787 to 1815. The years 1789–1799, however, mark a significant break in the administrative centralization of French politics and frame a struggling, highly controversial experiment in the democratization of French society.

The publication of caricatures and other graphic satires was encouraged during this period, as one side lampooned the other in debates over the position of the clergy, the role of the Third Estate, the authority of the monarchy, and the threatened return of the émigrés. Both anonymously produced and officially commissioned by the Committee of Public Safety, caricatures appeared in Hébert's *Le Père Duchesne*; were sold from established printshops and hawked in the garden of the Palais-Royal; were sometimes quickly and crudely engraved and other times finely etched with added mezzotint or hand coloring; were sold separately or in a series; and could be simple or sophisticated in conception. They were a vital part of a rich and prolific visual culture and were read side by side with propagandistic, historical, and allegorical prints, as well as calendars and representations of the constitution and the *droits de l'homme*. Caricatures and other graphic satires were central to the formation of the revolutionary character. No less than other prints, they represent republican principles and prescribe the demeanor of the free citizen.

Unfortunately, little has been written about the French caricature of the revolutionary period. Unlike its English counterpart, which has been the subject of numerous studies and exhibitions,[10] the caricature produced in France between 1789 and 1799 has long been neglected; and this despite the fact that the first study appeared within the revolutionary period. Disguised as a history of revolutionary caricature, the *Histoire des caricatures de la révolte des Français* (1792) by Boyer de Nîmes was in fact an impassioned, royalist critique of the Revolution. Caricature was perceived as merely one of the most vulgar and reprehensible products of the revolutionary temper; in the words of the author, "Caricatures were among those [means] that one employed most skillfully, consistently, and successfully in order to lead astray and agitate the people."[11]

The next substantial study of French revolutionary caricature was Champfleury's *Histoire de la caricature sous la République, l'Empire, et la Restauration* (1874). This was followed in 1916 by André Blum's *La Caricature révolutionnaire*, which remains an essential source for any further study of the subject, as does Champfleury's more encyclopedic account. Nevertheless, both Champfleury and Blum are only preliminary studies; they inquire into the circumstances of production of prints, identify certain of their leading makers, and describe many of their subjects. They do not, however, attempt to characterize their formal or generic qualities. French caricatures of this period are essentially of documentary interest to them. These authors make no effort at interpretation and, by their plain descriptive approach, fail to suggest how the images in question might have played the significant role in the Revolution that Boyer de Nîmes claimed for them.

The same is true of the most recent studies of French revolutionary caricature: *L'Art de l'estampe et la Révolution française*, the catalogue for the exhibition of 1977 held at the Musée Carnavalet, and Michel Vovelle's multivolume work, *La Révolution française: Images et récit, 1789–1799* (1986).[12] Both treat caricature as indistinct from other kinds of prints produced during the Revolution, never trying to define the particular contribution of satire, the way it appeals to the public's attitudes toward its subjects, the way it charges polemical issues with, in Baudelaire's words, "l'essence du rire."[13] By contrast, we propose in the present study to examine how these prints acquired definite and often threatening meanings between 1789 and 1799 and how the use of certain generic formulas uniquely charged their contributions to the polemical discourse of the Revolution. This is not to say that prints other than caricature have been banished from the exhibition or its catalogue. On the contrary, we have been sensitive throughout our study to the context in which revolutionary caricatures emerged and have attempted to explore their similarities to and differences from the many other kinds of prints that comprised the dynamic visual culture of the revolutionary period. For, it is only against this background, and in relationship to contemporary allegories, emblems, and propaganda and current event prints, that the mechanics of revolutionary caricatures can be fully understood and their importance truly appreciated.

Our study comprises six essays followed by full catalogue entries. The first is Michel Melot's examination of the reasons why caricature had been unable to develop in France before 1789. He argues that this was due in part to censorship but was also, more significantly, the result of the monarchy's equivocal attitude toward the bourgeoisie and its complicity in the struggle of that class to gain recognition and participate more fully in the political and economic life of France. Using the example of mid-eighteenth-century England, Melot claims that a full appreciation for the power and working of caricature requires a unitary consciousness capable of providing the bases for a true bourgeois culture. He proceeds to examine how the development of a flourishing commerce in prints and a fully defined taste for genre images, the democratized portrait, and engravings of current events provided a foundation upon which caricature could function and take on larger cultural meaning within revolutionary France.

Lynn Hunt then explores the political psychology of revolutionary caricatures, examining representations of gender differences in the context of both Condillac's eighteenth-century "sensationalist" psychology and Freud's modern notion of the "family romance." She examines the difficulties encountered in attempting to sustain the family romance once the parents (the king and queen) were gone, as well as the fragility of the social order that based itself on the concept of fraternity.

Claude Langlois turns to the subject of counterrevolutionary caricatures. He examines their iconography and the ways in which they derived from and transformed certain revolutionary and even prerevolutionary caricatures, suggesting how they participated in shaping the discourse of the period. Ronald Paulson then explores relationships between French and English caricatures of the Revolution, arguing that while English caricature occasionally influenced the "form" of its French counterpart, the French influenced the English by providing them with the facts, or the "content" for representations of the Revolution. Paulson focuses on beheading and its attendant metaphorical possibilities vis-à-vis both the French and the English public.

Albert Boime looks specifically at the caricatures of Jacques-Louis David and argues that rather than being discontinuous in his artistic production, they were dialectically related to the Neoclassical paintings and are critical to an understanding of David's participation in the revolutionary process. In a close study of select images from the exhibition, Boime touches upon issues crucial to its very thesis: the scatological nature of much of the caricature of the period, the ways in which this kind of humor served the political ambitions of those who made and identified with it, and most important, the role such humor played in the larger culture.

Finally, Klaus Herding's essay concludes our study by asking a number of essential questions: How do revolutionary intentions represent themselves visually? In what way are contemporary conflicts settled or covered up? How does this change the form of such representations? And on which political and didactic intentions does the changed form exert its influences? He explores answers to these questions by examining the prevalence of specific gestures and body language, the relationship between image and text, and the structural divergence between visual code and depicted action in revolutionary and counterrevolutionary caricatures.[14]

We have chosen to concentrate on French caricatures of the Revolution not only because they have received scant scholarly attention, but because they offer at once a rich and provocative index to the particular events and polemical issues of the period and, in their very functioning, embody the violent disregard for authority that came to characterize the revolutionary spirit itself. It is crucial, therefore, to consider, albeit briefly, the term *caricature* — its origins and applicability to the revolutionary prints under discussion — and to note the relation of this form of graphic satire to the early political print, specifically German examples produced during the height of the Protestant Reformation.

The term *caricatura* originated at the end of the sixteenth century and was first used among Bolognese artists in the circle of Annibale and Agostino Carracci to describe "portrait caricatures," as opposed to representations of comic or grotesque types.[15] The Italian word, as Denis Mahon has noted, "involves the idea of giving more weight (*carico*) or emphasis to the defects [of an individual's physiognomy] and thus exaggerating them."[16] This process of exaggeration, however, rather than disguising its subjects, renders them instantly recognizable. By isolating and stressing that which is unique and divesting the portrait of that which is superfluous, the caricature serves to unmask and reveal. Mahon also points out that the verb *caricare* could be used to mean "to load or to charge, in the sense of a firearm." While he comments that "this was probably not the original connotation of our use of the term," it was "eminently suitable for something which came to have a sting in it."[17]

Pure portrait caricatures were rarely produced during the Revolution, although two prerevolutionary examples are included in the present exhibition (figs. 1, 2) and show the distorted features of clerics as they were drawn by the painter Jean-Baptiste Jouvenet around 1655.[18] The dearth of such caricatures during the revolutionary era may be explained in part by their aristocratic, or elitist, origins.

Portrait caricatures were the creations of the cognoscenti whose uncomplimentary depictions of each other provided a source of entertainment for a privileged circle and, paradoxically, could even function as a form of flattery. To be the subject of such mild ridicule was, after all, to receive confirmation that one had achieved an elevated position and could be "brought down" wittily without any lasting threat of physical assault or permanent loss of authority. Such an "attack" was therefore actually capable of reinforcing the sitter's sense of invulnerability and confirming his status within an elite group whose members exclusively enjoyed the right to mock each other. Although the desire to undermine was certainly present in the

FIGURE 1. Anonymous French. *Figures de Jésuites ridicules et en caricature (Faces of Jesuits, Ridiculous and in Caricature),* ca. 1762, after Jean-Baptiste Jouvenet. (Cat. no. 4).

FIGURE 2. Anonymous French. *Figures de Jésuites ridicules et en caricature (Faces of Jesuits, Ridiculous and in Caricature),* ca. 1762, after Jean-Baptiste Jouvenet. (Cat. no. 5).

exaggeration of physical traits, it was in most cases tempered by the shared values of the caricaturist, subject, and audience. Thus, as Filippo Baldinucci could say of Bernini's caricatures:

> A particular product of his boldness in drawing was his work in that sort of sketch we call caricature or "charged strokes," which for a joke distort in an uncomplimentary way the appearance of others, without taking away the likeness or grandeur if the subjects were, as often happened, princes. Such personnages are inclined to be amused at such entertainment even when their own appearance is concerned and would pass around the drawings for other persons of rank to see.[19]

The popularity of this polite form of entertainment endured, and by the mid-eighteenth century Pier Leone Ghezzi, Thomas Patch, and Sir Joshua Reynolds could draw and paint caricatures of British tourists in Rome who wished to preserve them as souvenirs of their Grand Tours and evidence of a certain sophistication.[20] And the London printseller, Matthew Darly, could specialize in engraving and publishing of portrait caricatures drawn by aristocratic *amateurs,* such as Lady Durlington, Lady Di Beauclerk, Lady Craven, and Lord Bloton.[21]

At first glance, it may be difficult to discern any similarities between pure portrait caricature and the political caricature produced during the French Revolution. The two genres do, however, share certain fundamental characteristics, the most important among them being the exploitation of the subversive potential of humor. Clearly, this capacity can be used for different ends and with varying degrees of intensity, but it nonetheless remains an essential feature of all caricature and, within the context of the Revolution, sets it apart from other kinds of political prints.

Freud's remarks on the *joke* and its capacity to undermine or attack are essential for understanding the role humor plays within caricature.

> Where a joke is not an aim in itself — that is, where it is not an innocent one — there are only two purposes that it may serve, and these two can themselves be subsumed under a single heading. It is either a *hostile* joke (serving the purpose of aggressiveness, satire, or defence) or an *obscene* joke (serving the purpose of exposure).[22]

In hostile as well as in obscene jokes — and political caricature often employs both at once — humor makes possible the satisfaction of a desire in the face of a barrier imposed by an outside authority. It allows the exploitation of "something ridiculous in our enemy which we could not, on account of obstacles in the way, bring forward openly or consciously…the joke *will evade restrictions and open sources of pleasure that have become inaccessible.*"[23] More to the point, with regard to tendentious jokes — such as those that form the bases of political caricature — Freud claimed that humor permits one to experience the belittling of one's enemy as if one were actually, physically carrying out the implied assault.

The obscene images produced early in the Revolution clearly demonstrate how humor functions as an operative mechanism in political caricature.[24] In one print the traditional political "coupling" of the nobility and the clergy is ridiculed as the Abbé Maury and an aristocratic woman are shown fondling each other (fig. 3). In another, Marie-Antoinette compensates her hairdresser with sexual favors (fig. 4). Subjecting the clergyman and the queen to such humor is evidence of the special contempt their opponents had for them. As Freud wrote of obscenity, "It compels the person who is assailed to imagine the part of the body or the procedure in question and shows her [or him] that the assailant is himself [or herself] imagining it."[25] In these prints, the abbé and the queen could see themselves exposed and vulnerable, not only to rid-

FIGURE 4. Anonymous French. *Le Payement du coeffeur ou Toute Peine merite salaire (The Hairdresser's Payment; or, All Work Merits Reward)*, ca. 1789. Etching with hand coloring. Paris, Bibliothèque nationale.

icule but to an imagined and desired physical assault.

The jokes involved in these images work on many levels. They diminish the status of the queen and the privileged orders by showing them in intimate situations, thus ignoring the distance normally maintained between the monarchy, nobility, and clergy and those for whom such images were intended (the Third Estate and, perhaps, certain disaffected factions within the other orders). They also poke fun at their subjects' financial distress and suggest that the Revolution has forced them to resort to using sexual favors in lieu of proper payment. Finally, they assault specific, and heretofore extremely powerful, individuals *and* their roles.

In the revolutionary examples, the queen and the abbé are identifiable, but emphasis of prominent facial features does not contribute to recognition. Not even the revolutionary depiction of the Abbé Maury as a Medusa's head constructed of phalli and coupling figures (fig. 5) can qualify as pure portrait caricature; for, although exaggeration is certainly involved, there is no attempt at using the clergyman's own appearance as a foundation for it. His identification is made possible only by means of the print's inscription. A similar caricature, presumed to be of Marie-Antoinette (fig. 6), lacks even an identifying caption. It was, however,

FIGURE 3. Anonymous French. *L'Abbé réduit a la demie pension ou On ne fout pas pour six sols (The Abbé Reduced to Half Pension; or, One Cannot Screw for Six Sous)*, ca. 1789. Etching with hand coloring. Paris, Bibliothèque nationale.

FIGURE 5. Anonymous French. *L'Abbé M... / L'Original est vivant / son portrait est en vie (Abbé M... / The Original is Living / His Portrait is Alive)*, ca. 1789. Etching and mezzotint. Paris, Bibliothèque nationale.

widely accepted as representing the queen and her evil, licentious nature.[26]

As noted earlier, portrait caricature has as its aim the exaggeration of those aspects of a person's face and expression that are most essential, and the assumption that physiognomy is a valid indicator of character underlies this process. Political caricature similarly seeks to unveil and holds not only the subject, but everything that the subject stands for, up to ridicule. The general intention, if not the scope or intensity, is similar in each instance, but the means used to effect the desired revelation differ.

Political caricature of the French Revolution drew inspiration from a number of models, and there are numerous instances where elements or concepts taken from prerevolutionary prints have been transformed and reused in a context far different from that in which they emerged (figs. 7, 8). The first political prints, those produced in Germany at the height of the Protestant Reformation, are especially illuminating antecedents, not only because they provide evidence of direct borrowings, but because they indicate how *identification* functions within political caricature.

Interesting in this regard is a series of woodcuts designed by Lucas Cranach the Elder that contrasts the humanity of Christ to the vanity and greed of the pope in thirteen facing illustrations of Good and Evil (figs. 9, 10). These were cut by Cranach's son Hans, joined to texts by Philip Melanchthon and Johann Schwertfeger, and pub-

lished by Grunenberg in 1521 as the highly original and influential illustrated pamphlet *Passional Christi und Antichristi*. André Chastel has described this small volume as collecting, condensing, and circulating all of the objections raised against the papacy over the centuries, thus becoming the first step in the larger war of images that would be waged between the pope and his adversaries.[27] The woodcuts are indeed forceful, political images that criticize and even lampoon the papacy with an unprecedented vengeance. Humor is an essential ingredient and results from the startling juxtapositions that force the viewer to appreciate the discrepancy between the behavior that should inspire the pope and the abuses to which the office has been subjected over time. Nowhere in this collection, however, is there a pure portrait caricature of Pope Leo X. These prints constitute a broader form of caricature, one that is capable of satirizing the power and actions of *offices* or *institutions*, as opposed to focusing exclusively on individuals.[28]

The extraordinary image of the *Papstesel*, or *Pope-Ass* (fig. 11), of around 1523 represents an even closer conceptual link to revolutionary political caricature. First engraved by Wenzel von Olmütz and then copied as a woodcut by the Cranach workshop for inclusion in a pamphlet written by Luther and Melanchthon, this bizarre figure is comprised of a donkey's head, a woman's naked torso, a scaled body, one human hand and one hoof-hand, one griffin's foot and a hoof, and a face-ass from which protrudes the head of a dragon or griffin.[29] The accompanying text describes the animal as representing the spiritual body of the church deformed

FIGURE 6. Anonymous French. *Ah! Ah! Voila mon portrait (Oh! Oh! Here is My Portrait)*, ca. 1789. Etching and mezzotint. Paris, Bibliothèque nationale.

FIGURE 7. Anonymous French. *Les Jésuites passes au crible (The Jesuits Pass through the Sieve)*, ca. 1762. Engraving. Paris, Bibliothèque nationale.

by the earthly ambitions of the pope, who, as the head of the church, is represented as an ass oppressing, rather than ministering to, the souls of his flock.[30]

This compound image is a grotesque emblem which seeks to unmask the true nature not only of Leo x, but of the *office* of the pope (the papal flag is shown flying from the fortress in the background). This is accomplished by referring to and emphasizing the attributes of the various animals and mythical creatures whose combination has produced this monstrous and unique being. The members of the audience for whom this image was intended — unlike the elite circle that was traditionally entertained by portrait caricature — would have appreciated the overtly subversive humor and have seen themselves united as enemies of the values depicted. Rather than simply acknowledging resemblance, they were asked to make a series of figurative connections, to appreciate the many ways in which the pope is like an ass, a harlot, or a dragon. The accompanying text elaborates the various points of comparison, much as the detailed inscriptions that often appear in revolutionary caricature were used to clarify and drive home the message of the image.

Both portrait and political caricature depend on likeness. In the former, it is physical likeness; in the latter, official likeness. The crucial difference between them lies ultimately in the purpose and degree to which they apply ridicule. Jouvenet's Jesuit portrait caricatures were intended to diminish the status of specific individuals, but only slightly. In addition, they were meant to do so

within an elite group whose members — caricaturist, subject, and audience — shared certain values. In the revolutionary caricatures of the Abbé Maury, however, like the political prints they derive from, ridicule is intensified and politically motivated; it is used to assault and humiliate the abbé, uniting his adversaries — caricaturist and audience — in common opposition to his personal and professional ambitions. Similarly, as Lynn Hunt describes in her essay in the present catalogue, the attack on Marie-Antoinette is not motivated solely by hatred of an individual; rather, by raising the specter of illegitimacy, it becomes an attack on the monarchy, specifically the *role* of a queen.

When revolutionary era printmakers turned to political caricatures, the numerous German, Dutch, English, and French models available were readily used. It took only a monumental rupture in the social and political structure of France, the emergence of a powerful and liberated bourgeoisie, and the confusion of hastily articulated political ambitions to provide the stimulus and means for the rapid production and wide distribution of political caricatures. This was not the moment for the less strident portrait variety, which could prove ambiguous, *inflating* as well as deflating its subjects. Rather, it was the time for rigorous polemical exchanges intent not only on distorting and ridiculing opponents, but on shaping the revolutionary character, serving the cause of national integration and solidarity, and reconstituting the entire social

FIGURE 8. Anonymous French. *Le Crible de la Revolution (The Sieve of the Revolution)*, 1791. Etching and mezzotint. New York, The Metropolitan Museum of Art, The Elisha Whittelsey Collection, The Elisha Whittelsey Fund, 1962 (62.520.279).

FIGURE 9. Lucas Cranach the Elder (German, 1472–1553). *Christ Washing the Apostles' Feet,* ca. 1521. Woodcut from the *Passional Christi und Antichristi.*

and political world from the perspective of the new France.

In organizing this exhibition, it has been our goal to demonstrate how caricature, viewed within the larger context of revolutionary graphic production, set out to accomplish these monumental tasks. To achieve this end, we have marshaled a wide variety of revolutionary prints, arranging them thematically in eleven separate sections which follow a chronological progression.

We begin with prerevolutionary caricatures, focusing upon the principal satirical campaigns of the decades immediately preceding the Revolution; these include anti-Jesuit images, attacks on Mesmer, fashion caricatures, and criticisms of the English. Prints illustrating the taking of the Bastille, the single most dramatic and symbolic event of the early years of the Revolution, follow. The next section is devoted to caricatures of the three estates, tracing through images the emergence of the Third Estate as a political power. A section on the religious question examines reactions to the new strictures placed upon the clergy and the frustrated response of the papacy to the diminished status of the church. Images of the royal family range from those that belittle the king and queen, show outrage at their attempted flight from France, and delight in their beheading to those that express sympathy with their plight. These are followed by satirical allegories directed against the émigrés and counterrevolutionaries, images that are among the most beautiful and witty of the period. Portraits, historical prints, and allegories com-

memorating the assassination of Jean-Paul Marat appear next. These are followed by the bizarre and fantastic emblems of the new republican virtues — the revolutionary calendar, various representations of the Declaration of the Rights of Man and of the Citizen, and personifications of the new months. Images of the Terror — its institutions, personalities, rise and fall — are then presented. These are succeeded by prints created during the Directory period — images that react to the Terror and the new constitution, as well as examples of the revival of social and fashion caricature. The exhibition concludes with prints from the First Consulate of Napoleon — a lighter fare of café farces, Neoclassical allegories depicting the army's victorious campaigns, and sober and hagiographic portraits of the handsome young general. With these last images, the decade-long experiment in the democratization of French society had come to a close and with it the predominance of political caricature. Not until the final days of the Bourbon Restoration and the July Revolution of 1830 would French caricature reemerge as a powerful weapon in the service of political discourse.

———

Although through our study we hope to provide the reader with a vivid and coherent sense of French revolutionary caricature, its mechanisms and meanings, it is not our intention to present a single, consistent viewpoint. The essays and catalogue entries that follow respond in a number of ways to these prints, and our authors vary in their

FIGURE 10. Lucas Cranach the Elder (German, 1472–1553). *The Emperor Kissing the Pope's Toe,* ca. 1521. Woodcut from the *Passional Christi und Antichristi.*

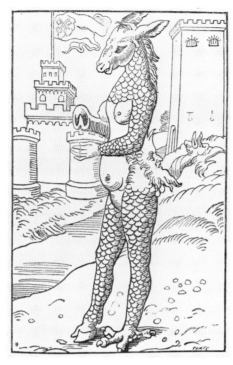

FIGURE 11. After Wenzel von Olmütz (German, active ca. 1523). *Pope-Ass*, ca. 1523. Woodcut reproduced in Champfleury, *Histoire de la caricature sous la Réforme et la Ligue, Louis XIII – Louis XVI* (1880).

perspectives, as do the scholars who confront the history of the Revolution itself. It is our hope that these differences of opinion will encourage further inquiry into the nature of French revolutionary caricature. For, although the historiography of revolutionary caricature is not yet as mature as that of the Revolution itself, and the debate not yet as refined, differences of interpretation are still keen. And if there seems to be a certain appropriateness in the existence of these differences, we do well to remember the heated political debates that gave rise to both the Revolution and its caricature.

James Cuno
Director
Grunwald Center for the Graphic Arts, UCLA

1. François Furet, *Interpreting the French Revolution,* trans. Elborg Forster (Cambridge: Cambridge University Press, 1981; originally published as *Penser la Révolution française*, Paris: Editions Gallimard, 1978), p. 1.

2. See Georges Lefebvre, *The Coming of the French Revolution,* trans. R. R. Palmer (Princeton: Princeton University Press, 1967; originally published as *Quatre-vingt-neuf*, Paris: Maison du livre français, 1939); Albert Soboul, *The Sans-Culottes,* trans. Remy Inglis Hall (Princeton: Princeton University Press, 1980; originally published as *Les Sans-Culottes parisiens en l'an II: Mouvement populaire et gouvernement révolutionnaire, 1793-1794,* Paris: Editions du Seuil, 1968); and idem, *The French Revolution, 1787-1799,* trans. Alan Forrest and Colin Jones (New York: Vintage Books, 1975; originally published as *La Révolution française*, Paris: Editions sociales, 1962). Challenges to this tradition will be mentioned in the text, but its recent defense should be noted here: George C. Comninel, *Rethinking the French Revolution: Marxism and the Revisionist Challenge* (London: Verso, 1987).

3. Alfred Cobban, *The Social Interpretation of the French Revolution* (Cambridge: Cambridge University Press, 1964), p. 9. Cobban launched his attack in a 1955 lecture on the occasion of the inauguration of a chair in French Revolutionary History at the University of London. He continued and refined it in the Wiles Lectures given in 1961-1962 and later published as the above-cited book.

4. The debate over the role of the bourgeoisie in the Revolution is anthologized quite usefully in Ralph W. Greenlaw, ed., *The Social Origins of the French Revolution* (Lexington, Mass.: D. C. Heath and Co., 1975). It is most clearly summarized in Colin Lucas, "Nobles, Bourgeois, and the Origins of the French Revolution," in *French Society and the Revolution,* ed. Douglas Johnson (Cambridge: Cambridge University Press, 1976), pp. 88-131.

5. Claude Mazauric, *Sur la Révolution française: Contributions à l'histoire de la révolution bourgeoise* (Paris: Editions sociales, 1970). See also, Jacques Godechot's review of Cobban's *The Social Interpretation of the French Revolution,* which appears in *Revue historique* 1 (1966), pp. 205-8.

6. See Jack R. Censer, "The Coming of a New Interpretation of the French Revolution," *Journal of Social History* 21, no. 2 (Winter 1987), pp. 295-309. The conference reviewed in Censer's article was held at the University of Chicago in September 1987 and was organized by Keith Baker, Mona Ozouf, Colin Lucas, and others, including Furet. By contrast, see the passionate defenses of Soboul's work by Sanford Elwitt and Claude Mazauric (and the measured critique of the same by Richard M. Andrews), who comprised the panel entitled "The Scholarly Work of Albert Soboul: An Attempt at an Appraisal," at the 1984 meeting of the Consortium on Revolutionary Europe held at Duke University; the panel's discussion was published in the Consortium's *Proceedings,* ed. Harold T. Parker (Athens, Ga.: N.p., 1986), pp. 315-70.

7. This is so much the case that it sometimes results in parody. See, for example, the American historian George V. Taylor's remarks: "A death has occurred — that of the class-struggle thesis of the French Revolution. This demise has never been announced. No funeral has been held. No obituaries have been published. But there is no doubt that the class-struggle thesis of the French Revolution has expired and is interred in the graveyard of lost paradigms assassinated by critical research." George V. Taylor, "Symposium: Caste, Class, Elites, and Revolution," in *Proceedings: The Consortium on Revolutionary Europe, 1750-1850,* ed. Owen Connelly (Athens, Ga.: N.p., 1979), p. 50.

8. This is from a report of Cobb's participation in London's South Bank "Romantics" Festival of summer 1981; see Judith Chernaik, "Romantic Logistics," *Times Literary Supplement,* 7 August 1981, p. 919.

9. Oddly left out of the debate is the work of Robert Darnton, whose studies of Grub Street journalism in the years just preceding the Revolution have been especially influential on art historians. See his *The Literary Underground of the Old Regime* (Cambridge: Harvard University Press, 1982). For evidence of Darnton's influence on the writing of art history, see especially Thomas E. Crow, "The *Oath of the Horatii* in 1785: Painting and Pre-Revolutionary Radicalism in France," *Art History* 1 (December 1978), pp. 424-71; idem, *Painters and Public Life in Eighteenth-Century Paris* (New Haven and London:

Yale University Press, 1985), pp. 92–96; and Albert Boime's contribution to the present catalogue.

10. The most important studies of English caricature are volumes 5 and 6 of the *Catalogue of Political and Personal Satires Preserved in the Department of Prints and Drawings in the British Museum*, prepared by Mary Dorothy George and published by the British Museum in 1935 and 1938 respectively. Draper Hill's books on the master caricaturist James Gillray are also essential in this regard — *Mr. Gillray the Caricaturist* (London: Phaidon Press, 1965) and *The Satirical Etchings of James Gillray* (New York: Dover Publications, 1976) — while the Victoria and Albert Museum's *English Caricature 1620 to the Present* (1984) is only the most recent popular exhibition to include numerous examples of English caricatures from the period.

11. The work was published in two volumes by the Imprimerie du *Journal du peuple* in Paris. It is extremely rare and was never completed. As evidence of the extent to which the study was more than a history of caricature, one should note that Boyer de Nîmes was condemned to death by a Revolutionary Tribunal in May 1793. Unless otherwise noted, translations from the French are mine.

12. Vovelle's five-volume work has a preface by Claude Mazauric and was published in Paris by Editions Messidor, Livre Club Diderot. For a convincing critique of the Musée Carnavalet exhibition, see Hannah Mitchell, "Art and the French Revolution: An Exhibition at the Musée Carnavalet," *History Workshop* 5 (Spring 1978), pp. 123-45.

13. Charles Baudelaire, "De l'essence du rire et généralement du comique dans les arts plastiques," in *Oeuvres complètes*, Bibliothèque de la Pléiade (Paris: Editions Gallimard, 1976), vol. 2, pp. 525-43. Although Baudelaire wrote on both English and French caricature, he limited his study of the latter to the nineteenth century. See his "Quelques caricaturistes français," in the above-cited volume, pp. 545-63.

14. The value of Herding's contribution lies not only in the originality of his thesis, but in the introduction of recent and significant German scholarship — too often neglected — to the study of the French Revolution and its graphic art.

15. See E. H. Gombrich and Ernst Kris, *Caricature* (Harmondsworth: Penguin Books, 1940); Werner Hofmann, *Caricature from Leonardo to Picasso* (New York: Crown Publishers, 1957); and Donald Posner, *Annibale Carracci* (New York: Phaidon Press, 1971), vol. 1, pp. 65-71.

16. Denis Mahon, *Studies in Seicento Art and Art Theory* (Westport, Conn.: Greenwood Press, 1971), p. 261.

17. Ibid.

18. It was at this time that Bernini introduced the term in France while he was at work on the bust of Louis XIV. The term was not officially accepted into the French language until 1762 when the Academy included it in the fourth edition of its *Dictionnaire*. Perhaps this accounts for the printing of Jouvenet's designs a century after their creation (cat. nos. 4, 5).

19. Filippo Baldinucci, *The Life of Bernini*, trans. E. Engass (University Park Pa.: Pennsylvania State University Press, 1966), p. 74.

20. Richard Godefrey, *English Caricature, 1620 to the Present*, exh. cat. (London: Victoria and Albert Museum, 1984), pp. 31-32.

21. Mary Dorothy George, *English Political Caricature to 1792: A Study of Opinion and Propaganda* (Oxford: Clarendon Press, 1959), pp. 147-49.

22. Sigmund Freud, *Jokes and Their Relation to the Unconscious*, trans. James Strachey (New York: W. W. Norton, 1960), pp. 96-97.

23. Ibid., p. 103.

24. All of the images in the group from which these examples are drawn are undated and anonymous. A number of them do appear to have come from a single series, however, as they are etched in a similar manner and bear a number in the upper right-hand corner.

25. Freud (supra, note 22), p. 98.

26. To my knowledge, these prints are unprecedented in the history of caricature, although they obviously derive from Arcimboldesque allegorical portraits (see Thomas Da Costa Kaufman, "Arcimboldo's Imperial Allegories," *Zeitschrift für Kunstgeschichte* [1976], pp. 275-96). Subsequent to these revolutionary prints, the German artist Johann Michael Voltz designed a popular caricature of Napoleon whose face was depicted as composed of naked corpses, the refuse of his early military defeats.

27. André Chastel, *The Sack of Rome, 1527*, trans. Beth Archer (Princeton: Princeton University Press, 1983), pp. 67-78. Significantly, one of these images, *The Fall of the Pope into Hell*, may have served as a distant model for the revolutionary caricature of Pope Pius VI being driven into hell (cat. no. 63).

28. This is true also of Cranach's illustrations for Luther's *September Testament* of 1522 and of Hans Holbein's woodcuts for Luther's translation of the Old Testament published by Thomas Wolff in Basel in 1523. These prints denounce the evils of the papacy and, by extension, of Rome by having the Great Whore of Babylon wear the papal tiara and by depicting the city of Babylon as Hartmann Schedel's *Imago romae* of 1493. Ibid. pp. 71-73.

29. The face-ass motif was used by David in his revolutionary caricature *Gouvernement anglois*. This image is discussed in detail by Albert Boime in his essay for this catalogue. F. W. H. Hollstein, *German Engravings, Etchings, and Woodcuts, 1400-1700* (Amsterdam: Menno Hertzberger, 1959), vol. 6, p. 161.

30. Reprinted in Champfleury, *Histoire de la caricature sous la Réforme et la Ligue, Louis XIII–Louis XVI* (Paris: Dentu, 1880), pp. 60-64.

Essays

CARICATURE AND THE REVOLUTION
The Situation in France in 1789

Michel Melot

Centre Georges Pompidou

aricature and *revolution* are words that seem to go together. Revolution is indeed a form of satire, and caricature, a form of revolt. It is possible, however, for one to exist without the other. Goya's satiric drawings were independent of any revolution, whereas the Revolution of 1917 was too prosaic to generate many caricatures. But sometimes the two reinforce each other in a simultaneous political and aesthetic explosion: this was the case during the French Revolution of 1789.

Before the Revolution, caricature was unable to develop in France at a pace comparable to that which had been experienced in Holland and England since the beginning of the eighteenth century. Caricature was certainly present in prerevolutionary France, but it was also repressed, censored by an absolute monarchic power. The monarchy contributed to the stifling of caricature in two ways: directly, through censorship, and indirectly, through its equivocal attitude toward the bourgeoisie and its complicity in the very struggle of this class to obtain recognition.

Censorship was an everyday reality. The art of engraving was unrestricted, but the sale of prints was closely regulated by the lieutenant general of police and fell under the control of the guild of booksellers. The authorities watched especially for fraudulent imitations and "indecent" prints, those which were harmful to "religion, the general good and the peace of the State, and the purity of morals." (Only a relatively short time had elapsed since a caricaturist had been burned alive for depicting Louis XIV with his mistresses.)[1] All academic studies of nudes were closely surveilled, as were all imports from England, whose political satires were more feared than her frivolities.

The Revolution could not immediately do away with this long-standing practice, which was perceived as a necessary evil. Thus, although censorship was solemnly abolished by the Declaration of the Rights of Man, Article 11, it was reintroduced with the appointment of a censor for caricatures in Paris as early as 31 July 1789. It was reaffirmed at the height of the Revolution on 17 April 1794 (28 germinal an II).[2]

In reaction to the measure adopted in July 1789, Millin sent a "letter to the representatives of the Commune of Paris on the danger of forbidding the publication of prints and engraved writings without the approval of the censor they had appointed."[3] On 20 January 1790, however, the Constituent Assembly again considered a "proposed decree against the violations resulting from printing and publishing engravings." The term *lèse-nation* replaced *lèse-majesté*, allowing the prosecution of "all authors, printers, and peddlers of writings inciting the People to insurrection against the laws, to the shedding of blood, and to the overthrow of the constitution."[4]

The practice of caricature presupposes conditions of freedom, but there are more profound explanations for the sudden awakening of revolution and caricature in France. Caricature is a subversive weapon whereby a political model is dismantled by means of an aesthetic model. The caricaturist perverts the rules of ideal representation in order to create the image of a human figure who is himself a representative of authority. Hence, in caricature there is transgression (of an aesthetic norm) for the purpose of aggression (against a social model).[5] In prerevolutionary France the various preconditions essential to this process were satisfied only occasionally and in limited fashion. The educated bourgeoisie, the class that supplied the audience and the infrastructure for caricature—and the sole group capable of appreciating its aesthetic transgression and the symbolic violence of its expression of political opposition—had little interest in a frontal attack on the monarchy.

The long-established alliance between the king and the high bourgeoisie against the nobility (which had permitted Louis XI to constitute France as a state and Louis XII to become the first absolute monarch) was still very effective in 1789. Only after the peace of Aix-la-Chapelle in 1748 had the king been attacked by caricaturists in a somewhat concerted fashion, and even during the Revolution the royal family did not become a prime target until after its flight to Varennes.

In view of the relationship between the king and the high bourgeoisie vis-à-vis the nobility, one might have suspected the latter to readily become the subject of caricature. The nobility was eventually attacked, but this was accomplished tardily, and in a global fashion, at the approach of the Revolution; for, in the end, why should the educated middle class, who enjoyed real power, have fought against the increasingly fictitious strength of a nobility that the king had indeed "domesticated" to the former's advantage? The high bourgeoisie

had come to exercise the nobility's responsibilities, perform its functions, and at times even hold its titles.

Caricature can only function satisfactorily in opposition. This is not surprising, for caricature can be defined formally as an upside-down academism, a way of *counterfeiting* the dominant taste. Before the Revolution, the French bourgeoisie could only attack the excesses of the aristocracy, not the aristocracy itself; this prevented caricature from becoming the locus of fundamental political demands. The great subjects of prerevolutionary French caricature were John Law's speculations, the extortions of the Jesuits (1761–1762), which led to their expulsion from the kingdom in 1762 (fig. 1),

Lc Crime puny

FIGURE 1. Anonymous French. *Le Crime puny (Crime Punished)*, ca. 1768. (Cat. no. 2).

or the animal magnetism of Mesmer (fig. 2). When caricature was finally wielded in France by a strong and structured opposition, this "opposition" was already in power as the Committee of Public Safety and directly attacked its political adversaries. But an opposition that holds power is no longer an opposition, and the official commissions for caricatures distributed to David and his circle on 12 September 1793 produced no results.[6] They had, nonetheless, been requested in a speech to the Jacobins that was as impassioned as it was determined: "All the artists will be employed in drawing the most disparaging caricatures against the enemies of the Jacobins."[7] A caricature, however, cannot be ordered; it is either spontaneous or it does not exist.

FIGURE 2. Anonymous French. *Le Doigt magique / ou le Magnétisme animal / simius semper simius (The Magic Finger; / or, Animal Magnetism / Once a Monkey Always a Monkey)*, ca. 1784. (Cat. no. 7).

There are other clear indications that the idea of caricature was not well established in eighteenth-century France prior to the Revolution. When prints were requested in official speeches, it was hoped that the efficacious "English" practice could find application in France.[8] It is probable that both the king and the revolutionaries viewed caricature as a product imported from England, and this was indeed the case, both from a strictly commercial standpoint (there was a large black market for English engravings in France) and from a political standpoint. Louis XIV's policies had stifled caricature in France, but, ironically, by supporting the partisans of King James, he had greatly encouraged its development, at his own expense, in England. A similar pattern occurred in Holland where the French had been guilty of numerous atrocities (fig. 3).

Thus, when the royalist, Boyer-Brun, known as Boyer de Nîmes,[9] undertook a veritable crusade against the revolutionary caricatures that invaded Paris after the flight to Varennes, he fixed upon a single idea, denouncing the plot of the Protestants whom he saw at work everywhere in the Revolution. This reaction, although aberrant, is nonetheless significant. It reveals the entire tradition from which caricature emerged in France: the religious wars where it had played a particularly active role for the last time in the kingdom; the reputation it had earned in the more liberated Holland and England as a weapon against France; and, finally,

through the power of imagery, the old and idolatrous beliefs that continued to exercise a profound influence on those who could rarely differentiate between the political and the religious.[10]

The first volleys of political caricatures occurred contemporaneously in France and in England between 1710 and 1720. Similarly, the word *caricature* appeared rather late in French dictionaries (*Dictionnaire de l'Académie*, 4th ed., 1762) and in their English counterparts (Samuel Johnson, *Dictionary of the English Language*, 1755). However, English caricature, unlike French, developed rapidly before 1760 with artists, a public, and organized sales and production networks. Both Frederick Antal and M. D. George have described the reason for this: the typically English importance of a "middle class" (distinct from the high bourgeoisie, which was linked to the aristocracy) with a strong collective self-consciousness, producing its own economic, moral, and aesthetic values.[11]

M. D. George justly notes that the absence of a middle class in other European countries astonished English travelers of the period. Thus, in England was born a true culture, or counterculture, of the middle class—a middle class more homogeneous than that in France, more conscious of its rights and its identity.[12]

The social existence of each individual (Tocqueville noted that in England everyone could be a "gentleman," while in France only the aristocrats "were born") is the primary condition for the existence of caricature, because it attacks the individual in his own image. Thus, in England personal attacks against prominent public figures of the day increased, while in France, caricature remained most often allegorical and abstract. Antal's pertinent observation should also be noted; he has

FIGURE 3. Romeyn de Hooghe (Dutch, 1645–1708). From *War Scenes and Cruelties of the French in the Netherlands*, 1672–1673. Reproduced from the *Kulturgeschichtliches Bilderbuch aus drei Jahrhunderten*.

stressed the absence in England of a strong artistic tradition, which allowed, in his view, the development of both courtly and popular engravings.[13]

In England, caricature was the weapon of the Whigs against the Tories who hoped for a Jacobite restoration. These positions within the bourgeoisie were well established. There was nothing comparable in France before the Revolution. M. D. George is perhaps hasty in writing that "class antagonism is not discoverable before the French Revolution."[14] It is true, nonetheless, that in France the traditional division of the three orders — nobility, clergy, and Third Estate — failed to reflect the real conflicts taking place within each, as was proven by the alliances formed during the Estates General.

Where can one find, in this fragmented and scandalously underrepresented Third Estate, an established, unitary consciousness and common interests capable of providing the bases for a true culture? This consciousness and culture were formed, or rather were improvised, in 1789 on the occasion of the Estates General, through its symbols, its attitudes, its speeches, its images.

As noted, the great commercial bourgeoisie, that of the art collectors (Jean de Julienne is an excellent example of this group in the history of collectors of engravings), had been culturally assimilated to the nobility since the Renaissance. At the other extreme of the middle classes included within the Third Estate, the petty bourgeoisie was practically without representation, and its members were often illiterate. Few prints are found in the inventories made subsequent to the deaths of small Parisian shopkeepers and artisans, and when they do exist, they are pious images linked with religious practices and sometimes with the oldest of superstitions. Neither art nor caricature was the concern of the lower middle class, which when it became mobilized, followed the model of Neoclassical virtue, of moral and aesthetic rigor that could alone replace the values of religion. Barring a few exceptions, therefore, it is not in this category that a public of patrons of caricature could be constituted before the Revolution. We should note, however, that a number of French revolutionary caricatures were abstract and austere, no doubt adapted for this naive public (fig. 4). As Champfleury observed: "A peculiar form of caricature, that of the Revolution. It is very close to symbolism; it is nevertheless caricature."[15]

Caricature was too sophisticated and perhaps suspected of a frivolity that was useless in the struggle of the lower classes. It found its public both in the comfortable and cultured segment of the bourgeoisie (when this group was not excessively puritanical), and in the rebellious faction of the

nobility, which was familiar with art and antagonistic toward absolute monarchy.

The most beautiful collection of eighteenth-century English caricatures preserved in France is found in the Bibliothèque nationale under the name of the Marquis de Biencourt. The marquis was a great amateur, a bibliophile, and, in the language of the period, an "antiquarian." He was the proprietor of the Château d'Azay-le-Rideau,[16] and one of the few noblemen who voted for the abolition of the privileges and adhered to the orders of the Assembly.

FIGURE 4. Anonymous French. *Le Despotisme terrassé (Despotism Overthrown)*, 1789. (Cat. no. 25).

The central role played in the early stages of the Revolution by Philippe d'Orléans is also well known. The royalists attributed to the Duc d'Orléans the presence of all the caricatures imported from England and aimed against the royal family, nor were they wrong in so doing. On his initiative and in order to escape censorship, the courtyard of the Palais-Royal became a true free-trade zone where revolutionary newspapers and prints were sold. The existence of this market was a thorn in the side of the monarchy.

But if these few rebellious aristocrats played a certain role in developing the taste for caricature in France, they could not profit from it even symbolically; fundamentally bound to their own class and ultimately submerged by the strength of the popular movement, they could not be the source of a new culture. (The Marquis de Biencourt's son finally defended the king at the Tuileries on 10 August.) One should, nonetheless, take note of the existence of this Anglophile current, which was manifested in the production of personalized, strongly anti-monarchist caricatures, more licentious than would have been permitted by the middle-class moral code (fig. 5).

The "natural" public of political caricatures was the enlightened bourgeoisie, the progressives whom the monarchy had formerly been able to absorb within its orbit through the sale of titles of nobility. Members of this class were to be found in the royal "offices"; in the liberal professions, working as professors, doctors, lawyers, and members of Parliament; and in everything referred to as *la robe*, or relating to the judiciary. It is certainly the culture of this social group that is expressed in the greater part of the very allegorical, often austere, caricatures that are directed more readily against the Jesuits than the king and emphasize scatology over licentiousness (fig. 6). To recall Champfleury once again, these caricatures are "very close to symbolism." In this precarious social situation, it becomes understandable that eighteenth-century French caricature did not enjoy the glory of English caricature whose pungent creations were appreciated by a truculent and pragmatic clientele of merchants and tradesmen.

———————

Little by little, however, the conditions in France changed so that an original caricatural style could develop before the Revolution, manifest itself in a disorderly fashion during the Revolution, and ripen along with the social class that carried it to its triumph in 1830. The signs auspicious to the development of French caricature during the prerevolu-

BRÉF DU PAPE EN 1791.

FIGURE 6. Anonymous French. *Bref du pape en 1791 (The Papal Brief in 1791)*, 1791. (Cat. no. 62).

tionary period are numerous. Only a few will be mentioned here: the flourishing of a true commerce (in the modern sense of the word) in prints; the predeliction for genre subjects; the banalization of the portrait; and the birth of the engraving of current events.

It was within the lower nobility and the intellectual middle classes composed of officers and counselors that prints found a large and obliging public in the middle of the eighteenth century. The phenomenon is general enough to have attracted the attention of historians, and it was marked by the invention or commercialization of new procedures capable either of industrializing engraving or of making it more attractive; the appearance of catalogues of prints for sale to the public and the first catalogues of works by individual artists; the appearance of specialized criticism and organized advertising; and even the appearance of the first subterfuges — the limitation of the number of printed copies, handwritten signatures, the constitution of amateurs' associations — capable of creating a market of scarcity for reproducible prints.

This movement was noted even by contemporaries, such as Charles François Joullain who, in his *Réflexions sur la peinture et la gravure...*, published in 1786, remarked that the "number of merchants increased... to the point of surprise, particularly since one could hardly imagine from where they might have emerged in such a short time."[17] The spectacular progress of the print market in France can be precisely situated between 1750 and the Revolution and is one of the signs of the intellectual movement that began to stir the middle classes around an art of reproduction. The engravings in

NOUVEAU PACTE DE LOUIS XVI.
avec le peuple le 20. Juin 1792. l'An 4.me de la liberté.

FIGURE 5. Anonymous French. *Nouveau Pacte de Louis XVI / avec le peuple le 20 juin 1792 l'an 4ᵐᵉ de la liberté (New Pact of Louis XVI / with the People 20 June 1792 the Fourth Year of Liberty)*, 1792. (Cat. no. 66).

FIGURE 7. Philibert-Louis Debucourt (French, 1755–1832). *Promenade de la gallerie du Palais-Royal (The Palais-Royal Gallery's-Walk)*, 1787. Etching and engraving. Washington, D.C., National Gallery of Art, Widener Collection, 1942.

question could be either refined or popular and for that reason were pleasing to a wide variety of amateurs who, although still unable to choose sides politically, could at least express their individual tastes. Of note, the strictly commercial and speculative movement that had been the impetus for many printshops and studios was halted by the Revolution, and a number of these establishments had no choice but to convert rapidly to revolutionary engraving, which was more popular and leaned more toward caricature.

Another factor contributing to the first great successes of caricature was the general preference for "genre" prints, as opposed to reproductions of historical paintings, which stood at the top of the hierarchy of genres. "Genre" engravings essentially reproduced the work of the minor Flemish and Dutch masters—at times exaggerated to the point of vulgarity. They included street scenes, fairs, beggars, "expressive" heads, licentiousness —all subjects that border on caricature and seem to yearn to belong to it.

A study of the documents of this period concerning prints reveals a contradiction. On the one hand, there was vigorous condemnation of genre subjects; on the other, they experienced a growing success. In this seeming paradox, the contrast between the real power of a segment of the population and its cultural nonexistence may be seen. French theories of good taste have always resisted the excesses of realism, the showy themes of which attract an easy clientele. France, however, has

always been surrounded by the "expressionist" realism of Flanders, Holland, Lorraine, Germany, and Italy. Although French amateurs cannot be said to have consistently resisted genre painting, when they did yield to it, this was done almost surreptitiously, as if they were hiding from academic doctrines. Although famous critics like Mariette and Caylus inveighed against the invasion of genre engravings and paintings, in the second half of the eighteenth century an entire public of bourgeois, officers, merchants, even nobles and priests, avidly sought them out. This laid the groundwork for caricature within a public still suspicious of it and disguised its use in the face of theories that continued to condemn it.

The appearance of a great school of French genre painters, accustomed to the taste of the national clientele, resulted from this demand. In July 1789 the most famous and popular artist working in engraving was undoubtedly Philibert-Louis Debucourt who had made the medium his specialty (fig. 7). This work was considered "good" genre by aristocrats who thought highly of the jocundity of genre prints but, in the name of aesthetics, rejected the vulgar genre of the Flemish. The middle class did the reverse, with the result that "genre" engravings in general and the so-called aristocratic engravings of "manners" had quite different clienteles and were equally subject to scorn. Wicar, in his famous speech of 22 April 1794 (3 floréal an II), given to the Popular and Republican Society for the Arts, demanded that these "infamous" prints be burned at the foot of the Tree of Liberty and condemned Louis-Léopold Boilly's entire oeuvre.

One must also take into account the extraordinary demand for portraits in the period preceding July 1789. The portrait had been exclusively reserved for the aristocracy. As noted previously, in France only the aristocrats were considered to have been "born." How could one paint the portrait of an individual, powerful or famous though he might be, who had no existence of his own in the social body? Artists who painted self-portraits were an exception to this rule as were, rarely, some powerful individuals assimilated to the nobility. In the course of the eighteenth century, however, the portrait became available to models of common origin. Rigaud painted Samuel Bernard, Louis XIV's banker, as well as his own mother. It is said that in 1715 Marguerite Bécaille, a benefactress of hospitals, became one of the first women to owe her portrait solely to her personal merit.[18]

A broad availability of portraits is indispensable to fertilizing the mode of caricature, which plays precisely on the specific features of the individual model. On the very eve of the Revolution, everyone, regardless of social class, pursued the "physionotrace" craze. This small identity portrait was drawn in a camera lucida and engraved with a pantograph; six copies were made and colored in minutes for the price of a few sous. It gained initial popularity at Versailles and very soon thereafter at the Palais-Royal where Gilles Louis Chrétien, its inventor, was residing—undoubtedly having realized that his clientele was far broader than that of the court.[19] This sudden democratization of the portrait was a small revolution in itself, a revolution in images that peacefully translated, on a reduced scale and in symbolic fashion, the disintegration of the social order and the abolishment of another privilege. Caricature was becoming inevitable under such conditions, just as the way was prepared directly for photography. Here again, however, it would be the July Monarchy that realized the hopes that the French bourgeoisie had expressed during the Revolution and in so sudden a manner that it astonished itself.

Yet another fundamental aesthetic development contributed to the emergence of caricature: the sudden transformation of traditional history painting into scenes of current events. The "event," for the artist, like the "character," had possessed only a sublimated meaning. The recent, daily event was disqualified as a subject just as the portrait of an ordinary individual would have been. The events of the Revolution brought about the birth of a new mode, that of reportage.[20] In this regard the account book for 1787–1789 of an obscure merchant named Vallée,[21] who sold mainly "genre engravings" to the nobles, officers of the king, and a few members of the clergy, is revealing. The Estates General provided him with the occasion to sell caricatures also. His account book is empty for 16 and 17 July 1789, but, beginning on 29 July, he sold several *Bastilles* a day.

The development of engraved current events was linked to that of the press. The revolutionary newspapers were sometimes illustrated, as was Camille Desmoulins' *Les Révolutions de France et de Brabant*. This was another platform offered to caricature, and it was utilized often, although not abused. The propaganda engravings that proliferated in 1793 and 1794 to glorify revolutionary events were published serially in the manner of periodicals. As Claudette Hould has clearly explained, they were intended to serve as illustrations to the *Recueil des actions héroïques et civiques des républicains français*, published by the Committee of Public Safety at the beginning of 1793, or to the *Recueil des traits héroïques et civiques*, a *daily* paper commissioned by the Convention in September.[22] These attempts to create timely imagery linked with the press constituted the beginnings of what the bourgeoisie of the July Monarchy would achieve forty years later with *Le Charivari*. By that time the French middle class had become self-conscious and could recognize itself in Daumier's caricatures. France had found its Hogarth, but for this to occur, a second revolution was necessary.

1. André Blum, *Louis XIV et l'imagerie satirique pendant les dernières années du XVII* siècle (N.p., n.d.), pp. 272–88.

2. Regarding the appointment of the censor on 31 July 1789, see André Blum, *La Caricature révolutionnaire* (Paris: Jouve et Cie, 1916), p. 13. On the great debate led by Wicar in germinal and floréal of Year II in the Société populaire et républicaine des arts sur la censure des estampes de moeurs, see Athanase Detournelle, "Aux armes et aux arts," *Journal de la Société républicaine des arts* (1794), pp. 380–81.

3. Aubin-Louis Millin, *Lettre aux représentans de la Commune de Paris sur les dangers de la défense qu'ils ont faite de publier des estampes et des écrits burinés sans l'approbation du censeur qu'ils ont nommé* (Paris: Lagrange, 1789), p. 7. This document is in the Bibliothèque nationale, Paris (8°Lb39 2241).

4. *Procès-verbaux de l'Assemblée nationale . . .* (Séance du 2 août 1790), vol. 26, no. 368, p. 18.

5. Michel Melot, "La Caricature ou l'imitation contrariée," in *L'Imitation, aliénation ou source de liberté: Rencontres de l'Ecole du Louvre* (Paris: La Documentation française, 1985), pp. 231–40.

6. Claudette Hould, "Les Commandes du Comité de salut public," in *Actes du colloque sur les images de la Révolution française tenu à la Sorbonne, Paris, 1985* (forthcoming). The reader is referred to Albert Boime's essay in this catalogue for further discussion of David's caricatures.

7. Alphonse Aulard, *La Société des Jacobins* (Paris: Librairie Jouaust, 1889), vol. 1, p. 477 (cited by Blum [supra, note 2], p. 23).

8. The French texts of the period on the subject of prints are, in fact, obsessed with the successes of English artists: "Thus England has little difficulty in taking away our clientele and our money, we are far from being able to say the same thing" (Charles François Joullain, *Réflexions sur la peinture et la gravure accompagnées d'une courte dissertation sur le commerce de la curiosité et les ventes en général* . . . [Metz: Imprimerie de C. Lamort, 1786], pp. 32–33; this book is in the collection of the Bibliothèque nationale, Paris [v 24806]). Pierre-François Basan does not disagree, "Over the last fifteen years, England has supplied us with a very large number of specialists in this genre who, by means of a new style of engraving, have succeeded in becoming popular throughout Europe" (*Dictionnaire des graveurs anciens et modernes depuis l'origine de la gravure*, 2nd ed. [Paris: L'Auteur, 1789], vol. 1, pp. 2–3). We may deduce that what was true of prints in general was also the case with caricature which was an English specialty.

9. Boyer de Nîmes [Jacques-Marie Boyer-Brun], *Histoire des caricatures de la révolte des français*, 2 vols. (Paris: Imprimerie du *Journal du peuple*, 1792). This text is in the collection of the Bibliothèque nationale, Paris (La32 29).

10. In view of these antecedents the introduction to the chapter on modern French caricature in Thomas Wright's history bears rereading: "Modern political caricature, born as we have seen in France, may be considered to have spent its infancy in Holland. The location of this country and the superior degree of freedom that it enjoyed made it, during the seventeenth century, the general refuge of political dissenters from other nations, and especially of the French who fled Louis XIV's tyranny." Thomas Wright, *Histoire de la caricature et du grotesque dans la littérature et dans l'art*, 2nd ed. (Paris: A. Delahays, 1875), p. 372. It should be recalled that until 1694, the monopoly of French copperplate engraving had been limited to Catholics. Regarding the organization of the practice of engraving, see Marianne Grivel *Le Commerce de l'estampe à Paris au XVIIe siècle* (Geneva: Droz, 1986). A dissertation by Pierre Casselle, *Sur le commerce de l'estampe à Paris dans la seconde moitié du XVIIIe siècle* (Ph.D. diss, Ecole nationale des chartes, 1976) has unfortunately not been published, see *Positions de thèses de l'Ecole nationale des chartes* (Paris: 1976), pp. 37–44.

11. Frederick Antal, *Hogarth and His Place in European Art* (London: Routledge and Kegan Paul, 1962).

12. George also remarks that lack of respect toward the royal family, a specifically English characteristic, was reinforced by the rupture brought about by the English Revolution and the arrival of the Hanoverian family. See Mary Dorothy George, *Hogarth to Cruikshank: Social Change in Graphic Satire* (London: Allen Lane, Penguin, 1967), pp. 13–17.

13. Antal (supra, note 11), chap. 2.

14. George (supra, note 12), p. 15.

15. Champfleury [Jules-François-Félix Husson], *Histoire de la caricature sous la République, l'Empire, et la Restauration* (Paris: Dentu, [1874]), p. 20.

16. Pierre Leveel, "Les Biencourt d'Azay," in *Bulletin de la Société archéologique de Touraine* 37 (1974), pp. 423–43.

17. Joullain (supra, note 8), pp. 126–27.

18. Jeanne Duportal, *La Gravure en France au XVIIe siècle* . . . (Paris: Librairie nationale d'art et d'histoire, 1926), p. 7.

19. René Hennequin, *Avant les photographies: Les Portraits gravés au physionotrace* (Troyes: J.L. Paton, 1932).

20. Laura Malvano, "Le Sujet politique en peinture: Evénements et histoire pendant les années de la Révolution," *Histoire et critique des arts* 13-14 (First Semester 1980), p. 65.

21. Jean Adhémar, "Vallée, marchand d'estampes à Paris en 1787–1789," in *Bulletin de la Société archéologique, historique et artistique Le Vieux Papier* 24, fasc. 213 (July 1965), p. 261–64.

22. Hould (supra, note 6).

The Political Psychology
of
Revolutionary Caricatures

Lynn Hunt

University of Pennsylvania

Behind the caricatures of the French Revolution lay certain assumptions about political psychology in a time of revolutionary change. The French were in the process of trying to revolutionize themselves, that is, re-form their political character. This reformation required an enormous effort at total political reeducation. As one local revolutionary exclaimed:

> A revolution is never made by halves; it must either be total or it will abort. All the revolutions which history has conserved for memory as well as those that have been attempted in our time have failed because people wanted to square new laws with old customs and rule new institutions with old men... REVOLUTIONARY means outside of all forms and all rules; REVOLUTIONARY means that which strengthens, consolidates the revolution, that which removes all the obstacles which impede its progress.[1]

Caricatures, like paintings, festivals, dress, porcelain, street names, and even the calendar itself could all be mobilized in the attempt to create a

"new man." They were all part of the endeavor to escape from the French past, that "history of a people which until now has hardly been anything other than the crimes of its kings."[2]

Like other visual forms, moreover, caricatures could be especially influential in a society in which half the adult men and three-quarters of the adult women could not read. They were one of the primary means for informing people of revolutionary events outside of their own neighborhoods, and they helped shape the collective memory of those events—on both the revolutionary and counter-revolutionary sides. For the illiterate populace, images fixed the impression of revolutionary happenings much more indelibly than the printed word. This may have been true for the literate population as well, for images captured on a single page a vision of events that could only be described at great length in newspapers or pamphlets.

Caricatures did more than convey information, however; they actively shaped views of events and personalities. Ridiculing the king and queen in printed images, for example, helped prepare the way for their executions in 1793. Bitter satirical cartoons of the clergy made the new church organization seem more justifiable. Caricatures of the nobility were part of the general attack on deference in revolutionary society. On the other side, mocking prints of revolutionary leaders or symbols helped undermine support for the new government.

Revolutionary officials were keenly aware of the power of images. Their views on the subject were best expressed by Henri Grégoire, a priest and leading deputy in many of the legislative assemblies of the revolutionary decade. In a speech given in January 1796, he captured the revolutionary enthusiasm for "signs":

> When one reconstructs a government anew, it is necessary to republicanize everything. The legislator who ignores the importance of the language of signs will fail at his mission; he should not let escape any occasion for grabbing hold of the senses, for awakening republican ideas. Soon the soul is penetrated by the objects reproduced constantly in front of its eyes; and this combination, this collection of principles, of facts, of emblems which retraces without cease for the citizen his rights and his duties, this collection forms, in a manner of speaking, the republican mold which gives him a national character and the demeanor of a free man.[3]

Although this passage might be taken to refer indiscriminately to words or images (e.g., "this collection of principles, of facts, of emblems"), Grégoire was referring in this speech to a very potent image, the seal of state. In the same report he argued against the view that seals were only necessary "to compensate for the ignorance or the imperfection of writing." On the contrary, the use of a seal was founded on reason because it was more easily recognized than a signature, more permanent, and more difficult to counterfeit. In short, images had uses that went far beyond the supplement to writing. All civilized people, Grégoire insisted, had found that "a sign, a type, was necessary to give a character of authenticity" to public acts.[4]

In Grégoire's usage, it is clear that "signs" were the vehicle for the production of political effects. Signs were the way that events or persons could be represented and understood in their operation; they made possible "grabbing hold of the senses" in order to awaken republican ideas. Signs, in other words (whether words or images), were essential ingredients in "the republican mold," which revolutionaries hoped to use to fashion a new human personality. Signs worked so effectively because, as Grégoire explained in an earlier speech, "In general, very few men act on principles; almost all of

them imitate: the character of most of them is more the product of the examples that have passed in front of their eyes than it is of the maxims which we have attempted to inculcate in them."[5] What "passed in front of their eyes," then, was all-important. The signs that grabbed hold of their senses were the ones that would determine the new political personality.

Grégoire's concept of the sign came out of Enlightenment thought and in particular out of the enormously influential work of the Abbé de Condillac, the French philosopher who died in 1780. In his *Essay on the Origins of Human Knowledge* (1746) and his *Treatise on Systems* (1749), Condillac developed Locke's principles of psychology in an even more "sensationalist" direction. For Condillac, man was a product of the reactions of his senses to the stimuli provided by the physical environment.[6] Reason, or the faculties of understanding, could be reduced to an analysis of signs, and the material for signs came from the sensations. The mind only organized information that came in through the senses. As Condillac argued in his *Essay*, "I am convinced that the use of signs is the principle which develops the germ of all of our ideas." He cited Bacon as one of his most important sources of inspiration because he had shown that "the origin and the progress of our knowledge depends entirely on the manner in which we use signs." As Condillac put it in the concluding passages of his *Essay*, "The senses are the sources of our knowledge . . . reflection and other operations put the material [provided by the senses] to work; signs to which we owe the exercise of these same operations are the instruments that they use."[7]

From our twentieth-century perspective, such views might seem less than radical, but in eighteenth-century France, Condillac was linked with Locke as the pioneer of a philosophical attitude that promised to revolutionize the understanding of perception, the sources of true knowledge, philosophy, and aesthetics (since aesthetics depended on the analysis of perception). Like Locke before him, Condillac helped shift attention away from metaphysical concerns with the abstract nature of knowledge toward an interest in the actual mechanics of thought and perception. Psychology and anthropology could now become important tools in understanding how the mind worked and how it was influenced by its environment. Most important, from the perspective of the revolutionaries, was Condillac's insistent emphasis on nature; nature and the natural operations of the mind were the true sources of knowledge rather than history, tradition, custom, or Scripture. These historical forms were more likely to distort true knowledge; they could not make up for a faulty connection between objects existing in nature and the usage of signs to represent them.

By the time of his death in 1780, Condillac had become a virtual household word in educated circles. His principles of psychology and logic were considered self-evident. The revolutionaries consequently referred to him frequently when they developed their ideas for a new order. In January 1791, for example, the noted intellectual La Harpe called for far-reaching changes in education, including the use of French rather than Latin in the schools. As for metaphysics, he insisted, Locke and Condillac were all that was necessary, for they were "the only two philosophers in whom one finds what it is possible for us to know about human understanding."[8] Political leaders such as Sieyès and Robespierre quoted Condillac on many occasions in their speeches.

Condillac's emphasis on the importance of signs to knowledge fit well with eighteenth-century aesthetic writing that underlined the ability of art to teach through the appeal to emotion. The visual arts provoked immediate bodily sensations in the viewer, and so they were much more efficient as educational vehicles than verbal descriptions could ever hope to be.[9] Painting, sculpture, engraving, architecture, and even the design of costumes could grab hold of the senses and encourage the development of republican ideals. In defending the use of official costume, for example, Grégoire assimilated it once again to the use of signs: "The language of signs has an eloquence of its own: distinctive costumes are part of this idiom for they arouse ideas and sentiments analogous to their object, especially when they take hold of the imagination with their vividness."[10] The capacity for vividness and the appeal to the emotions made art an excellent vehicle for political propaganda, and caricatures represent the most successful of propagandistic artistic forms that were used during the Revolution. Unfortunately for the revolutionaries, however, caricatures could be used to make any political point, and the French government could never hope to entirely control their production.[11]

Historians of the French Revolution have shown increased interest in caricatures in the last few years, not just as illustrations of important political events or personalities, but also as a new kind of documentation of political consciousness. Recent publications by historians have categorized the caricatures by their political intent — revolutionary or counterrevolutionary — and by their political reference. Michel Vovelle's multivolume edition of caricatures, *La Révolution française: Images et récit, 1789–1799,* arranges the images chronologically by the event of reference: the fall of the Bastille, the execution of the king, the struggle between Girondins and Jacobins, and the like.[12] Vovelle derives from the caricatures not only considerable information about events and persons but also an elaboration of the revolutionary vision of the ideal society.

The caricatures can be read in many other ways, however. At least as important as the commemoration of significant events, the portrayal of revolutionary heroes, or the attacks on enemies were the major silences or subjects not chosen. Vovelle points out, for example, that there were few prints made of the uprising in the Vendée, even though it was certainly one of the major events of the Revolution.[13] There were many representations of the execution of the king, but hardly any of these were French in origin; almost all of them were foreign prints made to arouse sympathy for the dead monarch. One of the major exceptions is the dramatic Medusa's head version printed by Villeneuve (cat. no. 90).[14]

In general, the representation of violence posed many problems for prorevolutionary engravers, and as the violence of the Revolution increased in 1793–1794, representations of it in any explicit way in France declined (of course, non-French printmakers did not avoid the subject in the same way). As a consequence, the most dramatic representations of violence are to be found in the first years of the Revolution, especially 1789, rather than during the period known as the Terror. Few of the later prints approached the horror of those that represented the deaths of Foulon de Doué and his son-in-law Bertier de Sauvigny, who was the intendant of the Paris region under the Old Regime. On 23 July 1789, an angry crowd first seized Foulon, hung him from a lantern post in front of city hall, decapitated him, mutilated the body, and then promenaded his head in front of Bertier, who soon suffered the same fate. The engravings of the moment captured some of the most disturbing details of the events.[15]

Rather than focusing on the explicit political themes of the caricatures or the trajectory of the representation of violence (which would be a fascinating subject in itself), this essay will discuss the less explicit, but no less important, uses of gender differences and familial imagery in the caricatures. Central to the psychology of the revolutionaries as they attempted to fashion a new order was an underlying preoccupation with such images as metaphors for political and social order. Representations of gender differences and familial order were, however, never front and center in the conscious expressions of the revolutionary leadership;

Robespierre and Saint-Just, for example, did not give speeches that took the family as their explicit frame of reference. Although the various revolutionary governments passed important and pathbreaking legislation about the family — instituting divorce, for instance, for the first time in French history — the relationship between images of the family and images of the political and social order remained largely unspoken amongst the revolutionaries.[16]

Some of the greatest critics of the Revolution, on the other hand, understood early on the connection between social order and gender imagery. The Englishman Edmund Burke, for instance, in his *Reflections on the Revolution in France* (1790), complained that the revolutionaries were tearing off "the decent drapery of life" and revealing "the naked shivering nature" of men. The "new conquering empire of light and reason" would destroy the traditional place of women in the moral imagination, reduce kings to men, and permit the dissolution of the social and political fabric:

> On this scheme of things, a king is but a man; a queen is but a woman; a woman is but an animal; and an animal not of the highest order. All homage paid to the sex in general as such, and without distinct views, is to be regarded as romance and folly. Regicide, and parricide, and sacrilege, are but fictions of superstition, corrupting jurisprudence by destroying its simplicity.[17]

The important thing to note here is the link made between the homage paid to women and the deference paid to royalty, between the elevation necessary to woman's position and the ability of society to resist regicide, parricide, and sacrilege. The "homage paid to the sex in general" was the invisible glue in the social and political order; without it, people became like animals, even animals "not of the highest order." In this passage from the earliest years of the Revolution, Burke expressed a nightmarish fantasy; without the "ancient opinions and rules of life," there would be no compass to govern society, and the result would be the destruction of order, the effacement of all manners, and ultimately anarchy, terror, and cannibalism. This nightmarish fantasy of revolution appeared as well in the work of many of the English caricaturists of the time.[18]

If caricature as a genre necessarily involves an element of fantasy or exaggeration, then it is not surprising if caricatures in a time of revolution tell us something about the fantasies of the moral and political imagination. English artists tended to express the nightmarish side of these fantasies; French artists in the service of the Revolution obviously had very different aims. In many respects,

French engravers were less free to express their fantasies of power; they, like the revolutionary leaders, were under great pressure to direct political and moral energies away from violent expression into more acceptable channels. Many of the official engravings, letterheads, and vignettes of the revolutionary period are consequently marked by stiffness in presentation and restriction of subject matter to a canonical set of emblems and allegories (see, for example, cat. nos. 127, 128, 134, 137).

We can nevertheless detect in the caricatures the expression of a kind of "family romance." When Freud used this term, he meant the neurotic's fantasy of "getting free from the parents of whom he now has a low opinion and of replacing them by others, who, as a rule, are of higher social standing."[19] When the child feels slighted by the parents, he (*he*, in particular, since Freud thought this tendency was much weaker in girls) retaliates by imagining that these are not in fact his real parents; his real parents are important landlords, aristocrats, even kings and queens. This notion of the family romance with its emphasis on revolt against the father was incorporated by Otto Rank into his psychological interpretation of mythology. According to Rank, "Myths are, therefore, created by adults, by means of retrograde childhood fantasies, the hero being credited with the myth-maker's personal infantile history."[20] Myths incorporated the same infantile rebellion against the father that was displayed in the family romance of neurotics.

It is not necessary to accept the entire Freudian framework in order to make use of the concept of family romance, by which I mean here more generally the development of unconscious fantasies about the familial order underlying revolutionary politics. No one print can capture all the nuances of the family romance at any given time, but taken as a whole, the caricatures do tell interesting tales about the revolutionary political imagination. The family romance operated on at least two different levels during the revolutionary decade: first, as a set of commentaries on the role of the king and queen and, second, after their fall from power, as a collective search for new models on which to base the republic. Schematically, these might be labeled the family romance of patriarchalism and the family romance of republican fraternity. The caricatures provided a medium through which the more unconscious and even threatening aspects of these family romances could be addressed. The caricatures can function, then, as the equivalent of dreamwork in psychoanalysis.

In the early years of the Revolution, the family romance had a much more literal meaning than later on because it was focused on the royal family, which was itself the model for political power. The king, in absolutist political theory, was the father of his people, though the role of the queen was less certainly identified. The king's role was God-given and quite literal in conception; the king was closer to God on the great chain of being, and as a father, he was superior in every way to his children. The first psychological step in the establishment of a republic, then, was the erasure of the distance between father and children. The original object of attack was the queen, Marie-Antoinette, who was vilified even before 1789 in pornographic caricatures that portrayed her as sexually promiscuous. She was shown in the embrace of innumerable men and women, including Cardinal de Rohan of the Diamond Necklace Affair and the king's own brother. Representations of the queen's presumed sexual promiscuity called into question the basis of the regime in certain genealogy; if the paternity of the king's heirs was in question, so was the notion of hereditary kingship itself. The weak link obviously was the queen, whose fidelity was essential to the purity of the line. An example of this pornographic genre is a caricature from the revolutionary decade known as *Ma Constitution* (fig. 1). By showing the queen with Lafayette in a suspect position,

FIGURE 1. Anonymous French. *Ma Constitution (My Constitution)*, 1798. Etching and aquatint. Paris, Bibliothèque nationale.

it undermines the credibility of the Hero of Two Worlds as much as it continues the attack on the queen herself. Lafayette is here quite graphically trying to put his hand on the center of power, but his action hardly seems heroic.

The king was never denigrated to the same extent as the queen, perhaps because the habit of thinking of him as sacred in his person made such attacks seem too sacrilegious even for the most ardent of the revolutionaries. Nevertheless, the caricatures do tell the story of his fall from that sacred status over time. Representations of the king wearing the cap of liberty and drinking to the health of the nation (fig. 2) showed that he was no longer a

FIGURE 2. Anonymous French. *Nouveau Pacte de Louis XVI / avec le peuple le 20 juin 1792 l'an 4me de la liberté (New Pact of Louis XVI / with the People 20 June 1792 the Fourth Year of Liberty)*, 1792. (Cat. no. 66).

distant, regal figure. He was now more familiar, more accessible, more like a good bourgeois and much less like a father. Even before these caricatures of 1792, however, the royal family as a unit had come under attack. The caricature of the royal family being brought back to Paris by the National Guard after the ill-starred flight to Varennes in June 1791 (fig. 3) depicted them as pigs being returned to the stable. Later, a similar theme was used to show the royal family being driven to their place of house arrest in the Temple in August 1792 (fig. 4). By now an important change had been registered. A figure clearly identifiable as a *sans-culotte* (he has the long trousers associated with the working men of the cities) is herding the royal family into their prison. With the king portrayed as a turkey and the queen as a she-wolf, the royal family can hardly function

FIGURE 3. Anonymous French. *La Famille des cochons ramenée dans l'étable (The Family of Pigs Brought Back to the Sty)*, ca. 1791. (Cat. no. 84).

FIGURE 4. Anonymous French. *Les Animaux rares / ou la Translation de la ménagerie royale au Temple (The Rare Animals; / or, The Transfer of the Royal Menagerie to the Temple)*, 1792. Etching and aquatint. Paris, Bibliothèque nationale.

any longer as a model for political and social order. On the contrary, their characterization in this way demonstrates that the world has been turned upside down; now the lowest on the great chain of being rule over the highest. Burke's prophecy of 1790 has been realized: "A king is but a man; a queen is but a woman; a woman is but an animal; and an animal not of the highest order." Any belief that reconciliation between the father and his sons was possible had by now been destroyed. The sons were driving out the father and his family.

The revolutionaries were hardly in a position to develop a family romance in strictly Freudian terms; they could not imagine a father who would be of a higher social standing than the king. But they could imagine a father who was more receptive to the revolutionary process. When the king refused that process and tried to flee the country, the revolutionaries turned on him. The execution of the king and queen was the final step in this destruction of the patriarchal family romance of the Old Regime. In the caricature entitled *Louis le traître lis ta sentence* (cat. no. 86), the turn around is clear and dramatic: the king is referred to in the familiar *tu* form, and he is denounced as a criminal. The family romance had veered off into tragedy, and the royal couple had to be sacrificed.

It was one thing to jettison the old family romance; it was another to imagine a new one altogether. When the new National Convention abolished royalty and proclaimed the republic in September 1792, it immediately chose for the emblem of its seal a female allegory based on the Roman goddess of liberty (fig. 5).[21] The choice occasioned little comment, probably because no one was certain that it would be definitive, but it was nonetheless momentous because it dominated

representations of the French Republic ever after. There were many reasons behind the choice: in iconographic tradition, most abstract qualities and concepts were represented by female figures, just as in the French language these qualities and concepts were feminine nouns; Catholicism made the French more receptive to figures that resembled the Virgin Mary (the figure on the seal was soon referred to derisively by opponents of the republic as "Marianne"); and the female figure was suitably distant both from the male head of state of the monarchy and from the particular male politicians of the revolutionary era. Most important, the abstract female of the allegory contrasted dramatically with the personal portrayals of the king on the coins and seals of the Old Regime. Where he was male, she was female. Where he was a specific individual of a unique family, she was general, intangible, and representative of collective ideals. Where his recognizable face stood for sacred power in its very being, she was unidentifiable, standing, armed, and, though not aggressive in demeanor,

FIGURE 5. Cast of the Seal of the First Republic, 1792. Paris, Archives nationales, Collection de sceaux, D 137.

clearly ready to act in the world. Finally, where he was a father figure, she was young, almost virginal, seemingly unconnected to any family.

In the years that followed, female representations of the republic, of liberty, equality, reason, wisdom and the like appeared everywhere from official documents to playing cards and porcelain. Rarely, however, was the female figure depicted as maternal. Even the more staid representations of the Directory period (fig. 6) showed a female allegory shorn of any maternal attributes. There were rarely children present in the allegories, even more

FIGURE 6. Barthélemy Joseph Fulcran Roger (French, 1767–1841). *Directoire exécutif (The Executive Directory)*, ca. 1798, after Jean-Claude Naigeon. (Cat. no. 161).

exceptionally did any male figure appear who might be construed as a husband, and there was never a father present. By the end of 1793, during the most radical period of the Revolution, the female figure had male company. The Convention voted to replace "Marianne" on the seal of the republic with a representation of Hercules, who was intended to stand for the French people (fig. 7). Marianne was not definitively displaced, but for the rest of the decade, she had to share some of the spotlight with the male figure.

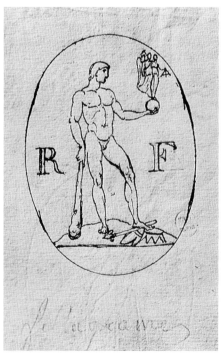

FIGURE 7. Augustin Dupré (French, 1748–1822). *Hercule R[épublique] F[rançaise] (Hercules F[rench] R[epublic])*, 1793. Ink drawing. Paris, Musée Carnavalet.

Hercules was not a paternal figure, however. On the seal of the republic, he was shown holding small female figures of Liberty and Equality in his hand, as if he was a big brother to them. Even on the coins of the Directory period, when Hercules is shown as not much bigger than Liberty and Equality, he still seems much more brotherly than paternal (fig. 8). In the caricatures of the republican period, then, the revolutionaries tended to portray themselves as young people without parents and without children. They imagined themselves as part of no lineage. In a sense, this was a family romance with the notion of parentage taken out; only brothers and sisters remained. The revolutionary slogan of liberty, equality, and *fraternity* had a very distinctive meaning. In place of the one father-king, there were now many, equal brothers.

But fraternity certainly did not mean that brothers and sisters were equal partners. The tiny stature of Liberty and Equality in the hands of Hercules made that clear. The brothers were there to protect

FIGURE 8. Drawing of Hercules Coin.

the orphaned sisters. Female figures were rarely shown accomplishing anything (fig. 9); they were there for their representative quality. The active figures were the young males, such as the one in figure 10 who is protecting the female figure of the Constitution. The elimination of the royal patriarchal couple did not automatically open the way for women to participate in public affairs; the proliferation of the female allegory was made possible, in fact, by the exclusion of women from public affairs. Woman could be representative of abstract qualities and collective dreams because women were not about to vote or govern.

The family romance without parents was very difficult to sustain, and a social order based on fraternity proved very fragile. Nevertheless, it is a measure of just how thoroughgoing the French Revolution was that it challenged even the unconscious bases of political power and social order. It is not possible in the brief space of an essay such as this to detail all the variations and developments in the familial iconography of the revolutionary epoch. It would be interesting, for example, to look more closely at the representations of the *sans-*

FIGURE 9. Antoine Quatremère de Quincy (French, active 1790s). *Projet de groupe a exécuter au fond du Panthéon français (Study for a Group to be Executed for the Back Wall of the Pantheon)*, 1794. Etching and aquatint. Paris, Bibliothèque nationale.

culottes as good family people and to contrast these with the attacks on the queen. I hope that I have been able to suggest in these few pages that there are many different ways to read the caricatures. Although at first glance, some of them may seem opaque and hard to decipher, they repay reviewing because they are an unusually rich source of documentation of the revolutionary view of the world.

FIGURE 10. Philippe-Auguste Hennequin (French, 1762–1833). *Allégorie de la constitution (Allegory of the Constitution)*, 1795. (Cat. no. 160).

1. Quoted from the "Discours prononcé à l'ouverture des séances du Comité des sans-culottes, par Marat-Mauger, président de ce Comité, et commissaire du Conseil éxécutif près le départment de la Meurthe" (not dated, but from the content and context, apparently late summer 1793). Archives nationales, F1c III Meurthe 15, Correspondance et divers, 1789–an v. Unless otherwise noted, all translations from the French are mine.

2. Henri Grégoire, *Rapport sur les moyens de rassembler les matériaux nécessaires à former les Annales du civisme, et sur la forme de cet ouvrage; par le citoyen Grégoire* (Séance du 28 septembre 1793).

3. Henri Grégoire, *Rapport fait au Conseil des cinq-cents, sur les sceaux de la République, par Grégoire* (Séance du 11 pluviôse an IV–31 janvier 1796).

4. Grégoire (supra, note 3). For a fuller discussion of the republican seal, see Lynn Hunt, *Politics, Culture, and Class in the French Revolution* (Berkeley and Los Angeles: University of California Press, 1984), pp. 87–119.

5. Grégoire (supra, note 2).

6. Isabel F. Knight, *The Geometric Spirit: The Abbé de Condillac and the French Enlightenment* (New Haven and London: Yale University Press, 1968).

7. E. B. de Condillac, *Essai sur l'origine des connaissances humaines précédé de L'Archéologie du frivole par Jacques Derrida* (Paris: Editions Galilée, 1973), pp. 103, 288, 289.

8. Marie Gustave Baguenault de Puchesse, *Condillac: Sa vie, sa philosophie, son influence* (Paris: Plon-Nourrit, 1910), p. 277.

9. See the illuminating remarks by Mary D. Sheriff, "On Fragonard's Enthusiasm," *The Eighteenth Century* 28 (1987), pp. 29–46.

10. Henri Grégoire, *Du costume des fonctionnaires publics: Rapport fait par Grégoire* (Séance du 28 fructidor an III–14 septembre 1795).

11. On the failures of artistic propaganda in France, see James A. Leith, *The Idea of Art as Propaganda in France, 1750–1799: A Study in the History of Ideas* (Toronto: University of Toronto Press, 1965).

12. Michel Vovelle, *La Révolution française: Images et récit, 1789–1799*, 5 vols. (Paris: Editions Messidor, Livre Club Diderot, 1986).

13. Ibid., vol. 1, p. 22.

14. See the fascinating argument by Neil Hertz, "Medusa's Head: Male Hysteria under Political Pressure," *Representations* 4 (1983), pp. 27–54.

15. The *Révolutions de Paris* did carry a series of very dramatic engravings of the September Massacres of 1792, but most of the representations of this event were printed either after the fall of Robespierre or by foreign presses. The violence of armed uprisings and of the war was most often very stylized in presentation. See Vovelle (supra, note 12), vol. 3.

16. There were certain moments, however, when the connection between social and political order on the one hand and gender differentiation and familial imagery on the other did come to the forefront. For a discussion of some of these, see Lynn Hunt, "Révolution française et vie privée," in *De la Révolution à la Grande Guerre* vol. 4 of *Histoire de la vie privée*, ed. Philippe Ariès and Georges Duby (Paris: Editions du Seuil, 1987), pp. 21–51.

17. Edmund Burke, *Reflections on the Revolution in France* (Garden City, N.Y.: Anchor Books, 1973), p. 90.

18. For further discussion of these fears and their treatment in English caricature, the reader is referred to Ronald Paulson's essay in this catalogue.

19. From "Family Romances," in *The Standard Edition of the Complete Psychological Works of Sigmund Freud*, trans. James Strachey (London: The Hogarth Press and the Institute of Psycho-Analysis, 1959), vol. 9, pp. 238–39.

20. Otto Rank, *The Myth of the Birth of the Hero: A Psychological Interpretation of Mythology*, trans. F. Robbins and Smith Ely Jelliffe (New York: R. Brunner, 1952), p. 82. Rank incorporated Freud's paper on family romance in this book, pp. 63–68.

21. For a discussion of the debates on the seal, see my *Politics, Culture, and Class in the French Revolution* (supra, note 4), pp. 87–119.

Counterrevolutionary
Iconography

Claude Langlois

Université de Rouen

istory is often written, and later interpreted, from the point of view of the victor. This is true of the French Revolution, and particularly an aspect of it that in recent years has become a little better known, the revolution in images.[1] Whether innovative or degrading, great paintings or hasty sketches, these images have been employed to form a homogeneous and, what is more, a consistently patriotic corpus.

This notion is, however, a tenacious and dangerous illusion, partly fostered by publications that, until very recently,[2] have presented to the general public—for aesthetic as well as pedagogical reasons—a confusion of the most heterogeneous works. One must, of course, take into consideration that unlike paintings, which can be easily traced from exhibition to exhibition, it is extremely difficult to keep track of a largely political body of engravings, most of which were produced without any indication of their artist, engraver, or even publisher. The situation becomes even more problem-

atic when this corpus suddenly expands and proliferates. Even when solid points of reference seem to exist, they often prove to be inadequate; thus, the order of the appearance of engravings in a well-known journal *Les Révolutions de Paris* often has no relationship whatsoever to the date of the event reproduced or to the number printed on the engraving, which refers to the date of publication of the journal itself (after August 1792 there is no record of how frequently this journal was issued). Similarly, the publication dates for the famous print series *Tableaux historiques de la Révolution française* can still not be ascertained; these images began to appear around mid-1791, but soon after, we lose track of them. Indeed, we do not even know which prints were published before and which after the fall of Robespierre.

As a consequence of these daunting, but not absolutely insurmountable, difficulties, the historian is frequently drawn to a practice that is as simple as it can be illusory. It consists of relating an engraving, and particularly a caricature, to the event it is supposed to describe[3] or treating icono-graphic elements as invariable without seriously examining the concrete marketing conditions under which a particular print comes into being.[4] An example of the latter is the treatment of the Phrygian cap. It is a matter of some importance whether this cap is at the end of a pike or on some-one's head, whether it is worn by the traditional allegorical feminine figure or by the new *sans-culotte* of 1792. In the latter instance, the wearing of the cap, as opposed to holding it, is not a whim of the engraver; each choice is a reference to a very specific situation occurring in April 1792.

Not only must the slow pace at which informa-tion traveled be recalled and the delay that could be occasioned if the engraving were at all elaborate, it is even more important to determine the condi-tions under which political engravings were pub-lished. The Oath of the Tennis Court provides an excellent example. Until the beginning of 1790, it was just one event among many. After 4 February when the king swore allegiance to the constitution at the Assembly and the oath "to the nation, to the law, to the king" was on everyone's lips, this situa-tion changed. At this point the patriots, in order to prevent the king's initiative from acquiring too

much symbolic significance, seized the opportu-nity to recall the *first* oath taken by the deputies. It was transformed into the founding gesture of the Revolution, an interpretation that was consecrated by David's drawing presented at the Salon of 1791.[5]

A quantitative approach, however cursory, quickly dispels the impression that political engrav-ing before the fall of Robespierre was largely com-mitted to the Revolution. The real situation was quite different. For a number of engravers who were striving above all to make a living, the Revolu-tion was a calamity. As a result of it, they found themselves unemployed. Clients had emigrated, certain speculations in progress before 1789 had been interrupted, and the market had, as a result, declined. The most astute attempted to make the best of the troubled times. One of the first to understand the situation was Jean-François Janinet, who by the end of 1789 had transformed his customary engraving activities and begun mar-keting the first, and for a considerable length of time the most famous, of the series representing the Revolution.[6] Others, like Charles Le Vachez and his son or Jean-Baptiste Vérité, concentrated on collections of portraits of deputies as a means of prospering or, at least, surviving while waiting for

FIGURE 1. Anonymous French. *Prise de la Bastille le 14 juillet 1789 (The Taking of the Bastille on 14 July 1789)*, 1789. (Cat. no. 19).

better days. Later, particularly after 1793, a few applied their talents to the service of the new allegories produced within the framework of the "Cultural Revolution" of Year II. Among the most famous of these were the engraver Jacques-Louis Copia and the painter Pierre Paul Prud'hon, who furnished drawings. It should be noted that during the first years of the Revolution, many famous engravers continued imperturbably to produce elaborate allegorical images in the style of those that the monarchy had commissioned in previous years.

One might oppose to this analysis the situation of popular political engraving. In publishing countless representations of the taking of the Bastille (fig. 1) and still more of the destruction of the Bastille, were the image makers of the rue Saint-Jacques moved by pure patriotism or were they merely seeking to satisfy the taste of the times? The considerable public consensus in favor of the destruction of the old prison-fortress, which had in fact become useless, makes ascertaining the engravers' motivations even more difficult.[7]

FIGURE 2. Anonymous French. *Le Noble Pas de deux (The Noble Pas de deux)*, 1789. (Cat. no. 42).

In the case of caricature, as one might guess, there was less ambiguity. It began with the representation of the three estates, at first fraternally united then quickly divided once the Third Estate had vanquished the others (fig. 2). The mass of true caricatures—including the deformation of features and of the body—which spread wildly and happily, was even more direct in its message. Such engravings returned to the old image of the dissolute monk, a glutton and tippler, and of the sleek cleric who is no better (fig. 3); these figures were, according to the artist's inspiration, thinned, undressed, relieved of their teeth, married,

FIGURE 3. Anonymous French. *Le Degraisseur patriote (The Patriotic Fat Remover)*, 1789. (Cat. no. 48).

deprived of their ration of "fresh flesh" (that is, the commerce in young girls), or stripped of their cowls and reclothed in the National Guard uniform.[8] Undoubtedly, this production evolved from a certain initial unanimity into a polemical work; aggressive or joyous, macabre or playful, it was intended as much to explain what had happened as to make the newly sovereign people conscious of their real power.

The repetition of a number of caricatural themes certainly lends them an incantatory aspect, as if they were intended to persuade the population of the "reality" of the change that had taken place. Well before festivals assumed this task, the political education of the people was accomplished through the sight of new colored engravings, posted day after day; thus, the Parisian population in particular learned to recognize its adversaries and their many guises. Above all, since these enemies appeared already vanquished in the caricatures, the citizenry learned to rid itself of its fear. During the Revolution ridicule truly killed or, rather, permitted one to put to death a political opponent. Equality was proclaimed by the Declaration of the Rights of Man, the privileges of the nobility and of the clergy were abolished during the night of 4 August 1789; but just as it would take many long years before the peasants succeeded in freeing themselves entirely from the feudal system, many months would be necessary before the governing classes lost their prestige in the eyes of the people.

The undermining work of caricature was, without a doubt, one of the most efficient means for achieving this end. One might even ask if the radicalism of the image, in its simplification, did not ultimately help to bring about extreme political solutions, which were certainly not desired by those who encouraged the production of such engravings during the early years. The combat intensified when, after having shown the spectacle of the fall of the privileged, the monks, and the wealthy clergy, caricature attacked the pope, who was hostile to the Civil Constitution, the king, who was rejected for treason, and finally the émigrés, who took up arms against the Revolution.

The foregoing description must, however, be qualified, as it refers specifically to Parisian caricature. Although one may justly counter that Paris had the monopoly of this production and therefore imposed its rapidly radicalized vision of the Revolution on the rest of France, this is only half true. Unfortunately, we know very little about the details of the circulation of the caricatures produced outside of Paris, but all evidence suggests that they reached primarily an urban public. In contrast, Parisian engravings, albeit filtered and selected, reached the greater part of the countryside, but with a reduced virulence. Two specific examples will serve to illustrate. The sole provincial engraver to imitate the Parisian production, and only a small part of it at that, was Letourmy (fig. 4). Although he was based in Orléans, he had established a liaison with Paris before the Revolution. When prints

arrived from the capital, he cut into wood a few of the most famous episodes, using a traditional technique, or copied certain famous caricatures. He put aside the most violent, however, and graced those that he did reproduce with floral garlands, which indeed attenuated their intensity.

More significant still is the case of the images reproduced on revolutionary faience, which was principally distributed from a number of centers located in the region of Burgundy.[9] The painters adopted as their basic model the agreement of the three estates, and with an astonishing consistency, they remained faithful to this iconographic theme, reproducing it with only minute variations. Thus, year after year, they distributed a political vision frozen in June 1789, that of the union of the three estates, celebrated in a political trinity, unceasingly reproduced: "The three are but one."

———————

Within the sphere of politically committed engravings, patriotic caricature initially occupied the field, to the extent of nearly having a monopoly for a considerable period of time. This was true,

FIGURE 4. Letourmy (French, active ca. 1791). *Tableaux mémorables qui ont donné lieu à la Révolution (Memorable Scenes That Gave Rise to the Revolution)*, 1791. (Cat. no. 32).

despite the fact that caricature during the first years of the Revolution did not at all reflect the bitterness of the political debate, whether ideological or simply polemic. In terms of the writing of the period, the situation was, in fact, entirely different. At the Assembly and in the press — through the newspaper and the pamphlet — the enemies of the Revolution made themselves widely heard, developing their arguments or mocking their adversaries.[10] The most scathing pens were wielded by the royalists, and this was almost to be expected, to the extent that the new power was represented by the Constituent Assembly where the patriots were dominant. Power was now in the hands of Bailly, Lafayette, Mirabeau, Orléans, and also of those less well-known constituents put forward by the press because they appeared to be the spokesmen of the new majority: Camus, Target, Montesquiou, Barnave, and many others. Royalist journalists normally treated the patriots as whipping boys, called them ridiculous names, unearthed stories from their pasts,[11] and placed them in embarrassing "situations," seeking to discredit with as much felicitous style as obvious bad faith.

The newspaper that best succeeded in this game was the famous *Actes des apôtres*, which set the tone and carried in its wake a host of imitators. It attacked the new political class with formulas that hit the mark and that a host of satirists would pick up with delight. The newspaper editors, hidden behind a transparent anonymity, brought into play every aspect of language, manipulated epigram or invective with brio, and knew when necessary how to be obscene with distinction.[12] Theirs was the very wit of Rivarol, placed in the service of class politics. The whip was repeatedly lashed on the shoulders of the "boors" and "louts" who believed that they could slip on the uniform of a noble officer and govern in his place. With a casual joy, the *Actes des apôtres* fanned all embers, wounded individuals at will, and gibed at all new ideas.

When a quarter's issues were nearly published, the reader was asked to hold off binding the copies into a single volume until he had received an engraving to place at the beginning of the book as a frontispiece. This frontispiece was traditionally allegorical, but it came to lean more and more toward caricature. The choice of subject skillfully permitted the artist to synthesize the political combat of the past months in one strong image. In order to assist the unskilled reader in deciphering the image and to help him to detect all the malicious allusions — as well as for the pure pleasure of fabricating stories based upon the engraving — the newspaper furnished, along with the frontispiece, an explanation that could run over ten pages in length. In this text, the author, caught up in the game, allowed his imagination to wander freely on the bases for the visual fiction and, so to speak, to redouble its message with his verbal delirium.[13]

During the first years of the Revolution the writing of the *Actes des apôtres* was the antithesis of patriotic caricatures. To the latter, which were rapidly drawn and most often tagged with only a word or a line, were opposed the abundant royalist texts, masterfully written material to which a rare and precious image was eventually joined. Early royalist caricature, as much in its inspiration as in its workmanship, remained narrowly dependent on the written form. It was, so to speak, the text's quintessence or emblem.[14] And yet, it is from this that the new counterrevolutionary caricature would emerge. Only a shock was required to make the royalists conscious of the importance of this new medium, which the patriots were already using with marked success. For the friends of the king this shock occurred with Varennes. The day following the attempted flight of Louis XVI, two political currents clearly imposed their message via caricatures. The partisans of the Duc d'Orléans proposed deposing Louis XVI in favor of his son and the solution of a regency.[15] The republicans sought above all to overthrow the monarchy and distributed shocking images of the pig-king brutally returned to the sty (cat. no. 84).[16] The affair of the Champ-de-Mars gave the royalty a reprieve. The constitution was finally approved, the royal power strengthened. The Constituent Assembly disappeared; with the new Legislative Assembly, the Revolution seemed to be institutionally concluded. Caricature, however, remained essential to the decisive new combats that were brewing.

In the context of the beginning of the Legislative Assembly and as a gesture of goodwill, Louis XVI consented to suppress the *Actes des apôtres*. In truth, the journal was beginning to fall apart by itself; but, despite this, it did not comply immediately, and the last issues were still appearing at the end of 1791, if not at the beginning of 1792. The gradual demise of this significant publication was offset by the appearance of new papers, which constituted a little royalist press. These new journals were written in popular language and were perhaps better adapted to the times than the *Actes des apôtres* with its more aristocratic tone. To the *Journal de la cour et de la ville*, which had not ceased publication, newcomers were soon added: the *Rocambole des journaux*, beginning in May 1791, which enrolled a part of the staff of the *Actes des apôtres*, the *Sabats jacobites* of François Marchant; and, soon after, the *Chant du coq*,[17] *A deux liards*, and finally the *Journal du peuple*. The latter, which was the last to appear among this informal group, was published by Boyer de Nîmes beginning in February 1792.

These new papers adopted the polemical style of the *Actes des apôtres*, but, as noted above, in a more popular tone. Desiring to be effective, they also took a serious interest in caricature. Beginning in October 1791, caricature had a real existence within the royalist camp.[18] At first, it made its appearance in the form of small vignettes that recalled a book format. These cleverly and successfully lampooned the "ancients," Bailly and Lafayette, who were, in fact standing aside at this time. They also attacked a few lesser-known figures, such as d'André, a member of parliament from Aix who had gone into the commerce in luxury foods (fig. 5), or Montesquiou who was asked to render his accounts, like all the members of the Constituent Assembly reaching the end of their terms.[19]

Soon this initial caricatural production changed its format and style. In November it affirmed itself, during the following months it asserted itself, and in March 1792 it reached its apogee and succeeded in producing a new caricature every day. Until the beginning of May it maintained its momentum but soon thereafter slowed down. From the middle of May on, caricatures became fewer and the obstacles to their distribution multiplied. After 10 August royalist caricature, along with royalist journalism, disappeared. All responsible parties were sought by the authorities, and those who persisted were reduced to engaging in clandestine activities. A total of approximately one hundred fifty different engravings had appeared over a period of nine months; of these, approximately one hundred have been preserved in various public collections.[20]

How can we determine the number and the dates of these royalist caricatures, as well as of their patriotic counterparts, when both are undated and unsigned? The answer is simple. Unlike patriotic caricature, the new royalist production maintained a close relationship to the royalist press, and above all, somewhat paradoxically, with the *Actes des apôtres*. This newspaper had remained influential in more ways than one. By 1790 it had come under the sway of English caricature, which had quite early on become hostile to the Revolution; and before disappearing, it gave its blessing to the new caricatural endeavor by incorporating in its last issues reproductions of the first royalist caricatures that were beginning to appear.[21] For a long time the authors of these new caricatures were to "see" their adversaries through the eyes of the journalists of the *Actes des apôtres*. The connection between this newspaper and royalist caricature is obvious, but the import of other journals should not be

FIGURE 5. Anonymous French. *Au Coq-André, rue de la Grande Tuanderie (At the Coq-André, rue de la Grande Tuanderie)*, 1791. Etching, aquatint, and stipple. Paris, Bibliothèque nationale.

neglected. Marchant, who regularly accompanied his pamphlets with appropriate engravings, particularly his famous *Jacobinéide*,[22] took up the tradition of the *Actes des apôtres* in his *Sabats jacobites* by using vigorous caricatures for frontispieces which did not require explanatory texts.[23] For their part, *A deux liards* and the *Rocambole des journaux* occasionally informed their readers about the new publications of royalist engravers.

———

Three individuals came to play essential roles in the development of counterrevolutionary caricature. Gautier de Syonnet, Jacques-Marie Boyer-Brun, known as Boyer de Nîmes, and Michel Webert have remained, nonetheless, relatively unknown to historians. The first was the editor of the *Petit Gautier*, the nickname usually applied to the *Journal de la cour et de la ville*, a paper which had begun anti-revolutionary combat as early as 1789. If one can believe his adversaries, Gautier de Syonnet should be numbered among those "Rousseaus of the gutter" discussed by Robert Darnton.[24] It suffices to read Gautier to know that he spared no one, not even his departing mistress.[25] As soon as the new caricature appeared, the *Petit Gautier* supported it. The paper announced the first publications, emphasized their originality, and described them sufficiently to give readers the urge to purchase. Gautier remained indefatigable in this effort. When the caricatures became too numerous, he grouped them and limited himself to indicating their titles; as soon as the flow became less abundant, after the middle of April 1792, he reverted to a more or less laconic description. It is to his dedication that we owe our knowledge of a production that has not been preserved after the middle of May. A closer look will reveal that the role of the *Petit Gautier* as a newspaper was still more important. The caricaturists, who had initially been nourished by reminiscences of the *Actes des apôtres*, quickly turned to this journal for inspiration; more than once, Gautier de Syonnet feigned a naive surprise at the role his journal had played, but no one was fooled by this stance, particularly not his readers. A fervent admirer of the new caricature, only rarely did he permit himself to be mildly critical, and this when an engraving differed too much, in his opinion, from the usual caricatural style.[26]

Boyer de Nîmes was also a journalist, and the Revolution afforded him the opportunity to work on several newspapers during his brief career. As his name would suggest, he began by writing for the *Journal de Nîmes*, where he claimed to have published a few caricatures.[27] He was forced to leave this paper following the serious incidents of 1790. Once in Paris, he would never forget either the events of the still-troubled south[28] or the Protestants who, in his opinion, were at the origin of all the ills of the Revolution. During the entire year of 1791, he served as the editor of the *Journal général de la France*, a position which the Abbé de Fontenai had left to found his own newspaper. In February 1792 Boyer de Nîmes in turn began his own *Journal du peuple*, which, as its title indicated, aimed to reach a more popular public than the *Journal général de la France*.[29] His success in this domain was, however, limited. In an attempt to reach his intended goal, Boyer de Nîmes paid great attention to the new caricatures. In cases where his descriptions of images can be compared to those of Gautier de Syonnet, it is Boyer de Nîmes who has the truer sense of the image's language.[30] The subject clearly excited him, and even though his newspaper had barely started, he planned a periodical publication of a new series that would group the best caricatures published since 1789. His *Histoire des caricatures de la révolte des Français* began to appear at the end of March 1792. Each week, in theory, he presented two new caricatures, one favoring the Revolution and the other opposing it. Thus, he cleverly gave a new impetus to the royalist caricatures that had only begun to appear a few months before and created a spurious sense of

equilibrium between the images of the two camps, which redounded to the benefit of the royalists. This periodical publication, which was obviously interrupted after 10 August, also allowed Boyer de Nîmes the opportunity to abandon himself to his anti-Protestant fantasies.[31] Nonetheless, it has given us irreplaceable testimony concerning the way in which certain contemporaries "saw" and understood caricature during the revolutionary period.

With the publicity from the *Petit Gautier* and the propaganda of Boyer de Nîmes, royalist caricature was not lacking in advantages. At the very outset, however, it had needed a publisher. It found one in the person of Michel Webert, known as Webert the German. Although he was the "kingpin" of the enterprise, Webert remains one of the least known of the figures responsible for the success of royalist caricature. Originally from Saverne in Alsace, he was twenty-one in 1790 and had been living in Paris for five years.[32] At that time, he was seized in one of the periodic raids of the Palais Royal and imprisoned for distributing pornographic literature.[33] With the intervention of his family, he was freed. Already a bookshop clerk, he soon became a bookseller at number 203 of the Palais-Royal. It was Webert who published the series of counterrevolutionary caricatures, and his name is found on several. The newspapers mentioned him often and, when publication was well advanced, they even announced that a collection of fifty, then of sixty, caricatures was for sale in his shop. He was not the only one who sold royalist caricatures. One could find them at the Palais-Royal, in the shop of Madame Lebel, on the quais, and undoubtedly in certain shops of the rue Saint-Jacques. Undeniably, however, Webert was the publisher and the principal distributor. He may have engraved some of the caricatures himself, but there is no doubt whatsoever that he functioned mainly as supervisor of operations, using a number of different artists and engravers. Unfortunately, none of these are known to us, although it remains possible, through allusions made in the newspapers, to discover that the central figure of the group was the author of the caricature known as *Gare au faux pas* (1791).[34]

The group responsible for royalist caricature was thus composed of Gautier, Boyer de Nîmes, and Webert; a few journalists and publicists, who produced propaganda; and a few technicians — among them an engraver of great talent — who conceived and realized the work. Through their efforts and in the space of a few weeks, the royalists were able to take hold in a kind of critique that until then had eluded them almost completely. This success was

FIGURE 6. Anonymous French. *En reviendra-t'elle? (Will She Survive?)*, 1790–1791. Etching with hand coloring. Paris, Bibliothèque nationale.

no doubt also encouraged by the temporarily more difficult situation in which revolutionary caricature found itself after the summer of 1791, which had been marked by anti-pontifical (May–June) and anti-royal (June–July) caricature. The disappearance of the patriotic *Révolutions de France et de Brabant* entailed the demise of the original caricatures that accompanied each week's issue.[35] *Les Révolutions de Paris*, another revolutionary organ, sequentially began to publish maps of the new French departments and, as a result, was not very interested in current events.[36] Furthermore, anti-royalist caricature was quickly stifled as part of the repression that followed the affair of the Champ-de-Mars in July 1791. A renewal occurred only with Villeneuve's new collection, composed principally of oval prints on a red background, and with the large and beautifully worked engravings devoted to the émigrés of Condé's army.

Everything would suggest that royalist caricature profited from these circumstances, gaining the acceptance and recognition that permitted it to

FIGURE 7. Anonymous French. *L'Expirante Targinette (The Dying Targinette)*, 1792. Etching and mezzotint. Paris, Bibliothèque nationale.

assert itself during the first quarter of 1792. It goes without saying that this astonishing reversal of the situation did not suffice to attract large numbers to the royalist camp, for these "new" caricatures arrived at the wrong moment and were, paradoxically, both archaic and ahead of their time. The royalists had learned quickly that in caricature it was necessary to simplify the stroke, to stress, to underline, to repeat, to hold a few individuals up to ridicule, and to drive home the point regularly. Mastering the rules of the new medium, however, had its downside: the political message, already very ideologically marked in contemporary journalism, became even more pronounced, while the plurality of targets—everything to the left of the most fervent royalists—introduced an element of confusion for the public.

FIGURE 8. Anonymous French. *Dernière Procession constitutionelle pour / l'enterrement du serment civique qui / se fera le...1792 (The Last Constitutional Procession for / the Burial of the Oath of Allegiance Which / Will Take Place on...1792)*, 1792. Etching, aquatint, and stipple. Paris, Bibliothèque nationale.

At first glance, this "new" caricature, which is easily identifiable, seems a little old-fashioned in comparison with the patriotic variety. It relied heavily on formal borrowings; it shamelessly copied opposing caricatures, took inspiration from old prints, and brazenly plagiarized the images provoked in the other camp by current events (compare fig. 6 [patriotic] and fig. 7 [royalist]).[37] It was also very much inspired by the English example; this is particularly apparent in the use of "phylacteries," which correspond to our modern "bubbles," to establish dialogues between the illustrated figures. On the other hand royalist caricature avoided, with rare exceptions, the more popular coloring of patriotic prints, striving to remain within the range of the semi-fine engraving and favoring aquatint, sometimes printed in sepia.[38]

It also obstinately refused the deformation of bodies and, more particularly, that of the face. This

FIGURE 9b. Detail of figure 9a.

FIGURE 9a. Anonymous French. *Grande Seance aux Jacobins en janvier 1792, ou l'on voit le grand effet interieure / que fit l'anonce de la guerre par le ministre Linote a la suite de son grand / tour qu'il venoit de faire (The Great Meeting of the Jacobins in January 1792, Where We See the Great Shock / Produced by the Announcement of War Made by the Minister Linote / Following His Grand Tour)*, 1792. Etching and mezzotint. Paris, Bibliothèque nationale.

can even be said of one royalist print where, despite the addition of grossly exaggerated noses, individual faces remain recognizable (fig. 8). Royalist caricature did not hesitate to use animal forms (body or head) for certain of its figures; Narbonne, for example, was regularly represented as a linnet (figs. 9a–b).[39] It sought, however, to make the political figures represented immediately identifiable. (It is important to remember that caricature in the modern sense of the term, that is, a deformation that accentuates the features and thereby makes the individual *more* recognizable, did not yet exist.)[40] Visual recognition continued to operate in the allegorical mode by means of the presence of a specific object, which could in an extreme case, for example that of Mirabeau-*tonneau* (Mirabeau-barrel), be identified with the personage himself. The result of these choices for royalist caricature was a certain awkwardness of the image; heads were often disproportionate to bodies and were frozen in the artificial attitude of portraits.

To these easily recognizable formal characteristics must be added a singularity in the choice of individuals, which was particularly perceptible in the first caricatures. The royalists chose to represent members of the Constituent Assembly who had just stepped aside and who, in certain cases, were no longer in the foreground of political life. Barely published, these new caricatures gave the impression of already being anachronistic. Did the royalist Sleeping Beauty, finally awakened, believe she was still in 1789? Did these newcomers deem it necessary, before following political events step-by-step, to recapitulate the Revolution through the

evocation of great names, such as Bailly, Lafayette, and Talleyrand, or of lesser-known figures, such as Camus (fig. 10), Target, or Montesquiou?

These somewhat anachronistic choices may be explained in part by inexperience and also by a desire to preserve and to summarize, which was linked to the late appearance of royalist caricature on the market. But this, undoubtedly, is not the essential point. To the desire to "stick" to the present, which could easily become tyrannical, counterrevolutionary caricature added an equally powerful need to constantly recapitulate the past while ceaselessly anticipating the future. This desire was openly professed and was even its principal characteristic. To better understand the originality of royalist caricature on this point, it is necessary to compare it to the model elaborated by patriotic caricature at its inception.

Patriotic caricature paradoxically erased the "present" of that which it represented. It put the event in parentheses, scarcely alluding to it visually.[41] Its authors no doubt supposed that the

FIGURE 10. Anonymous French. *Camus, Talleyrand, Rabaut-Saint-Etienne, la Religion livrée (Camus, Talleyrand, Rabaut-Saint-Etienne, Religion Handed Over)*, 1791. Etching and mezzotint. Paris, Bibliothèque nationale.

"present" was sufficiently embedded in the public's imagination. By ignoring the "now," it proposed an interpretation of the event that rested on a simple antinomic vision, opposing the departed "past" to an immediate, transformed "future." From this perspective, the Revolution becomes an all-powerful, but invisible, motor that sets History in motion and creates an irreversible progression, a view that is opposed to the circularity of the "world turned upside down."[42] Caricature may seem to borrow its visual themes from this popular old conception, but in fact, it breaks away from both its mirror effects and the rigidity of its models.

Royalist caricature, for its part, functioned in a very different manner, primarily because it did not use the same actors. From the beginning, patriotic engraving had recourse to "collective" figures through the representation of the three estates; later, to the noble, the monk, and the member of the Third Estate, would be added the aristocrat, the cleric, the emigrant, and the patriot. Royalist caricature, however, was primarily individualistic (figs. 11, 12). Out of one hundred fifty known caricatures, it has been possible to count more than one hundred thirty different individuals; more than forty of these were found in the foreground at least once or twice;[43] around sixty would have been easily identifiable for someone knowledgeable about political life and reasonably familiar with this production. The entire play of royalist caricature consisted of bringing together in fictitious scenes, borrowed from current events, personae who would normally be involved, as well as those who might have been present in a previous historical situation of the same type. In equal measure it anticipated what would occur, materializing hopes and fears in an often tragic tone that left little place for anything but grim humor or false laughter. Thus were engendered images of the death of the king,

FIGURE 11. Anonymous French. *Les Douleurs de Target, ou les Travaux d'Hercule (The Trials of Target; or, The Labors of Hercules)*, 1790. Etching. Paris, Bibliothèque nationale.

FIGURE 12. Anonymous French. *Les Couches de M^r. Target (Mr. Target's Confinement)*, 1791. Etching and mezzotint. Paris, Bibliothèque nationale.

shown crucified with his brothers (fig. 13); the execution of the Jacobins or of Lafayette, or the suicide of the Duc d'Orléans.

Patriotic caricature was intent upon making the new popular actors of the political scene conscious of the irreversibility of the Revolution and of the beneficial rupture in the course of history that it had introduced. The royalist production, in contrast, played the card of the immediate present, a present that was illuminated alternately by a ceaseless realignment of actors, an expanding genealogy of adversaries, and the projection into a desired or feared future of information gleaned from day to day. Thus, at the beginning of the Revolution, patriotic caricature was essentially instructive in function. It served to make the people conscious of the fact that the world had indeed changed, that the configuration of social relationships was basically modified because the respective place of the principal actors was no longer the same. It announced at once that the new world had arrived and that the Old Regime was no more.[44] Less ambitious in a certain sense, less naive as well, but consequently less capable of acquiring and mobilizing adherents, royalist political engraving insisted that the Revolution was not a rupture, nor was it irreversible or instantaneous; instead, it was a specific time, a present stretched out beyond measure, scarcely manageable and not easily understandable, which constantly required the evocation of the immediate past and the anticipation of the near future. Such a present threatened to escape at every moment from those who wished to grasp it. Within this difficult context, the job of caricature became making comprehensible what was not,

a risky substitution of reassuring fictions for a moving and changing reality.

Royalist caricature, which in many respects appeared to be armed with certitudes, was, therefore, replete with paradoxes. It multiplied condemnations and fired on "anything that moved" to its left; it did not spare Louis XVI but handled with care — or pretended to ignore — the Robespierrist Mountain; it did not know whether it despised most the Feuillants, who were ready to somehow compromise with the Revolution, or the Brissotins, who were capable of doing anything to obtain power and keep it. Its hatred was, however, directed above all at the nobility who were guilty of treason; Lafayette, Talleyrand, Villette, Ségur, Montmorency, and the other liberal nobles were all attacked, despite the fact that their ranks were then melting away like snow in the sun. The authors of royalist caricature did not pay attention to detail; they hoped to see all of the rebellious nobles hung by the eagerly anticipated coalition troops. They produced a type of truly "suicidal" caricature and would have liked nothing better than to have been out of work for lack of adversaries. Their production maintained an unvarying stance, a politics of the worst, a permanent one-upmanship, bad faith instituted as a fixed system.

And yet, for the first time in France — forty years before Grandville, Daumier, and the other collaborators of *Le Charivari* and *La Caricature* — a truly modern political caricature had appeared. In order to establish itself, it took advantage of the seemingly stagnant period of the Legislative Assembly,

FIGURE 13. Anonymous French. *Le Nouveau Calvaire (The New Calvary)*, 1792. Etching and Mezzotint. Paris, Bibliothèque nationale.

FIGURE 14. Anonymous French. *Grand Débandement de l'armée anticonstitutionelle (The Great Rout of the Anti-Constitutional Army)*, ca. 1792. (Cat. no. 109).

specifically the six months of apparent immobility between November 1791 and April 1792 when everything slowly capsized.[45] For the first time a homogeneous group used both the written press and caricature to follow political events from day to day.[46] It made known most of the new actors, and it furnished points of reference among the Legislative Assembly, the "political parties," and the existing military forces. For the first time, caricature reacted to a ministerial crisis, the fall of the Feuillant ministry in March 1792 and its replacement by the first Girondist ministry. For the first time, an opposition press campaigned through caricature, as well as through satire, to denounce the financial scandals of the regime and to attack the deputies who "fill their pockets"[47] or who "fight like ragpickers." Ministers were lampooned, heads of armies were accused of incompetence, mistresses were shown as discreetly pulling the strings (fig. 14). Protestants were blamed for everything, as Jews would be one hundred years later. The cynicism of opportunists who looked both right and left to determine advantage was also denounced.[48]

A perusal of royalist caricature can evoke the caricatures of the July Monarchy, or even the Third Republic. This illusion is engendered largely by the royalists' assiduous reading of the daily newspapers and the inspiration they derived from the longstanding practice of their English neighbors. Counterrevolutionary caricature sought each day to give new impetus to "the final struggle" and demonstrated clearly how it intended to do so. Before the declaration of war, it enjoyed a nearly total freedom of expression, and then, as a result of prudence or through unofficial pressure, it became more discreet. On 10 August 1792, it disappeared.

FIGURE 15. Anonymous French. *Domine salvum fac regnum (Lord Save His Reign)*, 1792. Etching, aquatint, and stipple. Paris, Bibliothèque nationale.

The effectiveness of this production has the verdict of History against it. The vanquished are necessarily held to be in the wrong. Although it was a popular form, royalist caricature was nonetheless produced by the official "political class," not the masses or the new leaders. It addressed itself in fact to the same public that Grandville and Daumier would find, the readers of the newspapers, the attentive connoisseurs of daily parliamentary developments; this was a potential clientele of a few tens of thousands at most. Through its ideological choices and even more through the "cultural" language in which it signified them (fig. 15), the counterrevolutionary press obviously narrowed its readership to a "party" of the right: the nobility and its hangers-on, the conservative urban bourgeoisie, and the fringe of traders and artisans who were either worried or simply royalist in their sympathies.[49] At any given moment, it could attract a larger clientele, seduced by the quality of the caricature, and even sometimes reached patriots to the extent that it occasionally fired on the same targets as the most extreme among them: first on the moderate Feuillants and then on the Girondists in power.

The success of this caricature, according to Boyer de Nîmes—who remains credible despite having played the role of judge and jury—was real. Approximately twenty caricatures made their mark for posterity, and their presence in collections attests to a large printing. Occasionally, historians have more difficulty understanding the impact made by certain small works dating from the beginning of the effort, such as the first caricatures directed against Lafayette (fig. 16), who was often referred to as *le Sans-tort,* and against Bailly (*Eh*

donc coqco).[50] They are more easily convinced of the quality of the caricatures published later, like *L'Homme aux assignats, Gare au faux pas,* or *Grand Convoi funèbre de leurs majestés les Jacobins.* The development of this kind of caricature is undeniably worthy of being reconstructed, and its images deserve to be incorporated in an as yet unwritten history of political caricature.

We must not forget, however, that caricature is primarily a weapon of combat and in this case, a struggle to the death. One might ask whether this caricature of intimidation did not have a stronger effect on its adversaries, who took it seriously, than on its partisans, whose basic defeatism made them difficult to mobilize. Ostensibly desirous of fighting the battle for a restored monarchy, instead it contributed to discrediting moderate solutions (the Feuillant ministry or the Fayettist proposal) and to communicating the image of a violent counterrevolution, as blind as it was ferocious in its repression.[51] Consciously or not, the king's caricaturists aided in making others see what a *true* counterrevolution would entail and to their rejecting it.

On the one hand, the hangings that the counterrevolutionaries promised in their engravings (fig. 17) were only the complement of the adornments to the political "lamppost" illustrated by the patriots.[52] There seem, however, to be essential differences between the macabre exhibitions of the respective combatants. Royalist caricature designated its victims by name and allowed it to be

FIGURE 16. Anonymous French. *Départ du général parisien / pour la fameuse nuit du 5 au 6 Octobre / Mes amis menez moi je vous prie coucher / a Versailles (Departure of the Parisian General / for the Famous Night of 5–6 October / My Friends Please Take Me to Versailles to Sleep)*, 1791. Etching and mezzotint. Paris, Bibliothèque nationale.

BRANLE D'AUTUN.

FIGURE 17. Anonymous French. *Branle d'Autun (Autun's Dance)*, 1792. Etching, aquatint, and stipple. Paris, Bibliothèque nationale.

understood that those indicated were only the first on the list. Moreover, in July 1792, at the moment when tension was becoming strongest, the *Manifeste de Brunswick* suddenly gave support to these images by suggesting that the coalition troops would soon be in Paris and that Brunswick would then act in reality as Bender had in Webert's caricatures (cat. no. 101).[53] These ambiguous images, the grimacing mirror of today, were suddenly transformed into the "certainty" of a nightmarish tomorrow. As in all good Westerns, however, victory does not belong to he who boasts and draws his weapon at any provocation, but to he who, at the right moment, fires first. This was the case in August 1792 and more so at the beginning of September.

The symbolic execution of adversaries is a useful outlet for democracies that are peaceful or, at least, only occasionally feverish. During times of revolution, however, this ploy quickly becomes a bomb, which can explode in the hands of those who inexpertly manipulate it. Truly, during the Revolution ridicule killed, and it did so in more than one fashion. The image under such conditions was necessarily murderous.

years later; on the contrary, the print that shows the king crucified (fig. 13) does not date from the time of his execution but from April 1792 (ibid., vol. 2, p. 153).

4. In contrast, we have Lynn Hunt's suggestive perspective of the Hercules *sans-culotte*. See her *Politics, Culture, and Class in the French Revolution* (London: Methuen and Co., 1986), pp. 87–122.

5. Philippe Bordes, *Le Serment du Jeu de paume de Jacques-Louis David* (Paris: Editions de la Réunion des Musées nationaux, 1983).

6. Janinet's series was entitled *Gravures historiques des principaux événements depuis l'ouverture des Etats généraux*. The publication began at the end of 1789. Other engravers joined the ranks thereafter, notably Sergent.

7. H.-J. Lusebrink and R. Reichardt, "'La Bastille' dans l'imaginaire social de la France, 1774–1799," *Revue d'histoire moderne et contemporaine* 30 (April–June 1983), pp. 196–234.

8. Antoine de Baecque, "Le Sang des héros: Figure du corps dans l'imaginaire politique de la Révolution française," *Revue d'histoire moderne et contemporaine* (October–December 1987), pp. 553–84.

9. R. Ajalbert and C. Bonnet, *Les Faïences révolutionnaires de la collection Louis Heitschel* (Paris: Austerlitz, 1985).

10. Jean-Paul Bertaud, *Les Amis du roi: Journaux et journalistes royalistes en France de 1789 à 1792* (Paris: Perrin, 1984).

11. This was particularly the case with Brissot. A campaign of lampoons in the summer of 1791 paradoxically contributed to making him better known.

12. For a discussion of the use of obscenity in the prerevolutionary press, the reader is referred to Albert Boime's essay in this catalogue.

13. See, for example, the engraving entitled *Royal Louis* that accompanies the eighth volume of the journal.

14. As a comparison, see Michel de Certeau's suggestive reading of a frontispiece, "Histoire et anthropologie chez Lafitau," in *Naissance de l'ethnologie?*, ed. C. Blanckaert (Paris: Cerf, 1985), pp. 63–90.

15. An original series of caricatures on the royal family portrayed the theme of the king who had reverted to childhood and the child who would be king.

16. A. Duprat, "La Dégradation de l'image royale dans la caricature révolutionnaire," in *Les Images de la Révolution française: Actes du colloque de 1985* (supra, note 1).

17. This journal was founded in July 1791: see Jean-Paul Bertaud (supra, note 10) and also Eugène Hatin, *Histoire politique et littéraire de la presse en France* (Paris, 1860), vol. 4, p. 83. A *deux liards* made its appearance in October 1791 and was subsidized by the court.

18. Claude Langlois, *La Caricature contre-révolutionnaire* (Paris: Presses du C.N.R.S., 1988).

19. A campaign of lampoons was orchestrated around the theme of the Constituent Assembly's rendering of its accounts at the end of its mandate. Montesquiou was especially targeted because he often reported on financial issues.

20. Not counted here are the various copies or the replications with slight variants of the same engraving. These caricatures are found in the principal collections (de Vinck, Qb1, etc.) of the Bibliothèque nationale (Cabinet des estampes) and of the Musée Carnavalet *(fonds Histoire)*.

21. This can be deduced from the presence of engravings that do not function as frontispieces, which accompany the last issues.

22. This anti-Jacobin pamphlet, as its names suggests, appeared in January 1792. It was accompanied by twelve engravings that are veritable small caricatures.

23. Three engravings appeared, one with each of the three bound volumes.

24. Robert Darnton, "The High Enlightenment and the Low-Life of Literature in Pre-Revolutionary France," in *French Society and Revolution*, ed. Douglas Johnson (Cambridge: Cambridge University Press, 1976), pp. 53, 87.

25. Jean-Paul Bertaud (supra, note 10), p. 32

26. For this development, as well as those that follow, please see my *La Caricature contre-révolutionnaire* (supra, note 18).

1. See *Les Images de la Révolution française: Actes du colloque de 1985* (Paris: Publications de la Sorbonne, 1988).

2. See Michel Vovelle, *La Révolution française: Images et récit, 1789-1799*, 5 vols. (Paris: Editions Messidor, Livre Club Diderot, 1986). This monumental work marks a change in the use of iconography. It is, nevertheless, mostly the historical narration that determines the place of the "images."

3. To mention only two examples from the corpus of counterrevolutionary caricatures: the engraving representing Lafayette as a centaur led by a patriot to Versailles in October 1789 (fig. 16) actually appeared two

27. Boyer de Nîmes, *Histoire des caricatures de la révolte des Français* (Paris: Imprimerie du *Journal du peuple*, 1792), vol. 1, p. 134. The caricatures supposedly appeared in the *Journal de Nîmes* of 28 February 1790. This journal has not been preserved for the period under study.

28. It is undoubtedly he who attracted attention to the Avignon massacres. This is already visible in the *Journal général de la France*. On the iconography of the subject, see Claude Langlois, "Les Massacres d'Avignon ou la Première Guerre des gravures," *Provence historique* 148 (1987), pp. 287–300.

29. This was the period when Marat's *Ami du peuple* was interrupted, from 15 December 1791 to 11 April 1792.

30. The only collection available of the *Journal du peuple* at the Bibliothèque nationale in Paris is unfortunately incomplete for the last months. Out of 193 numbers, about 40 are missing.

31. The explanation of the caricatures was always followed by general comments on the course of the Revolution, wherein the role of the Protestants becomes an obsession.

32. Archives nationales, W 369, tribunal révolutionnaire.

33. See the *Moniteur* of 14 February 1790.

34. This caricature (DV 4059) appeared at the beginning of December 1791, not long after the election of Pétion to the mayoralty of Paris. Several later caricatures are designated as "by the author of *Gare au faux pas*."

35. The journal lost its engraver, to whom we owe one of the first political caricatures that more or less followed the events of the day, at the end of July 1791, the same time that Camille Desmoulins left. The last engravings to appear were more allegorical. The journal's last issue was published in mid-December 1791.

36. Beginning in mid-July 1790, Prudhomme's journal delivered an engraving of one of the eighty-three French departments almost every week. It would return to illustrations of political events after 10 August 1792.

37. It is not always easy to ascertain who has copied whom, particularly since it is not possible to date patriotic caricature with the same accuracy.

38. The *Grand Convoi funèbre de leurs majestés les Jacobins* (DV 6479, 6480) was one of the exceptions. The newspapers enthusiastically insisted on the fact that this caricature was "illuminated." By this, "colored" should be understood.

39. This tendency was strong at the beginning. Later, it weakened, except in some cases, among them the representation of Narbonne, the minister of war, as a linnet.

40. At least this was the case in France, but it seems also that the same was true of Great Britain. Michel Jouve, *L'Age d'or de la caricature anglaise* (Paris: Presse de la Fondation nationale des sciences politiques, 1983), pp. 135–40.

41. Few caricatures that reproduce the theme of the three estates or specifically the victory of the Third Estate included events as points of reference. A notable exception is found in the caricature entitled *Réveil du tiers état* (cat. no. 27), where the destruction of the Bastille appears in the background.

42. F. Tristan and M. Lever, *Le Monde à l'envers* (Paris: Hachette-Massin, 1980).

43. These are personalities who, isolated or paired, are the subjects of caricatures.

44. Patriotic caricature contributed undeniably to the "creation" of the Old Regime as an immediately devalued past. On this subject, at greater length, see Pierre Goubert, *L'Ancien Régime* (Paris: A. Colin, 1969), vol. 1, pp. 10–28.

45. This period has been equally neglected by historians. The surest point of reference remains M. Reinhard, *La Chute de la royauté* (Paris: Editions Gallimard, 1969).

46. It should be noted that *Les Révolutions de France et de Brabant* had attempted this, in a rather halfhearted way, during 1790 and the beginning of 1791.

47. A popular expression that would have been more applicable to the anti-parliamentarism of the Third Republic, but which found undeniable graphic equivalents during this period. See especially the caricature entitled *L'Homme aux assignats* (DV 3130).

48. In fact this aspect is rather suggested by the image of the tightrope walker (see notably the caricatures *Gare au faux pas* and *Encore une fois gare au faux pas* [DV 4060]).

49. This is the generous estimate of the readership of the royalist press made by Jean-Paul Bertaud (supra, note 10), pp. 56–70.

50. These pieces relied upon plays-on-words that had been in circulation for a long time. Lafayette was called a "centaur" because he always presented himself as the commander of the National Guard on his white horse. He was also referred to as *le Sans-tort* (the never wrong) because he claimed, according to his adversaries, to be always in the right. The familiar formula "Eh donc Coqco" was attributed to Bailly's wife who was presented as a former cook. A play-on-words that is rather tentative (*coq/coco*) permitted Bailly to be represented as a rooster.

51. Lafayette was, along with the Duc d'Orléans, the principal victim of this caricature. It was only in August, much too late, that royalist caricature discovered that the ambitious general could be useful to its cause.

52. On another level, a significant break can be noticed between the fiction of caricature that has recourse to a traditional representation of the putting to death of the enemy by hanging and the new reality of the guillotine. See Daniel Arasse, *La Guillotine dans la Révolution*, exh. cat. (Vizille: Musée de la Révolution française, 1987).

53. For historians this kind of caricature may appear to be a shadow theater because it represents figures who would quickly disappear from history, particularly the generals who were supposed to aid the opposition like the French Rochambeau and Luckner, as well as Bender, the commander of the Austrian troops in Belgium.

THE SEVERED HEAD
The Impact of
French Revolutionary Caricatures
on England

Ronald Paulson

The Johns Hopkins University

The basic question addressed by this essay is: What impact did French caricatures of the Revolution have on English caricatures and English sensibility in general? Caricature will not be used solely in the limited sense of a charged likeness (Italian *caricatura*) but will refer as well to political prints, or graphic commentaries on political events. (One cannot call these latter works political *cartoons*, as that term was reserved for full-size drawings for large paintings or frescoes and was not applied to graphic political satire until after the cartoon competition for the decorations of the houses of Parliament in the nineteenth century.) The term French revolutionary caricature will be used to include both form *and* content, that is, the events or symbols represented by particular graphic artists, independent of the caricature tradition itself.

To answer the question of impact in terms of form, French revolutionary political prints had virtually no effect on English caricature. The influence flowed from the other direction, but even

then, the French did not depend to any great degree on caricature, let alone of the contemporary English variety. Instead, they drew most of their models from the sober political satire of the Netherlands and England prior to the 1780s. The great majority of the works collected in the present exhibition are therefore emblematic, and sometimes merely reportorial, representations of current events.

The northern tradition, represented at its best by Romeyn de Hooghe and other seventeenth-century draughtsmen, had been assimilated into France at the time of the Mississippi Bubble, as it had into England later with the South Sea Bubble;[1] prints were imported, copied, and adapted. These prints were in turn essentially adaptations of, or collages constructed from, the *Emblemata* of Alciati, the *Iconologia* of Ripa, and the Dutch rhymed emblem books of Jacob Cats.[2] In England the greatest benefactor of this tradition was William Hogarth, who developed its resources into a social codification of political events, advancing from the simple emblematic satire of *The South Sea Scheme* and *The Lottery* (1724) to the complex socio-political parallels of *A Harlot's Progress* (1732).

Caricature did not figure in these engravings, though Hogarth's genius for catching a likeness with minimal means (as in his *John Wilkes* [1763]) could forgivably be mistaken for such. The method he developed involved instead projecting analogies between contemporary social scenes, which were well documented in the newspapers, and the macrocosm of Walpolian politics. Meaning was conveyed through the metonymic relationships between a person and an animal, statue, painting, or some optical illusion, while never violating probability as the Dutch precursors had often done in their more purely emblematic satires. Graphic satire in France, intellectually very primitive compared to the work that Hogarth produced from the 1730s through the 1760s, remained at the stage of using emblems, for example, a figure of Liberty confronting a figure of Injustice.

Hogarth had resented the comparisons of his work to caricature because he regarded it as foreign derived, aristocratic, too easy, and altogether independent of good draughtsmanship. Perhaps most important to him, it was historically a toy of the elite young English gentlemen who went to Italy on their Grand Tours and brought back caricatures of each other, sometimes also developing a knack for drawing them in the process.[3] Caricature, which began in seventeenth-century Bologna as a sophisticated offshoot of the grand-style history painting of the Carracci studio, became in the eighteenth century the game of amateurs who were able to catch a likeness in a lucky scratch or two. After all, the facial resemblance had to be detectable by no one but the members of the small coterie in which the caricatures were circulated.

In the mid 1750s George Townshend, one of these aristocratic young men, began caricaturing his acquaintances in the government and thus produced the first political caricatures. Gradually, two or more of these visages were related by comparison or contrast, and perhaps vestigial bodies were added. These drawings were soon being etched and sold by printsellers, and the method was then adapted by professionals who earned a living by their pens and burins.

In the 1780s and 1790s two English artists of genius, Thomas Rowlandson and James Gillray, developed political caricature into an art form. They were followed in the next generation by a third, George Cruikshank, who carried the form through the Napoleonic period and up into the texts of Charles Dickens. Caricature was, one

might say, *the* major art form of the French revolutionary era, though not one for which the French themselves were distinguished. Rowlandson and Gillray, in their different ways, joined caricature heads to emblematic situations and figures in the manner of Hogarth and then, satisfying decorum, caricatured the bodies as well. Whereas, previously, the heads had been merely attached to tiny perfunctory bodies, Rowlandson and Gillray produced bodies that went with and were fantastic extensions of the exaggerated heads. Their experiments contributed in turn to the etchings and paintings Goya began to produce in Spain at the end of the century.

The English political caricature of Rowlandson and Gillray, although it was fully developed by 1789, had virtually no effect on French political prints of the Revolution. The only artist who seems to have benefited from English developments was David, who when the occasion arose demonstrated that he could draw in the crude manner of Isaac Cruikshank, George's father. These prints (cat. nos. 114, 115) are interesting and revealing because David has used the English style and graphic vocabulary to attack the English; both of his designs were aimed at the Pitt ministry's hostility to France. This suggests that David wished to tar the enemy with his own brush. Although through their work, Gillray and especially Isaac Cruikshank and the many lesser-known English caricaturists professed to express popular John Bullish English culture, not unrelated to that of the *sans-culottes* in France, David instead perceived their efforts as the attempts of the ruling class to exploit popular conservatism to its own ends. It is likely that he remembered caricature as an elite mode of expression and, as such, one totally inappropriate to the high ideals of the French Revolution.[4]

As David, more than anyone else, defined the visual representation of the French Revolution, the aim was to dignify and to legitimize revolutionary efforts by means of historical precedents. For this endeavor the appropriate style was his own and that of his students, beginning with *The Oath of the Horatii* (1785; Paris, Musée du Louvre) and continuing with his modern-dress version, *The Oath of the Tennis Court* (drawing; 1791; Château de Versailles), and his solemn hieratic Death of Marat (1793; Brussels, Musées royaux des beaux-arts). The appropriate mode was historical and emblematic or, on the popular side, when portraying *sans-culottes*, a kind of sentimental naturalism summed up in the style of Greuze's genre pieces. Even when attacking elements of the Revolution itself, as in the remarkable group of prints warning against

Robespierre in 1794, dignity was maintained. Robespierre was taken very seriously and in a way that David did not want the French to take the Pitt ministry and George III. The only appropriate use of the English mode of irreverent exaggeration, therefore, was when the foreigner himself was the subject.

Furthermore, caricature as an aristocratic form could only serve a purpose in the prerevolutionary phases when the aristocracy was jockeying for position vis-à-vis the monarch. During the stage of the aristocratic initiative, cliques hired artists to lampoon other cliques and the court party itself; the money came from the nobles who sponsored the satires, not the public who saw them in the printshops. Once the Revolution was underway, however, practical considerations called for emblematic, positive, nonaristocratic images. Only the enemies of the Revolution and the French Republic were suitable for the ignominy of caricature (later possibly the discredited Girondists or the Jacobins, as they seemed to exceed revolutionary aims in the Terror, would be added). Nevertheless, even these portrayals remained sober and emblematic. Humor, that primary ingredient of the English tradition, was lacking, and indeed, it is hard to detect this element in David's lugubrious adaptations of English caricature.

There was no Gillray in revolutionary France, nor could there have been. He would have gone into exile. But there was also less possibility of one because of the long-standing prominence of the Academy in France and the absence of a strong dissident tradition in art of the sort that flourished in England. If, as some think, Hogarth was ultimately an apologist for the status quo in English politics, it is nevertheless impossible to disregard the presence in England of a Hogarth followed by a Rowlandson and a Gillray, not to mention a Zoffany and, in certain respects, a Gainsborough and Reynolds — artists who were witty, comic, and subversive with patrons, sitters, and even academic authority (a case for which could be made even with Reynolds himself).

In France only two alternatives had emerged to the classical style that was being worked out successfully by David a few years before the outbreak of 1789. One was the sentimentalized version of Hogarth developed by Greuze, who thereafter sought unsuccessfully to absorb himself (as of course Hogarth had too) in the higher academic representations of Neoclassicism. The other was the lighthearted, though hardly comic, tradition of Boucher and Fragonard — the Rococo, associated with the amorous, decorative, and carefree, or

everything detested by the French Revolution and its spokesmen from Rousseau to David. If the official dignified style, based on the forms of David, was used for affairs of state, the popular Greuze idiom represented the lower orders, but soberly and without caricature. The aristocratic, unserious, largely discredited Rococo, with its connotations of *amor* and obscenity, was utilized only in order to attack the queen and court. The styles were, in short, appropriate and decorous, and there was no place in the representation of the French themselves for much development of the English type of caricature.[5]

The influence of the French on English caricaturists was virtually nil — certainly in terms of form and style — except in one important respect. The French graphic artists supplied their English observers with the facts, the narrative, the metaphors, and the donnée of their caricatures, and of much beyond caricature. Symbolically, every action, word, and image that passed from France to England was grist for the English caricaturist's mill, serving as fact, confirmation, and prediction. These were the sourcebooks for Gillray's caricatures and, in a different way, which also relied upon Gillray's mediation, for Blake's *America* (1793) and his other prorevolutionary prophetic books of 1790–1795.[6] (There may be an echo of the beheaded nudes in *Les Formes acerbes* [fig. 11] in Blake's strangely segmented nude bodies.)

The imagery itself, however, came primarily from French words — not from prints but from speeches, broadsides, and secondhand reports on which the English based their fearful perception of happenings in France. The words of Brissot and Robespierre and Vergniaud projected the graphic images expanded into caricature by Gillray and the others. Sometimes Burke's verbal caricature of the French in his *Reflections on the Revolution in France* (1790) served. He provided the images of the monstrous hags who marched on Versailles and clergymen hanging from the Parisian lampposts which were to reappear in caricatures by Rowlandson and Gillray, persisting into George Cruikshank's works of 1818–1819. William Windham, Burke's disciple, for example, spoke on 4 March 1790 in Commons against the English reformers: "Truly sorry am I to observe that swarms of these strange impracticable notions have lately been wafted over to us from the continent, to prey like locusts on the fair flowers of our soil....What would recommend you to repair your house in the hurricane season?"[7] The Gillray representations of swarms of locustlike creatures and crumbling architectural structures are projections of such words as

Windham's, which in turn expand upon the imagery of hurricanes and natural phenomena uttered by the French themselves.

From French graphic art then the English derived sometimes content, sometimes imagery, but not — as David had borrowed conversely — any form or style. The English saw the appropriateness of their charged or caricatured form to the representation of a French stereotype already venerable in the caricature tradition. For the French had long fitted into English categories of comedy and satire: literary ones such as the Swiftean madness of projectors and rationalists; literary and graphic ones such as the Francophobic depiction of the frog-eating fop who uses a dozen eggs when one would do and starves on fricassees as opposed to the Roast Beef of Old England. The Revolution itself conformed to English empiricism's aesthetic categories (preeminently Burkean after his publication of *A Philosophical Enquiry* in 1757) of the sublime and beautiful; or, as with Rowlandson, the picturesque; or, with Hogarth and Gillray, the pseudo-sublime or bathetic. It thus found images in the fragment, the ruined building, the disastrous avalanche or storm, the apocalypse of Revelation, and various versions of parricide.

But the particular fact that impressed itself on the English — not only on the caricatures but on the English sensibility in general — and helped to determine the forms taken by the models of apocalypse and parricide was beheading. Not hanging or shooting or drinking hemlock but a severance of the rational part of the body which had the effect of dehumanization — this caught the English, as well as the European, imagination.

After the severing, there was the holding up of the head, displaying it on a pike, carrying it in a procession. The public, popular, spectacular, scopophilic qualities were emphasized by the French in the press and in prints. From the French point of view, as the English recognized, the visual separation of head from body assured a spectator that the act was irreversible and that no trick was being played. The monarch was without question dead and had been subjected to the iconoclastic treatment dealt out to religious images in churches. In the model of the Body Politic the king is the "head" of the state, and so it is appropriate, indeed necessary, that his removal should be accomplished by decapitation.

The most horrible aspect of French beheading, however, was its basis in "reason." The word applied preeminently to the machine that distinguished French beheading, the guillotine.[8] Beheading with a machine suggested not only the rationalism of the *philosophes,* who were widely

regarded as fathers of the Revolution, but the factory of the Industrial Revolution and mass production. It carried a disquieting implication that the machine would continue to cut off heads, as a pin-maker continues to make pins, as long as it is supplied with bodies. The beheading of the king, followed by the queen, then by the Girondists, and by the mass of repetitions that characterized the so-called Terror implemented the idea of an unlimited series of beheadings. Furthermore, the beheaders were eventually beheaded themselves — first the Girondists, finally the Jacobins. The powerful, because desperate, prints of Robespierre's last days come as close as anything published during the Revolution to the eloquence of English graphic satire. One example shows the executioner himself as the only victim left for Robespierre to behead (cat. no. 146). Another, *Le Bourreau se guillotine lui-même* (fig. 1) shows the executioner, the last to have survived, at the moment after he has guillotined himself; his arm remains awkwardly upraised, grasping the cord that has released the blade.

These prints express not only the fear as to who will be next, but the anxiety of the open-ended. This open-endedness, as well as the machine's shape (a very different structure from the old axe and block) and function (once the cord is pulled, there is no stopping the blade from falling) caused the guillotine to be associated with the scythe of the Grim Reaper. See, for example, *Le Peuple fran-*

FIGURE 1. Anonymous French. *Le Bourreau se guillotine lui-même (The Executioner Guillotines Himself),* ca. 1794. Engraving with hand coloring. Paris, Musée Carnavalet. Photo: Musées de la Ville de Paris © by SPADEM 1988.

FIGURE 2. Anonymous French. *Le Marquis de Launay / gouverneur de la Bastille (The Marquis de Launay / Governor of the Bastille)*, 1789. Engraving with hand coloring. Paris, Bibliothèque nationale.

çais / où le Régime de Robespierre (cat. no. 147). The guillotine recalled Caligula's wish that all the Roman senators might have a single neck. It also suggested a connection between the savage image of Hercules *mangeur*, advocated by David and Robespierre in the last days of the Committee of Public Safety, and the task undertaken by Hercules of cutting off the Hydra's constantly regenerating heads (recalling the grimly proleptic print of 1789 *Le Despotisme terrassé* [cat. no. 25], where the aristocratic horde is portrayed as the Hydra). Seen from the other side of the Channel beheading by guillotine represented a kind of leveling process that recalled the Dance of Death. How could the good any longer be distinguished from the bad? With the extension of the Terror into the Napoleonic wars, the image of Death with his scythe appears on battlefields exchanging his secrets with Napoleon.[9]

Dismemberment itself became an obsessive notion. French artists took to isolating formally hands and heads that were not surgically removed. The portrait of the Marquis de Launay, head and shoulders encircled and isolated with the towers of the Bastille appearing in the background, has below it a reproduction of his severed head on a pike (fig. 2). One print shows a wall with an arm thrust through it, looking as if it were severed, a notion further lodged in the spectator's mind by the guillotine represented below it (fig. 3).

In England Blake makes much of detached, severed heads in his prophetic books, and as late as Byron's *Don Juan* (1819–1824), there is the projected

scenario of Juan's beheading, anticipated perhaps in the threat of circumcision and castration in the harem episode. The motif did not end with thermidor, extending into the Napoleonic period to the Cruikshank caricature of the Napoleonic family carrying their severed heads like crowns (1814; fig. 4), which recalls the decapitated figures carrying their heads in the *Réception de Louis Capet aux enfers* (1793; fig. 5). Perhaps the most amusing example of survival and memory is Gillray's *The Apples and the Horse-Turds* (1800; fig. 6), which shows Napoleon and his friends as horse turds and the crowned heads of Europe as apples floating down a river. Both groups resemble heads that have been decollated.

As Cruikshank's postrevolutionary caricatures show, the guillotine was the continuing symbol of radicalism for the English. *The Radical's Arms* (1819; fig. 7) represents English radicals as supporters of an escutcheon made of a guillotine, distinguished by a bend sinister formed by the diagonal of the blade poised over a world-in-flames (taken from "World's End" tavern signs). The Magna Carta, Bill of Rights, and laws of the land are being trampled underfoot by the *sans-culotte* supporters, but the guillotine remains the centerpiece.

Most striking and famous is Cruikshank's *A Radical Reformer, — (i e) a Neck or Nothing Man! Dedicated to the Heads of the Nation* (1819; fig. 8). In it the *sans-culotte* monster, who stands on huge apish feet, has a guillotine for a body, sharp feral teeth, a

FIGURE 3. Villeneuve (French, active 1789–1799). *Louis le traître lis ta sentence (Louis the Traitor Read Your Sentence)*, 1793. (Cat. no. 86).

FIGURE 4. George Cruikshank (British, 1792–1878). *The Imperial Family Going to the Devil*, 1814. Etching with hand coloring. San Marino, The Huntington Library.

liberty cap on his head, a dagger in one hand, and blood dripping from the other. The guillotine replaces his stomach, and from the hole for the victim's head, which represents the lower end of the monster's alimentary system, blood flows. By this time, however, the creature can be regarded as either the radical apocalypse or an apparition projected by the fears of the fleeing politicians and bishops. The fearfulness of the radical apocalypse is balanced by the perhaps justified paranoia of the heads of the nation, as had often happened in Gillray's caricatures of the French Revolution.

In Cruikshank's satires on the prince regent, beheading is introduced as a sly warning to foolish

FIGURE 5. Villeneuve (French, active 1789–1799). *Réception de Louis Capet aux enfers par grand nombres de brigands ci-devant couronnées (Reception of Louis Capet in Hell by a Large Number of Previously Crowned Bandits)*, 1793. (Cat. no. 92).

monarchs. In *Meditations amongst the Tombs* (1813; fig. 9), the Prince, present at the private opening of the tombs at Windsor, is shown Charles I, who seems to be holding up his own head as a warning to his descendant.

Dismembering was a process that, in Gillray's imagination, had combined with Vergniaud's notorious prophecy that the Revolution would devour its own children and with the French engraving *Le Peuple mangeur de rois*, showing Hercules as a *sansculotte* wearing a liberty cap while cooking a nobleman over a Roman fire preparatory to eating him.[10] In a print of 1792, *Un Petit Souper, à la parisiènne* (fig. 10), Gillray projects beheading into devourment; the public feasts on the dismembered bodies of aristocrats and, by implication, of all civilized Englishmen and women. Gillray has joined the old Francophobe caricature of the starving frog-eating Frenchman, now reduced to cannibalism (still operative in Byron's second canto of *Don Juan*), with the French print *Les Formes acerbes* (fig. 11) in which a man drinks from a steady fountain in the form of a guillotine. The image emerged most powerfully in Spain in Goya's *Saturn Devouring One of His Sons* (1820–1823; Madrid, Museo del Prado), but it is also present in the hovering dismembered heads with which Goya studded his prints and paintings.

In England, the reaction to beheading was intensified by the indigenous iconoclastic tradition. Laden with a much more complicated heritage than that of the French, English iconoclasm had been decreed by the monarch himself in the sixteenth century and had continued relatively unabated and with official sanction ever since. The reformers had knocked the heads off holy images all the way up to Charles I, the monarch himself, as an iconoclastic gesture — an act deriding idolatry which was defended magisterially by John Milton in *Eikonoklastes* (1649). This act was followed by the marginalizing of the monarch. As late as the 1720s the Calves' Head Club held an annual dinner in London on the anniversary of Charles I's beheading. The eating of the dolled-up calf's head signified different, but powerful, emotions to the anti-monarchists who ate, to the Tory-Jacobite crowds that mobbed the dinner, to the readers of newspaper accounts of both the dinner and the rioting, and to those viewing prints illustrating the event. The proceedings of the club may still have formed part of the context of Gillray's *Un Petit Souper.*

We should note that in England the famous case of beheading was royal. Beheading, as opposed to

FIGURE 6. James Gillray (British, 1757–1815). *The Apples and the Horse-Turds; — or — Buonaparte among the Golden Pippins,* 1800. Etching. San Marino, The Huntington Library.

hanging, was the mode of capital punishment reserved for the great, but the last beheading in England had taken place as long ago as 1747. In France by contrast the use of the guillotine on both king and commoners had served as a symbolic way to level the monarch with his subjects.

Gillray's boldness produced a bizarre consequence in England, which was in part the result of the strong physical resemblance that existed between George III and Louis XVI. In Gillray's work George III became the first English monarch to be individualized to the point of caricature (carried far beyond the idealization of the royal emblem). During the first of George III's fits of "madness" in 1788–1789, Gillray had portrayed him, in a brilliant imitation of Fuseli's *The Three Witches* (1783; Kunsthaus Zürich), as the dark side of the moon, a disembodied head isolated high in the sky (fig. 12).[11] Gillray's attitude toward politics was ambivalent, his prints were anti-French but displayed equal dis-

FIGURE 7. George Cruikshank (British, 1792–1878). *The Radical's Arms,* 1819. Etching with hand coloring. Los Angeles, Richard Vogler George Cruikshank Collection.

gust with the behavior of Pitt and the British monarch.

The result of these combined factors was Gillray's remarkable print *The Hopes of the Party, prior to July 14th* (1791; fig. 13), which portrayed the projected beheading of none other than George III — what would happen if the French revolutionary sympathizers in England gained their way.[12] The beheading takes place not on a guillotine, but on the more sinister, because more English, block. The print, a grim prophecy of the execution of the French monarch in 1793, becomes a reprise of the execution in London in 1649. Queen Charlotte, strung up to a lamppost (like one of the bishops in the later *Zenith of French Glory* [1793; fig. 14]) is

FIGURE 8. George Cruikshank (British, 1792–1878). *A Radical Reformer, — (i e) a Neck or Nothing Man! Dedicated to the Heads of the Nation,* 1819. Etching with hand coloring. Los Angeles, Richard Vogler George Cruikshank Collection.

FIGURE 9. George Cruikshank (British, 1792–1878). *Meditations amongst the Tombs*, 1813. Etching with hand coloring. San Marino, The Huntington Library.

FIGURE 10. James Gillray (British, 1757–1815). *Un Petit Souper, à la parisiènne; — or — A Family of Sans-Culotts Refreshing, after the Fatigues of the Day*, 1792. Etching. San Marino, The Huntington Library.

FIGURE 11. Jean-Baptiste-Marie Louvion (French, 1740–1804). *Les Formes acerbes (Bitter Forms)*, 1795, after M. Poirier de Dunkerque, avocat. (Cat. no. 152).

FIGURE 12. James Gillray (British, 1757–1815). *Wierd Sisters; Ministers of Darkness; Minions of the Moon*, ca. 1789. Aquatint. San Marino, The Huntington Library.

joined with Pitt in a sexually suggestive pose that forces the viewer to make the association of Charlotte with the French caricatures accusing Marie-Antoinette of sexual promiscuity. In this English caricature the sexual suggestiveness reaches further than the French. There is a strong indication that we are to see the dishonoring of the monarch as extending symbolically, if not literally, to a buggering by Horne Tooke.

An important English phenomenon was the development from respect to satire in the direct personal representations of George III between 1783 and the Revolution. The years 1792–1793, centering on the execution of Louis XVI, proved the watershed. Humor and grudging respect returned thereafter, as the horror of the events in France became more evident. Before that moment, however, it was possible for Gillray at least to represent George III in a particularly ambiguous way, as Byron was later able to do with the king's madness and death in *The Vision of Judgment* (1822).

FIGURE 13. James Gillray (British, 1757–1815). *The Hopes of the Party, prior to July 14th — "From Such Wicked Crown & Anchor-Dreams, Good Lord Deliver Us,"* 1791. Etching. San Marino, The Huntington Library.

The British monarch was also, of course, peripheral — at times no more than a scapegoat for his powerful ministers — compared to the monarch of France, and this allowed for a freedom, if not recklessness, that would have been unthinkable abroad. The features outlined thus far also come together in a coincidence, a confirmation perhaps, but also a strengthening, of an inbred quality of English caricature: the joining of surreal content with a surreal form.

The example of this that Neil Hertz has explored is the head held up immediately after beheading: both the monarch's, or the male's — from Hertz's

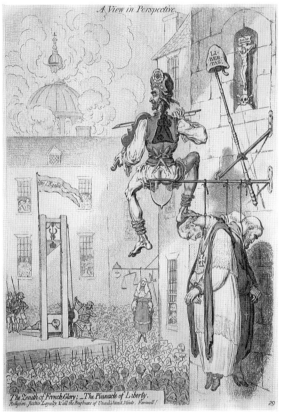

FIGURE 14. James Gillray (British, 1757–1815). *The Zenith of French Glory; — The Pinnacle of Liberty*, 1793. Etching. San Marino, The Huntington Library.

point of view — severed head and the paralyzing head of the Medusa (fig. 15; cat. no. 89).[13] He refers to a print — unattributed by him, but clearly by Rowlandson — *The Contrast* (fig. 16), which shows a Medusa-headed crone, the sort of monstrous woman Burke described in his *Reflections*. She carries a trident, the central prong of which impales a man's head, removed from a corpse in the foreground (another man is shown hanging from one of the lampposts also described in Burke's *Reflections*). Medusa, writes Hertz, is "here depicted as a beheader, her own head recognizably snaky yet still

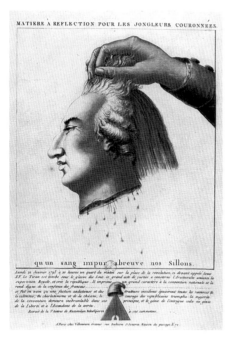

FIGURE 15. Villeneuve (French, active 1789–1799). *Matière à réflection pour les jongleurs couronnées / qu un sang impur abreuve nos sillons (Matter for Thought for Crowned Jugglers / May Our Fields Run with an Impure Blood)*, 1793. (Cat. no. 90).

firmly attached to her shoulders: Medusa usurping the pose of Cellini's Perseus, a decapitated male at her feet. Still another way—the print seems to suggest—in which the world has been turned upside down."[14]

What beheading and dismemberment offered was the *Unheimlich*, or uncanny, which was implicit in the facts coming out of France: the *Todestrieb* (the death drive) of the Terror, the Revolution devouring its own young (in effect itself), seen also in the *Wiederholungszwang* (the repetition compulsion) and of course in castration anxiety. The return of the repressed was the result of revolutionary doubling, ego splitting, recurrence, and repetition, at the bottom of which Freud would say lies castration anxiety —in England, entrenched in its own long-lasting version of iconoclasm, the beheading of statues, not only of saints but of noblemen and women on tombs, and finally of the king himself.

The public spectacle of the beheading of the monarch and subsequently of the queen strongly suggested the relationship of castration to ocular anxiety: the eye as both the surrogate for the sexual organ and the organ with which the crucial discovery of difference is made. The public guillotining presented the act of seeing the missing, the altered, the transposed. The threat was to the totality of one's body as well as to one's knowledge of the difference of the world, the breaking of one's monarch, who is the macrocosm of one's microcosm.

FIGURE 16. Thomas Rowlandson (British, 1756–1827). *The Contrast*, 1792. Etching with hand coloring. San Marino, The Huntington Library.

Our feeling before the great anti-revolutionary caricatures of Gillray is of something missing. We feel the mortal danger to the subject, which can dissolve into a fungus or a skeleton or a stone. Its integrity, its very identity, is at stake and already rendered suspect by the scratchy, overcharged, and monstrous style of the caricaturist. Revolution, we might say, makes fearful, real, and threatening a dimension that was already present in English political caricature, waiting for a subject.

1. The Mississippi Bubble, or Mississippi Company, was a speculative venture that became a subject of French and Dutch caricatures during the second decade of the eighteenth century. These caricatures first appeared in London in 1720, were rapidly copied, and served the following year as models for similar caricatures of the South Sea Company, or Bubble. The latter was a speculative, financial company that lured investors with the promise of immense capital gains in the South Sea trade, only to lose their money through mismanagement and skulduggery. "Bubble prints," as these caricatures were known, followed the Dutch tradition of including elaborate architectural settings and a mixture of real and allegorical figures. See my *Hogarth: His Life, Art, and Times* (New Haven and London: Yale University Press, 1971), vol. 1, pp. 70–77.

2. Ripa's *Iconologia* was first published in Rome in 1593 without illustrations; woodcut illustrations by Giuseppe Cesari were introduced in the 1603 edition. An English translation first appeared in 1709, while three other English editions were published by 1785. On Alciati, see F. W. G. Leeman *Alciatus' Emblemata: Denkbeelden en voorbeelden* (Groningen: Bouma's Boekhuis, 1984). On Jacob Cats, see Mario Praz, *Studies in Seventeenth-Century Imagery*, Studies of the Warburg Institute, vol. 3 (London: Warburg Institute, 1939); this text also provides general information on the history of emblem books.

3. See Richard Godefrey, *English Caricature, 1620 to the Present*, exh. cat. (London: Victoria and Albert Museum, 1984), pp. 14–15.

4. It has been argued by Ernst Gombrich (in a lecture given at Yale University in 1979, which is, as far as I am aware, unpublished) that the English mode of Gillray can be said, by its very overcharging, to fantasize, distance, and in effect emasculate its subjects, thereby making a Napoleon or a Pitt *less* menacing, containing them in effect in order

merely to amuse spectators. The question then becomes whether this strategy serves the purpose of the ruling elite or of the printseller and etcher, who are interested primarily in sales, or of both.

5. The English caricature of Gillray could, however, occasionally be incorporated in a French design, as in *Le Neuf Thermidor ou la Surprise angloise* (cat. no. 153), where the English are represented by a copy of Gillray's caricature of John Bull gourmandizing.

6. See David V. Erdman, *Blake: Prophet against Empire* (Princeton: Princeton University Press, 1954), pp. 149–97.

7. *Parliamentary History*, xxviii (1790), pp. 452–79.

8. See Daniel Arasse, *La Guillotine et l'imaginaire de la Terreur* (Paris: Flammarion, 1985), and Valérie Rousseau-Lagarde and Daniel Arasse, *La Guillotine dans la Révolution*, exh. cat. (Paris: Musée Carnavalet, 1987).

9. See both the endless Dance of Death drawings and prints that Rowlandson produced in the first decades of the nineteenth century (as well as his striking caricature of Death and Napoleon on the battlefield [British Library]) and the use of the Grim Reaper in the later cantos of Byron's *Don Juan*.

10. This engraving is illustrated in Lynn Hunt, *Politics, Culture, and Class in the French Revolution* (Berkeley and Los Angeles: University of California Press, 1984), p. 108, pl. 14. Hunt also cites the following from issue no. 217 of *Révolutions de Paris*, 30 November–8 December 1793 (10–18 frimaire an II): "Homer called the kings of his time *mangeurs de peuples*, we will write on the figures of the French sans-culottes these words: *Le Peuple Mangeur de Rois*" (p. 108).

11. Mary Dorothy George describes Gillray's *Wierd Sisters; Ministers of Darkness; Minions of the Moon* as being published 23 December 1791. In her entry, however, she notes, "Wraxall *(Memoirs,* 1884, v. 291) describes the print as appearing during the Regency Crisis, c. Feb. 1789, and it would seem to illustrate the situation at that time." See Mary Dorothy George, *Catalogue of Political and Personal Satires Preserved in the Department of Prints and Drawings in the British Museum* (London: British Museum Publications Limited, 1938; reprint, 1978), vol. 6, p. 834.

12. *The Hopes of the Party* should be compared to Gillray's later reportorial representation of the beheading of Louis xvi (1793) — a print with almost no equivalent inside France — followed by his second representation of it within a savage caricature of revolutionary terror in Paris, *The Zenith of French Glory* (1793; fig. 14).

13. Neil Hertz, "Medusa's Head," in *The End of the Line: Essays on Psychoanalysis and the Sublime* (New York: Columbia University Press, 1985), pp. 161–62.

14. Ibid., p. 162.

Jacques-Louis David,
Scatological Discourse in the French Revolution,
and the
Art of Caricature

Albert Boime

University of California, Los Angeles

David's political cartoons of the 1790s are the most astonishing specimens of his entire visual practice. Rarely discussed in detail in the abundant literature devoted to the master, they reveal a side of his work and his artistic personality that appears quite at odds with his magisterial Neoclassical productions.[1] The contrast between the serious purpose and the elevated themes of the painting and the vulgarity and fantasy of the cartoons might initially suggest the work of two radically different mind-sets. Far from being discontinuous in David's production or manifesting the marks of a schizoid personality, however, his monumental pictures and his modest caricatures are dialectically interrelated and critical to an understanding of his participation in the revolutionary process.

The political cartoon and its progeny stand at the crossroads of Neoclassicism and modern art.[2] When in eighteenth-century England charged portraits were first introduced into political prints, the caricature became a social weapon unmasking and ridiculing the pretensions of the powerful. The emergence of the modern political cartoon in the second half of the eighteenth century fixed it in a Neoclassical mode. It shared, along with the art of Mortimer, Blake, and David, clarity through emphasis on drawing and strong contours as well as a moralizing and didactic content expressed in allegorical terms. The pronounced topical allusions of most Neoclassical painting identify the past in terms of the present. Likewise, political caricature exploits anachronism, metonymy, and emblematic devices to convey the idea that all epochs are basically equivalent. The simple propagandistic aims of political caricature and its generally chauvinistic intent are identical with the seemingly high-minded representations of Neoclassicists.

The precise nature and extent of this relationship, however, requires clarification.[3] Political caricature would at first glance seem to be inimical to Neoclassicism at every point: where the former exaggerates and debunks, the latter moderates and idealizes; where one distorts, the other regulates; where one grasps at the gross material conditions of ordinary life, the other seeks perfection through a controlled visual experience. It is in precisely these polarities, however, that we are able to discover a dialectical tension existing between the caricatural delineation of political realities and the disguised Neoclassical version.

The political caricature is aimed generally at one's enemies; the Neoclassical painting, at one's heroes. In this sense, Neoclassicism may be seen in psychoanalytical terms as a sublimated expression of the Oedipal wish projection to be the mighty patriarch in place of the father, for example, the Socrates, the Belisarius (already blinded, i.e., castrated, by the parent-emperor), or the elder Horatius to whom the sons submit. The Oedipal complex constitutes the beginnings of the forms of political and social authority, the regulation and control through the superego or conscience. On the other hand, the political caricature permits the displaced manifestation of the repressed aggressive desire to oust the father. The political enemy, or the subject of distortion, becomes a projection of the hated parent and through caricature can be struck down. Political caricature allows for the gratification of the desire to eliminate the rival parent, which in Neoclassicism has been sublimated on behalf of a higher ideal. Thus, Neoclassicism can be understood as the imagined absence of the repressed enemy, while political caricature can be understood as the imagined absence of the parental prohibition. Both forms of representation established their graphic language during an age of revolution, when accepted institutional norms were exploded and opened to question.

The two visual forms often reached different audiences. The painting was primarily destined for elite exhibitions and appealed to an upper-class spectator, while the caricature could be cheaply reproduced and made available to the wider community. Both the Neoclassicist and the cartoonist, however, based their narratives on essentially medieval categories of Good and Evil, embodied in the images of the benevolent Father (God, the state) and the tyrannical Devil (hell, despotism). The objective representations of these categories, however, varied according to that portion of the public targeted by the artist.[4] Nevertheless, the appeal of both modes rested on a set of moral assumptions held in common by their respective audiences.

Caricatures have often been traced to medieval block books and moralizing prints, and the political cartoon, more than any other graphic medium, has preserved this tradition. Gombrich has pointed out the extent to which caricatures disclose the dominant role of the mythological imagination in our political thought.[5] The allegorical personifications of Good and Evil (under whatever guise) and a host of metaphorical and metonymic devices become the real substance of political persuasion and are therefore easily translated into the cartoonist's emblems. As noted previously, in this respect political caricature relates to Neoclassicism, which similarly conveys propagandistic material in allusive terms. The deeds and/or misdeeds of the past are exploited in the name of the present. Parodic iconography, like revolutionary Neoclassicism, was sustained by its topicality. When the bourgeoisie needed the support of, and pretended solidarity with, the popular classes, it employed caricature as the vehicle to manipulate their culture. In pretending to know what best appealed to the popular classes, however, the bourgeois artist betrayed his or her own entrenched biases.

The great revolutionary moment involved a long and persistent attack on the aristocratic character. The formula applied was not initially an indication of fundamental social revolution, but emphasized primarily the disappearance of symbols by which a certain class of people distinguished itself from the amorphous mass. The advocates of the Revolution ground out hundreds of caricatures, attempting to prepare the public for a new social order. By 1793, however, the focus had shifted from the demolition of the nobility. Once the king was guillotined in January of that year, the whole propaganda apparatus, including the caricaturists, had to be employed to ready the French people for foreign invasion and the domestic counterrevolution of royalist sympathizers. A proclamation issued by the National Convention two days after the king's execution advised: "Let us, through our union, avert the shame that domestic discord would bring upon our newborn republic. Let us, through our patriotism, avert those horrible shocks, those anarchical and disorderly movements which would soon overwhelm France with disturbances and grief, if our outside enemies, who are fomenting them, could profit therefrom."[6] The French now organized the Committee of Public Safety (Comité de salut public) to deal with invasion from without and civil war, which broke in the Vendée near the end of March. The Committee of Public Safety declared the intention of mobilizing all French resources — animate and inanimate — on behalf of the Revolution. As part of this mass effort, the fine arts and public education institutions were to deal with "the agitation of factions within the country and the efforts of a leagued Europe against us."[7]

During the interval between the voting of the Levy-in-Mass in August 1793 and the drafting of the draconian Law of Suspects in mid-September, the Committee of Public Safety, presided over by Carnot, requested the "Deputy David to employ

EXPLICATION.

N.º 1. *George Roi d'Angleterre commande en personne l'élite de son Armée Royal-Cruche N.º 2. Il est conduit par son Ministre Pitt ou Milor Dindon N.º 3 qui le tient par le Nez pour mieux lui prouver son attachement. L'avant-Garde de la Royal Armée N.º 4 reçoit un échec à la porte de la Ville N.º 5 qui est occasioné par la colique de quelques Sans-Culottes placés au haut de la Porte N.º 6. L'avant-Garde dans sa défaite brise les cruches, dont il ne sort que toutes sortes de Bêtes venimeuses N.º 7 qui est l'esprit qui les anime. Fox ou Milord Oie N.º 8 ferme la marche monté sur sa Trompette Angloise et qui témoin de l'échec sonne un rappel en arrière par prudence. Artillerie Angloise nouvelle N.º 9 qui a la vertu d'éteindre les incendies et de éclairer les fortifications.*

4391

FIGURE 1. Jacques-Louis David (French, 1748–1825). *L'Armée des cruches (The Army of Jugs)*, 1793–1794. (Cat. no. 114).

his talents and all the means in his power to augment the number of caricatures which could arouse the public spirit and make it perceive precisely how atrocious and ridiculous are the enemies of Liberty and the Republic."[8] David went to work developing his own cartoon ideas and stimulating others to do so as well. By May of the following year, he had submitted two designs and a list of expenses required to reproduce both black-and-white and colored versions. The Committee accepted the plan and on 18 May 1794 (29 floréal an II), decreed its execution, stipulating that the artist submit to the Committee five hundred copies of each version of the two cartoons (two thousand in all). The large printing indicates the great importance attached to these cartoons by the powerful Committee of Public Safety.

Both cartoons, which date from between 12 September 1793 and 18 May 1794, attack the English government.[9] The first mentioned in Carnot's decree was entitled *L'Armée des cruches (The Army of Jugs)*, showing "an army of crocks commanded by George III, who in turn is led by the nose by a turkey" (fig. 1). The cartoon constitutes a treasure trove of verbal and visual puns in addition to its pri-

mary function as carrier of a critical political message. George III, depicted as a potbellied pot, pitcher, jug, or crackpot—all terms contained in the French word *cruche*—steps out ahead of his troops, who are also depicted as jugs with spidery legs. The crocked troops carry two standards, one a pig's head surmounted by a royal crown and the other a combination of jester and Tower of London (perhaps a satiric allusion to the Tory government warning of a left-wing plot to take over the Tower in March 1793). The word *cruche* has a double meaning referring to a blockhead or dolt, as in the English "jughead." To behave like a crackpot in France is to utter *crucheries*, or utter nonsense. The English monarch wears donkey ears, and in place of a wig he sports a money bag fastened to the back of his head. A conspicuous Order of the Garter (the eight-pointed star) enwraps the pot. George is depicted as not only grossly stupid, but as a venal jackass blindly following a strutting turkey-cock.

The turkey, "Milor Dindon," who pulls George by a leash attached to his nose, is identified in the legend as Britain's prime minister, Pitt. The French word for turkey, *dindon*, carries the same double sense as *cruche*. The verb *dindonner* literally means "to dupe" and is associated with several popular expressions that designate a pompous, conceited fool. The musical meter of the French term with its accented second syllable had been exploited by Molière for his weak and doltish bourgeois character Georges Dandin (whose surname nearly reverses the nasal sounds of *dindon*). The word *dandin* itself had traditionally been used to designate a blockhead and closely resembles *ding ding dong*, the noise of a ringing bell. Other cartoons of this period, including one traditionally ascribed to David, actually identify the English king as "Georges Dandin" (figs. 2, 10). This nickname

FIGURE 2. Godefroid (French, active 1790s). *Le Jongleur Pitt soutenant avec une loterie l'equilibre de l'Angleterre et les subsides de la coalition (Pitt the Trickster-Juggler Trying to Balance England's Budget and the Subsidies of the Coalition with a Lottery)*, 1793–1794. Etching with hand coloring. Paris, Bibliothèque nationale.

would have been aptly applied since Molière's character was a farmer, and the English king was often referred to as "Farmer George" due to his spare-time activity at the Home Farm in Windsor. David thus plays ingeniously with the literary and verbal associations of *dindon-dandin*.

Bringing up the rear of the potted army is "Milord Oie," a goose wearing a Whig stovepipe hat and riding the back of an English citizen with a funnel-shaped trumpet protruding from between his buttocks. My Lord Goose is identified as Charles James Fox, one of the chiefs of the parliamentary opposition to George III's Tory party. His position at the "other end" of the troops refers as well to his seat on the opposing benches in the House of Commons. Riding his "English Trumpet," he observes the routing of the advance guard of the royal army by the *sans-culottes* and "sounds the call to retreat from the rear out of prudence." *Oie*, or goose, also means simpleton or ninny. Here the inane Goose-Fox emits an ineffectual warning

in the form of a loud fart. Flatulence in French, as in English, signifies both the expulsion of stomach gas and empty and pretentious speech. Since Fox had a reputation as an eloquent orator in behalf of the Whig opposition, the metaphor was an ingenious conceit.

Fox had tried to maintain Whig support of the French Revolution in its early stages despite Pitt's impending suppression of civil liberties and the dissolution of party unity due to the rightward swing of alarmist Whigs like Burke. By December 1792, however, many moderate supporters had deserted him because of his willingness to negotiate with the Jacobin government after the September Massacres, which he himself deplored. After Louis XVI's execution in January 1793, Fox came increasingly under the pressure of the conservatives who followed the government's push for the maintenance of law and order at home and resistance to the spread of French power and ideas abroad. The more violent and the more republican the Revolution became, the greater was the pressure to retreat to a more conservative position. His views, as a result, became increasingly confused and ambivalent. By the time of Marie-Antoinette's execution in August 1793—which Fox thought "more disgusting and detestable than any other murder recorded in history"—he had been virtually reduced to merely "tooting his horn" from the rear.[10]

David's Goose-Fox sounds the retreat in response to the blow sustained by the advance guard of the royal army at the gate of the city they attempt to siege. From the top of the gate, four *sans-culottes* squatting in a row with their buttocks bared (literally, "*sans*" *sans-culottes*) unload a salvo of shit on the English crocks. David's legend explains that this was occasioned by their "colic," punning on the term which in both French and English refers to abdominal and intestinal disorders and the temperament accompanying them. The face of the *sans-culotte* at the head of the row wears a subtle smile, reminding us that French toilet training of the period stressed that the expulsion of fecal matter produced *plaisir*.[11] The English crocks collapse under the onslaught of the falling excrement, one of them receiving it in his open mouth. The crocks and jugheads have been reduced to the level of *pots de chambre*. As they tumble to the ground and smash themselves, all sorts of slithering "venomous creatures" pour out and expose "the spirit that motivates them" to belligerence.

In the background stands a row of what David describes as "new English artillery which has the virtue of being able to extinguish fires and to delay fortifications." What first appear as enormous siege cannons are upon closer inspection revealed to be *seringues*, the famous syringe or clyster used to administer enemas. The body which held the pump portion of the clyster was actually referred to as a "cannon" in French. Hence, these particular cannons are indeed useful for "extinguishing fires and dissolving fortifications"—that is, putting out intestinal pains and preventing body waste from backing up. The clyster-cannons stand in opposition to the *sans-culottes*, whose application literally backfires on the royal English army.

David's second cartoon commissioned by the Committee of Public Safety, *Gouvernement anglois (The English Government)*, is also scatological, but this time George's actions backfire on his citizenry at home (fig. 3). A "flayed Devil" ("Diable écorché") symbolizing the English government, is suddenly stopped in his tracks by the explosion occurring in his anus. His monstrous head is enveloped by a nest of wriggling serpents, and his gaping mouth, which displays a set of fangs, contributes to an expression of shock. He lunges at his royal scepter for support as if it were a lame person's walker, as his posterior, elaborated into the head of George III, violently discharges a train of foul smoke and lightning shafts in the direction of a crowd of panic-stricken citizens. The ghoulish devil, wearing the royal crown and the Order of the Garter, is labeled

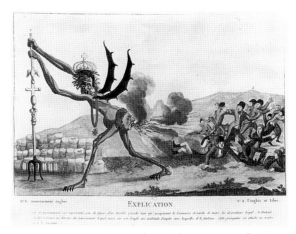

FIGURE 3. Jacques-Louis David (French, 1748–1825). *Gouvernement anglois (The English Government)*, 1793–1794. (Cat. no. 115).

as the "English Government," while the crowd on the opposite side is labeled "Freeborn English." David's legend reads: "This government is personified by the figure of a Devil skinned alive, monopolizing[12] commerce and covered with all the royal decorations. The portrait of the king is located at the rear end of the government which vomits on its people a myriad of taxes which overwhelm them. This prerogative is attached to the scepter and the crown."

David ingeniously suggests that, despite the apparent form of representative government, the English people, far from being free, are actually enslaved by the economic policies of the king. The bales and barrels at the right are labeled "taxes" and therefore remain unopened and unavailable to the overburdened society. The crown's monopoly of commerce in this period, restricting entry of would-be competitors, controlled the flow of revenue, and the resulting higher prices functioned as a kind of tax on commodities. The fetid smoke emerging from George's anus-mouth carries the inscription "English Liberty," while the lightning shafts blasted toward the fleeing crowd bear the names of several specific taxes—such as those for clothing, gaming, and sport (*jeux*)—and also include the vital life substances of air, earth, and water. This is the domestic trade-off for waging war against the French revolutionary government.[13]

David's representation of the emaciated, flayed devil, with grotesque bat wings and Janus-Anus, derives from medieval representations of the devil and his anal associations. He clearly took Jacques Callot's second version of *The Temptation of Saint Antony* (1635) as the model for his cartoon (figs. 4a–b). In the foreground of the famous engraving of hell, the chimerical armor-plated beast with wheels who emits barbed weapons and foul, sulphurous smoke from his mouth and anus inspired the George motif, and the horned beast with bat wings probably influenced the treatment of the devil. Callot's curious creatures, toads, and serpents indulge in anal games and probably served as prototypes for the "venomous" creatures of *The Army of Jugs* as well.[14]

As Norman O. Brown noted in *Life against Death*, psychoanalytic investigations of folklorish and literary allusions to the devil persistently reveal their anal character. The culmination of the ritual of the Witches' Sabbath was to kiss the devil's posterior or a facial mask attached to it. In the key ceremony of the Black Mass, the "sacred host" was prepared by kneading on the buttocks of the queen of the sabbath a mixture of feces, menstrual blood, urine, and various kinds of offal. Dante, whose devil sports batlike wings, makes Lucifer's anus the point of transition between hell and purgatory. Luther is unique in not only stressing the devil's anality, but in attacking him with anality. In one instance the theologian routed him "with a fart," while in other cases he threatened to defecate in his face or stuff him up his anus, "where he belongs."[15] Rabelaisian anality also takes this turn, as in the case of Panurge's malodorous concoction of fecal matter, which is so vile "that the devil could not have endured it."[16]

FIGURE 4a. Jacques Callot (French, 1592–1635). *La Tentation de Saint Antoine* (*The Temptation of Saint Antony*), 1635. Etching (second version). New York, The Metropolitan Museum of Art, Gift of Henry Walters, 1917. (17.37.149).

FIGURE 4b. Detail of figure 4a.

For both Luther and Rabelais the devil is a projection and condensation of their anal fixation, which is dealt with by returning it to where it originated. The devil in this sense is a component of the encoded process of the childhood environment. Excrement can then serve as a weapon to be flung in the face of the enemy, that is, the tyrannical father who is embodied in David's cartoons in the figure of George III and the English government. The scatological material of the cartoons may be seen as an instance of coprophilia—the obsession with excrement—associated with psychosexual infantilism.

Swift's writings, early translated into French, also contain many hints for David's cartoons. The Janus-Anus motif is already prefigured in Swift's poem *Strephon and Chloe*, where the pernicious backbiting of women is described: "You'd think she utter'd from behind / Or at her mouth was breaking wind." In *Gulliver's Travels* the bestial Yahoos are distinguished from all other creatures by their fascination with their own excrement. It is no mere waste product but a magical and ritualistic substance. At one point, the Yahoos leap up on a tree and discharge their excrement on Gulliver's head. This is analogous to the Yahoo ceremony for changing from one chief to another. When the old leader is discarded, his successor and the Yahoos of the district march in a body "and discharge their excrements upon him from Head to Foot."

According to Freudian theory, the human infant begins the anal phase at the time the libido gets concentrated in the anal zone. This infantile stage is marked by the attachment of symbolic meaning to bodily waste. Children bestow upon the anal product the status of their own original creation, which they now deploy to gain pleasure (feces as play), to attain the affection of another (feces as gift), to assert personal ownership (feces as property), or to act out hostility against another (feces as weapon). Thus, some of the most crucial areas of social behavior develop in the anal phase and retain their connection with it into adulthood. When infantile needs are ultimately repressed into sexuality, the symbolism initially associated with the anal product gets displaced to nonbodily cultural objects which function as secondhand replacements. The sublimation of feces into property, however, is not simply a transference from excrement to money; on the contrary, money remains excrement, because the anal associations, although repressed, continue in the unconscious. Indeed, there is no aspect of civilized exchange and its expression that is totally free of connections with anality.

It is no coincidence that the king spews out from his Janus-Anus the sublimated attributes of some of the categories of social behavior decisively affected by the anal stage of infantile sexuality. He discharges the symbolic replacements of anal-erotic enjoyment now taxed to subsidize the war against France. By attempting to monopolize commerce and tax the public on common items, George III betrays his anal compulsion to withhold liberty from his citizens and conversely to blast them with these taxes as if they were gifts. David's condensation, his visual and verbal puns, spring from the process of encoding and decoding his environment. The French terms for caricature are *charge* (noun) and *charger* (verb), meaning to charge or overcharge in the sense of exaggeration.[17] By surcharging or overloading a singular trait or feature, the hidden character of the person or complex of persons is revealed. Caricature serves the purpose of unmasking people and situations, not simply through degrading them and stripping away their facade, but in negating their self-perception and even sublimations. The disfiguration of a person in caricature could thus result in the discovery of a new truth.

The anal origins of the term *charger*, to caricature, symbolizing the heaping of satiric dirt on the subject-victim, should be clear. The overloading of the drawing is at the same time a form of *décharge*, that is, the expulsion of excrement upon the head of the victim. The caricaturist essentially eliminates unwanted subjects by discharging fecal matter at them. Enemies are seen as fallen and filthy,

and as in the case of Luther and the devil, the fight against them is expressed in the form of an anal counterattack.

The discharge in the form of a surcharge (*charger*) is a process of debunking, of exorcizing the Evil One by reducing him to a biological function generic to every living creature or besmearing him with the results of that process.[18] Traditionally, the devil was a great illusionist and trickster, and the job of the theologian was to unmask his multiple guises.[19] David's merging of the devil with the monstrous British government translates the punishments of hell into everyday terms and points to the material and political origin of evil. His dual attack on the political and religious emblems of the crown further serves to derobe the devil's supposed antithesis, the church. The anticlerical Jacobins never ceased coupling the church and the throne, and their attempt to dechristianize France had less to do with atheistic belief than with the desire to create a new religion suitable to the republic.[20] If religion is sublimated anality, then the devil's anality is the negation of religion through the exposure of its origin. Analogously, the equation devil = shit is the negation of classicism; by exposing the disguised (sublimated) anality behind Neoclassicism (rational state, organized religion, hierarchical authority), David reaffirmed the connections between political caricature and his high art.

One of the major sources for David's cartoons was the English caricaturist James Gillray.[21] Although Gillray's vitriolic pen supported the Tories, his caricatures of George III and Pitt were almost as savage as those of the Jacobins and of the parliamentary opposition. Nearly all of the French artists producing anti-British cartoons in 1793–1794 used Gillray's froglike depiction of the king's profile as the prototype for their image (fig. 5). David

FIGURE 5. James Gillray (British, 1757–1815). *Anti-Saccharrites, — or — John Bull and His Family Leaving off the Use of Sugar*, 1792. Etching. San Marino, The Huntington Library.

FIGURE 6. James Gillray (British, 1757–1815). *Lieu'. Gover'. Gall-Stone, Inspired by Alecto;—or—The Birth of Minerva*, 1790. Etching. San Marino, The Huntington Library.

was especially attracted to Gillray during the decade of the 1790s, and oddly enough, this admiration was mutual. The artist Landseer recalled that at an assembly of fellow English artists during the time of the French Revolution, Gillray proposed a toast to David, "the first painter and patriot in Europe."[22]

David based the figure of the devil in his *Gouvernement anglois* on Gillray's caricatures of the 1790s. The English cartoonist's *Lieu'. Gover'. Gall-Stone, Inspired by Alecto* (fig. 6) portrays a pair of emaciated, ghoulish figures with long bony arms close in physical type to David's image. The skeletal frame of Alecto is also winged, and her hair consists of a tangled mass of slithering vipers. An even closer parallel may be found in Gillray's *Sin, Death, and the Devil* (fig. 7), depicting the struggle between Pitt and his Lord High Chancellor, Thurlow, with Queen Charlotte throwing herself between them to shield Pitt from the fallen Thurlow's vengeance. Pitt as King Death is a bony creature whose emaciated body is articulated in a manner similar to that of the flayed devil in David's cartoon. In addition, he wears a crown through which a serpent glides and wields a scepter, which he grasps with both hands. The hair of the queen-Alecto is composed of a tangle of serpents, and the figures are enveloped in infernal smoke, fire, and lightning.

It is certain that David knew this cartoon—one that particularly offended the British royal family—because he used it again for his monumental *Intervention of the Sabine Women* in the late years of the decade (fig. 8).[23] The striking similarity between the three central characters of the cartoon and the protagonists of the *Sabine Women* leaves no doubt that David employed Gillray's cartoon in formulating his composition. The assimilation of the cartoon to David's picture, which alludes to the factionalization of French political life, again demonstrates the close affiliation of the political caricature and magisterial Neoclassical productions.

David must also have been familiar with Gillray's abundant scatological references. These extend from Pitt portrayed as a toadstool on the royal crown as dunghill (1791), to the king sitting on the toilet with a bad case of colic as he receives news of the assassination of the Swedish ruler (1792), and even to a nervous French king as he is separated from his wife and family (1793).[24] But the most important for David's work was the 1793 cartoon entitled *The French Invasion;—or—John Bull, Bombarding the Bum-Boats*, which depicts George III as the map of England defecating on a *sans-culotte* head developed out of the map of France, while from the latter's mouth—like a giant harbor—a fleet of ships depart to invade the English coast (fig. 9).[25] The idea of releasing a barrage of excrement on the enemy may have been the point of departure for an appropriate Davidian riposte.

In addition to the traditional association of caricature and scatology, a literary and ideological discourse of excremental metaphor paralleled and facilitated the bourgeois David's use of such references. Revolutionary rhetoric was distinctly anti-

FIGURE 7. James Gillray (British, 1757–1815). *Sin, Death, and the Devil. Vide Milton*, 1792. Etching. San Marino, The Huntington Library.

FIGURE 8. Jacques-Louis David (French, 1748–1825). *Enlèvement des Sabines (Intervention of the Sabine Women)*, 1799. Oil on canvas. Paris, Musée du Louvre. Photo: Cliché des Musées nationaux, Paris.

aristocratic and became an instrument of attack on the old society. This society had manifested itself through a privileged code of *politesse* and decorum, although its pornographic proclivities hinted at the pressures of excessive role-playing. The radical break with the past of feudal and aristocratic domination required a drastic transformation of speech, visual sign systems, dress codes, and body language. A discourse for the crowd was required to aid in encoding a new environment with an inclusive, nonprivileged space. The new discourse would derive from the street and even descend into the gutter where the mud could splash in all directions.

Scholars like myself investigating this material must, as Robert Darnton put it, dig "downward into intellectual history" and turn up the "dirt." Here the scholarly enterprise allows itself to come down from the summit and betray its own dynamic of anality. Darnton's delightful wordplay may itself be seen as a modern complement of the writing of those he calls the "Grub Street" intellectuals, writers whom David's friend Henri Grégoire classified

FIGURE 9. James Gillray (British, 1757–1815). *The French Invasion; — or — John Bull, Bombarding the Bum-Boats*, 1793. Etching. San Marino, The Huntington Library.

as geniuses "dwelling in basements and in seventh-story garrets." Grégoire noted that "true genius is almost always *sans-culotte*." Darnton, like David and Grégoire, has attempted to bring the Enlightenment "down to earth." Eighteenth-century authors were, after all, "men of flesh and blood, who wanted to fill their bellies, house their families, and make their way in the world."[26] Many of the revolutionary pamphleteers and activists such as Carra, Gorsas, and Fabre d'Eglantine were marginalized by the academicians of the pre-revolutionary epoch "as the excrement of literature." Their requests for government support were invariably refused in favor of those in good standing, that is, whose writings promoted the regime and the ideology of the dominant elite.

The closed world of high society had to explode to make room for the "vile rabble" previously contained in the Grub Street ghetto. Until then, these outcast writers had managed to survive by hustling pornographic writings and titillating those in private who condemned them publicly. At the same time, they vented their resentment against the cultural aristocracy who despotically dominated the world of letters. As Darnton notes, it was "in the depths of the intellectual underworld" that writers like Marat, Brissot, and Carra developed their revolutionary determination to stamp out the aristocratically polite worldview.

Grub Street had to confront the privileged and exclusive academic bodies that monopolized arts and letters and catered to polite society. Its smutty underworld *libelles* attacked the court, the church, the nobility, the academies, the salons, and every "respectable" Establishment institution, including the monarchy. Like the political caricaturists, these writers indicted the social order for its deviance, debauchery, and decadence, always stressing the connection between sexual and political corruption. Cartoons depicting Marie-Antoinette in the arms of the Comte d'Artois, the Duchesse de Polignac, and even Lafayette constituted a graphic equivalent of the literary pornographers.[27] They defamed and desanctified the sign system of social decorum and privilege, debunking the myths that legitimatized it in the public mind.[28] Their pornographic tirades and manifest tone of moral outrage succeeded in reaching the wider community, which was more or less impervious to the rarefied abstractions of Enlightenment philosophy. The scatology of their pamphlets set the stage for the anti-elitist discourse of the revolutionary epoch.

The author of the populist Jacobinical journal *Le Père Duchesne*, Jacques René Hébert, belonged to the literary canaille before the Revolution and found his voice in the plainspoken and quasi-obscene language of the popular classes — especially the Parisian *sans-culotterie*.[29] His newspaper enjoyed an enormous success from the time of its first appearance in November 1790 and provides a literary complement to David's caricatures.

The sobriquet "Père Duchesne" derived from a common figure of the popular imagination who became Hébert's notorious persona during the years 1790–1794. Hébert-Père Duchesne was identified in the mind of his large audience as coarse, candid, and jocular. He took as his model the mud-slinging texts of Rabelais, whom the Jacobins celebrated as the prophet of the Revolution for his desacralization of royal and clerical power. The journal's reports were deliberately couched in foul language to appeal to the crowd. Hébert was quite conscious of his use of language, at one point even praising the ghost of Marat in a dream for sharing his ability to "speak the language of the *sans-culottes*" (no. 264). He poured his unceasing venom on the nobility and wealthy commoners, joined the campaign to dechristianize France, and from late

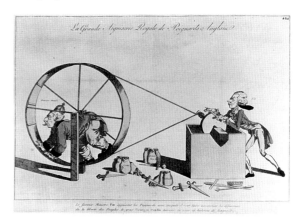

FIGURE 10. Dubois (French, active 1790s). *La Grande Aiguiserie royale de poignards anglais (The Great Royal Knife-Sharpening Establishment for English Daggers)*, 1793–1794. (Cat. no. 113).

1792 violently abused the monarchy, preached war against monopolists, hoarders, and speculators, and systematically excoriated the Girondists — who ultimately included former Grub Street denizens such as Carra, Brissot, and Gorsas. Hébert identified his literary persona with the poor and the *sans-culottes*, exploiting their economic problems to rally to his side the revolutionary cadres that inaugurated the Terror in September 1793.

From June 1793 to February 1794 Hébert, the mouthpiece of the *sans-culotte* movement, contributed to the consolidation of the revolutionary government and the organization of the dictatorship of the Committee of Public Safety. This period coincides roughly with the commissioning of David's cartoons and their execution. It was dominated by the popular assimilation of social and class conflict in which *Père Duchesne* and the *sans-culottes* played a significant role. In the Year II the customs, speech, costume, and gestures of the ancien régime were no longer acceptable. *Père Duchesne*'s obscenities were not only a leveling strategy, they also served to reprimand those who continued to maintain haughty airs and aristocratic appearances. Any gesture or sign that grated against the sense of equality could constitute grounds for arrest and worse. The *sans-culottes*, like the Grub Street boys, pitted themselves and their cultural expression against the pretended superiority of the elite. Eventually, this extended to a condemnation of all "respectable people" who exploited the underclasses and lived off unearned profits.

The *sans-culottes* formed the cadre that enabled the most advanced faction of the radical bourgeoisie to subdue the aristocracy and moderate commoners. The Jacobins exploited the antagonism between the rich and the *sans-culottes* to rally the people to their side. Attacks against commercial monopoly and hoarding were among the stock themes of *Père Duchesne*.

David's political caricatures are texts belonging to the same world of popular discourse. The visual texts, no less than the written, carry scatological metaphors which heap scorn and more on the counterrevolutionary forces at home and abroad. David swears in graphic language as colorful as the profanity of Hébert's journal. In fact, *Père Duchesne* employed many of the same figurative devices that David made use of, including the mitered demon (no. 35), the infestation of institutions with toads, lizards, and other "venomous beasts" that require purification (nos. 46, 176), soldiers getting pissed on (no. 56), kings being led by the nose by unscrupulous politicians (no. 149), the stupid *dindon* (nos. 15, 99, 117, 128, 182, 183), and Georges Dandin. Hébert first uses the latter sobriquet as early as issue 14, and it recurs with increasing frequency from 1792 to the end of the publication.[30] At one point he calls Pitt the "Seeing Eye dog for the blind king Georges Dandin." (An explicit case of Hébert's contribution to the imagery of revolutionary caricature is found in the anonymous print of ca. 1791 *Grande Armée / du ci devt prince de Condé* [cat. no. 103]. There a dog is shown pissing on counterrevolutionary soldiers and wearing a collar which bears the inscription "J'appartiens du Père Duchesne" ["I belong to Père Duchesne"]. This suggests that Hébert's influence was widespread among revolutionary caricatures, that it was not limited to David, and that it was felt throughout the entire cartoon-making industry.)

Père Duchesne also attacks the English for trying to ruin French commerce, inciting the Girondins and the Vendéens to civil war, and hiring assassins to kill revolutionary leaders. He accuses Pitt and George III of sharpening the daggers to assassinate the French chiefs, a phrase he repeats often and which inspired another popular cartoon of the epoch entitled *La Grande Aiguiserie royale de poignards anglais (The Great Royal Knife-Sharpening Establishment for English Daggers*; fig. 10).[31] Often attributed to David, it was designed by Dubois and shows an obese and panting George III (labeled "Georges Dandin") crouching on all fours like a squirrel or chipmunk inside a wheel which drives the grinder's stone on which a diabolical Pitt sharpens a blade.[32] The fiendish-looking fop is surrounded by daggers and sacks of money destined for assassins, including one labeled "Cordai." The legend reads: "The famous minister Pitt sharpening the daggers with which he intends to murder the defenders of the People's liberty. The fat Georges Dandin turning the wheel and panting from exhaustion." *Père Duchesne* warns the *sans-culottes* that Georges Dandin is paying agents to vilify and even to destroy them and that they alone provide the means to stop him (nos. 245, 268). Hébert admonishes them to follow the example of the republican armies standing up valiantly to the coalition of English, Prussian, and Austrian troops subsidized by Pitt and Georges Dandin and to war unceasingly against their domestic counterparts, "the royalists, moderates, aristocrats, and conspirators of every stamp." He reminds them that the English murdered the *sans-culottes* of Toulon and their Parisian brothers must avenge them in an open war in which "either France or England perishes." David's heroic *sans-culottes* gushing excrement on the royal army and Hébert's linkage between domestic and foreign struggle affirm a common perception of *sans-culottisme*. They acknowledged that the popular movement made possible the formation of the revolutionary government, thus quelling counterrevolution at home and the English-subsidized coalition abroad.

Above all, however, it is *Père Duchesne*'s scatological imagery and anality that link Hébert's "scribbling" to the Grub Street crowd and to David's political caricatures. In one of his more endearing moments, he reduces the ill French king to basic human dimension by pleading with the court physicians to "clyster him, purge him, and heal him quickly" (no. 42). Later, referring to the king's veto power during the early stages of the Revolution, he rails against the "vile scoundrels who toady to Monsieur Veto to persuade him to shove down the toilet [foutre à la chaise percée] the most salutory law ever written" (no. 99). He admonishes the lawmakers of the National Assembly "to purge France of all the excrements of despotism and aristocracy" (no. 153), while the "chronic indigestion" of the enemies of the people have made the Constituent Assembly "belch out and throw up these stinking excrements of the Club of 89 and the Feuillants [i.e., constitutional royalists]" (no. 134). Indeed, "this diseased club has been discharged through the anus of the nobility" (no. 140). Given the right amount of troops and adequate provisions, the civil war in the Vendée could be suppressed and "all the excrements of royalty, aristocracy and the church will be swept away" (no. 252). The Girondins "ooze from the muck of the swamp . . . they are the vile excrements of royalism and Brissotism" (no. 330). When *Père Duchesne* pours verbal abuse on royal tyrants and emperors, he is at his Rabelaisian best:

> You believe yourself to be an all-powerful being because you rule over two or three kingdoms, so be it, fuckhead! A simple stove merchant, a poor bugger who possesses only a pike, is a thousand times more powerful than you. Yes, Père Duchesne at the head of the brave *sans-culottes*, even before he reaches the age of a puppy, will tread on the skull of all the kings, and will shit [fera caca] on all their thrones. (no. 117)

This is the language of David's cartoons and the *sans-culotte* discourse that the Committee of Public Safety wanted to incorporate into its public message during the critical period of September 1793.[33]

Ironically, however, by the time David began finalizing his designs, the danger posed by Hébert and his popular movement persuaded the Jacobins to terminate his career. Just two months before David submitted his cartoons to the Committee for approval, Hébert was guillotined on the basis of circumstantial evidence and hearsay. Among the jurors that declared him guilty was the artist Topino-Lebrun, David's student.[34] This violent end to the *sans-culotte* mouthpiece and the deliberately propagandistic intent of the political caricatures help to further clarify the wellsprings of David's expression of anality.

The direct association of the *sans-culottes* with excrement is not only the complement of the direct language of *Père Duchesne*. It carries a subtext as well of the bourgeois counterattack against the *sans-culottes* on the part of David and his Jacobin colleagues. The affiliation of the *sans-culottes* and muck is a put-down of the vile rabble that the Jacobins now wanted to suppress. One clue to the breakup is the economic signification of David's *English Government*, with its all-out warfare on tax-

ation and controls. On this issue the *sans-culottes* and the Jacobin bourgeoisie fundamentally differed.[35] The *sans-culottes* actually advocated taxation and controls, while the revolutionary bourgeoisie favored economic freedom—an opposition between consumer and producer. The artisan and small shopkeeper class suspected those who defended freedom of enterprise; they insisted on fixed wages and prices rather than market fluctuations and heavy taxation of merchant capital. Hence, they espoused a social ideal that contradicted economic growth. But the members of the Committee of Public Safety were mainly free traders and rejected a controlled economy as a permanent policy. They resigned themselves temporarily to the situation only because they were unable to carry on the war without price-fixing. David's anus-faced George III and his retched-up excremental taxes are also, therefore, a concealed critique of *sans-culotte* economics.

I have argued for the close connections between the cartoons and the magisterial Neoclassical productions. I want to conclude with a discussion of David's painting of 1793–1794 to clarify my arguments. Shortly after Louis XVI's execution, *Père Duchesne* featured a mock funeral oration for its *sans-culotte* audience. It chronicled a lurid family history of cuckoldry, buggery, sadism, and corruption which justified the king's punishment. Hébert warned that it was now up to the republicans to finish their task and

> purge France of all the fucking scoundrels [jean-foutres] who participated in the crimes of this tyrant. There remain a great number including his wife and his bugger of a race which still survive: believe me, you will never be able to rest until they are destroyed. Little fish become large, so take guard, fucker, *liberty hangs by a hair* [italics mine]. (no. 212)[36]

Père Duchesne's prophecy was fulfilled almost immediately after publication, for the next issue mourns the passing of Lepelletier de Saint-Fargeau, a deputy who voted for the king's death. Lepelletier was stabbed by a former royal guard on the eve of Louis XVI's execution and died shortly afterward. *Père Duchesne* called his assassin "one the vilest of scoundrels," and expressed the fear that this act would encourage the royalists to further assassinations. Hébert praised Lepelletier as a "brave bugger whose only blemish was his nobility, but who overcame this handicap by enrolling for life in the *sans-culotterie* and dying in the service of liberty." He also lavished praise on the magnificent cortege that transported Lepelletier's remains to the Panthéon and contrasted the crowd's rever-

FIGURE 11. Anatole Devosge (French, 1770–1850). *Lepelletier de Saint-Fargeau*, 1793, after Jacques-Louis David. Black crayon drawing. Dijon, Musée des beaux-arts.

ence for the deputy with its disdain for the funeral of Louis XVI.

It was David who arranged the ceremonies for Lepelletier, together with the musician Gossec. Lepelletier's body was placed on public view, on the pedestal of the destroyed statue of Louis XIV.[37] The pedestal was flanked by steps adorned with candelabra and incense burners. A plaque on the pedestal quoted the martyr's last words: "I am content to have spilled my blood for my country. I hope that it will serve to consolidate liberty and equality and expose their adversaries."[38] *Père Duchesne*'s call for self-sacrifice and all-out warfare on traitors who threatened the people was thematically echoed in the ceremonies organized by David.

David further decided to commemorate the event with a portrait of the martyr based on the public viewing of the corpse. In his speech to the National Convention declaring his intention, he imagined an aged patriarch explaining to his large family the motifs underlying the representation of freedom's hero: "Do you see the sword hanging over his head by just a hair? Well, children, that shows how much courage Michel Lepelletier and his noble companions needed to rout the evil tyrant who had oppressed us for so long, for, had they set a foot wrong, the hair would have been broken and they would all have been killed."[39] David's portrait (now known only from a drawn copy by Anatole Devosge [fig. 11] and miscellaneous fragments, the original having been destroyed) clearly abandoned topical realism to introduce the metaphorical sword suspended by a hair—a device bor-

rowed from *Père Duchesne*. The journalist used the phrase "la liberté ne tient qu'à un cheveu," which the artist reinterpreted as "cette épée... qui n'est retenue que par un cheveu." Uttered in nearly identical contexts, David's representation of the text slips in the direction of political caricature. The huge sword, dripping with blood, whose pommel has been elaborated into the head of a Gallic cock, dominates the upper half of the image and pierces a card which reads "I voted for the tyrant's death." These metonymic devices transform the picture into a political tract as declamatory and propagandistic as the images of *Père Duchesne* and Gillray (fig. 12).

The dripping blood, the gaping wound, and the suspended sword dangling over the nude torso do more; they create an agglomeration of motifs bordering on anal eroticism. The love of the martyr's body has been represented in the objectified form of a fetish together with the instrument of his martyrdom. The will to apotheosis is negated by the release of libidinous energy displaced onto the objects and the infantile fascination with bodily cavities and secretions. Something similar occurred in the making of the *Death of Marat* (fig. 13), where the diseased body, gaping wound, and bloodstained instruments are almost perversely presented as objects of tender regard and saintliness.[40] The dechristianization of Jacobin imagery

FIGURE 12. James Gillray (British, 1757–1815). *The Dagger-Scene; — or — The Plot Discover'd*, 1792. Etching. San Marino, The Huntington Library.

FIGURE 13. Jacques-Louis David (French, 1748–1825). *Marat assassiné* (*Death of Marat*), 1793. Oil on canvas. Brussels, Musées royaux des beaux-arts.

broke through the repressed anality and allowed this material to come to the surface of cultural practice.

What happens in this period of crisis is the dissolution of the boundaries between high and low art. Under the pressures of the Terror and the setbacks of utopian projections, the once heroic, idealized space is transgressed by the heretofore excluded other. Classic Neoclassicism was marked by the absence of the enemy, but in the later stage the painting is noted for the metonymic presence of the adversary. David's *Hector and Andromache* is often juxtaposed with the *Lepelletier* and *Marat* to suggest continuity, when in fact they are a Revolution apart. Save for Homeric allusions to the Trojan War, the enemy other is absent from the earlier work, and Hector is embalmed and puffed up to heroic dimensions. In the later images the instruments of the protagonist's demise, representing the metaphorical presence of the enemy, are foregrounded in his traditionally exclusive space. Hence, the greater degree of realism and regression in the later painting. David's incorporation of texts vital to the narrative and the iconic rendering of objects such as swords, knives, pens, an inkwell, and a trompe-l'oeil wooden crate gave to his martyr portraits the vernacular language of *Père Duchesne* and the emblematic power of Gillray's cartoons.[41]

This is true as well of the *Death of Bara* (fig. 14). The ordinariness of the adolescent protagonist and propagandistic intent of the work forced David to seek a symbolic characterization. The painter came up with an androgynous being compressed into a national icon. The prostrate, naked hero

clutches his tricolored cockade to his breast with both hands as the last act of his young life. He wears an expression akin to rapture. What is most curious about the figure is its effeminate character; both the face and the body resemble more a pubescent female than an adolescent male. Bara has been transformed into the fairytale Cinderella, the nascent version of "Marianne"—the virginal figure on the seal of the republic—only to be sadistically raped and murdered. David's manipulation of the historical facts and the picture's emblematic qualities again attest to the breakdown of the traditional categories.

David executed several terrifying images of cruelty and mutilation in the years 1793–1794, including the *Triumph of the French People*, showing two ferocious *sans-culottes* stabbing fallen kings, and a portrayal of the revolutionary General Dampierre in battle supporting his right leg, which has been severed below the knee. These images evoke the writings of David's contemporary the Marquis de Sade, with the Bara in particular recalling the youthful victims of de Sade's *The 120 Days of Sodom*. An aristocratic denizen of Grub Street, de Sade became radicalized during his long imprisonment in the Bastille and at Charenton. In March 1790 the Constituent Assembly ordered the release of all prisoners held by lettre de cachet (the hated royal prerogative), and with his liberation de Sade enthusiastically embraced the Revolution in its early stages. He became secretary and speaker for the Section des Piques (formerly Vendôme), to which Robespierre belonged. It was in the latter function that he was chosen to compose a funeral oration for Lepelletier and Marat, which enjoyed so much success that it was printed and distributed at public expense.[42]

De Sade's writings have a strong affinity with Grub Street; his libertines all belong to the upper classes and include princes, nobles, bishops, and wealthy commoners.[43] They are evildoers and criminals who have gained their wealth by exploiting the poor. And almost invariably they sodomize, are sodomized, and possess abundant coprophagous appetites (La Duclos, the storyteller of *The 120 Days*, recounts a hundred stories concerning excremental orgies). De Sade's sexual character was essentially anal, and he openly acknowledged his coprophilia. He attempted to subvert the conventions of polite society with his scatological language and perversely erotic behavior. He inundates his aristocratic characters and their victims with shit, vomit, and snot. His sexual lexicon is as crude as that of *Père Duchesne*, and he joins pornographic material to spheres of experience normally kept separated by socio-moral taboo. In the middle

FIGURE 14. Jacques-Louis David (French, 1748–1825). *La Mort de Bara* (*Death of Bara*), 1794. Oil on canvas. Avignon, Musée Calvet.

of his notorious *Philosophy in the Boudoir* (1795), he abruptly introduces a political tract entitled "Yet Another Effort, Frenchmen, If You Would Become Republicans," which rages against religion and monarchy. Clerics in his opinion should be "treated as charlatans and jeered at, ridiculed, covered with filth in all the public squares and marketplaces in France's largest cities."[44] Here de Sade conjoins the anality of the caricatural tradition with the revolutionary discourse central to David's cartoons.

Ironically, the onset of the Terror forced de Sade to recognize his humanity, while David discovered his anal-sadism. Unlike David, de Sade refused to authorize executions when the head of his section and was jailed for his *modérantisme*. It was while de Sade languished in prison that David produced his two cartoons and painted his image of Bara. This inversion of the two personalities under revolutionary pressures and their expression in high and low art constitute the themes of Peter Weiss's play *The Persecution and Assassination of Marat As Performed by the Inmates of the Asylum of Charenton under the Direction of the Marquis de Sade*. Contrasting the revolutionary idealism of Marat with the shrewder cynicism of de Sade, Weiss signals the dangers of infantile regression within an institutionalized surrogate for society. His own extensive use of scatological metaphor acknowledges the ideological discourse of de Sade and its indictment of a corrupt ruling class. At the end of the play, the stage directions call for Marat's body to reproduce the David painting with one arm slung over the edge of the bath, the quill pen still in one hand, and the messages in the other. Weiss's play depends on anachronism and metonymy to transmit its political message, strategies harvested from his researches into eighteenth-century political caricature and Neoclassicism.[45]

I am very grateful to the following friends and colleagues whose advice and suggestions were decisive in the development of this paper: Philippe Bordes, Ronald Grazioni, Draper Hill, David Kunzle, David Lubin, Robert Maniquis, Debora Silverman, and Dora Weiner. Unless otherwise noted, all translations from the French are mine.

1. See André Blum, *La Caricature révolutionnaire* (Paris: Jouve et Cie, 1916), pp. 195–96; J. Lortel, "David caricaturiste," *L'Art et les artistes* 18 (March 1914), pp. 273–75; G. Wildenstein, "David, auteur de caricatures contre les Anglais commandées par la Convention," in *Omagiu lui George Oprescu: Cu prilejul împlinirii a 80 de anii*, ed. T. Vianu and M. Popescu (Bucharest: Academia Republicii Populare Romine, 1961), pp. 595–97. See also Jules Renouvier, *Histoire de l'art pendant la Révolution* (Paris: Vve Jules Renouard, 1863), vol. 1, pp. 76–85, vol. 2, pp. 481–96, who while publishing long sections on both David and caricature in the French Revolution never links the two.

2. I have in the past tentatively advanced the claim that Neoclassical imagery and political caricature share the same station in the development of modern art. See my articles "Thomas Nast and French Art," *American Art Journal* 4 (Spring 1972), pp. 57–58, and "The Comic Stripped and Ash Canned: A Review Essay," *Art Journal* 32, no. 1 (Fall 1972), pp. 22–23.

3. Ronald Paulson, *Representations of Revolution (1789–1820)* (New Haven and London: Yale University Press, 1983), p. 182. Paulson's chapter "The Grotesque, Gillray, and Political Caricature," pp. 168–211, was invaluable for my study.

4. David Kunzle, *The Early Comic Strip* (Berkeley and Los Angeles: University of California Press, 1973), pp. 3–4, 11–39.

5. E. H. Gombrich, *Art and Illusion* (London: Phaidon Press, 1959), pp. 279–303.

6. Leo Gershoy, *The Era of the French Revolution, 1789–1799* (Princeton: Van Nostrand, 1957), pp. 153–54.

7. Ibid., p. 156. On the basis of a report drawn up by the Committee of Public Safety, the National Convention proclaimed a Levy-in-Mass in August 1793. Of note, Jacobin sexism entered into the formulation: "Women, who at long last are to take their rightful place in the revolution and follow their true destiny, will forget their futile tasks: their delicate hands will work at making clothes for soldiers; they will make tents and they will extend their tender care to shelters where the defenders of the *Patrie* will receive the help that their wounds require" (ibid., pp. 156–57). For further discussion of the image of women during the Revolution, the reader is referred to Lynn Hunt's essay in this catalogue.

8. Blum (supra, note 1), p. 195. See also Hannah Mitchell, "Art and the French Revolution: An Exhibition at the Musée Carnavalet," *History Workshop* 5 (Spring 1978), pp. 123–45; Lynn Hunt, "Engraving the Republic: Prints and Propaganda in the French Republic," *History Today* 30 (October 1980), pp. 11–17. On the same day that David was commissioned to do his cartoons, Loysel, head of the Committee on Assignats and Monies, proposed to the National Convention to represent the highlights of the Revolution on paper currency and, by so doing, insure that the images of the love of liberty, the horror of tyrants, and the regeneration of society will be in everyone's hands. See *Réimpression de l'Ancien Moniteur* 17 (1860), p. 643.

9. This was the beginning of a widespread crackdown on the English presence in France. On 9 October the National Convention completely prohibited the selling or wearing of English goods, and all subjects of Great Britain were to be placed under house arrest; if absent, all their belongings were to be confiscated for the benefit of the republic. See "Affairs of France," *The Universal Magazine* 93 (October 1793), pp. 306–7.

10. For the Whigs and the French Revolution, see L. G. Mitchell, *Charles James Fox and the Disintegration of the Whig Party 1782–1794* (London: Oxford University Press, 1971), pp. 153–238; J. W. Derry, *Charles James Fox* (London: Batsford, 1972), pp. 325–26. David's friend Barère, who also hated Pitt, was more sympathetic to Fox; see Bertrand Barère, *Memoirs of Bertrand Barère, Chairman of the Committee of Public Safety during the Revolution* (London: H. S. Nichols, 1896), vol. 4, pp. 175–78.

11. *Dictionnaire des sciences médicales* (Paris: 1812–1820), vol. 9, p. 446, s. v. "digestion."

12. The term *accapareur* carried sinister connotations for the *sans-culottes*, and one risked being put into this category. See Oscar Browning, ed., *The Despatches of Earl Gower, English Ambassador at Paris from June 1790 to August 1792* (Cambridge: Cambridge University Press, 1885), p. 357.

13. David's cartoon literally embodies the ideological protest of the Jacobins against the English in this period; see *Réimpression de l'Ancien Moniteur* 17 (1860), pp. 640, 645, 722–23, and vol. 20 (1870), p. 41, as well as Barère (supra, note 10), vol. 4, pp. 107–8, 322–23. Publications with titles such as *Discours sur les crimes du gouvernement britannique et sur les vices de la constitution anglaise* and *Discours sur les crimes du gouvernement anglais et les vices de ses finances* repeatedly refer to the enormous taxes oppressing the English people. The writer Laveaux noted that "poverty presently makes the English slaves, despite the fact that nature created them free." After briefly describing the composition of Parliament and the role of the king, he concluded: "Such is the monstrous assemblage of powers that is called the English Constitution." See J.-C. Laveaux, *Discours sur les vices de la constitution anglaise* (Paris: Imprimerie des sans-culottes, 1794), pp. 7, 13. (This was a speech given on 20 January [1 pluviôse].) Similarly, Lachevardière noted that in "the eyes of republicans every king is guilty," but George III had become "a monster in the eyes of the universe." See A. L. Lachevardière, *Discours sur la constitution et le gouvernement d'Angleterre* (Paris: Imprimerie des sans-culottes, 1794), pp. 20–23.

14. For the scatological tradition associated with imagery of Saint Antony and other pertinent issues bearing on my thesis, see M. N. Myers, "Ensor's 'The Tribulations of Saint Anthony': Permutations of the Excremental Vision," *Arts Magazine* 54 (December 1979), pp. 84–89.

15. Norman O. Brown, *Life against Death* (Middletown, Conn.: Wesleyan University Press, 1959), pp. 179–304.

16. For Rabelaisian scatology, see M. Bakhtin, *Rabelais and His World* (Cambridge, Mass.: M.I.T. Press, 1965), pp. 145–52, 175–76, 368–436.

17. Ernst Kris, *Psychoanalytic Explorations in Art* (London: G. Allen and Unwin, 1953), pp. 173–203.

18. See Bakhtin (supra, note 16), pp. 145–52, for the use of excrement in the besmirching and debasing process.

19. David Nicholls, "The Devil in Renaissance France," *History Today* 30 (November 1980), pp. 25–30.

20. For the Jacobin's use of language to discredit religion, see J.-E. de La Harpe, *Du fanatisme dans la langue révolutionnaire, ou De la persécution*, in *Oeuvres* (Geneva: Slatkine Reprints, 1968), vol. 5, pp. 496–500. This process has an ancient pedigree; see Bakhtin (supra, note 16), pp. 81, 89, 147.

21. For Gillray, see Thomas Wright and Joseph Grego, *The Works of James Gillray, the Caricaturist* (London: Chatto and Windus, 1873); Draper Hill, *Mr. Gillray the Caricaturist* (London: Phaidon Press, 1965); Draper Hill, *Fashionable Contrasts: Caricatures by James Gillray* (London: Phaidon Press, 1966); Kunzle (supra, note 4), pp. 378–79.

22. "Mr. Landseer's Apology for James Gillray," *The Athenaeum* 15 (October 1831), p. 667.

23. Karen Domenici, "James Gillray: An English Source for David's *Les Sabines*," *Art Bulletin* 65 (1983), pp. 493–95. Domenici also called attention to the connection between the devil in David's *Gouvernement anglois* and Gillray's Pitt. I apologize to Domenici for overlooking her article in my discussion of David and Gillray in *Art in an Age of Revolution* (Chicago: University of Chicago Press, 1987), p. 487.

24. Paulson (supra, note 3), p. 200.

25. Mary Dorothy George, *Catalogue of Political and Personal Satires Preserved in the Department of Prints and Drawings in the British Museum* (London: British Museum Publications Limited, 1942; reprint, 1978), vol. 7, no. 8346; Hill, 1965 (supra, note 21), p. 53.

26. Robert Darnton, "The High Enlightenment and the Low-Life of Literature in Pre-Revolutionary France," *Past and Present* 51 (May 1971), pp. 81–115. See also Lynn Hunt, *Politics, Culture, and Class in the French Revolution* (Berkeley and Los Angeles: University of California Press, 1984), p. 50; Thomas E. Crow, *Painters and Public Life in Eighteenth-Century Paris*, (New Haven and London: Yale University Press, 1985), pp. 92–96.

27. Blum (supra, note 1), pp. 176–80.

28. Bakhtin (supra, note 16), pp. 81, 89, 145–52.

29. I have used the series edited by Albert Soboul with an important introduction by him: Jacques René Hébert, *Le Père Duchesne*, 10 vols. (Paris: Edhis, 1969). I have also profited from Soboul's *The Sans-Culottes* (Princeton: Princeton University Press, 1980).

30. Refer to issue nos. 191, 203, 216, 218, 219, 232, 234, 242–45, 249, 257, 274, 275, 282, 285, 287, 294, 297, 302, 305, 314, 316, 320, 322, 327, 334, 336, and 340.

31. This was standard rhetoric for the Jacobins. See also Bertrand Barère, *Rapport fait au nom du Comité de salut public, sur les victoires remportées par les armées de la Moselle, du Rhin, de Sambre-et-Meuse, et du Nord* (Paris: Imprimerie nationale, 1794), p. 13. In this speech given on 18 July 1794 (30 messidor an II), Barère stated: "L'Aiguiserie royale des poignards a Londres fonde plus l'espoir des tyrans de la Tamise, que tous les arsenaux & toutes les manufactures des gouvernemens européens."

32. I follow André Blum's attribution (supra, note 1), p. 192, no. 594. Ralph E. Shikes, *The Indignant Eye: The Artist as Social Critic in Prints and Drawings from the Fifteenth Century to Picasso* (Boston: Beacon Press, 1969), pp. 136–38, and Mitchell (supra, note 8), p. 130, attribute the cartoon to David.

33. Refer also to the cartoon entitled *Bombardement de tous les trônes de l'Europe, / et la chûte des tyrans pour le bonheur de l'univers* (cat. no. 110). It too was executed in the mode of Père Duchesne's discourse. Figure 2 of this essay shows George III's throne as a closestool into which the crown is about to fall. The use of excrement in "smear tactics" was not confined solely to representation; for Bailly's execution the guillotine was removed to a dunghill. See J. F. Nourrisson, *Trois Révolutionnaires, Turgot, Necker, Bailly* (Paris: Perrin, 1886), p. 328.

34. *Procès instruit et jugé au tribunal révolutionnaire, contre Jacques-René Hébert…*, in *Le Père Duchesne* (supra, note 29), vol. 10, p. 2.

35. Soboul, 1980 (supra, note 29), pp. 8, 14, 20, 62, 253.

36. The repeated use of foutre ("to fuck") or foutu ("to be fucked") throughout *Père Duchesne* is both an index of working-class identification and a metaphorical device to frame the messages the author transmits. (It was never used in polite society, and even the trial brief used only the letter *f* to designate Hébert's favorite word.) In the French and in English equivalents the positive sexual signifier relates as well to a negative signified. Hébert's obsessional *foutre* (which is eventually neutralized through repetition) broadly caricatures the revolutionary text in the way that David's metonymic devices and scatological metaphors caricture political life.

37. See E.-J. Delécluze, *Louis David, son école et son temps: Souvenirs* (Paris: Didier et Cie, 1860), pp. 148–53; Antoine Schnapper, *David* (New York: Alpine Fine Arts Collection, 1982), pp. 149–53.

38. Schnapper (supra, note 37), p. 149.

39. Delécluze (supra, note 37), p. 151.

40. The cult aspects of Marat's body have been discussed in Klaus Herding, "Davids *Marat* als 'dernier appel à l'unité révolutionnaire'," *Idea* 2 (1983), pp. 89–112.

41. Marrinan approaches this idea with his dual claim that David has physically "written [Corday] out," but at the same time she is "written" into the message, referring to her name on the note held by the expiring Marat. But her metonymic presence is key to understanding the new direction in David's work for the Revolution. See M. Marrinan, "Images and Ideas of Charlotte Corday: Texts and Contexts of an Assassination," *Arts Magazine* 54 (April 1980), p. 161. Bryson, in his important study of the painter, calls this new direction David's "populist vision." See Norman Bryson, *Tradition and Desire* (Cambridge: Cambridge University Press, 1984), p. 96.

42. Geoffrey Gorer, *The Revolutionary Ideas of the Marquis de Sade* (London: Wishart and Co., 1934), pp. 56–57.

43. I benefited here from Roland Barthes, *Sade, Fourier, Loyola*, (New York: Hill and Wang, 1976), pp. 15–37, 123–71; Maurice Blanchot, "Sade," in L.-D.-F.-A. de Sade, *The Complete Justine, Philosophy in the Bedroom, and Other Writings* (New York: Grove Press, 1965), pp. 37–72.

44. Sade, ibid., p. 306.

45. See K. Braun, ed., *Materialen zu Peter Weiss' 'Marat/Sade'* (Frankfurt am Main: Suhrkamp, 1976), pp. 16, 22, 58, 60, 63, 67, 71, 102–14, 161, 176–77.

Visual Codes in the Graphic Art
of the
French Revolution

Klaus Herding

Universität Hamburg

revious research on the graphic art of the revolutionary decade focused primarily on its effects as propaganda.[1] The artistic achievement of this genre is, however, obscured rather than clarified by an exclusively iconological and often ideologically predetermined approach. When examining the historical determinants and the visual structure, it seems more appropriate to speak of "visual codes" in which the interests of both the producer and the consumer are refracted and concentrated. The often underestimated revolutionary engravings and broadsides are more productive for such research than many a harmonious painting.

The initial questions to be asked, therefore, are: How are revolutionary intentions depicted in this context? how are contemporary conflicts dealt with or covered up? how does this, in turn, change the form? and on which political or didactic intentions does this changed form exert influence?[2] In viewing the most important examples of French revolutionary art, three phenomena appear as leitmotivs to help arrive at answers: specific gestures

and body language, the linking of picture and text, and the structural divergence between code and action. It follows even from these few points that engravings of events (as in the series produced by Pierre-Gabriel Berthault and others)[3] are less valuable for this kind of study than those in which iconic symbols combine, often contradictorily, with narrative fragments. Such antagonistic combinations especially call for innovative codes, which, as implicit emblematic guidelines, create a new cohesion, charging the form with historical content.

The following examples will develop this thesis further. The first, *Le Nouvel Astre français*, embodies the dialectic strategy of the Montagnards at the beginning of 1793 and links very different conceptions of the Revolution (fig. 1a). The print combines the old astronomical notion of revolution with the new historical-political concept; it advocates a system established by violent action yet continues to refer to nature. The dethroning of kings becomes part of the pattern of the unchanging cycle of the stars and as such demands a singular, irrefutable

FIGURE 1a. Anonymous French. *Le Nouvel Astre français ou la Cocarde tricolore suivant le cour du zodiaque* (*The New French Star; or, The Tricolor Cockade Following the Course of the Zodiac*), 1793. (Cat. no. 111).

validity for which a graphic legitimation is required. Corresponding to this ambiguous intention, the engraving argues historically (through the circle of kings), naturally (through the rays of the sun and the darkness that it expels), and astronomically (through the twelve signs of the zodiac). According to Griewank, the astronomical argument—the reference to the eternally changing course of the stars—could only be used conventionally "in the sense of the circular movement of sovereign power,"[4] and therefore in favor of the return of the absolutist regime. In contrast, the engraving shows a dual break: first, a *new* star ("nouvel astre") is announced; second, it is Time, or Chronos, as the natural authority, and not the king, who brings the "circular movement" to an end.

In spite of the engraving's apparent didactic simplicity, its components are quite complicated and require closer examination. Divided into an earthly and a heavenly realm, the print evokes traditional bipartite pictorial structure. Below, there is a circle of twelve rulers whose flames of life are being extinguished by Chronos. This scene, removed from all definite determinations, is given a non-narrative ambience. The rulers stand in a no-man's-land and are thus removed from historical time. In the zenith below the zodiac the revolutionary cockade covers a sun whose rays illuminate the entire space. Some of these rays carry verbal messages and thus indicate the insufficiency of the pictorial means. Above the picture is inscribed, "Le Nouvel Astre français ou la Cocarde tricolore *suivant* le cour du zodiaque [italics mine]"—the cockade *follows* the zodiac, the course of nature; it does not change it. The entire engraving, however, is by no means organized in a natural fashion. The bottom inscription reads, "Peuples *rentres* dans vos droits [italics mine]." Here, too, the Revolution is interpreted as the reestablishment of a previous condition according to natural laws. Underneath, however, the text continues, "Sous peu il n'y aura plus de tirans, le tems trop juste vous donne la liberté et l'égalité." Chronos, who puts an end to the life of the individual, is declared the protagonist of history. This is clarified in a supplement at the lower left, which is detached from any implications of natural law. Time speaks here as "No. 1" (which may refer to a series of prints): "Que je détruise enfin cette cohorte d'ambitieux, ces vils usurpateurs des droits de leurs semblables." The role of Time as avenger is decidedly political in formulation.

So far the engraving has referred to four authorities, zodiac, stars, kings, and time. An additional verbal concordance is established between these four areas. The rays elucidate: "Avis aux siecles futurs / L'orgueil les forma, la raison les détruit. / L'oeuvre du tems ou le préjugé vaincu / Triomphe de la philosophie et de la raison." The repetition of *raison* clearly shows that revolutionary violence is still being justified by the philosophy of the Enlightenment. At the same time, however, the ray-sentences point forward. They describe the Revolution as if completed. Prejudice is vanquished; revolutionary reason has become the model for the future. On this basis Robespierre was able to declare in 1792, "Postérité naissante, c'est à toi de croître et d'amener les jours de la prospérité et du bonheur."[5]

As distant times are brought to bear in the engraving, so are distant spaces. Nevertheless, the foreground is concerned with Louis xvi. "Louis xvi. le traitre et le dernier" reads the base of his pedestal from which the fleurs-de-lis have fallen. His image has been replaced by the altar of the fatherland on which the fire of patriotism burns. The flames from the altar very nearly devour the cap of freedom — an insinuation which the engraver seems to have made unintentionally. Although the altar's inscription — "Egalité / République française" — also bears the date 1792, Louis's flame has already been extinguished. This suggests that the engraving was made immediately after his execution on 21 January 1793.

The other represented rulers are drawn from all of Europe, and the pope and the sultan are included as well. Chronos, who has inverted his scythe, transforming it into an acolyte's candle-snuffer (a good example of the Revolution's mixed symbolism) has just reached Gustavus iii of Sweden (fig. 1b), who was assassinated in 1792. Chronos has already put the cap of the Jacobins on Joseph ii of Austria, who retracted his reforms on his deathbed

FIGURE 1b. Detail of figure 1a.

in 1790, and on his brother and successor, Leopold ii, who died in 1792 after forming a counterrevolutionary alliance with Prussia. Leopold's Prussian ally, Frederick William ii (r. 1786–1797), who had unsuccessfully campaigned against France, is next in line. Pius vi (r. 1775–1799), who campaigned against Jansenism and Febronianism, has a bent candle, signifying that he could not prevail in the face of the revolutionary cockade-sun (Pius vi was actually imprisoned in France in 1798). Why his candle is not entwined by the snakes that symbolize malicious rulership remains an unanswered question. Catherine ii of Russia (r. 1762–1796) appears after the Ottoman sultan Selim iii (incorrectly identified as Selim ii), who came to power in 1789 and was murdered in 1808. Catherine's bare breasts hint at her unrestrained sensuality (fig. 1c). The Russian ruler's domestic policy was contradictory; on the one hand, she enforced serfdom, and on the other, she was an enthusiastic supporter of the French Enlightenment. This may explain why her candle has been attached in such a manner that her crown hangs down the back of her head. Stanislaw ii August Poniatowski of Poland (r. 1764–1795), who in his youth was Catherine's lover, seems to smile expectantly at the revolutionary sun (Kościuszko's unsuccessful insurrection of 1794 took place during his reign). Maria i Francesca Elisabeth of Portugal (who came to power in 1777 and became insane in 1792) and Victor Amadeus iii, duke of Savoy and king of Sardinia (r. 1773–1796), one of the fiercest opponents of the Revolution and partner in the First Coalition against France, follow (fig. 1d).

Below is George III of England (r. 1776–1820), who was regarded as the inflexible advocate of the policy that led to the independence of the North American colonies in 1783. Thereafter, George III left the government to his prime minister, Pitt; hence, the light of his candle has already been extinguished, and his crown has split in two. One of the snakes is missing, suggesting that George was a ruler "without bite." Charles IV of Spain (r. 1788–1808) experienced a similar situation; although he was not deposed, he was completely controlled by his immoral wife Maria Luisa of Parma who managed to put her lover Godoy in charge of the affairs of state in November of 1792. Thus, drifts of smoke announce the king's loss of power.

FIGURE 1c. Detail of figure 1a.

The etching is, therefore, historically accurate and, at the same time, offers an early satirical example of the devaluation of absolutist monuments. The tendency toward mockery is evident in the depiction of the rulers, who resemble chess pieces[6] and are so small that no one, using Chronos for scale, would have to look up to them.

In its potential for inversion, *Le Nouvel Astre français* far surpasses the satirical "overthrow" staged in *The Double Trumpet* (1791), an engraving created on the occasion of the removal of Voltaire's remains to the Panthéon (fig. 2). Here the king is replaced by the civic hero, and absolute rule is dramatically superseded by enlightened rule. The memorial to the king has been dishonored, a lewd genius topples the "faux pas" with a kick. To Voltaire, "l'homme immortel," however, a temple of fame and a *mons gloriae*, the attributes of a ruler, are dedicated. The reason for the degradation of the king's image is supplied by the banner at the genius's back, which records the date of Louis's attempt to escape. The engraving refers, therefore, to two events: the bringing back of the monarch from Varennes on 21 June and the reinterment of Voltaire on 11 July 1791.

FIGURE 1d. Detail of figure 1a.

As in *Le Nouvel Astre français*, the pictorial inversion receives verbal support. "Ce monstre votre idole horreur du genre humain / Que votre orgueil trompé veut retablir en vain." The question of what kind of respect is still owed the king is addressed here. The answer suggested approximates the contemporary saying, "Whosoever mocks Louis shall be thrashed; whosoever hails him shall be hanged." The two lines on the right, "Tous les vrais citoyens ont enfin rappellé la liberté publique / Nous ne redoutons plus le pouvoir tirannique," function on a different level. This rhetoric, removed from the events of the day, corresponds to the inscription on the banner held in front of the

FIGURE 2. Anonymous French. *Voltaire au Panthéon* (*Voltaire at the Panthéon* or *The Double Trumpet*), 1791. Etching with hand coloring. Paris, Bibliothèque nationale.

genius; recalling Voltaire's writings, it reads, "Un roi n'est plus qu'un homme avec un titre auguste / Premier sujet des loix et forcé d'etre juste."[7] The monarchy itself is not questioned here.

The etching's political statement combines two contradictory views: that of Voltaire, for whom the monarchy was a legitimate political institution,[8] and that of the second phase of the Revolution, for which Voltaire (as guarantor of a progressive tie to the past) could no longer serve as a model. In contrast to Voltaire, the print clearly calls for the overthrow of the monarchy. *The Double Trumpet*

FIGURE 3. Hendrik Goltzius (Dutch, 1558–1617). *Fame and History*, 1586. Engraving. Princeton, The Art Museum, Princeton University, Junius S. Morgan Collection.

heralds the step from the monarchy to the rule of enlightened citizens, fulfilling the function of *relevance* as well as a broadside's second possible function, that of *prediction*. It anticipates the actual overthrow of the king by one and a half years. The etching also prefigures the iconoclasm that began in the fall of 1792; no statues of kings had been overturned prior to that time. Furthermore, just as during later acts of actual iconoclasm, substitutes for the destroyed works are offered. As the king is replaced here by a civic hero, so David would actu-

FIGURE 4. Anonymous French. *La Double Trompette: Poètes et épigones (The Double Trumpet: Poets and Epigones)*, 1874. Wood engraving after an etching of 1761.

ally propose the replacement of François Girardon's equestrian statue of Louis XIV with a classicistic reclining statue of Lepelletier a year later.[9]

Despite the drastic inversion of values in the print, its graphic language is hardly innovative. Goltzius had already used a double trumpet to indicate historical change in 1586 (fig. 3), and the basic semantic content survives. The transformation of the trumpet of glory into one of defamation has antecedents as well. Champfleury used an example of this instrument dating from 1761 to illustrate his satire directed against poets and epigones (fig. 4).

In *Le Nouvel Astre français* the relationship between object and symbol is questioned more fundamentally than in *The Double Trumpet*. The whole system of reference within the former print seems to be muddled, making a new examination necessary. Should Chronos be interpreted as protagonist or assistant? How do the cockade and the sun relate to each other? What is the covering of the first symbol by the second supposed to mean? Is Voltaire's conception of revolution still the basis here? Specifically, is "revolution"—still used by Voltaire in Jean Bodin's sense—to be understood as a reversion of conditions in favor of a centralized monarchy?

The emblem of Louis XIV, whose rule came closest to perfection according to Voltaire, was the sun. Although the sun is covered by the revolutionary cockade, its rays are not extinguished; the cockade "borrows" its rays from the sun. Such a "cover phenomenon" requires an examination that takes into account older graphic patterns, especially since research on the wealth of imagination found in the art of the Revolution still proceeds on the whole ahistorically, that is, the revolutionary decade is interpreted only in terms of itself. One previous model, for example, is to be found in *The Great Eclipse of the Sun*, an English satire from 1706, which alludes to the "eclipsing" of the royal house by the "gentry."[10] If in the French etching the sun is not actually eclipsed, then it is at least cautiously concealed. One intention of the French print is to propagate these relationships: the covering up of absolute power by philosophy; the strange "new star" filled with reason and wisdom as the renewed power of the sun; absolutism based on Enlightenment. Certainly, however, this Voltairian ideology contradicts the action of Chronos, a paradox that appeared more simplistically in the symbol of the *Double Trumpet* (at once a graphic tribute to Voltaire and a verbal negation of his teachings). Serving reason, Chronos subjugates all potentates to his power, thus articulating the French Revolution's claim to be, in principle, worldwide. The engraving depicts the revolutionary break as both national and universal. This was a unique phenomenon. The American Revolution was far from making the missionary claim that the French Chronos makes in walking around the circle of kings, which serves as a symbol of the entire world.

This representation of the world as a circle of people is based on tradition. Andreas Frölich had combined the four elements with a circle of historical figures as early as 1667.[11] The mixture of narrative and symbolic-allegorical elements as well as the mythological-natural component — Apollo's sunchariot breaking through the clouds — had also been employed by Frölich. Even the devaluation of the figures in the circle incorporates older ideas. A moralizing seventeenth-century broadside from

FIGURE 5. Dominicus Custos (German, after 1550–1612). *Tanz der Narren um die Frau Welt (Dance of the Fools around Lady World)*, ca. 1603. Engraving. Bamberg, Staatsbibliothek.

G.1010; Rö.33 Wheel of Fortune [172 × 261] 1534 Erlangen

FIGURE 6. Georg Pencz (German, ca. 1500–1550). *Fortunas Rad (Wheel of Fortune)*, 1534. Woodcut. Erlangen, Universität.

Augsburg reads, "In this picture the world in all its splendor is presented" (fig. 5). The focal point in these representations, however, is always uncontested; in spite of all the foolish turbulence, a static center is presupposed.[12] Yet in *Le Nouvel Astre français*, restless Time does not replace confidence in a long-lasting political system. That is why the circle scene needs to be supplemented; it literally requires encouragement from the cosmic cover, which in turn needs the additional legitimation provided by the historical core.

Another motif of political iconography is involved here, that of the wheel of fortune and fate. Chronos's rotation engenders a pervading sense of instability: everyone will fall. This is exactly what Georg Pencz was suggesting with his *Wheel of Fortune* of 1534 (fig. 6). The wheel of fortune in Venetian engravings of the sixteenth century[13] is similarly unstable, and the complex of problems they address involves the entire world. The wheel of fortune, one is told, turns blindly, unless there is a prince at the helm, holding it with a steady hand (as Ferdinand II does in an Augsburg broadside of 1620).[14] Such representations of absolutist monarchs in the form of the *rota regia* comprise another point of departure for *Le Nouvel Astre français*.[15]

The striking manner in which the designer of *Le Nouvel Astre français* made his inversion effective, can be more closely determined by looking at the print *The Solemn Election of the German King and His Coronation as Emperor in the Prince's Temple, 1792* (fig. 7). It shows an open rotunda, supported by eight pillars bearing medallions with portraits of ecclesiastical and secular electors. They are grouped around the bust of Francis II of the House of Habsburg, the last ruler of the Holy Roman Empire, who was forced to abdicate by Napoleon in 1806. The iconography of the rotunda goes back to the so-called Emperor's Memorial commissioned by Maximilian in 1514 for the tomb of the German emperors (fig. 8). How well this project was remembered and could be varied upon is demonstrated by an engraving entitled *Theatrum virorum eruditione singulari clarorum* of 1678 (fig. 9), which may serve as a link. Contemporaries of the French Revolution experienced the events of their own epoch as theater, one more reason for engravers wishing to portray inversion to recur to older representations of this kind.

The Solemn Election of the German King (fig. 7) appeals for unity. It legitimizes the emperor (before the backdrop of the coronation city of Frankfurt) by means of the transfiguring light descending from above, as well as the fire on the altar, which probably is meant to counter the French altar of the fatherland (as is the choice of 14 July as coronation

FIGURE 7. Anonymous German. *Deutschlands Fürsten-Tempel (The Solemn Election of the German King and His Coronation as Emperor in the Prince's Temple, 1792), 1792*. Stipple engraving. Vienna, Österreichische Nationalbibliothek.

day). In contrast to *Le Nouvel Astre français*, the German engraving is programmatically static; although Time is involved, his wings are bound by two geniuses, signifying that he is to stand still. The moment of coronation is understood as *fulfillment*, guaranteed by the allegories of warlike Virtue and Imperial Power (Minerva and Majestas). Paradoxically, the German engraving, which calls for the observance of the old order, is, at least in part, a possible model for the French staging of the new order.

In *Le Nouvel Astre français* the inversion itself is less surprising than the combination of elements

FIGURE 8. Planned Emperor's Memorial for the Cathedral of Speyer, 1514. Modern reconstructed drawing by Philipp Maria Halm of Hans Valkenauer's project.

that it manages to integrate without being overloaded. Among the many new features that are incorporated are such abstractions as the reactivation of time and the dislocation of the kings from their history. The words are part of this abstraction; of undetermined origin, they nonetheless suggest divine power. In the differentiation between the kings, in the clouds, and in the smoke from the candles, however, we find an overdefinition that verges on caricature. The sky is definite, the enemy is defi-

FIGURE 9. Johann Franck (German, active seventeenth century). Frontispiece for Paul Freher's *Theatrum virorum eruditione singulari clarorum*, 1678. Engraving. Münster, Westfälisches Landesmuseum für Kunst und Kulturgeschichte, Porträtarchiv Diepenbroick.

FIGURE 10. Anonymous French. *Le Crible de la Revolution (The Sieve of the Revolution)*, 1791. Etching and mezzotint. New York, The Metropolitan Museum of Art, The Elisha Whittelsey Collection, The Elisha Whittelsey Fund, 1962 (62.520.279).

nite; the future and the earth are thought of abstractly. There are two results as far as form is concerned: first the *épuration*, the purification, of the surface of the picture—a tabula rasa effect, which Rosenblum has described as the most promising aspect of revolutionary art when considered in terms of its legacy;[16] second, a distinct pleasure in details with all the characteristics of, for example, Hogarth's narrative structure. This dualism is intensified by the disturbing use of writing in both of these formal structures. The demand for harmony seen in the German print has been swept away.

How differently such a repertoire of motifs could be treated, is shown in two counter-revolutionary French etchings. *Le Crible de la Revolution* (fig. 10) shows Chronos as the cynical sifter of the Revolution, the antithesis of Saint Michael, the Christian weigher of souls. Several members of the clergy and nobility, the Duc d'Orléans first of all, have already fallen through the sieve, that is, they have gone over to the Revolution, and a terri-

LA CAUSE DES ROIS.

1. la Victoire terrassant les rebelles, 2 la Fay.... 3 Roch...... 4 .Luck... 5. la Paix ramenent l'Abondance .6. le Peuple.

FIGURE 11. Anonymous French. *La Cause des rois (The Affair of the Kings)*, 1792. Etching and mezzotint. New York, The Metropolitan Museum of Art, The Elisha Whittelsey Collection, The Elisha Whittelsey Fund, 1962 (62.520.148).

FIGURE 12. Anonymous Italian. *La Colossal Repubblica francese (The Colossal French Republic)*, 1799. Etching and engraving with hand coloring. Venice, Museo del Risorgimento. Photo: Reale Fotografia Giacomelli, Venice.

ble end is predicted for them.[17] The royal family, including the dauphin, has been temporarily saved (after the return from Varennes),[18] and its members await their fate. The print must have been made in the middle of 1791. The sieve is tied to three poles, which in mockery of the alliance between the three estates, are entwined by a snake and held together by a sword. The tops of two of the poles are decorated with a visor and miter respectively, and the third is shaped like a spade. In contrast to *Le Nouvel Astre français*, there can be no discussion of a new language of signs emerging here.

The other counterrevolutionary print (fig. 11) presents *La Cause des rois* (1792). It combines allegories and representations of contemporary persons. In so doing, it does not set itself apart from the common standard of revolutionary graphic art. The designer hardly tries to integrate new structures, and he summons up old contents. On the zodiac appear the rulers who were united in the First Coalition against France. They are named once again on the pyramid on the right: the Prince de Condé from the House of Bourbon, Monsieur d'Artois, the Empress of Russia, the German emperor, and the kings of Spain, Prussia, and Sardinia. They call for peace and prosperity, and the people profit from their horn of plenty. Trade

flourishes, and the church stands as a mighty fortress. The rebels Lafayette, Rochambeau, and Luckner are overcome by Victoria and with them the corruptive currents of "anarchy," "democracy," and, explicitly, "republican ideas." The Revolution has overthrown its own generals.[19] Victoria raises her sword toward the kings, to whose natural order she owes her power. So closes this awkward circle, in the center of which the monarchic sun shines as always.

Despite the two foregoing examples, the abstractive system of codes operative in *Le Nouvel Astre français* did not remain without effect. The didactics of revolutionary imagery would ultimately have lasting consequences in antirevolutionary engravings as well. In the Venetian print *La Colossal Repubblica francese* of 1799 (fig. 12), the pictorial structure is established solely by an abstract linear connection of rays. The divine light (alpha and omega) shines its rays onto a mirror emblazoned with the crests of the Second Coalition against France (Russia, Austria, Turkey, and England). Reflected by the mirror, the light gains the strength to melt the six descendants of the republican idea, while Bravery chisels the shattered fleurs-de-lis back into the crest of France. As in *The Double Trumpet* (fig. 2), the didactics of the

FIGURE 13a. Anonymous French. *La Régénération de la nation française en 1789 (The Renewal of France in the Year 1789)*, 1790. Engraving. Paris, Bibliothèque nationale.

imagery are very closely connected with icono-clasm. *La Colossal Repubblica francese* is an abstractive allegorical print which presupposes an audience with both a highly developed ability to translate the historical process into new forms of the artistic process and widespread practice in the reception of a suitable system of codes.

In order to understand the genesis of this sys-tem, it is necessary to go back to its beginning. The difficulty encountered in replacing the old narra-tive structures is shown, for example, in a print addressed, with a dedication,[20] to the National Assembly, *La Régénération de la nation française en 1789* (fig. 13a). The extensive panorama represented is so varied that it is initially impossible to decipher just what the renewal entails. The Old and the New World (France and America), separated only by a narrow ditch, form the foundation upon which a rich allegorical interpretation of image and word can unfold on entirely different levels. At the top, in place of God, floats a round temple full of light,

FIGURE 13b. Detail of figure 13a.

the symbol of brotherhood; within it appears a snake biting its tail, a sign of eternal allegiance. To the right Victoria reclines on a cloud bank engraving the words "France libre, Louis XVI, 1er roi des François" on a shield with a lance. To the left is Chronos who brings Truth, already revealed; she opens the book of knowledge from which the rays of reason burst forth. They illuminate the allegory of France and ignite (alluding to Franklin's theory of electricity) a cluster of rays from which lightning bolts flash to strike the enemies of the fatherland. At the same time, however, the sun of reason offers the revolutionary-minded countryman warmth and light (fig. 13b). The result is a very complex system of communication which, incidentally, begins to dispense with the king. Although Louis XVI maintains his stand on French soil and is touched by the rays of reason, he is clearly subordinate to Francia. Helpless, *sine potestate*, he draws his sword, but against whom is he to wield it? The allegories have long since wrested power from him. If there is a center at all, he does not create it, but rather nature does, in the form of light and darkness.

This brings us back to the previously mentioned leitmotiv of gesture and body language. A radical change reveals itself in the loss of the conventions of gesture.[21] Where nature is the director, people become marionettes. Even the powerful Francia, who stretches her right hand toward the unredeemed continents, while hurling lightning bolts at the powers of darkness with her left, appears like a policewoman directing traffic, dependent on lights and props such as a globe or scale. Neither the half-freed Indians to the left nor the personified "evils" to the right achieve anything above bit parts. In other words, a specific body language for the representation of the civic individual is not yet in sight. Revolutionary renewal in the graphic medium still finds refuge in old methods. But the radicalization and the intensification of the metaphors for the "light" of the Enlightenment and the conflict between *codes* for nature and the *appearance* of nature, characterize the Revolution as a phase in which the harmonious observance of old standards is literally impossible — signal of a productive crisis in art.

The complicated structure of *La Régénération de la nation française* contains both a semiotic and a semantic break with the past. The driving forces that bring a code into such a visual context and define it, turn it around, or change it, remain unknown. Imagery alone, however, does not often convey explicitness. Thus, an engraving may depend heavily on written explanations and on

FIGURE 14. Anonymous French. *Le Temt découvre la Vérité (Time Reveals Truth)*, ca. 1794. (Cat. no. 171).

framing annotations, which are not subject to emblematic restrictions. This applies to *La Régénération de la nation française* as well as to the much less polished engraving from the post-Thermidorian era *Le Temt découvre la Vérité* (fig. 14). Here, too, a complex mythological apparatus is evoked. Beneath a cockade declared to be the "soleil national," Chronos, Veritas, Libertas (a mixed figure), and Hercules, as the allegory for the people, drive out shadows and monsters of the ancien régime.[22]

If the action was still comprehensible in *La Régénération*, here it appears quite muddled. It is unclear if the national sun only drives away the clouds of the ancien régime or if it is a protagonist. Chronos and the allegory of Liberty, Equality, and Loyalty are degraded to accessory figures; Truth holds a burning glass whose self-generated rays lend Hercules the strength to defeat the Hydra of the Triumvirate. This sequence of events throws light on the complexity and contradiction inherent in the structure of this visual interconnection. One must turn to the side stage as well. To the left, the four continents dance around the Tree of Liberty in anticipation of salvation. The annotation completes the confusion; it speaks of "nations réunis" instead of the allegories of the continents. If body language and the logic of imagery are not successfully integrated in this engraving, then the other side of the crisis — the growing abstraction in the development of the new system of codes — is carried to the extreme in an engraving created in 1790 on the occasion of the Oath of Alliance (fig. 15).

The center of this engraving is composed of a disc or sphere decorated with the fleurs-de-lis of the Bourbons behind which rays of light shine forth. In concentric half-circles around the fleurs-de-lis the credo of the first phase of the Revolution,

FIGURE 15. Anonymous French. *Serment fédératif et national prononcé au Champ de Mars, le 14 juillet 1790 (The Oath of Alliance of 1790)*, 1790 (completed 1791). Etching and mezzotint. Paris, Bibliothèque nationale.

the *entente* between ruler and people, is proclaimed. It is the king who speaks, although he is not depicted; only his words are represented. He swears to respect the constitution.[23] At the same time, Minerva swears the oath for the sciences, Mercury for trade, and Apollo for the arts. Above them, the genius of fame heralds the oath to all the world, while to the left, the *public*—the word appears for the first time—announces the cry of the people ("le cri du peuple").

This etching has survived in two states which show the degree to which the problem of overloading and overlapping of motifs was struggled with in the graphic rendering of revolutionary ideas. In the first state,[24] an attempt was made to do without the "broadcasting" effect of the king's speech, but in the absence of his person, the decisive political moment, the commitment of the regent to the constitution, was missing. The fleurs-de-lis were insufficient. Because the historical situation was unprecedented, no wealth of imagery was available to portray it; thus, the resort to writing in the second state.

The consequences of the dualistic relationship between abstraction and definition, image and writing, are illustrated in an engraving that deals with a conflict within the Revolution, a broadside prompted by the conspiracy of Babeuf in the beginning of 1796 (fig. 16). The plot is interpreted here as an attack on the Constitution of 1795, thus "l'an 3" is inscribed in the middle of the sun. The print treats the revolt in a montage. A scene in the foreground appears at first to be reportorial, or narra-

tive. A soldier stabs a person who is about to stab two others. On closer inspection, however, one realizes that non-narrative components predominate. On the one hand, isolated mythologies are interspersed without continuation in the action; on the other, the action itself is interrupted by symbols and letters. One of these symbols is the lance which dominates the scene, a weapon of grotesquely excessive length. Near its tip, the head of a snake appears to break through the body of the victim, and snakes entwine her head as well. The seemingly arbitrary nakedness (between two clothed figures) and the sagging breasts define this figure as a fury, but a fury who, robbed of her mythological context, intrudes into everyday life. This shock effect is exactly what the engraver wants to achieve. Babeuf's conspiracy is characterized as the onset of blind hate in the structural order of post-Thermidorian society. The soldier embodies the courage and loyalty of the revolutionary army whose glory is demonstrated by a temple in the background. The two daggers in the fury's hands are aimed at a radiant young woman with a child. They are personifications of France and the Revolution, illuminated by the new constitution. At this point, an abstract form breaks into the narrative discourse again. Writing (a listing of the new *départements*) surfaces abruptly as well. This intrusion constitutes a destruction of the narrative that surpasses the degree of abstraction in *Le Nouvel Astre français*. Thus, on one side of the print, the sky can be spotted with clouds and conform to conventional experience, and on the other, the sun can be the background for the inscription. The break runs through the middle of the composition. The innovation lies in the *purified montage character*, in the juxtaposition of traditional illusions of body and depth and the extensive field of writing-image, which at most hints at illusionistic visualization, for example in the incense which wafts from the *départements* to the constitution-sun.

The contradiction between symbolic abbreviation and "lifelike" rendition of individual objects is not resolved in such prints. One of the achievements of revolutionary graphic art is to have made this break visible. This assertion should not, however, be misinterpreted as an attempt to raise this particular print to the stature of a graphic masterpiece. It does not, for instance, succeed in mediating between the new division of space, the "révision de l'espace" that Michel Vovelle describes, and the experience of everyday life. Obviously, expectations for the future—the structural administrative measures that refer to them as well—have not been experienced sufficiently to allow them to be treated in a traditional manner, nor have they been stimulating enough to warrant visualization in an entirely new manner (for example, by giving in to symbolic abstraction). One could also say, along with Umberto Eco, that manifest in these cross-medial entities is an overcodification of dual insufficiency. On the one hand, there is a reciprocal insufficiency of imagery and writing, that is, one medium relies on the help of the other (as in a sign which *symbolically* conveys the message "smoking prohibited" but, because of constant violations, adds the message *verbally*. On the other hand, there is an insufficiency of reception; the recipients have too little experience with symbols and need the supplement of traditional narrative structures. Furthermore, several temporal levels intermesh in such engravings; the historical process is made comprehensible by the graphic simultaneity of chronologically distinct events.

The underlying problem confronted by all of these engravings was to find a visual formula for an unprecedented historical change, a formula that did not remain in the narrative and did not content itself with the account of an incredible event. To conclude this series, an engraving will be presented which deals with the historical process itself. In the engraving *L'Espoir du bonheur dédié à la nation* cre-

FIGURE 16. Anonymous French. *Le Complot de Babeuf (The Conspiracy of Babeuf)*, 1796. Etching and aquatint. Paris, Bibliothèque nationale.

ated in 1789/1790, we find an allegory of the three Times focused on the difficult conditions of the present epoch (fig. 17).[25] Three framed pictures are shown to Louis XVI while Necker steps out of the ship of state and, in so doing, crushes the head of a gracile Hydra. The pictures give the king insight into the course of time. Their presentation means nothing other than the gradual replacement of historic time by a time of salvation. Chronos is again the active authority; he points the past and present events toward a transhistoric goal of eternal happiness (fig. 17b). While Chronos mercifully covers the bad past and a younger genius attempts to show his

thorn-entwined picture of the present, the king desires to see the picture of the future toward which his minister of finance, accompanied by Truth, has rushed, ahead of everyone else. (This unceremonial behavior suggests Necker's love of truth and the promising future of his politics; it also demonstrates that he only left the ship of state for a short time and for the benefit of the country's future.[26] While on the picture of the past Arrogance and Hypocrisy rob Earth of her fruits and burden her with a cross, the picture of the future shows Vigilance in the form of a soldier, Piety as a priest, and Diligence as a countryman. It is a picture of unity and order endowed with sun and a rain of gold. The picture of the present portrays the Revolution as crisis; unfavorable winds blow, a ship (trade) is struck by lightning, a merchant plaintively raises his hands, and nobility and clergy insist on their privileges. The engraving thus connects the idealistic vision of the future with the material problems of the Revolution, which are blamed on the intrigues of the nobility and the clergy. Chronos himself is a part of the process of this allegory of the three Times. As the bearer of the past, he is represented as an old man; of the present, as an adult; of the future, as a childlike genius. The iconography of *light as truth* is also integrated as Truth's rays illuminate the pictures of the three Times. For the question of how the historical process is transformed into a visual process, it is significant that Truth uses pictures as media to support her vision; whereas otherwise — as in the engraving of the *Régénération de la nation française* — an often excessively allegorical "reality" was itself declared to be the emanation of truth.

The engraving of the three Times shows the position that imagery held in the French Revolution. It was not limited solely to agitational graphic art, which had to use pithy phrases; rather, the *framed picture* was expressly understood as the vehicle of the idea of the state, as the guarantor for the departure from the past, and as the vision of the future. Although turning away from the old and turning toward new ideas is the content of every revolutionary change of paradigms, the crucial point of 1789 was that this change manifested itself decisively by means of visual imagery. The French Revolution thus belongs to those epochs in which art could still represent what Hegel termed "the highest form of truth," in which it could still be the embodiment, and not only the reproduction, of what it portrayed. Whereas during the ancien régime, especially in the eighteenth century, art was valued as mere *art*, the Revolution reintroduced an appreciation for art that demanded not only respect for the form but also veneration for the

FIGURE 17a. Pézant (French, active ca. 1789/1790). *L'Espoir du bonheur dédié à la nation (The Hope for Happier Times Dedicated to the Nation)*, 1789/1790. Engraving. Paris, Bibliothèque nationale.

contents. However, the continuing confidence in the truth of visual imagery as the truth of salvation contains a threat to the world of imagery: if the image embodies the truth, then false conceptions had to be wiped out in the end by the image. The veneration of the image and the destruction of the image are very closely connected. Thus, the Venetian engraving (fig. 12), in which the statues of the Revolution are "executed" by a ray of light, is an inversion of the veneration of art which is manifested in the engraving of the three Times.

So far we have dealt with engravings in which abstractive codes, supported by writing, compete with mythological, allegorical, and realistic codes. The consequence of this intermixing was a complicated, at times even confusing, structure. This

result is basically paradoxical, especially when considered from the standpoint of the history of graphic art. First established in England in the eighteenth century, this medium was intended for the persuasion of the public. One could, therefore, have expected didactic explicitness — even "woodcutlike" simplification instead of additional coding — and a breaking of the formerly predominant iconographic secret language, rather than its reinforcement.

In reality, the graphic arts seemed to deal with the historic process in all its contradictions, whereas painting was apparently able to represent this process in a purified and simplified manner, as in David's *Death of Marat* (1793) or Regnault's *Liberty or Death* (1794). In the first picture (see p. 80),

FIGURE 17b. Detail of figure 17a.

the topical event is transferred beyond all narration to an iconic presentation; in the second (fig. 18), a historically significant disjunctive question without any narrative qualities is symbolically visualized.[27] Such a commitment to *one* code or *one* sign is probably found so seldom in graphic art because extremely different needs had to be satisfied by this marketable medium. During the entire seventeenth and eighteenth centuries graphic art had served either as a primary medium to document historic events or as an expression of emblematically, allegorically, or mythologically formed codes. The distinction between these two realms is parti-

FIGURE 18. Jean-Baptiste Regnault (French, 1754–1829). *La Liberté ou la Mort (Liberty or Death)*, 1794. Oil on canvas. Hamburg, Hamburger Kunsthalle.

ally resolved in the Revolution. This contamination, however, forces the squaring of the circle: it is necessary to absorb the "high" realms of graphic coding yet speak a comprehensible language. The examples in which both ends are successfully achieved can be counted on the fingers of one hand.

Jacques Louis Perée's engraving *L'Homme régénéré* of 1795 (fig. 19) is an especially effective example. The prototype of revolutionary renewal is presented to us as a man who is unclothed, that is, heroic or in the original state of creation, and whose base is the world. Admittedly, this engraving is overcodified as well; the new Adam, lifting his grateful eyes to heaven, holds up the attested human rights, while a flash of lightning breaks through the dark storm clouds and strikes a crown,

FIGURE 19. Jacques Louis Perée (French, 1769–unknown). *L'Homme régénéré (The New Man)* 1795. Engraving. Paris, Bibliothèque nationale.

the symbol of the ancien régime. On the fallen tree where the revolutionary places his foot (the old sign of triumph over the adversary) hang crests of the nobility; a censer and a fleur-de-lis scepter lie broken beside it — luxury, superstition, and privileges have been felled. The new natural man has accomplished this with his own hands; he wields a pickax, and the destruction of the Old Regime is expressly condoned. It is not fortuitous that the sun rises behind the pick at the bottom left. Despite all the overloading, this synopsis of revolutionary virtues is brought together in a single figure. As finely woven as the metaphors may be, they are portrayed nevertheless simply enough to be grasped at once and thus to satisfy their didactic intention.

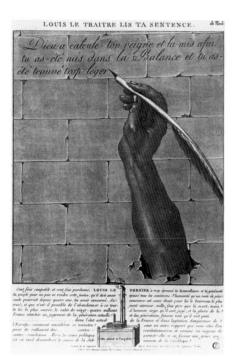

LOUIS LE TRAITRE LIS TA SENTENCE.

Dieu a calculé ton reigne et la mis afin tu as-été mis dans la Balance et tu as-été trouvé trop léger

FIGURE 20. Villeneuve (French, active 1789–1799). *Louis le traître lis ta sentence (Louis the Traitor Read Your Sentence)*, 1793. (Cat. no. 86).

Another example *Louis le traître lis ta sentence* of 1793 (fig. 20) is temporally closer to *Le Nouvel Astre français*. As the inscriptions indicate, it must have been made between the conviction and execution of Louis XVI.[28] Villeneuve's etching is formally an extreme contrast to *Le Nouvel Astre français*. In the latter there are many small forms and the simultaneous abstraction of anecdotal details; in the former, *one* very definite symbol which dominates the entire picture. "Louis the traitor read your sentence" says the inscription, which is used like a lemma, or caption, and corresponds like an icon to the representation of the hand. Both of these components are explicated in an epigram underneath the picture, which culminates in the reproduction of a guillotine with the inscription, "Elle attend le coupable." I am using the emblematic terms *lemma, icon,* and *epigram* here fully intentionally. The transformation and decoding of the emblem represent *one* of the possibilities through which the gap between different expectations regarding the graphic arts may be closed. Educational demands can be satisfied, and at the same time, the intended political agitation of the masses can be achieved.

The central icon, a paraphrase of the banquet of Belshazzar, especially deserves our attention. The use of "Mene-tekel-peres" (Daniel 5: 26–28) in the criticism of contemporary rule becomes common in the nineteenth century.[29] It is not, however, the

divine hand of the Scriptures that seals the fate of Louis's rule here. Three specific qualities transform the representation into a revolutionary symbol. First of all, the arm breaks through the wall from below; it is the arm of the people, not the judgment of God but a human verdict (an obvious contradiction to the inscription borrowed from the Old Testament). Second, the act of breaking through the wall suggests that force is to be used against the king and his palace.[30] Finally, the wall is full of cracks; as in contemporary caricatures, the collapse of the rule is indicated by decay. This implies that action against the king at best accelerates the natural process of decay, but basically only fulfills it. It is thus both natural and inevitable that the old must pass.[31]

This conception connects Villeneuve's print with that of Perée. The large main image is a shared *signum*. In each instance the unburdening of the background contributes to the effectiveness. Both images can be understood from a distance. If we could reconstruct the murals[32] of the French Revolution, then Villeneuve's print would have to be placed at the beginning.

1. See among others, David L. Dowd, "Jacobinism and the Fine Arts: The Revolutionary Careers of Bougier, Sergent, and David," *The Art Quarterly* 16 (1953), pp. 195–214; idem, *Pageant Master of the Republic: Jacques-Louis David and the French Revolution* (Lincoln: University of Nebraska Press, 1948); James A. Leith, *The Idea of Art as Propaganda in France, 1750–1799: A Study in the History of Ideas* (Toronto: University of Toronto Press, 1965).

2. Some aspects of this topic were discussed during a colloquium in Hamburg in 1983; see my essay, "Thesen zur Graphik der Französischen Revolution," in *Modelle für eine semiotische Rekonstruktion der Geschichte der Aesthetik*, ed. Heinz Paetzold (Aachen: Rader, 1987), pp. 249–62.

3. See the *Collection complète des tableaux historiques de la Révolution française*, 3 vols. (Paris: 1802), partly reproduced in *Freiheit, Gleichheit, Brüderlichkeit: Bilder von der Französischen Revolution*, ed. Ingo Groth (Dortmund: Harenberg, 1982). The best-known German collection is: Franz Eugen Freiherr von Seida und Landensberg, *Denkbuch der Französischen Revolution* (Memmingen: Müller, 1817, rev. ed. 1818).

4. Karl Griewank, *Der neuzeitliche Revolutionsbegriff* (Frankfurt am Main: Suhrkamp, 1973), pp. 144–45.

5. Maximilien Robespierre, *Oeuvres* (Paris: Presses universitaires de France, 1953), vol. 8, p. 115; this passage is from a speech of 11 January 1792.

6. The iconography inherent in the game of chess was taken especially literally in the political caricature of the nineteenth century. Examples from 1814 and 1833 (with Napoleon and Louis-Philippe among the chess pieces) can be found in the exhibition catalogue *La Caricature* (Landesmuseum Münster, 1980/1981), no. 74, ill.

7. This should be compared to the inscription on the altar to the fatherland decorated by Jean Guillaume Moitte: "Les mortels sont égaux, ce n'est point la naissance / C'est la seule vertu qui fait la différence. / La loi, dans tout état, doit être universelle; / Les mortels quels qu'ils soient sont égaux devant elle." Thomas E. Crow in *Painters and Public Life in Eighteenth-Century Paris* (New Haven and London: Yale Uni-

versity Press, 1985), p. 121, shows that "the 'great' remonstrances issued by the Paris Parlement in 1753 contained the following proposition: 'If subjects owe obedience to their kings, then kings, on their side, owe their obedience to the laws, the disregard of which prepares revolutions'."

8. See Voltaire's *Le Siècle de Louis xiv* (1752).

9. For the rededication of the base on the occasion of the celebration in honor of Lepelletier, see Antoine Schnapper, *Jacques-Louis David, témoin de son temps* (Fribourg: Office du livre, 1980), p. 149.

10. London, British Museum; see M. W. Jones, *A Cartoon History of the Monarchy* (London: Macmillan, 1978), fig. 18.

11. Andreas Frölich, *Kavalkade, die vier Elemente darstellend*, 1667, illustrated in F. W. H. Hollstein, *German Engravings, Etchings, and Woodcuts, 1400–1700*. (Amsterdam: Van Gendt and Co., 1975), vol. 9, p. 14.

12. By calling the figure in the center Vanity, the step toward effacing has already been made. To give at least one more example, this shows up very clearly in an engraving by P. Baltens after Abraham Bosse, *Tanz um die Frau Welt*, ca. 1585, illustrated in John B. Knipping, *Iconography of the Counter-Revolution in the Netherlands* (Leiden/Niewkoop: de Graaf, 1974), vol. 1, p. 43, pl. 35.

13. A fine example of 1518 appears in Julius v. Pflugk-Harttung, *Im Morgenrot der Reformation* (Stuttgart: Herget, 1926), p. 472; see also the broadside *Oculi omnium in te sperunt* (1572), reproduced in Wolfgang Harms, *Deutsche illustrierte Flugblätter…* (Munich: Kraus, 1980), vol. 2, p. 57.

14. Illustrated in Harms (supra, note 13), vol. 2, p. 289.

15. Even when no single definite "model" is apparent, associations should be made with sixteenth- and seventeenth-century graphic traditions. This is essential in light of the "factual" resorts to the past, as, for instance, the practice of denouncing princes as monsters, which dates back to Luther's engravers and their mocking of popery.

16. Robert Rosenblum, *Modern Painting and the Northern Romantic Tradition: Friedrich to Rothko* (London: Thames and Hudson, 1975).

17. This was not without reason. Philippe Egalité, who had enrolled as a member of the Jacobins on 23 June 1791, was guillotined in November 1793.

18. See Philippe Sagnac and Jean Robiquet, *La Révolution de 1789* (Paris: Editions nationales, 1934), vol. 1, p. 296.

19. The engraving condenses and simplifies a very complex historical situation. Lafayette had condemned the storming of the Tuileries on 10 August 1792. In so doing, he incurred the persecution of the Montagnards, whom he escaped by fleeing to Flanders. Jean-Baptiste de Rochambeau lost the trust of the leaders of the Revolution in 1792 because he advocated a defensive military policy at the outbreak of the war. He was arrested after the overthrow of the Gironde and escaped the guillotine only because of Robespierre's execution. Luckner, who had become the highest-ranking army general after Lafayette's flight, failed to raise a reserve army near Châlons-sur-Marne. He had to defend himself before the Revolutionary Tribunal and was sentenced to death and guillotined on 4 January 1794.

20. The dedication inscription reads, "Dédiée et présentée par M[r]. le Cointre Président du d[r]. de la Seine et de l'Oise à l'Assemblée nationale le 13 juillet 1790, comme pouvant etre le modele d'un monument public." How such a composition could be turned into a monument remains an open question. The medallion beneath the area of the picture, nevertheless, gives a hint. Erected in the midst of the National Assembly meeting room is an altar to the fatherland upon a three-tiered base, which is patterned after the one in the engraving. The word "decrets" on the tabletop indicates that the resolutions of the National Assembly were to be ceremoniously deposited there. The minute inscription around the top of the medallion reads accordingly, "Hommage au patriotisme des représentants de la nation." Below the dedication of the main engraving is the following explanation: "Le Tems amène une nouvelle administration, désignée par la balance: il la tient pour en marquer la durée. La *Vérité* éclaire la *France* et la *Foi* sur les droits éternels des nations. La *France* foule aux pieds ses chaines que des génies immortels l'ont excité à rompre et qu'ils achevent de briser: elle excerce sa force et sa puissance, et foudroye la *Bastille*, les *tirans* et tous les abus, en formant son admirable constitution, que la *Foi* fait exécuter. Une famille de *laboureurs*, des *prison-*

niers et des *vainqueurs* de la *Bastille*, expriment tous les sentimens qu'inspire l'heureuse *Révolution* qui s'opere. *L'agriculture* et le *commerce*, offrent l'image de la richesse du royaume: ils sont sous la protection de la *Vigilance* appuyée sur la *Force*. La *Sagesse* armée grave ce grand événement sur l'ecusson de la *France* et va le déposer au *Temple de Mémoire* pour y être un monument de l'héroisme de la *nation* et du *monarque* qui l'ont operé. La *Renommée*, la *cocarde française* à la main, étonne l'*univers*, dont les *quatre parties*, enchainées emblematiquement par les préjugés et les erreurs, témoignent tout ce que leur fait éprouver le triomphe de la *France*." The contamination of different levels of argumentation continues in the annotation, especially where the deviation from a naturalistic understanding is marked by the word "emblematiquement." The overcoding of the engraving shows itself, finally, in inscriptions that are only barely visible: to the left, "Liberté" and "France"; above, "Raison"; on the shield, "France libre, Louis xvi, 1er roi des François"; inscribed in the scales, "Récompense et mérite" and "punition aux fautes"; the king holds a scroll with the inscription, "Constitution"; the inscriptions on the medallions on the altar read, "Droits de l'homme et du citoyen. Pouvoirs législatif, judiciaire, exécutif et administratif. Monarchie héréditaire," and "Dieu, la nation, la loi, le roi." On the altar plate appears, "Patrie"; below, "Constitution"; on the notes struck by lightning, "Anarchie victorieuse, impots arbitraires, privilèges, esclavage, superstition, ordres, lettres de cachet"; on the scrolls on the ground and on the banderoles of the geniuses, "Voltaire, Locke, Montaigne; Franklin, *Negociations politiques*; Raynal, *Histoires Philosophiques*; Mably, *Considérations sur l'histoire*; Rousseau, *Contrat social*."

21. The engraving thus shows the historical situation immediately preceding that final devaluation of courtly gestures which reveals itself in Goya's *Family of Charles iv* (1800/1801). Martin Warnke has observed how stiffly, almost helplessly, Goya portrays the attempt of the royal family to comply with traditional norms of courtly gesture ("Goya's Gesten" in Werner Hofmann et al., *Goya: "Alle werden fallen"* [Frankfurt: EVA, 1981], pp. 115–41). If in Goya's painting "every courtly culture of gestures is gotten rid of," so that "after omission of the courtly apparatus of gestures… an emptiness" results (p. 127), then the necessity of repealing the old norms in the light of their revolutionary content becomes even more glaringly evident in the French engraving.

22. The legend reads: "Le Temt 1. découvre la Vérité, 2. qui foule aux pieds la féodalité, 3. elle est soutenüe par la Liberté, l'Egalité et la bonne foi, représentées sous une seule figure, 4. est désignées par les symboles suivans, le coeur, le niveau, la pique et le bonnet. Le peuple représenté sous la figure d'Hercule, 5. terrassant l'hydre du Triumvirat, 6. dans le fonds sont les nations réunis, 7. dansant au tour de l'arbre de la Liberté." Here, as in several other engravings, the merchant's name and address are given. Sales practices cannot be examined closely here, no matter how important they may be — this topic will be left to be researched separately. On the iconography of Hercules, see Lynn Hunt, "Hercules and the Radical Image in the French Revolution," *Representations* 1/2 (Spring 1983), pp. 95–117; Lynn Hunt, *Politics, Culture, and Class in the French Revolution* (Berkeley and Los Angeles: University of California Press, 1984).

23. The engraving bears the date of 14 July 1790. Since Louis xvi did not swear the oath to the constitution until 14 September 1791, the wording of the oath must have been inserted afterward. It reads, "Moi, roi des Français, je jure à la nation d'employer tout le pouvoir qui m'a été délégué par la loi constitutionelle de l'Etat, maintenir la constitution décrétée par l'Assemblée nationale et acceptée par moi, et faire exécuter les loix." On the scrolls below, the regions which have joined the Oath of Alliance are named: Alsace, Poitou, Aunis, Provence, Dauphiné, Languedoc, and Maine (with illegible accompanying text), Franche-Comté, Normandie, Boulonnois, Bretagne, Flandre. Below the picture, following the title line, the wording of the oath of the confederates is given: "Nous jurons d'être fideles à la nation, à la loi et au roi et de maintenir de tout notre pouvoir la constitution décrétée par l'Assemblée nationale et acceptée par le roi, de proteger en particulier la sureté des personnes et des propriétés, la libre circulation des subsistances, la perception des impôts et de demeurer réunis à tous les Français par les liens indissolubles de la fraternité." This liberal program is supplemented by the following legend: "Après le dépôt fait au sanctuaire de la nation et vérification faite des pouvoirs de la nation, les trois divinités qui la caracterisent, Minerve pour les sciences, Mercure pour le commerce, et Apollon pour les arts, pro-

noncent le serment que le génie de la Renommée proclame, celui du public annonce le cri du peuple. Du contre de ce dépôt, le disque de la lumiere aux armes de France, répand ses rayons pour revivifier toutes les parties de l'administration qui sont dans l'abattement. L'abondance, la gloire nationale, l'agriculture, le commerce, la navigation, la justice, les arts et autres; du même disque éclate un foudre qui precipite les génies malfaisants, tels que la Fraude, l'Envie, la Jalousie etc. etc." There has seldom existed a more favorable point of departure for the cooperation of the sciences and the fine arts in any state.

24. Illustrated in the exhibition catalogue *Goya: Das Zeitalter der Revolutionen* (Hamburger Kunsthalle: 1980/1981), p. 12. The second state is illustrated here.

25. The legend (underneath the title line) reads: "Louis seize conduit par la Bonté; Monsieur Necker par la Vérité, qui avec son miroir éclaire les tableaux des trois Tems. Le roi aussitôt qu'il les voit désire le tableau de l'avenir, quoiqu'un mauvais génie dont la structure est lassamblage de toutes sortes de monstres, lui designe le tableau du vieux tems (qui parait le couvrir d'un voile épais) mais il ne l'écoute pas. Et Monsieur Necker qui a vû le désir du roi s'empresse de sortir de la barque, pour écraser les serpents de l'envie et dérober à lavenir son tableau fortuné. Sous ce tableau, il parait se lever un soleil sans nuage, et l'on y voit une mer sans écoeuil. La barque désigne la France dans laquelle ils ont parcouru une mer pleine decoeuils. / Le Vieux Tems que s'enfuit / Son tableau représente la figure de la terre; à ses cotés est l'orgeuil qui attaque ses tours de son épée et lui dérobe de ses fruits, de l'autre coté est l'hipocrisie, qui lui dérobe aussi de ses fruits, et la charge de sa croix, sous le faix de la quelle elle parâit courbée. / Le Tems present qui est sur terre / Son tableau qui est entouré d'epines, représente les vents à l'opposé, qui se contrarient et forment un nuage épais dont nait la foudre qui finit par tomber sur le commerce; un noble et un prélat paroissent disputer chacun leurs droits, un négotiant se désole de toutes ses contrariétes. / Le Tems à venir qui descend / Son tableau qui est entouré de fleurs représente un brave officier qui garde ses bastions; un bon prêtre qui prie, un païsant qui ceuille du bled, le soleil qui luit annonce la paix et la tranquillité; une pluye d'or parait tomber du ciel. Ce tableau ne doit être que tracé." If the nobility and the clergy are attacked in picture and text, then the monarchic unity of the three estates in the form of the fleurs-de-lis of the House of Bourbon is entreated even more: "Roi," "Clergé," "Noblesse" are held together by the ties of the people ("Peuple"); the annotation refers once more to the emblematic tradition.

26. Here, as in other cases, the engraver's verbal explanations (see supra, note 22) fall behind the complexity of the graphic contents; eagerness alone can hardly explain Necker's behavior. The leaving of the ship of state might well allude to the second dismissal of Necker on 11 July 1789, which was repealed a few days later with the triumphal return of the minister. The iconography of the ship of state obviously reached new significance during the French Revolution or, more precisely, in the renewal of contrary traditions, above all the ecclesiastical. (See Mathias Gerung, "Christ's Ship," in Hollstein [supra, note 11], vol. 10, p. 44, no. 53; and Mathis Zündt, "The Apostles' Ship," in *Die Reformation in Nürnberg*, exh. cat. [Nuremberg: GNM, 1979], p. 144; cf. as well as Cornelis Galle "The Church's Ship" in Knipping [supra, note 12], vol. 2, p. 356.) The inversive resort to Christian iconography — despite the tradition of the ship of state — is also obvious in the king leading a lamb, symbol of Christ's innocence. A posteriori it would seem as if the king is thus already designated as the sacrificial lamb; in the year 1789, however, this can only refer to the self-sacrificing work for the good of the state.

27. On the program of the picture by Regnault, see the exhibition catalogue *Goya* (supra, note 24), p. 371, fig. 322; on David's painting, see my essay "Davids Marat als 'dernier appel à l'unité révolutionnaire'," *Idea* 2 (1983), pp. 89–112.

28. Since the inscriptions are readable in the reproduction, only the legend underneath the picture is repeated here: "Cent fois coupable et cent fois pardonné, Louis le dernier à trop éprouvé la bienveillance et la générosité du peuple pour ne pas se rendre cette justice, qu'il doit avoir épuisé tous les sentiments d'humanité qu'un reste de pitié seule pourroit depuis quatre ans, lui avoir conservé. Sa conscience est sans doute pour lui le bourreau le plus cruel; et que n'est-il possible de l'abandonner à ce tourment interieur, mille fois pire que la mort; mais la loi la plus sacrée, le salut de vingt-quatre millions d'hommes exige

qu'il soit jugé; et la gloire de la France attachée au jugement de la génération actuelle et des générations futures veut qu'il soit puni . . . dans l'état actuel de la France et dans lagitation dangereuse de l'Europe, comment considérer se monstre sous un autre rapport que sous celui d'un point de ralliment des . . . contre-revolutionnaires et comme un noyeau de contre-revolution. Alors la saine politique permet-elle en sa faveur une grace qui tot ou tard deviendroit la cause de la subversion de la république. — Extrait de la réponce de C. Durocher au réflection de l'agioteur Necker." Instead of an explanation, we have an attempt at justification. The last allusion refers to Necker's writing *Réflexions présentées à la nation française* (Paris, 1792), in which the king is defended.

29. See, for example, Heine's poem "Belsatzar" and Traviès's lithograph *Festin de Balthazar* in *La Caricature* of 24 April 1834; also see the illustration in the exhibition catalogue *La Caricature* (supra, note 6), p. 212, no. 86.

30. This corresponds to the violence of the torsion of the arm. The inside of the lower arm is shown frontally as if the hand were about to make a fist, but the hand itself is turned in profile while writing. The position of the hand physiologically demands a parallel movement of the lower arm.

31. Sagnac and Robiquet (supra, note 18), vol. 2, p. 124, show a version which appeared on 21 November 1792 in the newspaper *La Sentinelle*. The arm motif is employed in the same manner that Villeneuve used it but without any aquatint coloring. Of all the inscriptions, however, only the passage from the Bible is reproduced. The wall is made up of smaller stone blocks without any traces of decay.

32. During the French Revolution numerous murals were painted on the exteriors of Parisian homes. They are now, of course, all lost. Prints like that of Villeneuve, however, undoubtedly reflect the appearance of these wall paintings, not only through the witty introduction of a "wall" as the background to the print, but in their use of a scale that would enable them to be deciphered at a considerable distance, as opposed to the considerable detail seen in many other engravings.

Plates

LOUIS SEIZE

ROI DES FRANCEAIS

Né à Versailles le 23 Août 1754. Marié le 16 May 1770 et Sacré à Reims le 11 Juin 1775.

Bonnet de la Liberté, Présenté au Roi par le peuple Français, le 20 Juin 1792.

Anonymous French. *Louis seize (Louis XVI)*, 1792, after Joseph
Boze. (Cat. no. 65).

Anonymous French. *Réveil du tiers état (Awakening of the Third Estate)*, 1789. (Cat. no. 27).

Anonymous French. *Francs et généreux sans détour / les François inápreciables… (Truly Gallant and Brave / the Invaluable French …)*, 1790. (Cat. no. 43).

Anonymous French. *Adieu Bastille (Goodbye Bastille)*, 1789.
(Cat. no. 28).

le Calculateur Patriote.

Anonymous French. *Le Calculateur patriote (The Patriotic Calculator)*, 1789. (Cat. no. 24).

La Rage soufle par sa bouche et l'Enfer est dans son coeur.

Anonymous French. *La Rage soufle par sa bouche et l'enfer est dans son coeur (Rage Blows through His Mouth and Hell Is in His Heart)*, 1790. (Cat. no. 56).

Anonymous French. *Les Deux Diables en fureur (The Two Infuriated Devils)*, 1790. (Cat. no. 58).

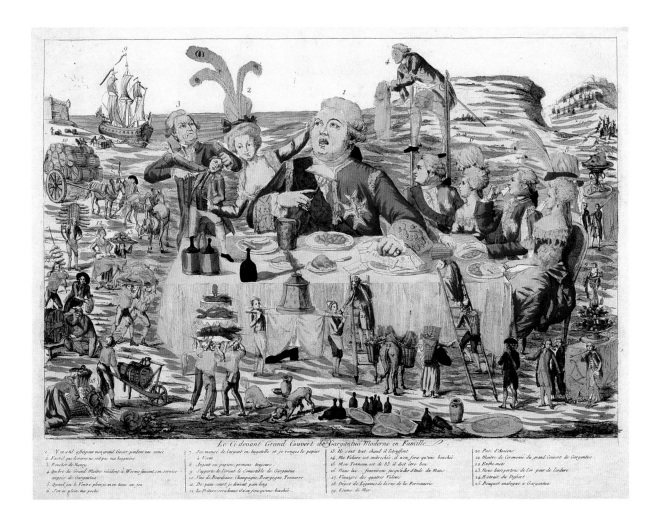

Anonymous French. *Le Ci Devant Grand Couvert de Gargantua moderne en famille* (*The Ci-Devant Great Family Feast of the Modern Gargantua*), ca. 1791. (Cat. no. 68).

Anonymous French. *Grande Armée / du cidev¹. prince de Condé*
(*The Great Army / of the Ci-Devant Prince de Condé*), ca. 1791.
(Cat. no. 103).

Anonymous French. *Le Conseil / électoral (The Electoral Council)*, ca. 1791. (Cat. no. 96).

Anonymous French. *Grand Conseil / des émigrans (The Great Council / of the Emigrants)*, ca. 1791. (Cat no. 97).

Jacques-Louis David (French, 1748–1825). *L'Armée des cruches*
(*The Army of Jugs*), 1793–1794. (Cat. no. 114).

N.º 1. Gouvernement Anglois.

EXPLICATION.

N.º 2. l'Anglois né Libre.

Ce Gouvernement est représenté sous la figure d'un Diable écorché tout vif, accaparant le Commerce et revêtu de toutes les décorations Royal, le Portrait
du Roi se trouve au derriere du Gouvernement lequel vomit sur son Peuple une multitude d'impôts avec lesquelles il le foudroye. Cette prerogative est attaché au Sceptre
et à la Couronne.

Se trouve A Paris chez Basset, Rue S.ᵗ Jacques n.º 64.

Jacques-Louis David (French, 1748–1825). *Gouvernement
anglois (The English Government)*, 1793–1794. (Cat. no. 115).

Jean-François Janinet (French, 1752–1814). *Liberté (Liberty)*, 1792,
after Jean Guillaume Moitte. (Cat. no. 130).

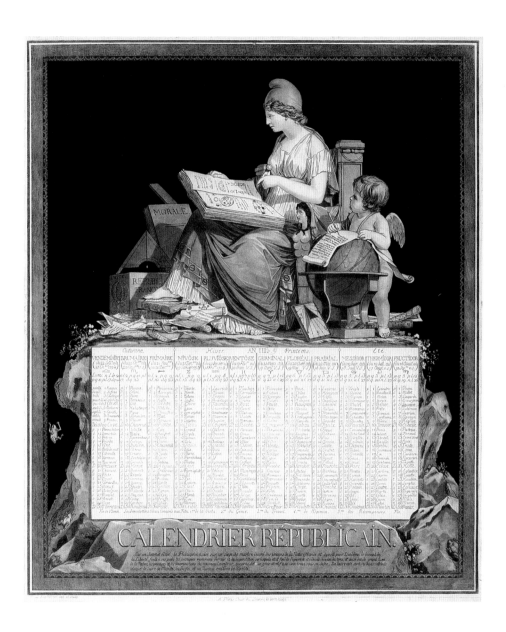

Philibert-Louis Debucourt (French, 1755–1832). *Calendrier républicain (Republican Calendar)*, 1794. (Cat. no. 127).

Philibert-Louis Debucourt (French, 1755–1832). *La Paix / à Bonaparte pacificateur / dix huit brumaire (Peace / to Bonaparte the Peacemaker / Eighteenth of Brumaire)*, 1801. (Cat. no. 187).

Chronology

A Chronological Outline
of the Revolution

*We hold our crown from God alone. The right to make laws by which our subjects
shall be governed belongs to us and to us alone; we neither share this right
nor are we answerable to anyone.*

—Louis XV (1770)

1789

JANUARY	The Abbé Sieyès publishes the provocative pamphlet *What is the Third Estate?*, defining the Third Estate as the entire nation, "the strong, vigorous man whose arm is still in chains."
24 JANUARY	The new electoral regulation favoring the Third Estate is issued.
5 MAY	The Estates General convenes at Versailles with 291 deputies from the clergy, 270 from the nobility, and 571 from the Third Estate. The structure of the Estates General becomes a central issue. Organized in independent orders with each of the three estates voting as a group, it would benefit the alliance of the nobility and the clergy; as a single body with individuals voting, it would benefit the numerically superior Third Estate.
6 MAY	The deputies of the Third Estate refuse to meet as an independent order. By contrast, the nobility votes 141 to 47 to reject individual voting as favored by the Third Estate; the clergy also rejects it, 133 to 114.
17 JUNE	The deputies of the Third Estate reject the title of Estates General and establish themselves as the National Assembly.
20 JUNE	The Oath of the Tennis Court is taken by members of the Third Estate, who, locked out of their meeting place at Versailles by the king, withdraw and swear never to dissolve until the constitution is passed and established on firm foundations.
23 JUNE	The king overrules the decrees of the Third Estate. The Third Estate responds by rejecting monarchical authority and declaring itself in open rebellion against the king.
7 JULY	The National Assembly creates a Constitutional Committee to formulate the principles of constitutional government. Two days later the National Assembly establishes itself as the National Constituent Assembly.
11 JULY	The king dismisses the popular minister Jacques Necker, who is associated with the failure of the Estates General, and replaces him with an overt counterrevolutionary, the Baron de Breteuil.

12 JULY	Riots break out in Paris after the news of Necker's dismissal reaches the city from Versailles.
13 JULY	The electors of Paris, who have been traditionally opposed to the monarchy, form a standing committee and a citizens' militia.
14 JULY	The Bastille is attacked and falls.
15 JULY	The Paris Commune is established with Jean-Sylvain Bailly, deputy to the National Assembly, elected mayor. The Marquis de Lafayette is nominated to the post of commander of the bourgeois militia, which will soon adopt the title of National Guard.
16 JULY	Hoping to regain control over events, Louis XVI recalls the popular Necker to the Ministry of Finances.
17 JULY	The king agrees to go to Paris and is met at the Hôtel de ville by Bailly who presents him with the red, white, and blue cockade, a symbol of "alliance between the King and the people."
4 AUGUST	The Constituent Assembly abolishes feudalism and certain seigneurial rights.
26 AUGUST	The Assembly adopts the Declaration of the Rights of Man and of the Citizen, "granted to all men by natural justice."
22 SEPTEMBER	The Assembly decrees that while the government of France is a monarchy, "there is no authority in France that is above the law; that the King reigns only by virtue of the law and that it is only in terms of the law that he can demand obedience from his subjects."
5 OCTOBER	Six to seven thousand women from the lower-class faubourg Saint-Antoine and the area around Les Halles gather outside the Hôtel de ville of Paris and demand bread. They decide to take their grievances directly to the king and so march on Versailles.
	The king and his family return to the Palais des Tuileries in Paris.
2 NOVEMBER	The Assembly decrees that all property owned by the church should be placed at the disposal of the nation.

1790

13 FEBRUARY	The Assembly abolishes religious orders except for those engaged in teaching and charitable acts; monastic vows are prohibited.
13 APRIL	The Assembly refuses to recognize Catholicism as the state religion.
14 MAY	National lands are divided into lots for auction.
19 JUNE	The nobility's hereditary titles and coats of arms are abolished.
12 JULY	The Assembly adopts the Civil Constitution of the Clergy. Bishops and curés are to be elected like other public officials; bishops are no longer to be installed by the pope; and papal briefs are to be censored by the government. Curés are to read out the decrees of the Assembly from the pulpit.

14 JULY	On the Champ-de-Mars, in front of 300,000 spectators, Lafayette celebrates the National Federation by pronouncing the oath which "binds Frenchmen to one another, and to their King in the defense of liberty, the Constitution, and the law." The king, in his turn, swears an oath of fealty to the nation and the law.
27 NOVEMBER	The Assembly demands that all French priests take an oath of loyalty to the Civil Constitution.

1791

3 JANUARY	Priests refusing to take the oath of loyalty are barred from exercising their ministry in public.
FEBRUARY	A group of nobles, calling themselves the Chevaliers du poignard, attempts to kidnap the king at the Tuileries, a sign of the rising counterrevolutionary activity among aristocrats, émigrés, and refractory priests.
10 MARCH	A papal brief condemns the Civil Constitution of the Clergy, as well as revolutionary principles. A second brief would be issued in April.
27 APRIL	Robespierre condemns the exclusion of the poor from the National Guard (the bourgeois militia) declaring that "to be armed for self-defense is the right of everyone without distinction, and to be armed for the defense of the nation is the right of every citizen."
21 JUNE	Dressed as a manservant, Louis XVI, who had attempted to flee France, is arrested at Varennes and returned under guard to Paris with his family. Before departing, the king had drafted a proclamation addressed to the people of France. In it he explained how he intended to join the Austrian army in the Netherlands, return to Paris, dissolve the Assembly, and restore his absolute power.
17 JULY	The radical Cordeliers Club, or Friends of the Rights of Man, whose leaders include Marat, meets on the Champ-de-Mars to sign a republican petition on the altar of France. The National Guard fires on the crowd without warning, resulting in what will be called the Champ-de-Mars Massacre. The Cordeliers Club is closed.
3 SEPTEMBER	The Assembly approves the definitive text of a constitution that has been in preparation since 7 July 1789. This will become known as the Constitution of 1791 and will substantially reduce the power of the monarchy by, among other things, forbidding the king to declare war or sign treaties without first obtaining the consent of the Assembly.
13 SEPTEMBER	Louis XVI approves the revised constitution.
30 SEPTEMBER	The Constituent Assembly is dissolved to shouts of "long live the King and the Nation."
1 OCTOBER	The new Legislative Assembly meets for the first time. It comprises 745 deputies, none of whom, by decree, had served in the Constituent Assembly.

29 NOVEMBER	Priests refusing to take the oath of loyalty to the Civil Constitution are declared suspect.
DECEMBER	The king secretly pleads for a European war and the invasion of France by his allies. In a letter to the Baron de Breteuil, his liaison with the courts of Europe, Louis XVI writes: "In place of a civil war there would be a political war in Europe and this change would greatly improve the situation. The physical and moral condition of France is such as to make it impossible for her to resist even a partial campaign."
	Jacques Pierre Brissot, leader of the moderate Girondin faction in the Assembly, argues for a political war in which a free France would bring the Revolution to its logical conclusion by toppling the monarchies of Europe.

1792

JANUARY	Robespierre emerges as the most vocal opponent of a political war. In a series of speeches before the Jacobin Club, he attacks Brissot and argues that before striking down the aristocrats in other countries, it is essential to destroy those remaining in France, to master the court, and to purge the army.
1 MARCH	The Holy Roman Emperor Leopold II, Marie-Antoinette's brother, dies. The queen had perceived him to be—along with the émigrés—an important ally in the effort to restore the French monarchy. Leopold is succeeded by his son, Francis II.
20 APRIL	Louis XVI goes in person to the Assembly to propose that war be declared against Francis II as the first step in the larger European war he had earlier described (see above, December 1791). War is declared. It will last almost continuously until the fall of Napoleon in 1815.
MAY	The war goes badly. The army is in total disarray and while retreating from the Austrians, soldiers lynch the Comte de Dillon, one of their commanding generals. On 18 May the military commanders advise the king to make peace immediately.
27 MAY	The Assembly decrees that all refractory priests are liable to be banished from France.
29 MAY	The Assembly dissolves the king's personal guard on the grounds that it is manned by aristocrats.
8 JUNE	The Assembly decrees the establishment of a camp of 20,000 *fédérés*, or National Guardsmen, outside Paris. They are meant to protect the city and resist any military coup.
11 JUNE	The king vetoes the decrees of 27 May and 8 June against the advice of his advisors, who claim that this will result in serious social upheaval by suggesting that he is devoted to the cause of the émigrés and the enemy.
20 JUNE	The people invade the Palais des Tuileries and force the king to wear the liberty cap and drink to the health of the nation. He refuses, however, to retract his veto.

JULY	Supported by an army of French émigrés under the command of the Prince de Condé, the Prussian army prepares to invade France. Given the immediacy of the danger, Robespierre and Brissot issue a joint call for unity and the Assembly declares: "Large concentrations of troops are advancing on our frontiers, and all those who regard liberty with horror are taking up arms to destroy our Constitution. Citizens! *La Patrie est en danger.*"
27 JULY	The properties of the émigrés are confiscated.
END OF JULY	Led by Robespierre, the assembled *fédérés* present petitions to the Assembly demanding that the king be stripped of his office. Robespierre further demands the dissolution of the Assembly and the revision of the constitution.
10 AUGUST	The revolutionary Commune of Paris is established.
	The *fédérés* march on the Tuileries and are fired upon by the Swiss guards. The king orders the troops to stop firing, and the crowd captures the palace. The king and his family are imprisoned in the Temple, and the monarchy is effectively overthrown.
28 AUGUST	Under intense pressure from the Commune of Paris, the Assembly agrees to authorize house-to-house searches for arms held by citizens whose political attitudes make them suspect. Exceptional powers are gradually granted to the government to meet the rapidly growing domestic and foreign crises of 1792.
2 SEPTEMBER	Word reaches Paris that Verdun, the last fortified town between Paris and the eastern frontier, is under siege. The Commune calls the citizens of Paris to arms and to form infantry batallions. Massacres of prisoners, three-quarters of whom had committed no political offense, occur in nine Parisian prisons. More than 1,400 prisoners are killed, escalating the crisis and marking the first days of the Terror.
21 SEPTEMBER	The first session of the National Convention is held with the purpose of giving France a new constitution.
	The monarchy is abolished and the republic is declared.
22 SEPTEMBER	Over a year later, this date will be established as the beginning of Year I of the republic. Rivalry between revolutionary factions in the Convention intensifies.
11 DECEMBER	The trial of Louis XVI by the Convention is opened. The Girondins, led by Brissot, divide on the matter of expelling the king or sentencing him to death. The left-wing Montagnards, on the other hand, call for the king's immediate execution.

1793

16–17 JANUARY	The Convention votes by a roll call lasting more than 24 hours for the death of the king. The vote is 387 to 334.
18 JANUARY	The Convention defeats a motion for a reprieve of the king's execution by a vote of 380 to 310. The Girondins are defeated.

21 January	Louis XVI is guillotined. The day before, a deputy of the Convention had written: "We are fully committed now. The paths have been cut off behind us and we have no choice but to go forward whether we like it or not. Now as never before we can truly say that we shall live as free men or die."
1 February	The Convention declares war on Great Britain and Holland.
23 February	The Convention decrees a mass conscription of 300,000 men.
7 March	The Convention declares war on Spain. A break in relations with various Italian rulers follows. With the exception of Switzerland and the Scandinavian states, France is at war with all of Europe. A decree issued by the Convention the previous November, declaring support of all peoples who wish to regain their liberty, now acquires a military dimension; and Brissot's declaration is now fact, "We can only be at peace once Europe, and the whole of Europe at that, is blazing from end to end."
10 March	The Revolutionary Tribunal is created to "take account of all counter-revolutionary activities, all outrages against liberty, equality, the unity and indivisibility of the Republic, the internal and external security of the State, and all plots aiming at the restoration of the monarchy."
11 March	Civil war breaks out in the Vendée, to the west of Paris. It is fueled by the extraordinary conscription of 300,000 men that had been decreed in February.
21 March	The Committees of Revolutionary Surveillance are established by decree of the Convention.
28 March	The laws against émigrés are codified and made more severe. Emigrés are banished for life from French territory and officially deemed to be dead in the eyes of the law. Their property reverts to the republic.
6 April	The Committee for Public Safety is formed to protect the nation from insurrection and foreign invasion. Marat proclaims, "It is by means of violence that liberty must be established, and the moment has come for organizing instantaneously the despotism of liberty in order to crush the despotism of kings."
31 May	The Montagnards, led by Robespierre, step up their attack on the Girondins, who are unable to stem the combined threat from within and without France.
2 June	The Convention orders the arrest of 29 Girondin deputies, marking the triumph of the Montagnards.
24 June	A new constitution is adopted by the Convention, preceded by a new Declaration of Rights, which includes the right to insurrection, "When the government violates the rights of the people, then insurrection, both for the people as a whole and for each group amongst the people, is the most sacred and necessary of duties" (Article 35).
13 July	Marat is assassinated by Charlotte Corday, a young royalist from Normandy.

27 JULY	Robespierre is elected to the Committee of Public Safety.
23 AUGUST	Mass conscription is decreed in accordance with the mentality of the *sans-culottes*, who seek numerical advantage over enemy armies.
5 SEPTEMBER	*Sans-culottes* march on the Convention and demand bread, calling for "war on tyrants! War on aristocrats! War on hoarders!" The Convention concedes and orders the arrest of all suspects and a purge of the revolutionary committees. The Terror is made the order of the day, acknowledging the triumph of the *sans-culottes*.
17 SEPTEMBER	The Law of Suspects is adopted, defining *suspects* as all those who, by word or deed, show themselves to be "supporters of tyranny or of federalism and therefore enemies of liberty."
5 OCTOBER	The republican calendar is adopted.

YEAR II

19 VENDÉMIAIRE	10 OCTOBER. The Convention declares that the government of France will remain revolutionary until peace is secured. The Committee of Public Safety is given sole responsibility for the coordination of emergency measures.
25 VENDÉMIAIRE	16 OCTOBER. Marie-Antoinette is guillotined.
BRUMAIRE–FRIMAIRE	NOVEMBER–DECEMBER. The dechristianization of France begins with the closing of the first churches in and around Paris and the sanctioning of the cult of the "martyrs of liberty," who include Marat and Lepelletier.
14 FRIMAIRE	4 DECEMBER. The revolutionary government is established, centralizing authority over administrative, economic, and military matters for the duration of the war and spelling the end of liberty of action for the popular movement. The needs of national defense are put above all others.

1794

17 PLUVIÔSE	5 FEBRUARY. Reporting on the principles of political morality that should guide the Convention, Robespierre defines the principle of *terror*: "If the sphere of popular government in peacetime is virtue, in revolution it is at one and the same time virtue and terror; virtue, without which terror is quite deadly; and terror, without which virtue is powerless. Terror is nothing more than rapid, severe, and inflexible justice; it is therefore something that emanates from virtue."
23–24 VENTÔSE	13–14 MARCH. Following months of outspoken criticism of both the Dantonist-led right wing of the Jacobins and the followers of Robespierre, the Hébertist leaders are arrested. They are tried before the Revolutionary Tribunal and guillotined on 24 March (4 germinal). The Hébertists were a loose group to the political left of Danton and Robes-

pierre. Their name derived from Jacques René Hébert, who publicized their views in his journal, *Le Père Duchesne*. They were among the strongest supporters of dechristianization, the Terror, and the revolutionizing of Europe through continued foreign wars.

9–10 GERMINAL

29–30 MARCH. Georges-Jacques Danton is arrested. Danton was, with Marat, an early leader of the revolutionary Cordeliers Club. Later, disassociating himself from Marat, Danton was elected to the Committee of Public Safety. Two months later the Committee was reorganized; Danton was removed and Robespierre was elected in his place. Danton continued to oppose both Hébert and Robespierre and to criticize the Terror. Following his arrest, he will be tried and convicted of, among other things, conspiring to restore the monarchy. He will be executed on 5 April (16 germinal).

18 FLORÉAL

7 MAY. A decree recognizes the existence of the Supreme Being and the immortality of the soul. Four great religious festivals are instituted, including the Festival of the Supreme Being and of Nature, which is to be held on 8 June (20 prairial) to inaugurate the new revolutionary religion. As president of the Convention, Robespierre will preside over the festival, which will be designed and choreographed by the painter Jacques-Louis David.

22 PRAIRIAL

10 JUNE. The Great Terror is established with the passage of the Law of 22 Prairial, which defined the categories of "enemies of the Republic," and decreed that "it is not so much a question of punishing them as of wiping them out."

THERMIDOR

JULY–AUGUST. The popular movement is drifting away from the revolutionary government and is increasingly alienated by the dictatorial powers of the Terror and the scale of its slaughter. Economic crises continue. Food prices rise while wages are strictly controlled. Discontent among the working population erupts at just the moment when Robespierre and his followers most desperately need its support.

8 THERMIDOR

26 JULY. Robespierre attacks his opponents before the Convention. The following day, he and many of his supporters are arrested. They will be executed the next day 28 July (10 thermidor) without trial. On the following day 71 men will be put to death in the largest mass execution of the Revolution.

11 THERMIDOR

29 JULY. The government committees are reorganized. A quarter of their members are to be replaced every month, and retiring members are eligible for reappointment only after the interval of a month. This effectively destroys the stability of the government.

7 FRUCTIDOR

24 AUGUST. Centralization of power within the government is weakened as the Committee of Public Safety, the Committee of General Security, and the Committee of Legislation are given distinct powers.

Decentralization of the government and the freeing of large numbers of political prisoners, which had occurred on 5–10 August (18–23 thermidor) effectively bring an end to the Terror. In the space of a month, all of the government personnel from Year II will have been eliminated.

YEAR III

22 BRUMAIRE

12 NOVEMBER.   The Jacobin Club is closed by decree of the Convention.

FRIMAIRE

DECEMBER.   *Sans-culotte* militants are systematically investigated, arrested, and tried for the political excesses of the Terror. Deprived of their political rights, they are condemned to "public contempt."

1795

21 PLUVIÔSE

9 FEBRUARY.   The busts of the "martyrs of liberty" Marat and Lepelletier, as well as David's paintings of them, are removed from the hall of the Convention. The remains of Marat are removed from the Panthéon.

3 VENTÔSE

21 FEBRUARY.   Freedom of worship and separation of church and state are granted by decree.

12 GERMINAL

1 APRIL.   In a late and desperate attempt, members of the popular movement invade the Convention and demand the enforcement of the Constitution of 1793. They are dispersed by the National Guard, and their disorganization is evident. Popular uprisings will follow a month later but will be quickly suppressed by the National Guard. The leaders of the riots will be imprisoned. Sentences are passed on 149, of whom 36 will be put to death. A purge of the rebellious sections follows and, in the eyes of many historians, the Revolution is brought to an end.

GERMINAL-FLORÉAL

APRIL–MAY.   Peace treaties between France and Prussia (Treaty of Basel, 4–5 April [15–16 germinal]) and between France and Holland (Treaty of The Hague, 16 May [27 floréal]) are signed. Two months later, a treaty with Spain (Treaty of Basel, 22 July [4 thermidor]) will be signed, leaving France at war only with Austria and England.

5 MESSIDOR

23 JUNE.   François-Antoine Boissy d'Anglas, spokesman for the coalition of moderates who control the Convention, writes in the preamble to a draft of a new constitution: "Finally, you must guarantee the property of the wealthy. . . . Absolute equality is a chimera: its existence would posit a complete equality in intelligence, virtue, physical strength, education and fortune in all men. . . . We must be ruled by the best citizens. . . . Now, with very few exceptions, you will find such men only amongst those who own some property, and are thus attached to the land in which it lies, to the laws which protect it and to the public order which maintains it." The rights of the bourgeoisie are thus secured over those of members of the popular movement.

5 FRUCTIDOR

22 AUGUST.   The Convention adopts the new constitution, and a regime of Notables is inaugurated. Executive power is entrusted to a Directory comprising five members appointed by the Council of Ancients (upper house of legislature) and from a short list of ten names drawn up by the Council of Five Hundred (lower house). Separation of the legislature into two houses represents a significant departure from

previous constitutions. The members of the Council of Ancients are older than the Five Hundred and are meant to act as a conservative check on the lower house. The two houses are separate and equal; neither is allowed to intervene in the affairs of the other. The Five Hundred initiate legislation, but the Ancients must approve it.

YEAR IV

3 BRUMAIRE

25 OCTOBER. Consistent with the Convention's desire to break completely with the aristocracy and prevent a return to the ancien régime, a law is passed prohibiting the relatives of émigrés from holding public office.

4 BRUMAIRE

26 OCTOBER. The Convention, having existed for more than three years, breaks up to cries of "long live the Republic!"

14 BRUMAIRE

5 NOVEMBER. The Directory issues a proclamation defining the government's program as intending "to wage an active war on royalism, to revive patriotism, vigorously to suppress all factions, to extinguish all party spirit, to destroy all desire for vengeance, to make harmony reign and to restore peace."

9 FRIMAIRE

30 NOVEMBER. François Noël Babeuf publishes the "Manifesto of the Plebians" in his journal, *Tribun du peuple*. It calls for the suppression of individual property and the attachment of each man "to the employment or occupation with which he is acquainted." All men are to place the fruits of their labor in a common store, and a simple administration of food supplies is to be established according to the most scrupulous equality.

1796

12 VENTÔSE

2 MARCH. Napoleon Bonaparte is appointed commander in chief of the army of Italy. His campaigns are successful, and two months later he will defeat the Austrians at the bridge of Lodi. Almost a year later he will defeat them in battles around Arcole and Mantua, leaving the road to Vienna wide open.

10 GERMINAL

30 MARCH. Babeuf establishes an insurrectionary committee, which launches a propaganda campaign to argue for his "communist" platform.

27 GERMINAL

16 APRIL. The two councils of the legislature decree the death penalty for calling for the division of private property. Nevertheless, Babeuf plans his Conspiracy of Equals, which seeks to overthrow the Directory.

21 FLORÉAL

10 MAY. Babeuf and his fellow conspirators are arrested. Their trial will not begin until almost one year later, and Babeuf will be executed on 28 May 1797 (9 prairial an v). With the arrest of Babeuf, the "Conspiracy of Equals" is crushed and the Directory moves further to the right.

YEAR V
1797

GERMINAL

APRIL.   Elections are held to replace the first third of the deputies in the Councils. Only eleven former deputies are reelected. The new third considerably strengthens the renewed right wing. Measures are passed in favor of the émigrés and the clergy.

18 FRUCTIDOR

4 SEPTEMBER.   Moderates are expelled from the Directory and right-wing deputies are purged from the legislative councils in a bloodless coup. The following day, laws are passed expelling émigrés, who had been provisionally readmitted to France, and reinstating harsh measures against refractory priests. The April election results are nullified.

Isolated from both the conservative Notables and the lower classes, the Directory becomes increasingly dependent on the generals and their armies.

YEAR VI

5 BRUMAIRE

26 OCTOBER.   The impending peace with Austria leaves France at war with only England. The Directory forms an army to invade England under Bonaparte's command.

6 BRUMAIRE

27 OCTOBER.   The Treaty of Campoformio is signed between France and Austria. It resulted from Bonaparte's attacks on Austrian crown lands the previous March. In April he had signed a preliminary peace treaty with the Habsburgs that, in contrast with the desires of the Directory, accepted his reorganization of Italy into satellite governments of France. In exchange, he offered them Venice and did not, as the Directory wanted him to do, lay claim to Belgium and the Rhineland. The October treaty confirms Bonaparte's growing independence from the Directory and acknowledges his Italian victories.

1798

30 NIVÔSE

19 JANUARY.   Repressive laws are enacted that have come to be called collectively the Directorial Terror. Stemming from the republican coup of the previous September, raids on houses, violation of the privacy of correspondence, restrictions on freedom of the press, supervision of theaters, and further purges of government personnel are utilized. The two main targets are émigrés and priests. During the course of the year, 160 returning émigrés will be executed, and 1,800 priests will either be shot or deported to Guiana (1,000 more will remain imprisoned).

VENTÔSE

FEBRUARY.   The English invasion plan is shelved on the recommendation of Bonaparte who is planning his Egyptian campaign as a means of securing Mediterranean colonies and staging areas for future operations against India, England's major overseas holding.

30 FLORÉAL	19 MAY. Bonaparte embarks for Egypt with a squadron of 55 ships and 280 transport vessels, 38,000 soldiers, and 187 scholars, writers, and artists. The highly strategic island of Malta is captured on 11–12 June (23–24 prairial). Escaping from the British fleet under the command of Admiral Nelson, Bonaparte captures Alexandria on 30 June (12 messidor) and immediately sets out for Cairo, which he captures on 22 July (4 thermidor). The French are now in control of the lower Nile, and their armies pursue the rest of Egypt.
14–15 THERMIDOR	1–2 AUGUST. Admiral Nelson attacks and destroys the entire French fleet off the Egyptian coast, isolating Bonaparte and the French army within Egypt. Austria is brought back into war with France, while the Ottoman Empire, which claims sovereignty over Egypt, declares war. The Egyptian campaign marks a turning point in the history of revolutionary France. Until this time, its efforts had been primarily limited to Europe. Now it expands to include the Mediterranean, drawing not only the Ottoman Empire but also Russia into a Second Coalition with England, which will later be joined by Austria and Sweden.

YEAR VII
1799

FRUCTIDOR	AUGUST. Still engaged in his conquest of Egypt and hearing of alarming French defeats at the hands of the Second Coalition, Bonaparte leaves his command to Kléber and departs from Egypt secretly, escaping the English blockade. He lands in France on October 8 (16 vendémiaire) and arrives in Paris a week later. The news of his arrival causes a public sensation. The journal *Le Moniteur universel* exclaims: "Everyone is intoxicated. Victory, which is Bonaparte's constant companion, has anticipated him this time, and he arrives in time to strike the final blows against the dying Coalition."

YEAR VIII

18 BRUMAIRE	9 NOVEMBER. As part of a planned coup d'état, Bonaparte is illegally named commander of the troops in Paris. The councils of Ancients and Five Hundred, the latter under the presidency of Napoleon's brother Lucien Bonaparte, are transferred to Saint-Cloud, away from the turmoils of Paris. General Bonaparte rides with a military cortege to the Tuileries where he accepts his command and declares that France will have a republic founded on true liberty, equality, and national representation. The three Directors involved in the coup resign, while the two others are held under guard at the Palais du Luxembourg until they yield their posts. The Directory is officially ended.
19 BRUMAIRE	10 NOVEMBER. Bonaparte appears before the legislative councils and declares that the Directory no longer exists and constitutional changes have to be made. Opposed by great numbers in both houses, he has grenadiers with fixed bayonets clear the Council of Five Hundred. Later in the evening, 60 members of the Council of Five Hundred are

rounded up and vote to accept Bonaparte, the Abbé Sieyès, and the Comte Ducos as provisional consuls with the authority to undertake constitutional revision. The Council of Ancients approves the measure.

4 NIVÔSE   25 DECEMBER.   The Constitution of Year VIII is proclaimed with Bonaparte as First Consul. His powers are far greater than those given Sieyès and Ducos. He directly influences appointments to the Senate. He appoints and presides over a Council of State and, in effect, directly chooses and can remove all high officials.

The revolutionary era is thus brought to a close; consolidation is achieved. The *Moniteur* of 14 November 1799 (23 brumaire an VIII) quoted from a placard posted in Paris: "France wants something great and long-lasting. Instability has been her downfall, and she now invokes steadiness. She has no desire for a monarchy, which remains therefore proscribed; but she does want unity in the action of the power executing laws. . . . She wants to enjoy the benefits accruing from ten years of sacrifices."[1]

---

1. The following sources have been consulted in the preparation of this chronology: François Furet and Denis Richet, *French Revolution*, trans. Stephen Hardman (New York: The Macmillan Company, 1970); Georges Lefebvre, *The French Revolution*, trans. Elizabeth Moss Evanson, (N.Y.: Columbia University Press, 1964), vol. 1 *(From Its Origins to 1793)*; Idem, *The French Revolution*, trans. John Hall Stewart and James Friguglietti (N.Y.: Columbia University Press, 1964), vol. 2 *(From 1793 to 1799)*; Samuel F. Scott and Barry Rothaus, eds. *Historical Dictionary of the French Revolution, 1789–1799,* 2 vols. (Westport, Conn.: Greenwood Press, 1985); Albert Soboul, *The French Revolution, 1789–1799,* trans. Alan Forrest and Colin Jones (New York: Random House, 1975); and Michel Vovelle, *The Fall of the French Monarchy, 1787–1792,* trans. Susan Burke (Cambridge and New York: Cambridge University Press, 1984).

Catalogue

Catalogue of the Exhibition

Cynthia Burlingham and James Cuno
Grunwald Center for the Graphic Arts

NOTES TO THE READER

When available and appropriate the following information has been supplied for each of the prints included in the exhibition: artist's name, followed by nationality and birth and death dates; title given in French followed by an English translation in parentheses; date of execution; name of the artist who designed the image from which the print was made; technique; catalogue raisonné references; dimensions; Bibliothèque nationale collection number; Bibliothèque nationale microfiche reference number.

In the majority of cases the *Collection de Vinck* catalogue has been used as a source for titles of individual prints. Peculiarities of eighteenth-century spelling and irregularities in the use of diacritical marks have been maintained as far as possible. Capitalization has, however, been modernized, and appropriate accents have been inserted when capital letters have been transcribed as lowercase. A close examination of the prints reveals discrepancies in the descriptions of technique found in the de Vinck catalogue, and thus it has not been relied upon for this information. The

following abbreviations have been employed in citing catalogue raisonné references:

DV = François-Louis Bruel, *Collection de Vinck: Inventaire analytique,* 6 vols. (Paris: Imprimerie nationale, 1914)

H = Georges Duplessis, *Collection Michel Hennin,* 5 vols. (Paris: H. Menu, 1877–1884)

B = André Blum, *La Caricature révolutionnaire* (Paris: Jouve et Cie, 1916).

A bracketed catalogue raisonné reference indicates a variation of an image included in the exhibition. Dimensions are given in millimeters with plate size preceding sheet size and height preceding width in each instance. Within the entries footnote references are given in short form and correlate with the bibliography at the end of the catalogue.

In a very few instances it was determined after careful consideration that prints originally selected for the exhibition should not travel. As these images are significant to our study, we have reproduced them in the catalogue adding the notation "not in exhibition."

I. PREREVOLUTIONARY CARICATURES

ANTI-JESUIT

The Society of Jesus was founded by Saint Ignatius of Loyola, a Spanish priest, and was granted approbation by Pope Paul III on 27 September 1540. Within forty years, the Jesuits, as members of the society soon became known, numbered 5,000 and operated 144 colleges. In France alone there were more than 300 Jesuits conducting 15 colleges. The spread of Jesuit influence in France, however, was frequently checked by the Gallican Parlement of Paris, and two centuries after its founding, the

Society of Jesus was expelled, its buildings and estates confiscated.

The issue that prompted the expulsion in 1762 centered on Antoine Lavalette, the Jesuit superior of the mission in Martinique. Seeking to relieve the financial problems of the mission, Lavalette began to expand its role in the island's trade with France. He was soon forced to borrow heavily without the knowledge of his superiors in France and Rome. Eventually, his creditors brought action against the society, claiming that the French Jesuits as a body were responsible for Lavalette's debts. Certain lower courts upheld the creditors' position, and on 8 May 1761 the Parlement of Paris sustained the lower courts' judgment.

Three weeks later, Louis xv appointed a special commission of the Royal Council to study the situation. In the fall, however, the Parlement of Paris resumed its attack on the society, ordering the works of twenty-three Jesuits burned and decreeing that the society must close its colleges by 1 October. Again the king intervened, suspending the Parlement's resolution for a year, until 6 August 1762. Parlement responded by assigning 1 April 1762 as the date for execution of the decree, and despite continued volleys between Parlement and the king, this date was met. Four months after the closing of the colleges, Parlement announced that the Society of Jesus was banned from France, but a royal edict of November 1764 allowed the Jesuits to remain in the country on the condition that they live as good and faithful subjects under the spiritual authority of French bishops. The battles between the Jesuits and Parlement were comparable to those that occurred between France and the papacy during the early years of the Revolution; and just as the Jesuits were the subject of numerous biting satires in 1762, members of the clergy would be attacked throughout the Revolution.

1. ANONYMOUS
French
*Condamnation de la Société des Jésuites
(Condemnation of the Jesuits),* ca. 1762
Engraving
296 x 444 (sheet)
Bibliothèque nationale, Qb1 6 août 1762
[M97434]
(Not in exhibition)

In this complex allegorical satire, a robed Jesuit (Antoine Lavalette) covers the face of a regal lion (Louis xv) with a cloak inscribed "false persuasion" and exclaims, "He is easily muzzled." At the left a weakened Pope Clement xiii dictates a brief to a scribe seated at a writing desk; a Jesuit to the pope's right hears a confession, and a shadowy figure, perhaps a creditor, approaches on his left. In the distance a lion sits between two figures who gesture in opposite directions; a runaway horse pulls a cart labeled "foolish rumors," which rolls toward a raging fire; and a figure at the far right wheels goods into the courtyard of a Jesuit college. In the right foreground, forceful anti-Jesuit Gallican bishops, who are depicted as dogs or foxes, join forces with lions representing the Bourbon monarchs Charles iii of Spain, Philippe of Parma, and Ferdinand i of Naples, who by 1768 would banish the Jesuits from their kingdoms. The coastal setting is not specific, but it suggests both Lavalette's mission in Martinique and the environs of Marseilles, where the Jesuit had been highly regarded for his commercial skills and where the lower courts later upheld the complaints of his creditors.

Originally accompanied by a key that identified its figures, this allegory is comparable in composition and manner of engraving to the northern tradition of emblematic satire that had influenced French caricature earlier on (see pp. 18, 55–56). A particularly apt example of this tradition may be found in the anonymous anti-Jansenist caricatures of the mid-seventeenth century, which favored Louis xiv's alliance with the Jesuits in the conflict over religious tolerance (Shikes, p. 36). Here, however, it is the alliance between the Jesuits and the monarchy that is the subject of satire and, specifically, the strain put on that relationship in 1762 by Lavalette's financial misdealings.

2. ANONYMOUS
French
Le Crime puny (Crime Punished), ca. 1768
Etching
388 x 257, 421 x 264
Bibliothèque nationale, Qb1 6 août 1762
[M97519]

Far more direct than the preceding satire, this image represents the suppression of the Society of Jesus in the Bourbon courts of Spain, Naples, and Parma, which took place from 1762 to 1768. Following a popular uprising against the government of Charles iii of Spain on 26 March 1766, a special

1

2

3. ANONYMOUS
French
Les Jésuites, arbitres de trônes et de couronnes
(The Jesuits, Arbiters of Thrones and Crowns), ca.
1762
Etching
202 x 262, 204 x 265
Bibliothèque nationale, Qb1 6 août 1762
[M97520]

3

court known as the Extraordinary Council of Castile concluded that the Jesuits had incited the people to riot against the crown. On 27 February 1767, the king concurred and issued a secret decree banishing the Jesuits and seizing their property. Nine months later, Ferdinand I of Naples, pressured by the Marchese Bernardo Tanucci and his Commission of Abuses, followed the lead of his father, Charles III, and expelled the Jesuits from his kingdom. Finally, on 7–8 February 1768, the troops of King Philippe surrounded the Jesuit houses in Parma and marched 170 Jesuits to its border, forbidding them to return. In France, however, as has been described in the introduction to this section, the campaign against the Jesuits was by no means so decisive.

In this caricature, the three Bourbon courts are shown triumphant, driving black-robed Jesuits into the clutches of sharp-tongued devils engulfed in flames. In the lower right, a screaming figure is being fitted with a crown that is both a royal diadem and an instrument of torture. This is Louis XV, and the caricature stands, in effect, as a warning from the Parlement to the king: through his interventions on behalf of the Jesuits, he too will fall from grace and burn in hell.

Raised on a dais, a Jesuit priest sits beneath a portrait of the order's founder, Saint Ignatius of Loyola. In his left hand he raises a key, the traditional attribute of Saint Peter, thus recalling that Jesus had referred to his apostle as the rock upon which the church would be built and had given him the keys to the kingdom of heaven (Matthew 16:15–19). Fellow Jesuits kneel beside their general, joined by natives of the New World who represent the society's many missions. To the left and right, crowned figures approach the dais to pay tribute to the religious order that legitimizes the authority of their secular governments, while three Jesuits in the foreground spin crowns and scepters. Charges of extreme influence over the courts of Europe were frequently made by opponents of the Jesuits and contributed significantly to popular suspicion of the order and its eventual suppression in France and the Bourbon courts of Spain, Naples, and Parma.

4. ANONYMOUS
French
Figures de Jésuites ridicules et en caricature
(Faces of Jesuits, Ridiculous and in Caricature),
ca. 1762, after Jean-Baptiste Jouvenet
Etching
186 x 113, 190 x 115
Bibliothèque nationale, Qb1 6 août 1762
[M97535]

5. ANONYMOUS
French
Figures de Jésuites ridicules et en caricature
(Faces of Jesuits, Ridiculous and in Caricature),
ca. 1762, after Jean-Baptiste Jouvenet
Etching
185 x 110, 190 x 119
Bibliothèque nationale, Qb1 6 août 1762
[M97536]

The origin of caricature dates to the end of the sixteenth century and credit for its invention is given to the painter Annibale Carracci. Strictly speaking, a caricature is a "charged portrait" in which one purposefully distorts and exaggerates the subject's features with the dual intention of poking fun and revealing "true" character (see pp. 15–18). This practice appears to have started as a kind of visual game within the Carracci circle in Bologna and quickly became a sport of the cognoscenti in Rome, where such artists as Bernini, Domenichino, and Guercino drew caricatures of their patrons for their mutual delight and amusement. It was, in fact, Bernini who first introduced the term *caricature* in France in 1665, while he was working on his bust of Louis XIV.

It was undoubtedly around this time that the young painter Jean-Baptiste Jouvenet drew the caricatures reproduced here. Jouvenet was born in Rouen in 1644 and entered the studio of Charles Le Brun shortly after arriving in Paris in 1661. Among his most important works were decorations for the Salon de Mars at Versailles, executed between 1671 and 1674. His drawings typically reveal an incisive quality of line that is also evident here. These are typical examples of pure caricature: facial features are quickly sketched; noses, cheekbones, eyes, and the size and shape of the head are most often exaggerated; and the subjects are held up to mild ridicule. The depictions are neither grotesque nor humiliating, they only serve to unmask their subjects. Unfortunately, little is known about the history of these caricatures, and one can only assume that the drawings survived from the seventeenth

4

century and were etched during the Jesuit controversies of the eighteenth century as part of the general enthusiasm for images critical of the order.

MESMER

In February 1778 Franz Anton Mesmer, a medical doctor trained in Vienna, arrived in Paris and proclaimed his discovery of a superfine fluid that permeated all living things. This substance, if obstructed, could result in illness. Mesmer believed that health could be restored by "mesmerizing," or massaging, the body's "poles"—the fingers, the nose, and especially the "hypochondria," or the sides of the upper abdomen—with iron rods, which were attached to a tub filled with iron filings and mesmerized water. The rods supposedly transferred the fluid from the container to the patients, who were tied both to the tub and to each other with ropes. Thus configured, they formed a mesmeric chain, which was presumed to act as an electrical circuit and send a restorative force coursing through the entire clinic.

Though Mesmer sought acceptance from academicians, he was ignored and forced to rely on the

5

financial support of bourgeois patrons and aristocratic converts, together with the encouragement
of a growing number of fashionable amateur scientists. As Robert Darnton has shown, the significance of Mesmer's ideas for the revolutionary era
lay in their challenge to the scientific establishment. Such political radicals as Jacques Pierre Brissot, Jean-Louis Carra, and Jean-Paul Marat had
ambitions early on to become recognized philosophers and scientists. These were thwarted, however, by the institutionalized authority of the
Academy of Sciences, the Royal Society of Medicine, and the faculty of medicine of the University
of Paris. Through their public support of mesmerism, these radicals were venting anger at being
excluded from what they felt was their rightful
place among the leading Parisian philosophers and
scientists. Mesmer's plight paralleled that of
Marat, his friend Brissot, and the younger Carra, all
of whom sympathized with the Viennese doctor
and adopted his struggle as their own (Darnton,
1968; Blum, 1910, pp. 447–54 [December]).

6. ANONYMOUS
French
*Le Mesmerisme a tous les diables (One Hell of a
Mesmerism)*, ca. 1784
Etching
190 x 288, 258 x 340
Bibliothèque nationale, Qb1 1784
[M98124]

As the caption below this image relates, Mesmer
is being carried away by a devil whom he attempts
to "mesmerize." Gold coins fall from his pockets
into a mesmerizing tub below; these were given to
the charlatan by the angry men and women in the
background, who hurl musical instruments, cords,
and rods into the tub. To the left, a clergyman, ridiculed for having written in support of Mesmer, is
being attacked by three devils, two of whom whip
him with his own belts as a third blows evil words
into his ear. To the right, three devils pull at the
medical robes of Charles Deslon, who shouts out in
frustration at having lost his authority in France.

Deslon, *docteur régent* of the medical faculty of
the University of Paris and physician to the Comte
d'Artois, the king's brother, was an early champion
of Mesmer. He joined him after being expelled
from his faculty position in 1781. A year later, disillu-
sioned with Mesmer's unwillingness to divulge his
ultimate doctrinal secrets, Deslon established his
own mesmerizing practice. In the spring of 1784 he
was a principal subject of the royal commission's
investigation into mesmerism (cat. no. 8); and in
November of that year, he was lampooned in a
comic play at the Comédie-Italienne, entitled *Les
Docteurs modernes*.

In the lower center of the caricature, a puckish,
winged "god of mockery" is shown resting on a
book by Mesmer and laughing at the French, all
of whom he describes in the caption as suckers
and charlatans.

6

7. ANONYMOUS
French
Le Doigt magique / ou le Magnétisme ani-mal / simius semper simius (The Magic Fin-ger; / or, Animal Magnetism / Once a Monkey Always a Monkey), ca. 1784
Etching with hand coloring
H 10019
225 x 164, 293 x 208
Bibliothèque nationale, Qb1 1784
[M98130]

LE DOIGT MAGIQUE
OU LE MAGNÉTISME ANIMAL
Simius Semper Simius

7

A mesmerist healed his patient by massaging the "poles" of the body. This was presumed to remove obstacles preventing a healthy flow of the super-fine fluid that Mesmer believed to be the primeval agent of nature, bathing all of the universe. Typi-cally, a mesmerist sat with his patient's knees between his own and ran his fingers over the sub-ject's body, especially the sides of the upper abdo-men. This occurred in a "clinic" decorated with heavy carpets and astrological ornaments, suffused with a somber light, and closed off from the outside world by drawn curtains. Sometimes patients col-lapsed writhing on the floor and were carried into mattress-lined "crisis rooms" to recover. Other

times, they supposedly fell into a deep sleep and communicated with distant spirits. The mesmer-ist's touch and the sensual ambience of the clinic encouraged widespread gossip about "sexual mag-netism."

In this caricature, a jackass-mesmerist, his pocket filled with money, is putting his female patient into a hypnotic trance. The spirits with whom she is about to communicate take the form of a handsome, and apparently unclad, angel and a beautiful, bare-breasted siren or perhaps Echidna. Half-woman, half-serpent, Echidna bore the Hydra, and her inclusion here may suggest the cari-caturist's view of the multiheaded, monstrous problems that result from being duped by mesmer-ists. The point of the satire is further elaborated in the Latin inscription below, which may be trans-lated, "Once a monkey always a monkey."

8. ANONYMOUS
Le Magnétisme dévoilé (Magnetism Unveiled), ca. 1784
Etching
258 x 302, 297 x 329
Bibliothèque nationale, H 10026
[G161323]

In the spring of 1784 Louis XVI appointed a com-mission to investigate mesmerism. Comprising four prominent doctors from the faculty of medi-cine of the University of Paris and five members of the Academy of Sciences, including Jean-Sylvain Bailly, Antoine Laurent de Lavoisier, and Ben-

Le Magnétisme dévoilé

8

jamin Franklin, the commission was prestigious and, in the eyes of the scientific establishment, authoritative. It spent weeks listening to the theories of Charles Deslon, an early convert to mesmerism who had been expelled from the medical faculty of the University of Paris for promoting the new theory, only to later run afoul of Mesmer for setting up his own clinic and proclaiming schismatic ideas about animal magnetism.

Members of the commission also submitted to continuous mesmerizing themselves and tested the operation of mesmerized fluid furnished by Deslon outside the clinic in a series of controlled experiments. The commission concluded that such fluid did not exist and that its "effects" could be attributed to the charged atmosphere of the clinics and the overheated imaginations of the mesmerists.

In this caricature, Franklin is shown leading the commission into a clinic brandishing its report in front of him. The power of enlightened science emanates from the report and sends the charlatan mesmerists fleeing the room on broomsticks, while a mesmerizing tub crashes to the floor beneath the weight of a blindfolded figure of Truth and an owl, a symbol of deceit, hovers above.

9. ANONYMOUS
French
Untitled, ca. 1784
Etching
209 x 301, 212 x 306
Bibliothèque nationale, H 10025
[G161322]

A mesmerist's clinic is shown in the throes of a convulsive crisis. The tub filled with mesmerized fluid stands in the center of the room. Having already performed their magic, the rods through which the liquid passes are now idle. The patients remain tied to the tub, while three women in the center of the room form a mesmeric "chain" by linking thumbs and index fingers. The erotic implications of the cure are evident in the way men grope at women seeking to touch the "poles" of their bodies. The entire affair is charged by the presence of the donkey-headed mesmerist whose very body enriches the passage of fluid throughout the room, while astrological beams break through clouds of smoke to bring additional magic to the séance. A wry commentary on the scene is offered in the painting over the door where a cupid dispenses his own fluid into a chamber pot.

9

SOCIAL CARICATURES

In the immediate prerevolutionary period, French caricature was just as preoccupied with manned balloon flights and the peculiarities of high fashion as it was with the Jesuits, the English, and Mesmer's eccentricities.

As Robert Darnton has noted, the first balloon flight in 1783 inspired the French with an almost religious awe and an unparalleled enthusiasm for man's ability to harness the power of nature. A crowd of nearly one hundred thousand wept, cheered, and even fainted as *aéronautes* ascended over Nantes one afternoon. Peasants met balloonists shouting, "Are you men or gods?"; while one aristocrat imagined seeing "the gods of antiquity carried on clouds; myths have come to life in the marvels of physics." Such responses led to the questions posed in the *Journal de Bruxelles* in 1784, "Who knows how far we can go? What mortal would dare set limits to the human mind?" (Darnton, 1968, pp. 22–23). Queries such as these provided ample opportunities for caricaturists to mock the hubris of their peers.

Around 1740 French couture attained dominance throughout Europe, establishing the most fashionable modes of dress and trading in the best fabrics and accessories. The industry also published the most influential fashion journals; these contained plates designed by a number of important artists, among them Hubert François Gravelot, Jean Michel Moreau *le jeune*, and Augustin de Saint-Aubin. The latter's *Gallerie des modes et des costumes français* comprised a set of 342 colored fashion plates published from 1778 to 1787, which not only illustrated the most current fashions, but also gave the names of the most highly regarded tailors. Emphasis upon stylish dress had played an important part in the regulation and civilizing of behavior at the end of the seventeenth century. By the third quarter of the eighteenth century, however, highly stylized, exaggerated, and eccentric dress was a means of demonstrating individuality, the desperate display of which encouraged numerous caricatures (Ribeiro, pp. 13–19, 43–65).

10. ANONYMOUS
French
Aux amateurs de physique (For Devotees of Physics), ca. 1783
Etching and engraving with hand coloring
241 x 301, 298 x 344
Bibliothèque nationale, H 9948
[G161244]
(Not in exhibition)

On 15 October 1783 Pilâtre de Rozier and the Marquis d'Arlandes rose into the air over Metz in northeastern France, carried by a hot-air balloon. This and other early manned flights ignited the imaginations of Frenchmen. Poets wrote odes to balloon flights; engineers offered treatises on the

Aux Amateurs de Physique.

10

construction of balloons, seeking prizes sponsored by the Academy of Sciences; and celebrated *aéronautes* were paraded through towns and cities where their portraits were printed and sold in the streets. A report in the *Journal de Bruxelles* of 31 January 1784 described a balloon flight, "The women in tears, the common people raising their hands toward the sky in deep silence; the passengers, leaning out of the gallery, waving and crying out in joy . . . you follow them with your eyes, you call to them as if they could hear, and the feeling of fright gives way to one of wonder" (Darnton, 1968, p. 20).

Such flights were both a public spectacle, accompanied by military music and firecrackers, and a confirmation of man's ability to harness the laws of nature by means of his powers of reason. This caricature celebrates the spectacle, poking fun at the crowd which, in a desperate attempt to follow the balloon in the distance, clambers awkwardly over a wall, men pulling up women whose dresses, when lifted, offer a sight that obviously resonates with the air-filled orb floating in the sky above.

11. ANONYMOUS
French
Untitled, ca. 1780
Etching
300 x 220, 306 x 224
Bibliothèque nationale, H 9787
[G161078]

11

Depictions of newsmongers appeared in French prints as early as 1751 with Gabriel-Jacques de Saint-Aubin's celebrated etching *Les Nouvellistes* (Carlson and Ittman, no. 32). There, numerous men are depicted as gathered in a café, sitting or standing around a stove, discussing the news of the day. The atmosphere is heated not only by the smoke of the stove, but by the expressions and postures of those engaged in serious conversation.

In this untitled etching of almost thirty years later, the newsmongers are shown in a garden, standing beside and seated beneath a tree, gathered about a central figure who reads from a journal labeled *Gazette*. The intensity of the audience's interest in the news is conveyed by strained looks and stunned expressions. The seated figure to the left clenches his jaw and grips his walking stick; the standing figure behind the reader leans forward, his eyes and mouth wide open; and the figure in the dark cape to the right gazes upward as if startled, his lips drawn down to complete this impression. The print illustrates how news was disseminated in the years just prior to the Revolution and how popular newsmongering was among those who frequented the cafés and gardens of Paris.

12. ANONYMOUS
French
L'Incendie des coeffures (The Burning of the Coiffures), ca. 1780
Etching
260 x 174, 290 x 189
Bibliothèque nationale, Tf 18
[R079848]

AU CAFFÉ ROYAL D'ALEXANDRE

L'INCENDIE DES COEFFURES

12

Like fashionable dress, hairstyles were susceptible to the most extraordinary exaggeration during the reign of Louis XVI. Contemporary accounts describe women's hair as reaching such a height that it often prevented them from riding in closed carriages or forced them to ride with their hair protruding from the window (Blum, 1910, pp. 461–62 [December]). Such hairstyles were encouraged by Marie-Antoinette, whose hairdresser created the *coiffure à la hérisson*, which concluded in spiked ends resembling the back of a hedgehog or sea urchin, and the *coiffure en pouf*, which was decorated with ornamental birds, butterflies, animals, and even a tree branch, fruit, or vegetables. Other hairstyles resembled gondolas, windmills, gardens, and mountain forests, causing an English witness to remark, "Parisian ladies wear high towers with an extraordinary number of flowers, pads and ribbons. The English find such boundless display extremely ill-bred, and if any such lady comes to London, people hiss and throw mud on her" (Godefrey, 1984, p. 61).

In this caricature a fashionable young woman gazes into the eyes of her beau, failing to notice that her mountainous hair has brushed up against a candelabra and caught on fire. Two attendants clamber up a ladder with a pitcher and a bucket to douse the flames. Wholly preoccupied with themselves and the possibilities for entertainment at hand in the highly fashionable Café royal d'Alexandre, the young man and woman continue their exchange ignorant of the disaster that has been narrowly averted.

illogical extreme and subjects the young woman and the artifice of fashion to an attack from nature, that of the barnyard.

13

13. ANONYMOUS
French
Vengeange de la valaille deplumée contre la coiffure emplumee de Mlle des Soupirs (The Vengeance of the Deplumed Birds against the Feathered Hairdo of Mlle of Sighs), ca. 1780
Etching and engraving
310 x 238, 330 x 258
Bibliothèque nationale, H 9813
[G161104]

Her hair piled high and adorned with peacock and ostrich feathers, a highly fashionable young woman is assaulted by vengeful, deplumed birds who squawk at and bite her. Their master, however, ignores the irate fowl and fondles the young woman's plumage admiringly. This wonderfully ludicrous image takes the coiffures of the time to their

14. ANONYMOUS
French
Le Triomphe de la coquetterie (The Triumph of Coquetry), ca. 1780
Etching
340 x 480, 356 x 491
Bibliothèque nationale, H 9825
[G161118]

In a sort of jousting tournament, a dazzling young woman, elegantly dressed and coiffed, has triumphed over her challengers, pushing them one by one into the water, while an audience composed of equally elegant people watch the contest and flirt in the background as an orchestra plays an accompaniment. It is a charming satire that depicts the daily competition in the realm of fashion as a grand public spectacle where bountiful hairstyles

LE TRIOMPHE DE LA COQUETTERIE

14

and jaunty hoopskirts decorate the scene in place of ribbons and banners.

The power that fashion had to attract attention in France is demonstrated by the circumstances surrounding the introduction of the hoopskirt toward the end of Louis XIV's reign. Two English women appeared one day wearing the broad, full skirts in the Tuileries gardens. An astonished and curious Parisian crowd gathered about them in such numbers that they were nearly trampled to death and were saved only by passing military officers who escorted them to safety. The skirts quickly became fashionable and were a target of official church criticism. A treatise on the indecency of hoopskirts was published in 1724, followed by another in 1735 entitled *Indignité et extravagance des paniers pour des femmes sensées et chrétiennes.* Charges were made against "round-table" and "barrel" skirts that lifted up with the slightest movement to reveal a woman's ankle and calf. In 1736 skirts, while maintaining their rigid infrastructure, were flattened and extended to enormous widths, forcing their wearers to walk sideways through doors. In Paris it became necessary to forbid the wearing of skirts wider than a four-wheel

carriage. By 1770 the hoopskirt had disappeared except at court or for the most formal occasions. As fashion was serious business, however, such occasions proved frequent.

ANTI-ENGLISH

Tension between Britain and its American colonies increased dramatically during the second half of 1775. On 23 August, Britain prohibited all foreign commerce with the Americans; on 19 October, it specifically prohibited the sale of ammunition to the colonists; and on 22 December, it again prohibited commerce of any kind with the colonies effective as of 1 March 1776.

France's interest in the colonies was in great part driven by its desire to end the British monopoly over American and West Indian trade. On 22 August Louis XVI ordered the preparation of sufficient warships to counter any British attempt to restrict the transport of French arms to the colonists, and eleven months later he signed a treaty of defensive alliance with the United States.

Ironically, the engagement of the French in America's war with England seriously undermined the strength of the French monarchy and resulted in a debt that threw the government into an irreparable financial crisis in the years just preceding the French Revolution (Dull, pp. 336–44; Blum, 1910, pp. 111–14 [August]).

15. ANONYMOUS
French
Les Rieurs sont pour nous, l'Anglois est bien malade, / Et graces au déstin, nous tenons la Grenade (We Have the Last Laugh, the Englishman Is Very Sick / Thanks to Fate, We Hold Grenada), ca. 1779
Etching with hand coloring
225 x 197, 258 x 198
Bibliothèque nationale, Qb1 6 juillet 1779
[M97913]

16. ANONYMOUS
French
Les Anglois, chassées de la Grenade (The English, Expelled from Grenada), ca. 1779
Etching with hand coloring
DV 1177
176 x 291
Bibliothèque nationale, Qb1 4 juillet 1779
(Not in exhibition)

A strategic base for French trade and military campaigns in the West Indies, Grenada was captured by the British by 1758; they also captured the valuable islands of Guadeloupe, Martinique, Saint Vincent, and Saint Lucia around this time. These French losses, together with those suffered to the British in Canada, spelled the end of the foreign policy ambitions of the Abbé Bernis, a friend of Madame de Pompadour. The Duc de Choiseul, another of Madame de Pompadour's favorites, was made secretary of state for foreign affairs in 1758, and by 1763 he had become minister of war and the marine. In that year he concluded a peace treaty with the British and extricated France from further fighting in the West Indies. The loss of France's first colonial empire was thereby acknowledged.

In July 1779, however, France revenged itself upon the British when the Comte d'Estaing undertook to defend French interests in the Western hemisphere once again. He drove the British from Grenada after recapturing Martinique and Saint Vincent. From Grenada, d'Estaing sailed on to Saint Lucia and restored French dominance in the

Les rieurs sont pour nous, l'Anglois est bien malade, / Et graces au Déstin, Nous tenons la Grenade.

15

West Indies. This campaign entailed England's worst naval defeat in nearly one hundred years, and French caricaturists celebrated with numerous satires, such as the two reproduced here.

In the first caricature, two battle weary French soldiers celebrate the defeat of the British fleet. They carry the spoils of war, a bag that seems to contain pomegranates (*grenades*), a pun on the name of the island they have conquered. *Grenade* was also the name of a small, hand- or machine-hurled explosive device that had been in existence since the sixteenth century and resembled a pomegranate in shape. Grenades were used in naval warfare, and this may explain the sinking fleet, depicted in the background on the left. In addition,

Les Anglois, Chassées de la Grenade.

16

the pomegranate tree lent its name to a special regiment of French soldiers established by Louis XIV, *les grenadiers*, thus further extending the wordplay.

A pun is also used to enrich the second caricature, wherein a French soldier drives the British, who are depicted as turkeys, from Grenada. As Albert Boime points out in his essay in the present catalogue (p. 69), the French word for turkey, *dindon*, carries a double meaning which derives from its closeness to the verb *dindonner* (literally, to dupe) and from a resemblance to *dandin* (traditionally used to designate a blockhead). In this case, the British are depicted as fools driven into retreat by the French and whipped by the jester-like figure of mockery, who flies above taunting and humiliating them in their defeat.

Martinique but initially failed in attempts to weaken the British stronghold in the West Indies. In July 1779 he captured the strategic island of Grenada and, although ordered to return to France, responded to requests for assistance from the American Continental Congress. He attacked the British at Savannah, Georgia, and later forced them to abandon Newport in favor of New York.

In this caricature, d'Estaing is shown as a personification of Destiny who, having muzzled the ferocious British beasts, presents a palm of victory to America, represented by an Indian chief holding a staff topped by a Phrygian cap. Fame is shown at the right as a figure of victory heralding d'Estaing's heroic exploits, while America sits proudly on bountiful bales of tobacco and rice destined for European markets.

17. ANONYMOUS
French
Le Destin molestant les Anglois (Destiny Molesting the English), ca. 1780
Etching
DV 1176
212 X 312, 243 X 331
Bibliothèque nationale, H 9781
[G161071]

17

In the spring of 1778 the Comte d'Estaing, senior active officer in the French Navy, commanded the royal fleet in its effort to protect French possessions in the Western hemisphere and assist the American colonies in their War of Independence against Britain.

D'Estaing arrived off the Delaware capes in July and succeeded in blockading the British garrison at Newport, Rhode Island. In November, he left for

18. JEAN CHARLES LEVASSEUR
French, 1734–1816
L'Amérique indépendante (Independent America), ca. 1783, after Antoine Borel
Etching and engraving
DV 1221
434 X 350, 501 X 377
Bibliothèque nationale, H 9703
[G160992]

Wearing the laurel wreath of victory, Benjamin Franklin acknowledges the triumphant and free America, represented by an Indian maiden kneeling before a statue of Liberty. Above Franklin and supported by clouds, a figure of military might draws his lance and prepares to assist a club-wielding warrior in liberating an enchained colonial. Throughout, enlightenment or reason, in the guise of myriad antique references, ennobles and sustains the natural order of the idealized native American.

In December 1776 Benjamin Franklin had been sent by the Americans to negotiate a treaty of amity and commerce with the French monarchy. Highly regarded in France as central to this alliance, Franklin was also respected for his knowledge of science and was appointed to the royal commission investigating mesmerism in the spring of 1784 (cat. no. 8).

Antoine Borel was a painter and etcher and was active between 1780 and 1785 (Le Blanc, vol. 1, pp. 465–66). Jean Charles Levasseur was a prominent engraver, admitted to the Academy in 1771; he exhibited in the royal salons from 1765 to 1789 and often engraved prints after designs and paintings by Jean Restout, François Boucher, and Jean-Baptiste Greuze, among others (Le Blanc, vol. 2, pp. 547–48).

L'AMÉRIQUE INDÉPENDANTE

Dédiée au Congrès des États unis de l'Amérique

18

The Bastille was a fortress-prison constructed in 1370 to defend the entrance to Paris at the faubourg Saint-Antoine on the eastern edge of the city. Since the reign of Louis XIV, it had been used as a state prison in which the king could incarcerate anyone for an indefinite period of time without a trial, and although in 1789 it housed only seven prisoners, the Bastille had become a prominent symbol of despotism. Its destruction, however, was far from merely symbolic; it was a desperate gesture made in the midst of very real economic and social crises.

By the summer of 1789, the price of wheat had reached its highest level since 1715, and the number of unemployed had increased dramatically. On 12 July riots broke out in Paris following the news that the king had dismissed the popular minister Jacques Necker. The following day, the Parlement of Paris, which had traditionally opposed the monarchy, created a bourgeois militia of 48,000 men, which it then had to arm. Word spread among the angry populace that guns and cannons were stored in the Invalides and powder and balls at the Bastille.

On 14 July a crowd of 20,000 to 30,000 stormed the Invalides and seized 40,000 muskets and 12 cannons. At the same time, another crowd demanded the 250 barrels of powder stored at the Bastille. The cannons taken from the Invalides were ultimately used to attack the fortress. Its governor, the Marquis de Launay, capitulated, and the mob stormed the Bastille, disarming its guards, freeing its prisoners, and arresting de Launay. In all, 98 people were killed and 73 were wounded. As de Launay was being conducted to the Hôtel de ville, he was taken from his captors, killed, and then decapitated; his head was impaled on a pike and paraded through the city. The destruction of the Bastille, symbol of the ancien régime, represented the triumph of the people over the monarchy and was thus depicted in numerous caricatures and current event prints throughout the Revolution.

19. Anonymous
French
Prise de la Bastille le 14 juillet 1789 (The Taking of the Bastille on 14 July 1789), 1789
Etching and engraving with hand coloring
DV 1564
336 x 510, 359 x 516
Bibliothèque nationale, Qb1 14 juillet 1789
[M98613]

PRISE DE LA BASTILLE LE 14 JUILLET 1789.

19

This print is typical of the recently developed engraving of current events (p. 31). It was produced following the taking of the Bastille, an occurrence of such dramatic import that it inspired more patriotic or symbolic prints than satires (Champfleury, 1874, p. 39). Here, the final moments of the assault are seen from the interior of the Cour de l'Orme. Cannons captured from the Invalides earlier in the day fire on the main structure of the fortress, and the uniformed Gardes françaises sweep through the gates of the Bastille to assist the citizens' militia in its attack. In the background at the right, the house of the Marquis de Launay, the governor of the Bastille, is in flames; while in the right foreground, he himself is placed under arrest.

20. ANONYMOUS
French
Démolition de la Bastille (Demolition of the Bastille), 1789
Etching with hand coloring
H 10404
217 x 178 (oval), 277 x 193
Bibliothèque nationale, Qb1 15–17 juillet 1789
[M98862]

DEMOLITION DE LA BASTILLE

20

On 15 July 1789 the Permanent Committee of the Constituent Assembly decided to demolish the Bastille. Two architects were engaged to supervise the project, and over one thousand workmen were hired, a large number of whom were drawn from the ranks of the unemployed. Once removed, the individual stones that had composed the structure were carved and transformed into souvenirs. They were distributed to the provinces by so-called apostles of liberty or conquerors of the Bastille, and great demonstrations were organized to welcome them. The last remaining stone was presented to the Assembly on 6 February 1790.

This print at first appears to be a typical historical depiction of the event; however, a closer examination indicates that the watching crowd is composed primarily of aristocrats. According to the inscription, these "deputies of the nobility" include the Marquis de Lusignan, a colonel of the Regiment of Flanders stationed at Versailles (one of the regiments that failed to come to the defense of the Bastille). Here the marquis is referred to as one of the "generous citizens" who assisted in the demolition of the Bastille. However, Lusignan was criticized by members of his own class for betraying the ancien régime and was not entirely trusted or accepted by the new ruling order of the Third Estate. The general tone of the inscription suggests a critical view of such aristocrats.

21. ANONYMOUS
French
Destruction de la Bastille apres la victoire remporté sur les ennemis de la liberté le 14 juil^et. 1789 (Destruction of the Bastille Following the Victory Gained over the Enemies of Liberty on 14 July 1789), ca. 1789
Etching with hand coloring on blue paper
DV 1672, B 94
170 x 261, 171 x 266
Bibliothèque nationale, Qb1 15–17 juillet 1789
[M98861]

At the center of this print, a member of the Third Estate holds a pike surmounted by a Phrygian cap and adorned with a banderole reading "Long live liberty." With his left hand he wields a sword with which he is about to cut off the last remaining head of the Hydra of despotism. To the left an abbé and a noble flee, while in the background the demolition of the Bastille is under way.

Destruction de la Bastille après la Victoire remporté sur les Ennemis de la Liberté le 14 Juil.er 1789

21

The inscription in the upper right gives the history of the Bastille and recounts details pertaining to the circumstances of its construction and its fall. Thus, a documentary representation of the destruction of the prison-fortress is combined with the symbolic killing of the Hydra by the Third Estate, a modern Hercules who destroys the despotism of the Old Regime and claims power and liberty for the French people. (On the representation of revolutionary France as Hercules, see pp. 38–39.)

22. ANONYMOUS
French
Pro patria vincere aut mori dédié à la nation (To Conquer or Die for the Fatherland Dedicated to the Nation), 1789
Etching with hand coloring
212 x 136 (sheet)
Bibliothèque nationale, Qb1 14 juillet 1789
[M98615]

This print, although simple in depiction and composition, is accompanied by an inscription that notes every detail of a relatively minor episode in the taking of the Bastille. It is an example of the propagandistic images that proliferated in the days following 14 July; such prints glorified the heroism of ordinary citizens and emphasized their role in this first great act of the Revolution.

In this case, one J. B. Cretaine, sixty years of age, is assisted by a younger comrade, after having suffered a broken wrist while fighting before the bridge of Tours at the Bastille. Despite his injury, and with only a piece of his sword, Cretaine had managed to capture an officer and turn him over to the Gardes françaises. His, we are made to believe,

was a heroic act to be emulated by all citizens, an example of one man's willingness to fight, and if necessary to die, for the fatherland.

PRO PATRIA VINCERE AUT MORI   DEDIÉ A LA NATION

J. B. Cretaine agé de 60 ans quoi qu'ayant eu le poignet droit entièrement meurtri à la Bascule du 1.er Pont de la Bastille se releva fut devant le grand Pont des Tours, ou l'epée nue à la main il Somma par 3 fois, l'ennemi de se rendre La lame de son epée fut cassée d'une balle un homme fut tué à ses cotés et malgré ses blessures il fut assez heureux de prendre le Major, le fit son Prisonnier le remit à 2 Gardes Françaises entre les deux Ponts.
Ce 14 Juillet 1789.

22

23. ANONYMOUS
French
Le Calculateur patriote (The Patriotic Calculator), 1789
Etching and mezzotint
DV 1616, [B 566]
148 x 110, 174 x 119
Bibliothèque nationale, Qb1 7 octobre 1789
[M99479]

24. ANONYMOUS
French
Le Calculateur patriote (The Patriotic Calculator), 1789
Etching and mezzotint on blue paper
DV 1618, [B 566]
242 x 172, 272 x 196
Bibliothèque nationale, Qb1 7 octobre 1789
[M99481]

These caricatures are part of a group of prints that were well-known through numerous copies and versions; they take a grim view of the Revolution, whose patriotic accountant is shown keeping a record of the heads that have been taken in payment and those that are still due. Champfleury sug-

le Calculateur Patriote.

24

gests that the accountant may be the Duc d'Orléans, accused by royalists of inciting the disturbances associated with the fall of the Bastille (Champfleury, 1874, p. 79). De Vinck, on the other hand, and less convincingly, sees Marat as the accountant. (Marat was famous for his frequent calls for public executions, but these occurred much later.)

According to de Vinck, the first caricature (cat. no. 23) includes the heads of J. F. Foulon de Doué, Jacques de Flesselles, Bertier de Sauvigny, and the Marquis de Launay, all massacred during the uprisings of July 1789. Succeeding states of this print were reworked to increase the number of heads paid to twenty-nine.

Le Calculateur Patriote.

23

25. Anonymous

French

*Le Despotisme terrassé (Despotism
Overthrown)*, 1789

Etching and mezzotint

DV 1696

179 x 272, 233 x 294

Bibliothèque nationale, Qb1 14 juillet 1789

[M98810]

26. Anonymous

French

*L'Hydre aristocratique (The Aristocratic
Hydra)*, 1789

Etching with hand coloring

DV 1697

173 x 264, 245 x 309

Bibliothèque nationale, Qb1 14 juillet 1789

[M98812]

Sunday, 12 July 1789, marked the beginning of a
series of uprisings that led to the fall of the Bastille.
News of the dismissal of the popular minister
Jacques Necker and his replacement by the Baron
de Breteuil, an ardent royalist, spread throughout
Paris. Fearing the dissolution of the Constituent

LE DESPOTISME TERRASSE

26

Assembly, as well as potential famine due to
increases in the price of bread, large groups of demonstrators quickly formed and marched through
the city. A clash with the king's troops occurred in
the gardens of the Palais des Tuileries, after which
the royal forces withdrew to camps at the Invalides
and Champ-de-Mars. On 13 July the electors of
Paris met at the Hôtel de ville, formed a Permanent
Committee, and created a citizen's militia which
attacked the Bastille the following day.

L'Hydre Aristocratique

26

In each version of this popular allegory on the
taking of the Bastille, a citizens' militia is shown
decapitating the many-headed Hydra of despotism. In *Le Despotisme terrassé*, the figure of France,
crowned and robed, responds to this act of insurrection by reflecting mournfully on its larger implications; while, in *L'Hydre aristocratique*, she tries to
escape by crawling away from the scene, slinking
along the ground like the snakes that surround her.

The caption below each print relates how this
monster of the aristocratic species was found en
route from Versailles to Paris on 12 July, determined
to come and ravage the capital. Citizens armed
themselves and ran to search for the beast. Finding
that it had withdrawn to a lair within the Bastille,
they were forced to cut off all its heads to prevent
them from growing back.

Le Despotisme terrassé and *L'Hydre aristocratique*
both employ the format of the current event prints
that were produced in such great numbers following 14 July (cat. no. 19). Here, however, the taking of
the Bastille is represented allegorically, and in this
respect, these images resemble catalogue number
69, which represents Marie-Antoinette as a fantastic beast while including a matter-of-fact description of the subject in the caption below.

27. ANONYMOUS
French
Réveil du tiers état (Awakening of the Third Estate), 1789
Etching with hand coloring on blue paper
DV 1674, H 10375, [B 39]
201 x 245 (sheet)
Bibliothèque nationale, Qb1 14 juillet 1789
[M98807]

A nobleman and a clergyman run away in horror as a man of the Third Estate awakens from his "nightmare" and trades for weapons the chains that have oppressed him. This moment of awakening is identified with the destruction of the Bastille, seen in the distance, and the choice of weapons foretells the imminent, violent overthrow of the ancien régime.

This print recalls a passage in the provocative pamphlet by the Abbé Sieyès entitled *What is the Third Estate?* In it the Third Estate is described as "the strong, vigorous man whose arm is still in chains" (Soboul, 1975, p. 43). The pamphlet advocated the position that the people constituted a sovereign power, superior even to that of the king, and concluded that "if the privileged order were to be removed, the nation would be greater, and not lesser, for its removal" (Soboul, 1975, p. 43).

REVEIL DU TIERS ETAT.

27

28. ANONYMOUS
French
Adieu Bastille (Goodbye Bastille), 1789
Etching with hand coloring
DV 1671, B 90
173 x 255, 187 x 270
Bibliothèque nationale, Qb1 14 juillet 1789
[M98808]

ADIEU BASTILLE

28

A member of the Third Estate, dressed in the costume of a Parisian street hawker, plays his bagpipe and causes two marionettes, dressed as a nobleman and clergyman, to dance to his tune. The chained lion at his feet represents the monarchy, now tamed by the Third Estate. The adieu to the Bastille, which is shown being demolished in the background, is also a farewell to the nobles and clergy who prospered under the despotic ancien régime. They are to be replaced by a new government of the Third Estate and a harmless, constitutional monarchy.

French society was divided politically into three estates, or orders: the clergy, the nobility, and the Third Estate. The latter group, comprised chiefly of merchants, financiers, entrepreneurs, professionals, government officials, and members of the legal profession, accounted for over ninety percent of the total French population of twenty-five million in the year 1789. Its political power was, however, in no way commensurate with its numbers.

The political ambitions of the Third Estate were given their clearest voice in a pamphlet entitled *What is the Third Estate?* written by the Abbé Sieyès and published in January 1789. This text concluded in its first three sections that the Third Estate was all-important, even though it was denied a position in the political process, and it warned that the order would henceforth seek a role worthy of its true significance. The pamphlet's influence was considerable, and its underlying assumption, that sovereign power in the nation belonged to the people as a whole, provided the Third Estate with its strongest rallying point at the meeting of the Estates General that was called in the summer of 1789.

The Estates General was a parliamentary assembly of the three estates, each of which met separately and voted as a unit. It had last assembled in 1614 and was convoked in May 1789 to contend with issues of ministerial despotism and to put an end to financial mismanagement. During the meetings, the voting procedure became an issue, as the traditional voting by orders favored the numerically inferior nobility who would form an alliance with the clergy. Voting as individuals, however, would favor the Third Estate. On 17 June the deputies of the Third Estate rejected the title of Estates General and separately established themselves as the National Assembly. Three days later, in the celebrated Oath of the Tennis Court, they swore not to dissolve until a constitution was passed and established on firm foundations. Strained relations between the three estates were a common subject of caricature in the early months of the Revolution.

29. Anonymous
French
Nuit du 4 au 5 août 1789 / ou le Délire patriotique (The Night of 4-5 August; / or, Patriotic Delirium), 1789
Etching and mezzotint with hand coloring
DV 2770, B 102
176 x 231, 191 x 245
Bibliothèque nationale, Qb1 4 août 1789
[M99036]

NUIT DU 4 AU 5 AOÛT 1789
OU LE DÉLIRE PATRIOTIQUE.

29

In this print four citizens, armed with flails, destroy swords, shields, armor, and bishops' miters, emblems of the aristocracy and clergy. Their patriotic fury has been inspired by the legislative reforms of 4-5 August 1789. On those nights, in response to the crisis created by recent peasant insurrections, the National Assembly voted to abolish feudalism, including tax exemptions, seigneurial rights, and the entire system of privileges that sustained the Old Regime.

In a mood characterized at the time as one of "drunkeness" and "delirium," speaker after speaker ascended the Assembly podium and with great emotion described the horrors of feudalism; each man either offered to sacrifice his own privileges or proposed reforms (Scott and Rothaus, p. 408). When the session broke up at two in the morning on 5 August, the privilege-based system of the ancien régime had been transformed into one based on the equality of the three orders.

30. ANONYMOUS
French
*Le Temps passé les plus utiles etoient foulés
aux pieds (In the Past the Most Useful Were
Trampled under Foot)*, 1789
Etching with hand coloring on blue paper
DV 2786
186 x 245, 209 x 263
Bibliothèque nationale, Qb1 4 août 1789
[M99024]

31. ANONYMOUS
French
*Le Temps present veut que chacun suporte le
grand fardeau &c (In These Times Everyone
Must Bear the Great Burden Etc.)*, 1789
Etching with hand coloring on blue paper
DV 2788, [B 84]
185 x 244, 209 x 265
Bibliothèque nationale, Qb1 4 août 1789
[M99054]

The first image reproduced here (cat. no. 30) represents the ancient régime and shows the aristocracy and the clergy crushing the Third Estate under the weight of taxes and the national debt (the nobility and clergy were exempt from this oppressive burden as a result of their privileged positions). The second image (cat. no. 31), however, shows the three estates bearing the burden together, carrying it forward into the future. The latter is an optimistic view of the new political order following the legislative reforms of 4-5 August 1789 (cat. no. 29), yet it contains signs of trouble or possibly a warning. The aristocrat on the left looks back at a severed tree — a sign of the violence that initiated the reforms — while the clergyman

appears less than pleased with his new role. Subsequent caricatures would show members of the Third Estate subjecting the aristocracy and clergy to the humiliation they themselves had suffered earlier (cat. nos. 38, 39).

Le temps present veut que chacun suporte le grand Fardeau &c

31

32. LETOURMY
French, active ca. 1791
*Tableaux mémorables qui ont donné lieu à la
Révolution (Memorable Scenes That Gave
Rise to the Revolution)*, 1791
Woodcut with hand coloring
545 x 736 (sheet)
Bibliothèque nationale, Qb1 août 1789

This grand, hand-colored woodcut is evidence of the widespread commerce in and popularity of images representing memorable moments from the early days of the Revolution. It reproduces four individual prints included in this exhibition (cat. nos. 27, 29, 30, 31), presenting them in a narrative order. In the upper left-hand corner, the aristocracy and the clergy are shown crushing the Third Estate under the weight of taxes and the national debt. To the right, the man of the Third Estate breaks his chains and awakens to his power, just as the Bastille is being destroyed behind him. Below, on the left, four members of the Third Estate destroy emblems of the feudal system. The fourth image shows the three orders equally bearing the burden of the past forward into the future of the new France.

Significantly, this woodcut was produced in Orléans and thus documents the dissemination of Parisian revolutionary images to the provinces (p. 44). Images such as this one sought to give

Le temps passé les plus utiles etoient foulés aux pieds

30

dans le temps passé foulée aux pieds le tiers | TAILLE IMPOTS-CORVÉE 1 | les plus utille étoient etat portoit tout le fardeau

ils y a trop longtemps de mes ennemis je veux | REVEIL DU TIER-ETAT 2 | que je vis sous loppression enfin brisser mes fers

lanoblesse est abolie pour comte marquis baron chevalier AORLEANS CHEZ | SUPRESSION DES ARMOIRIE 3 | toujours les titres de prince duc de monseigneur sont suprimés LE TOURMI

le temps present veut que fardeau des impots | DETTE NATIONAL 4 | chaqun suporte legrand de la france

32

order and legitimacy to the Revolution and to suggest that there was a natural progression in its events. This print is thus an early visual history of the Revolution.

Le souhait accompli.
V'là comme j'avions toujours désiré que ça fut.

33. ANONYMOUS
French
Le Souhait accompli / V'là comme j'avions toujours désiré que ça fut (The Granted Wish / That's How I Always Wanted It to Be), 1789
Etching with hand coloring on blue paper
DV 2056, B 87
180 x 155, 241 x 161
Bibliothèque nationale, Qb1 4 août 1789
[M98997]

A nobleman, a clergyman, and a member of the Third Estate embrace as they trample and overcome their respective limitations in order to work together as a united nation. The aristocracy sup-

33

presses its pride; the clergy, its privileges; and the Third Estate, its hatred for the other orders. It is an image of short-lived harmony, however, as subsequent caricatures reveal (cat. nos. 42, 44, 45).

34. ANONYMOUS
French
Tôt tôt tôt / battez chaud / tôt tôt tôt / bon courrage / il faut avoir coeur a l'ouvrage
(Soon Soon Soon / Beat the Iron While It's Hot / Soon Soon Soon / Have Courage / Our Heart Must Be in Our Work), 1789
Etching with hand coloring on blue paper
DV 2072
186 x 181, 188 x 184
Bibliothèque nationale, Qb1 25 août 1789
[M99139]

In this image the nobility and clergy join with a blacksmith from the Third Estate to forge a constitution for the new government based upon equality. Drawn up by the National Assembly beginning in July 1789, the constitution would not be accepted until September 1791, more than two years after the legislative reforms of 4-5 August 1789. Significantly, the forging of the constitution recalls the Third Estate's destruction of the symbols of feudalism represented in *Nuit du 4 au 5 août 1789* (cat. no. 29), thus acknowledging the August reforms as the basis of the new constitutional order.

34

35. ANONYMOUS
French
A bas les impiots (Down with Taxes), 1789
Etching with hand coloring on blue paper
DV 2839, H 10593, B 100
223 x 289, 235 x 299
Bibliothèque nationale, Qb1 4 août 1789
[M99041]

35

Prior to the Revolution, in addition to tithes to support the church and other feudal dues and obligations, peasants had to pay a vast array of government taxes, including those on property, income, and salt. In this image, which recalls allegories representing the destruction of the Hydra of despotism (cat. nos. 25, 26), two members of the Third Estate kill a serpent symbolic of taxation. The cutting off of its many heads is a reference to the form that popular violence assumed in the early days of the Revolution.

36. ANONYMOUS
French
A faut espérer q'eu jeu la finira ben tôt
(I've Got to Hope I'll Be Done Soon), 1789
Etching with hand coloring on blue paper
DV 2793, B 3
193 x 137, 251 x 164
Bibliothèque nationale, Qb1 mai 1789
[M98369]

37. ANONYMOUS
French
Je les donne au diable / de bon coeur / Extrait
d'un auteur patriotique (I Give Them to the
Devil / Gladly / Extract from a Patriotic
Author), 1789
Etching with hand coloring on blue paper
DV 2790, B 19
193 x 137, 240 x 158
Bibliothèque nationale, Qb1 mai 1789
[M98373]

38. ANONYMOUS
French
Vive le roi, vive la nation / j'savois ben qu'jau-
rions not tour (Long Live the King, Long Live
the Nation / I Knew Our Turn Would Come),
1789
Etching with hand coloring on blue paper
DV 2796
230 x 179, 278 x 208
Bibliothèque nationale, Qb1 4 août 1789
[M99061]

39. ANONYMOUS
French
Vive le roi, vive la nation / j'savois ben qu'jau-
rions not tour (Long Live the King, Long Live
the Nation / I Knew Our Turn Would Come),
1789
Etching with hand coloring on blue paper
DV 2797
230 x 175, 275 x 202
Bibliothèque nationale, Qb1 4 août 1789
[M99060]

A FAUT ESPERER Q'EU JEU LA FINIRA BEN TOT.
l'auteur en Campagne Ap. 1780.

36

In the first pair of images (cat. nos. 36, 37), the inequities of the ancien régime are represented by a
man and woman of the Third Estate who literally
support the nobility and clergy. In the first print
(cat. no. 36), the pockets of the privileged orders are
brimming with the taxes, tithes, and pensions paid
by the weary peasant, whose meager harvest is consumed by rabbits and birds. Similarly, in catalogue
number 37, a simple woman of the Third Estate
bears upon her back representatives of the other
orders, who smile smuggly, unconcerned with her
toil.

The tables are turned, however, in the subsequent prints. Following the abolition of feudalism,
the Third Estate is supported by the nobility and
clergy (cat. nos. 38, 39). In the first of these images,
the male peasant, who has killed one of the scav-
enging rabbits, carries messages of peace and con-
cord and is armed with a sword to enforce the new
order and protect the nation. The abbé carries the
scales of justice which balance equality and liberty
with the lightened load of the people. In the female
version of this image (cat. no. 39), the rosary carried

Je les donne au Diable
de bon cœur
Extrait d'un Auteur Patriotique

37

by the abbess seems almost to bind her hands. She leads a noblewoman, who must now bear the weight of the woman of the Third Estate suckling a child of the new France.

The inscriptions on the latter two prints — "Long live the king, long live the nation"—suggest that monarchy is still compatible with liberty and the new democratic order, but, at the same time, stress that the king's powers are not greater than those of the people.

Vive le Roi, Vive la Nation.

Isavois ben Qu'aurions not tour.

39

J.SAVOIS BEN QU'AURIONS NOT TOUR.

38

40. ANONYMOUS
French
J'suis du tiers-état (I'm from the Third Estate),
1789
Etching, mezzotint, and stipple on blue
paper
DV 2024
180 x 118, 213 x 136
Bibliothèque nationale, Qb1 5 mai 1789
[M98361]

As if answering the question posed by the Abbé
Sieyès' pamphlet *What is the Third Estate?*, a jocular cobbler proudly toasts the achievement of his
order. Derived from an image of a cobbler and a
peasant woman, the simplicity and directness of
this print is far removed from the solemn dignity of
official portraiture and suggests rather an obvious
delight in newly won freedoms. The informality of
the figure's pose stands in marked contrast to the
awkwardness that characterizes a representation of
Louis XVI (cat. no. 66), who was forced to utter a
similar toast in 1792, following the *journée*, or
demonstration, of 20 June.

J'suis du Tiers-état.

41. ANONYMOUS
French
Bon, nous voila d'accord (Good, We Agree), 1789
Etching with hand coloring on blue paper
DV 2051, [B 78]
143 x 136 (sheet)
Bibliothèque nationale, Qb1 4 août 1789
[M99000]

Bon, nous voila d'accord.

41

Recalling catalogue number 33, this caricature
ostensibly represents the unity of the three orders.
Yet there is a tension in this print that is not evident
in the earlier image. There, the three orders
appeared to have rushed together in a mutually
supportive embrace, each man staring expectantly
into the eyes of the other. Here, although the figures act in concert, their postures are uneasy and
their eyes filled with suspicion. The clergy and
nobility look to each other for support, isolating the
Third Estate who casts his eye upon the smug
cleric whose horn will turn into a writhing snake in
a later caricature of Abbé Maury (cat. no. 56). In a
subsequent print, *Le Noble Pas de deux* (cat. no. 42),
the man of the Third Estate will make the other
orders dance to his tune; while, in another (cat. no.
43), he will fiddle as the clergy and nobility burn
in hell.

40

42. ANONYMOUS
French
Le Noble Pas de deux (The Noble Pas de deux),
1789
Etching with hand coloring on blue paper
DV 2016, B 20
171 X 233, 210 X 242
Bibliothèque nationale, Qb1 2 novembre 1789
[M99549]

42

A nobleman gives his hand to an abbé, who grimaces as he dances to the tune of a violinist in the uniform of the Gardes françaises (the former ceremonial regiment of the royal household troops, which joined the cause of the Third Estate).

On 2 November 1789 the Constituent Assembly decreed that all property owned by the church be placed at the disposal of the nation. Prior to that time, a considerable part of the clergy's wealth was derived from rents collected from its landholdings. The abbé's grimace and the inscription below the image indicate the clergy's unwillingness to "dance" with goodwill and in accord with others in the name of liberty.

This image should be compared with earlier prints which represented equal relations among the three orders (cat. no. 33). By this time, the emphasis on equality had given way to representations suggesting the preeminence of the Third Estate.

43. ANONYMOUS
French
Francs et généreux sans détour / les François inápreciables . . . (Truly Gallant and Brave / the Invaluable French . . .), 1790
Etching with hand coloring on blue paper
DV 3654, B 158
159 X 270, 188 X 289
Bibliothèque nationale, Qb1 19 juin 1790
[M100043]

As in the previous two caricatures, the Third Estate is depicted playing the violin in the company of representatives of the other orders. Only here, he seems to have used his instrument as a weapon for driving the nobility and clergy into hell, literally fiddling while they burn.

The musical metaphor is a particularly flexible one that can suggest harmony (cat. no. 41), authority (cat. no. 42), or, as in this print, potentially destructive power. In addition, the association of the Third Estate with the violin recalls the powerful and popular rhythms of that instrument, just as members of the clergy are connected with the serpent-shaped, and often bellicose, horn (cat. no. 56), and the nobility with the more delicate and refined reed instruments (cat. no. 41).

The image of the nobility and clergy dragged into hell by winged devils and assorted monsters evokes numerous other prerevolutionary, as well as revolutionary, caricatures (cat. nos. 2, 63). It derives ultimately from Reformation political prints, such as *The Fall of the Pope into Hell* from the *Passional Christi und Antichristi* designed by Lucas Cranach the Elder and published in 1521 (Hollstein, no. 66z). It is a device that turned the threat of damnation against the very institutions that had often used it to subjugate others.

Francs et généreux sans détour
Les François inapreciables ;

De bon cœur donnent chaque jour,
Les aristocrates aux Diables.

43

44. ANONYMOUS
French
*Patience Margot j'auront ben-tot 3 fois 8
(Patience Margot I'll Soon Have Three
Times Eight)*, 1789
Etching with hand coloring on blue paper
DV 2066, B 88
187 x 174, 200 x 179
Bibliothèque nationale, Qb1 4 août 1789
[M98980]

The harmony of the three orders is questioned in this forceful image drawn by the unknown, but obviously competent, artist who has signed his work A. P. (compare cat. no. 46). A poor cobbler calls out to his wife not to worry for better times lie ahead. The woman holds symbols of the three orders in her hands, as if each played an equal part in a nourishing meal. Yet it is clear that the three foodstuffs are not equal. The clergy is symbolized by a *cruche*, or pitcher, of wine. While this could evoke the Holy Communion, it also suggests drunkeness, and in common parlance, *cruche* could be used to mean a dolt or a dunce. The nobility is represented by a cut of meat suspended by a

PATIENCE MARGOT JAURONT BEN-TOT 3 FOIS 8.

44

rope; this may be intended to suggest a bestial nature. The Third Estate, however, is embodied in the crucial loaf of bread, the staff of life for which the women of Paris marched to Versailles.

To the right a cat plays with a mouse on a table from which hangs a sheet of paper listing the price of bread, meat, and wine as eight *sous* each. The strength of the cobbler's arms and his fierce expression lend a threatening air to his promise of good times to come. The Third Estate, this print suggests, will emerge as the dominant order, the cat who will ultimately destroy the mouse.

45. ANONYMOUS
French
Cette Fois ci, la justice est du côté du plus fort
(This Time, Justice Sides with the Strongest),
1789
Etching with hand coloring
DV 2783, B 41
193 x 239 (sheet)
Bibliothèque nationale, 4 août 1789
[M98993]

This image clearly marks the transition in the political power of the Third Estate. Often represented as having been a lower order suppressed by the nobility and clergy (cat. no. 30), it had also been depicted as sharing the burdens of the new nation with the other two groups (cat. no. 31). In this print, however, the Third Estate, with Justice tipping the scale in its favor, controls the fates of the nobles and churchmen, holding them effectively hostage. The now powerful Third Estate, backed by the sword of Justice and armed with a rifle signifying insurrection, has brought about a complete reversal of the political orders.

45

46. ANONYMOUS
French
Ma Finte pour ce coup cy y nen reviendrons
jamais (Upon My Word They'll Never Survive
This Blow), 1790
Etching with hand coloring
DV 1521
177 x 254, 190 x 266
Bibliothèque nationale, Qb1 19 juin 1790
[M10039]

46

In this crudely executed but wittily conceived image by the caricaturist who signed himself A. P. (compare cat. no. 44), a soldier of the Gardes françaises, formerly a royal regiment, squats on the rue de la Liberté and defecates on the nobility and clergy as they are swept by in the gutter along with the other sewage. To the right, wearing the revolutionary cockade and applauding the soldier, is a typical figure of the Third Estate. The buildings in the background bear signs indicating the state to which the nobility and clergy have been reduced: "Property of the clergy for sale" and "Dead end of the aristocrats." According to de Vinck, decorating the wall in the center are the heads of Jacques de Flesselles, the Marquis de Launay, and de Losme de Salbray, all massacred on 14 July; J. F. Foulon de Doué, and Bertier de Sauvigny, killed 23 July; Deshuttes and Varicourt, bodyguards at Versailles, murdered in the *journée*, or demonstration, of 6 October; and the baker François, killed 21 October. At the end of the cul-de-sac the Hôtel de Broglie, home of the Duc de Broglie, an émigré, is for sale.

47. ANONYMOUS
French
Untitled, 1789
Etching with hand coloring on blue paper
350 x 247 (sheet)
Bibliothèque nationale, Qb1 4 août 1789
[M99003]

An anthology of some of the most popular images produced during the early days of the Revolution, this print incorporates several examples included in the present exhibition (cat. nos. 33, 34, 36, 38, 44). Unlike another early visual history of the Revolution that incorporates a number of popular prints (cat. no. 32), however, the arrangement of the individual images in this instance is neither chronological nor narrative. Rather, it is unified thematically and focuses on the relations between the three estates. The taking of the Bastille — the first sign of the growing insurrection of the Third Estate — is represented by two images in the lower left-hand corner; the tense and temporary equality that came to exist among the three orders, by six images scattered across the print; and the eventual triumph of the Third Estate, by the remaining eight randomly ordered images. The inclusion of these particular prints is evidence of their high visibility during this period and of the role that they played in forming the revolutionary self-image.

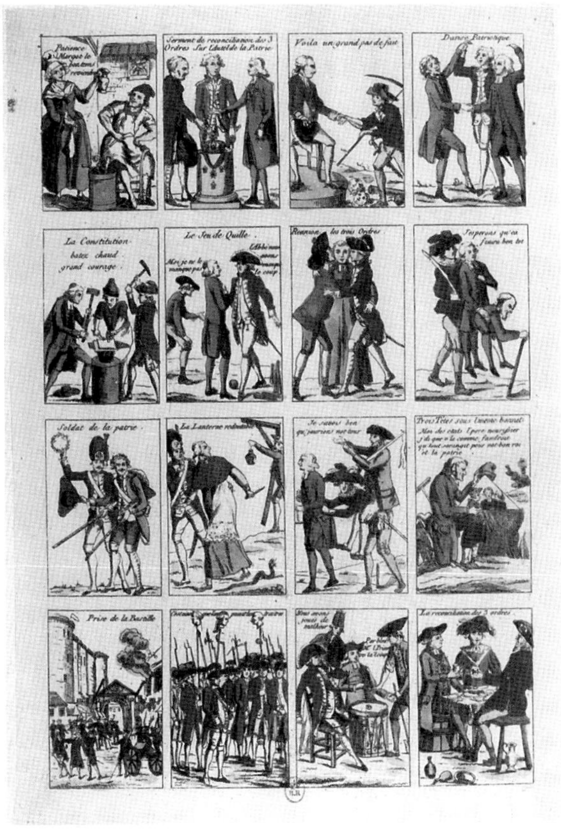

47

On 4 August 1789 the Constituent Assembly abolished feudalism and certain seigneurial rights. The following day, it appointed an ecclesiastical committee to reorganize the French church on the basis of newly proclaimed social and political principles. The committee's report was presented to the Assembly in May 1790. Two months later it was adopted as the Civil Constitution of the Clergy and completely reorganized the ecclesiastical structure. Dioceses were reduced in number, one to each governmental department; bishops were to be elected, like other departmental officers, by taxpaying citizens; and the clergy was to be salaried and to perform its services without charge.

On 27 November 1790 the Assembly required all clergy in public service to take an oath in support of the Civil Constitution. Large numbers of clergymen refused, however, and they were encouraged to do so by Pius vi in two papal briefs published in March and April 1791. In these the pope condemned not only the Civil Constitution, but also the revolutionary government's support of religious toleration, freedom of the press, and human equality, all of which he considered contrary to the principles of the church.

The pope's emissary and advisor on the situation in France was the Abbé Maury, the son of a cobbler, who had risen to prominence as an orator and deputy, first to the Estates General and then to the Assembly. Maury emigrated late in 1791 and was soon after sent by Pius vi as papal nuncio to Frankfurt, where the imperial electors were meeting to choose the successor to the Holy Roman Emperor Leopold ii, brother of Marie-Antoinette. Maury's appointment was a clear signal to the French revolutionaries that the pope was now wholly committed to the extinction of their regime. It also provided French caricaturists with a special target. For, although they had been lampooning the clergy's general discomfort with the Civil Constitution since its introduction in 1790, they did not have a prominent figure on which to concentrate. The Abbé Maury became that figure, and as he had betrayed his plebeian origins for personal gain, he was especially disliked. He represented not only the stubborness of the clergy, but the very real threat of counterrevolution.

48. Anonymous
French
Le Degraisseur patriote (The Patriotic Fat Remover), 1789
Etching with hand coloring
DV 3055, [B 126]
137 X 229, 171 X 252
Bibliothèque nationale, Qb1 2 novembre 1789
[M99607]

49. Anonymous
French
L'Abbé d'autre-fois — L'Abbé d'aujourd'hui (The Priest of Yesterday — The Priest of Today), 1789
Etching with hand coloring
DV 3058, [B 343]
206 x 147 (sheet)
Bibliothèque nationale, Qb1 2 novembre 1789
[M99585]

As the first of a series of ecclesiastical reforms intended to reorganize the church according to the principles of equality, the Constituent Assembly

48

decreed the confiscation of church property on 2 November 1789. This gave rise to numerous caricatures making fun of the recently reduced status of the clergy. In *Le Degraisseur patriote* (cat. no. 48) a National Guardsman and a representative of the Third Estate lead a corpulent and richly dressed priest toward a press wherein a fellow clergyman is forced to disgorge his wealth. To the right, two plain, skeletal figures, a monk and a priest, walk away in despair, having already experienced the effects of the Assembly's decree.

L'Abbé d'Autre-fois, | *L'Abbé d'Aujourd'hui*.

49

This same subject is given a more economical treatment in *L'Abbé d'autre-fois — L'Abbé d'aujourd'hui* (cat. no. 49), as an elegantly robed, porcine "priest of yesterday" is contrasted with a thin, disgruntled "priest of today." The reduction in status is humorously reinforced by the distance maintained between each clergyman's hands. The priest of today is capable of joining his hands, as in prayer, and is thus clearly more suited to performing the functions of his office.

50. Anonymous
  French
  Mgr après une si longue et si grosse indigestion, les medecins de la nation vous ordonnent la diette (Monsignor after Such a Long and Severe Indigestion, the Nation's Doctors Prescribe a Diet), 1789
  Etching with hand coloring
  DV 3052
  159 x 228, 183 x 242
  Bibliothèque nationale, Qb1 2 novembre 1789
  [M99617]

51. Anonymous
  French
  Ah! Monseigneur! on veut donc nous faire rendre tout / Je vous avait cependant conseillé en jouant de faire atout (Ah! Monsignor! It Seems That They Want Us to Give Everything Back / Yet While in the Game I Had Advised You to Play Trumps), 1789
  Etching with hand coloring
  DV 3075
  130 x 209, 146 x 221
  Bibliothèque nationale, Qb1 2 novembre 1789
  [M99614]

Further variations on the subject of catalogue numbers 48 and 49, these caricatures lampoon the new status of the clergy following the confiscation of church property as decreed on 2 November 1789. In the first image (cat. no. 50), a bishop of the

Mgr après une si longue et si grosse Indigestion, les Medecins de la Nation vous ordonnent la Diette.

50

ancien régime is assisted by a representative of the Third Estate and by other "doctors of the nation" as he expels the benefices and canonries that he had consumed before the Revolution. In the second print (cat. no. 51), a priest is similarly relieved of his privileges, however, this time it is via an enema administered by an apothecary of the Third Estate; the unwilling clergyman is shown bewailing his situation to a member of the nobility.

The joke in both prints, as in catalogue numbers 48 and 49, is the representation of the clergy as corpulent figures with voracious appetites for personal gain. In these prints, however, unlike the previous pair, the clergymen are placed in extremely humiliating situations. In the first example, a bishop is shown vomiting as a result of a strict diet forced upon him by his new secular superiors, while in the second, a priest is shown uncontrolla-

Ah' Monseigneur; on veut bien nous faire rendre tout.
Je vous avait cependant conseillé en Jouant de faire Atout.

51

bly relieving himself as a result of the laxative powers of the legislative clyster. More than simply poking fun at the diminished status of the clergy during the Revolution, these caricatures violently attack members of the religious community and expose them to public embarrassment of the crudest kind.

52. ANONYMOUS
French
Ils ne mont laisse que deux chicots (They Only Left Me Two Bad Teeth), 1789
Etching with hand coloring
DV 3073
223 x 172, 267 x 198
Bibliothèque nationale, Qb1 2 novembre 1789
[M99601]

Old, impoverished, and leaning on a cane, a near-toothless priest bemoans his reduced state following the decree of 2 November 1789. This print is directly related to a group of caricatures depicting patriotic "dentists" pulling the teeth of their clerical patients (DV 3066–68) and is more generally connected to the numerous caricatures that represent the diminution of the clergy's status in French society as a form of physical loss (cat. nos. 48–51). In this case, the clergyman has been deprived of his wealth, nobility, and political bite.

Despite the numerous and increasingly aggressive caricatures depicting impoverished churchmen, the majority of the clergy were only moderately affected by the Assembly's decree. In fact, the decree provided for the maintenance of the clergy in an honorable manner, with the state furnishing facilities for worship and assistance to the poor (formerly responsiblities undertaken by

the priests themselves). *Curés,* or parish priests, were given an annual stipend of 1,200 *livres,* an improvement over the 750 *livres* per annum dispensed under the ancien régime; members of the higher clergy made substantially more than this (Stewart, p. 179). Still, the stipends did not match the former incomes of the higher clergy, many of whom had made several thousand *livres* per annum in tithe payments and income from property. The caricatures reproduced in this section, therefore, represent a more aggressive assault on the clergy than that posed by the actual reforms.

Ils ne mont laisse que deux Chicots

52

53. ANONYMOUS
French
Prêtre aristocrate / fuyant le serment civique (Aristocratic Priest / Fleeing the Oath of Allegiance), 1790
Etching and mezzotint, background printed in red
H 10857
102 x 82 (oval), 133 x 96
Bibliothèque nationale, Qb1 27 novembre 1790
[M100400]

54. ANONYMOUS
French
Prêtre patriote / prêtant de bonne foi le ser-
ment civique (Patriotic Priest / Taking in Good
Faith the Oath of Allegiance), 1790
Etching and mezzotint, background printed
in red
H 10858
107 x 87 (oval), 134 x 97
Bibliothèque nationale, Qb1 27 novembre 1790
[M100401]

On 27 November 1790 the Constituent Assembly demanded that all priests swear an oath to the
Civil Constitution of the Clergy, which had been
adopted in July of that year. This measure effectively transferred authority over the French church
from Rome and the pope to Paris and the revolutionary government. Only seven bishops took the
oath, however, and members of the parish clergy,
although initially supportive of the Revolution,
were equally divided over the issue.

Acceptance or rejection of the oath varied
widely according to geographical region and within
the various social strata of the church. Many members of the lower clergy welcomed the oath as it
abolished long-established hierarchies and hence

PRETRE PATRIOTE
prêtant de bonne foi le serment Civique.

54

promised to improve their lot. Even prior to the
Revolution, parish priests in certain regions, the
Dauphiné for example, had mobilized to confront
inequities within the church, rejecting higher
ecclesiastical authority in favor of control by the
state.

These prints contrast the priest of the ancien
régime, who stubbornly refuses to take the oath,
with the new patriotic priest who respects his duty
to the government and the Revolution. The
skeleton-like aristocratic clergyman (cat. no. 53),
newly deprived of his wealth and privileges, is left
to wander aimlessly. In contrast, the patriotic priest
(cat. no. 54) gladly pledges his loyalty to the new
national church and renounces the emblems of the
old order and higher clergy.

PRETRE ARISTOCRATE
fuyant le serment Civique.

53

55. ANONYMOUS
French
Retour de l'Abbé M...chez son pere (Return of Abbé M...to His Father's House), 1790
Etching with hand coloring on blue paper
DV 1999, B 434*bis*
270 x 184, 300 x 195
Bibliothèque nationale, Qb1 22 janvier 1790
[M99692]

Abbé Jean Siffrein Maury, the son of a provincial cobbler, rose to prominence as a vehement defender of aristocratic privilege, first as a deputy to the Estates General and then to the National Assembly. In so doing, he rejected his origins, turning his back on the petite bourgeoisie. For this, he was particularly despised by the revolutionaries and came to represent the peculiar position of the clergy, which, as a political order, included both aristocrats and members of the Third Estate. Here the Abbé Maury is shown being beaten by his father and scolded for having become an aristocrat, a cruel twist on the theme of the prodigal son.

56. ANONYMOUS
French
La Rage soufle par sa bouche et l'enfer est dans son coeur (Rage Blows through His Mouth and Hell Is in His Heart), 1790
Etching with hand coloring
DV 1984
255 x 184 (sheet)
Bibliothèque nationale, Qb1 22 janvier 1790
[M99688]

La Rage soufle par sa bouche et l'Enfer est dans son Cœur.

56

Abbé Maury was famous for the outspoken and vigorous speeches opposing the Civil Constitution of the Clergy that he delivered in the Assembly. Here he is shown clutching a snake in his left hand and speaking the words of the devil through the serpent of evil—using a second snake as if it were a horn. (An early, sinuously curved, wind instrument was called a *serpent*.) Behind the abbé, appearing startled by his bellicose preaching, a hen protects her eggs from the threat presented by the snakes; the cluster of eggs possibly represents the fraternity that will characterize the new French nation.

55

57. ANONYMOUS
French
L'Abbé M…chassé des enfers (Abbé M…
Expelled from Hell), 1790
Etching with hand coloring
DV 2003, B 431*bis*
201 x 165 (oval), 253 x 209
Bibliothèque nationale, Qb1 22 janvier 1790
[M99683]
(Not in exhibition)

Wearing only his ecclesiastical collar as a kind of loincloth, a bald Abbé Maury is chased from hell by two fire-breathing devils, while in the background two priests desperately gesture, as if to warn him. As implied by the caption, the Abbé cannot be accepted into hell because, in addition to incurring the wrath of the revolutionaries, he also wrought discord among his fellow clerics. Maury's relentless support of royalist principles and aristocratic privileges kept the clergy in the spotlight of political controversy throughout the early years of the Revolution.

L'Abbé M…. Chassé des Enfers .

Impie Errant, Tourment des humains proscrit de Dieu et chassé des Enfers
Fuit Combustible Heretique ne vient plus ici mettre la Discorde entre tes Confreres .

57

58. ANONYMOUS
French
Les Deux Diables en fureur (The Two
Infuriated Devils), 1790
Etching with hand coloring
DV 1989, B 439
375 x 246, 412 x 288
Bibliothèque nationale, Qb1 13 avril 1790
[M99878]

Les deux Diables en fureur

Le 13 Avril 1790 deux Diables Volant

58

Two of the most outspoken opponents of the National Assembly's refusal to recognize Catholicism as the state religion were the Abbé Maury and Jean-Jacques d'Eprémesnil. D'Eprémesnil, former deputy of the nobility to the Estates General, was also a staunch supporter of the rights and privileges of the clergy under the ancien régime. Both men were well-known for their biting tirades against the revolutionaries. They are shown here being defecated by winged devils, one feet first and the other head first. The poem below the image describes the humiliating scene:

> On 13 April 1790 two flying devils
> Made a bet
> Who would shit most foul
> On human nature
> One shat the Abbé M…y
> The other paled
> And dropped D'E…y
> And his entire clique

Il ne sçait sur quel pied Danser.

Danse Aristocrate

59

59. ANONYMOUS
French
Danse aristocrate (Dance Aristocrat), 1790
Etching with hand coloring on blue paper
DV 1991, B 429
216 x 310 (sheet)
Bibliothèque nationale, Qb1 13 avril 1790
[M99890]

As if entertaining the aristocrats to the left and
the National Guardsman and the citizens to the
right, the Abbé Maury walks a tightrope between
them. He is assisted by a Punchinello-like devil and
compelled by the tune played on the violin of the
Third Estate. Provocative and economical, the caricature depicts the precarious position of Maury,
who, as in early images where the nobility and the
clergy dance to the tune of of the Third Estate (cat.
no. 42), is portrayed as a puppet of others.

60. ANONYMOUS
French
*M^{rs}. les Noirs lancent leur venin anti-
constitutionel contre les decrets de l'auguste /
Assemblée nationale sur l'abolition des
pouvoirs temporels du clergé. / M^{rs}. les
Evèques du côté gauche prononcent le ser-
ment civique décreté le 27 9bre / etc. (Mssrs. the
Noirs Spew Their Anti-Constitutional Venom
at the Decrees of the Illustrious / National
Assembly upon the Abolition of the Temporal
Powers of the Clergy. / The Bishops on the
Left Take the Oath of Allegiance Decreed on
27 November / etc.)*, 1790
Etching with hand coloring
DV 3477, B 340
213 x 330, 239 x 348
Bibliothèque nationale, Qb1 27 novembre 1790
[M100393]

At right, the bishops Talleyrand-Périgord of
Autun and Jean-Baptiste Joseph Gobel of Paris take
the oath to the Civil Constitution of the Clergy
beneath a radiant triangle, which is at once a secular sign of equality and a holy symbol of the

60

The debate between rival factions of the clergy over whether to take the oath required by the Civil Constitution is here portrayed as a struggle between good and evil. Accompanied by bats, owls, and other attributes of darkness and deceit, the Noirs attempt to speak with serpent tongues but are silenced by the spiritual light of the new order of reason, which strikes with the force of lightning and the authority of the Holy Spirit.

Trinity. Their calm and noble postures place them in sharp contrast to the clergy at the left, who, as Noirs (a conservative faction within the Assembly), favor the institutions of the ancien régime and oppose the Civil Constitution. Among the Noirs are the Archbishop Juigné of Paris; the Abbé Royou, who published the royalist newspaper *Les Amis du roi*; and the Abbé Maury, who, as in many other caricatures (cat. nos. 55–59), is signaled out for special abuse.

61. ANONYMOUS
French
Reponce à l'auteur de la chronique, qui appelle bombe, la bulle du pape (Reply to the Author of the Chronicle, Who Calls the Papal Brief a Bomb), 1791
Etching with hand coloring on blue paper
DV 3441, B 254
276 x 418, 331 x 427
Bibliothèque nationale, Qb1 4 mai 1791
[M100605]

61

In March and April 1791, Pius VI issued two papal briefs that formalized the schism within the church over the revolutionary government's requirement that French priests take an oath of loyalty to the Civil Constitution of the Clergy. In this satire, the pope is shown seated on his throne issuing briefs (*bulles* in French) by blowing bubbles (also *bulles*), which are immediately popped by an allegorical figure of France. Drawing on a conceit popular in French caricature, the pope's authority is lampooned as fragile and insubstantial.

The inscription below emphasizes the role played by good citizens and good Christians in producing the print; thus, it was intended to act as a propagandistic image in support of the good French clergy who accepted the authority of the revolutionary government over that of Rome.

62. ANONYMOUS
French
Bref du pape en 1791 (The Papal Brief in 1791),
1791
Etching with hand coloring
DV 3452, B 255
210 x 187, 265 x 218
Bibliothèque nationale, Qb1 4 mai 1791
[M100617]

Sneering, a member of the Third Estate finds an appropriate use for the papal bulls of 1791, which bear the signatures of Abbé Royou, publisher of the royalist newspaper *Les Amis du roi,* and Abbé Juigné, the archbishop of Paris. In the background Pius VI is burned in effigy—an event that actually occurred in the garden of the Palais-Royal on 6 April 1791—while a magpie, or *pie* in french, preceded by the numerals VI, flies overhead.

Two ecclesiastics, identified by de Vinck as the Abbé Royou and the Cardinal de La Rochefoucauld, observe the disrespectful citizen through a telescope. Such scatological imagery was common in revolutionary caricatures (compare cat. nos. 46, 51, 58, 114, 115), and its assault on refined taste and the pictorial conventions of decorum, carried a direct challenge to authority.

BRÉF. DU. PAPE. EN. 1791.

62

63. ANONYMOUS
French
Arrivée du pape aux enfers (Arrival of the Pope in Hell), 1791
Etching with hand coloring
DV 3464, B 265
158 x 210, 192 x 228
Bibliothèque nationale, Qb1 4 mai 1791
[M100623]

In contrast to the caricature of Abbé Maury driven from hell (cat. no. 57), Pope Pius VI is here welcomed by devils. Taunting and mocking, they inform him that he will be joined by many of his disciples and colleagues and will surely be well grilled for disregarding his sacred obligations and failing to uphold the laws of Saint Peter.

Caricatures directed against the pope and the clergy often raised the specter of eternal damnation (Vovelle, 1986, vol. 2, p. 260), thus turning the tables on religious leaders who frequently used this threat against others. Significantly, the pope was actually burned in effigy in a public demonstration at the Palais-Royal (cat. no. 62).

There are prerevolutionary French precedents for caricatures suggesting that church authorities will burn in hell (cat. no. 2). An even earlier source for this tradition can be found in anti-papal prints of the Reformation, such as *The Fall of the Pope into Hell* in *Passional Christi und Antichristi* (1521) designed by Lucas Cranach the Elder (Hollstein, no. 66z).

Arrivée du Pape aux Enfers

Venez, Venez St Pere vous alle voir bon nombre de vos Confreres, beaucoup de vos diciples et surtout de ceux qui portoit la Crosse et la Mitre doré, ce nétoit pas la coque St Pierre vous avoit recommandé, et pour avoir foulé aux pieds tous les devoirs les plus sacrés vous alle être bien grillé.

63

Born on 23 August 1754, Louis XVI, the grandson of Louis XV, became dauphin in 1765, following the death of his father and two elder brothers. He was married to Marie-Antoinette of Austria at age sixteen and was crowned king in 1774. It soon became obvious that he was ill prepared to deal with the various financial and political crises that he had inherited, and he seems to have lacked a true understanding of the discontent of the Third Estate or the intensity of the forces that led to the Revolution. Marie-Antoinette, whose extravagant personal expenditures and tendency to intrigue fueled gossip concerning her vanity and licentiousness, seems to have been equally uninformed. The queen's involvement in plots to save the monarchy in the face of mounting revolutionary pressure served to deepen the popular suspicion and hatred directed against her.

Following the fall of the Bastille in July 1789, the king's authority was weakened by a series of legislative acts passed by the Constituent Assembly, including the adoption of the Declaration of the Rights of Man on 26 August 1789. Hostile opposition to Louis XVI and the institution of the monarchy mounted over the following year, and in the autumn of 1790, through various emissaries, the king and queen appealed to European monarchs for money and troops to help restore the former power of the French throne.

In late 1790 a plan was conceived whereby the royal family would take refuge near France's eastern frontier under the protection of the Marquis de Bouillé. Montmédy, close to the Luxembourg border, was selected as the rendezvous point with detachments from the émigré army. The king and his family fled Paris on the night of 20–21 June 1791 but were soon recognized, arrested, and returned under military guard. In September the king approved the new constitution, thereby establishing a constitutional monarchy; all along, however, he continued to plead secretly with his European allies for the invasion of France.

In December 1792 it was discovered that on the night of his flight from Paris during the previous year, Louis had left documents in an iron safe in the Palais des Tuileries that declared his opposition to the Revolution, as well as correspondence with foreign powers outlining additional royal intrigues. This new evidence was pivotal in the National Convention's decision to try the king; it compounded the effect of the dramatic flight to Varennes and sub-sequent arrest, turning the tide of opinion against Louis XVI and signaling the end of the monarchy.

The trial of Louis XVI began on 11 December and ended on 7 January 1793. A week later, three questions were put to a roll call in the Convention: Was the king guilty of conspiring against the nation? Should judgment be submitted to the people? And should execution by guillotine be his penalty? On the first question, Louis was declared guilty by a unanimous vote, while the second question was opposed by a strong majority of the Convention's members. On the ultimate issue of the death penalty, 387 members voted affirmative, but a question of reprieve was attached to 26 of the votes. This meant that the death penalty received only 361 unconditional votes, as opposed to 360 negative votes and votes with a reprieve stipulated. A vote on the reprieve was then called, and it was rejected by a vote of 380 to 310. On 21 January 1793, Louis XVI was guillotined.

Following the king's execution, Marie-Antoinette remained imprisoned in the Temple with her family until she was transferred to the Conciergerie in August 1793. Two months later she was brought to trial and charged with secretly communicating with the enemy, supporting the counterrevolutionary activities of the émigrés with large sums of French money, plotting the royal family's attempted escape to Varennes, various acts of salacious behavior, and exerting a malign influence on the king. She was found guilty of treasonous contact with enemies of France and plotting a civil war and was executed on 16 October, nine months after her husband.

LOUIS XVI

64. ANONYMOUS
French
Louis seize (Louis XVI), 1775, after Joseph Boze
Stipple engraving
DV 396
233 x 158, 349 x 238
Bibliothèque nationale, N2, Louis XVI, t.2, 92

65. ANONYMOUS
French
Louis seize (Louis XVI), 1792, after Joseph Boze
Stipple engraving with hand coloring
DV 397
233 x 158, 288 x 174
Bibliothèque nationale, Qb1 20 juin 1792
[M101224]

Executed in 1775 during the early years of Louis XVI's reign, the original version of this engraving (cat. no. 64) is a typical formal portrait of the monarch with a caption noting his title and the dates of his birth, marriage, and coronation. It was engraved

65

after a painting by Joseph Boze (1744–1826), the *peintre monarchique*, who enjoyed an active career at court painting portraits of members of the royal family and their circle.

In the version from the revolutionary period (cat. no. 65), the plate was reworked, and the dignified portrait transformed into a caricature; Louis now wears the Phrygian cap of liberty, which, as noted in the new caption, was presented to the king by the people of France during the *journée*, or demonstration, of 20 June 1792 (see cat. no. 66). His title has also been changed, referring to the Constituent Assembly's decree of 19 October 1789, which proclaimed Louis XVI "king of the French," as opposed to the traditional title of "king of France and Navarre."

64

66. ANONYMOUS

French

Nouveau Pacte de Louis XVI / avec le peuple le 20 juin 1792 l'an 4ᵐᵉ de la liberté (New Pact of Louis XVI / with the People 20 June 1792 the Fourth Year of Liberty), 1792

Etching and mezzotint with hand coloring

DV 4877, H 1180, [B 474]

208 x 141, 238 x 173

Bibliothèque nationale, Qb1 20 juin 1792

[M101233]

On 20 June 1792, the anniversary of the Oath of the Tennis Court and the flight to Varennes, the *sans-culottes* of Paris staged a great demonstration, or *journée*, invading first the Legislative Assembly and then the Palais des Tuileries. Brandishing pikes and wearing red liberty caps, the crowd sought to pressure the king to withdraw his power of veto over the Assembly's decrees and to recall the Girondin ministers that he had dismissed. After gathering in the place du Carrousel, the crowd made its way into the palace where it confronted

Louis XVI with cries of "down with the veto." The king donned the Phrygian cap of liberty and drank to the health of the nation, though he refused either to withdraw the veto or recall the Girondin ministers.

Numerous images record this event, and they range from royalist depictions of *sans-culottes* threatening the dignified royal family to satiric representations of the king. The king is often portrayed as a common man of the people, much in the spirit of representations of members of the Third Estate (cat. no. 40). As Lynn Hunt notes, in her essay in the present catalogue, such representations of the king as a more familiar, accessible figure, as opposed to the regal and distant images of official portraits (cat. no. 64), served to undermine the idea of the God-given role of the monarch as the father of the French people (p. 37).

The humorous portrayal of the king's "new pact" with the French people that is reproduced here bears only a weak "vive la nation," as if muttered under the monarch's breath, and an inscription recording the date of the event. A slight stiffness in Louis's stance could be suggestive of a perceived insincerity in his toast. Variants of this print show more hostile and openly antimonarchical representations of the king. Villeneuve produced a similar version with additional commentary (DV 4878), as well as an image of the king drinking and surrounded by wine bottles — less the good bourgeois than the foolish drunkard dangerous to the survival of the nation.

*Vive
la Nation*

NOUVEAU PACTE DE LOUIS XVI.
avec le Peuple le 20. Juin 1792. l'An 4ᵐᵉ de la liberté.

66

67. ANONYMOUS

French

Le Gargantua du siècle / ou / l'Oracle de la dive bouteille (The Gargantua of the Century; / or, / The Oracle of the Divine Bottle), ca. 1790

Etching with hand coloring on blue paper

DV 3398, B 476

350 x 546, 426 x 577

Bibliothèque nationale, Qb1 16 février 1790

[M99733]

Portrayed as Gargantua, "the famous glutton," a corpulent Louis XVI sits astride a tiny horse, having come to hear the "Oracle of the Divine Bottle" foretell future events. The king is stunned by the words on the tablets that hang on the trees before him: "The yoke of the oppression of France will be opened" and "A people, fully free to win its Liberty." According to the inscription, however, he

LE GARGANTUA DU SIECLE
OU
L'ORACLE DE LA DIVE BOUTEILLE.

67

persists and asks to know the secrets of the bottle. After a frightful boom, the bottle pops its cork and pronounces, "Trinkc," an onomatopoeic pun on *trinque*, meaning "drink" or, in the familiar sense, "to get the worst of it"—certainly not what the monarch had hoped to hear.

By representing the king as Gargantua, this caricature follows a long tradition of portraying the politically powerful as gluttonous giants feeding on the labor and property of their subjects. In this case, the representation is enriched by the many references to the king's drunkeness and by his association with a bevy of clerical birds, who, as the caption tells us, are "very dirty, stinky, conceited, and voracious" (one holds a document bearing the words, "Live for yourself").

Significantly absent from this image is Marie-Antoinette, who, more than the king, was known for capricious spending, ostentation, and self-aggrandizement. Her absence, however, only emphasizes the ridiculous nature of the king, who is alone, cuckolded, and reduced to look for answers in a cracked bottle of mossy champagne. The red-faced Louis, whose horse wears bells to

warn everyone of his approach, has become a foolish and inept clown on whom the crowned figures in the background can no longer depend.

68. ANONYMOUS
French
Le Ci Devant Grand Couvert de Gargantua moderne en famille (The Ci-Devant Great Family Feast of the Modern Gargantua), ca. 1791
Etching with hand coloring on blue paper
B 477
356 x 528, 422 x 549
Bibliothèque nationale, Qb1 18 février 1791
[M100480]

As in the preceding caricature, Louis XVI is portrayed as Gargantua, the gluttonous giant. Only here he is at table, about to eat an entire pig as his subjects struggle to satisfy his appetite for the kingdom's plentiful produce and game. He turns to the

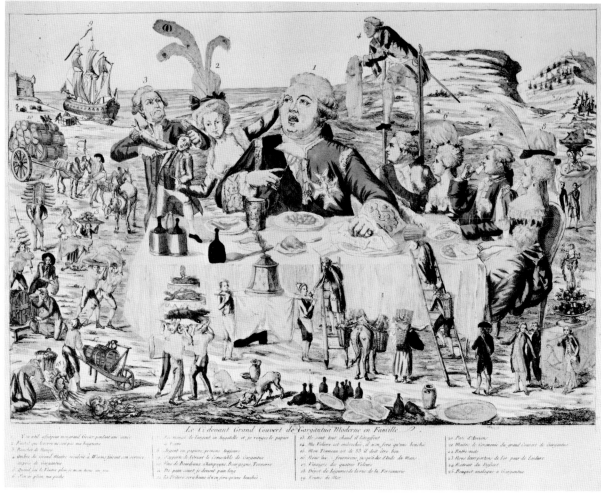

Le Ci devant Grand Couvert de Gargantua Moderne en Famille

68

Marquis de Bouillé (3) and asks if there is enough to fill his great gullet for a year. (Bouillé is identified in the caption as the "Butcher of Nancy" for his role in the violent repression of the mutiny that occurred in that city in 1790; this explains his attack on the neck of the young soldier.) Marie-Antoinette (2) interrupts, however, asking if the blood filling her glass will not also serve as her bath. The implication is that the blood the royal family has sucked from its subjects in the form of goods and currency will lead to its own violent downfall. The fates of the king and his family will, therefore, ultimately be intertwined with that of the young soldier.

MARIE-ANTOINETTE

69. ANONYMOUS
French
Ce Monstre à été trouvé au royaume de Santa Fe au Perou...(This Monster Was Found in the Kingdom of Santa Fe in Peru...), ca. 1784
Etching and engraving
DV 1150
233 x 313, 327 x 365
Bibliothèque nationale, Qb1 1784
[M98135]

70. ANONYMOUS
French
Description de ce monstre unique se saisissant de sa proye...(Description of This Unique Monster Seizing Its Prey...), ca. 1784
Etching
H 10011
213 × 320, 304 × 357
Bibliothèque nationale, Qb1 1784
[M98137]

70

In 1784 the *Courrier de l'Europe* reported the capture of a Chilean monster with a man's face, lion's mane, snake's scales, bull's horns, bat's wings, and two tails (cat. no. 70). Although an obvious hoax intended to attract attention to the newspaper, it also offered scientists an opportunity to test out new theories of sexual reproduction (there were reports at this time that Frederick II had produced

69

centaurs and satyrs through experiments with sodomy [Darnton, 1968, pp. 30–32]). Numerous prints of the *Courrier*'s monster circulated in Paris, making it the talk of the town.

Not long after its advent, the monster became a symbol of Marie-Antoinette and acquired a more feminine appearance, losing its beard and coming to resemble a harpy, a popular characterization of the queen (cat. no. 69; see also DV 1148, 1149, 1151–57, B 532). The detailed description of the beast also became a veiled satire, "This unique monster seizing its prey...emerged during the night to devour the swine, cows, and bulls of the area...its mouth is as wide as its face...it has ears like an ass...[it was brought as a gift] to the royal family...it is hoped that the female will be captured...the species

seems to be that of harpies, heretofore considered legendary."

These prints are but two of many that portrayed the queen as a composite figure (cat. no. 81). One print, entitled *La Panthère autrichienne voué au mépris et à la exécration de la nation française dans sa posterité la plus reculée* (1792), describes her as "this dreadful Messalina, fruit of licentious concubinage...composed of heterogeneous matter, fabricated of many races" and goes on to emphasize her fiery tresses recalling those of Judas, her nose and cheek bloated and made purple by corrupt blood, and her fetid and infected mouth. All such images — some of which are much more subtle than others — were intended to discredit the legitimacy and character of the queen by emphasizing her bestial nature. In this respect, they were part of a long tradition of printed images which began with Wenzel von Olmütz's *Papstesel (Pope-Ass)* of 1523 (p. 21), a Reformation lampoon of Pope Leo X.

71. ANONYMOUS
French
Représentation exacte du grand collier en brillants, des S.'^ Boëhmer et Bassange (Exact Representation of the Famous Diamond Necklace, by MM. Boëhmer and Bassange), ca. 1786
Etching and mezzotint
DV 1046
292 × 226, 327 × 235
Bibliothèque nationale, Qb1 1 août 1785
[M98156]

By 1786, with France beset by famine and the monarchy bankrupt, it was widely believed that "Madame Deficit," as Marie-Antoinette came to

REPRÉSENTATION EXACTE DU GRAND COLLIER EN BRILLANTS ,
DES S.rs BOËHMER ET BASSANGE .

71

be known, had squandered the nation's finances on lavish personal expenditures. The so-called Diamond Necklace Affair focused attention on the queen's pursuit of expensive pleasures and also appealed to the public's delight in her frequently rumored sexual adventures.

The central figures in the scandal were Cardinal Louis-René-Edouard de Rohan, grand almoner of France and former ambassador to Austria, who had long sought favor with the queen for personal gain, and Jeanne de Luy de Saint-Remy de Valois, the comtesse de Lamotte, an adventuress who wished to exploit Rohan's ambitions to her own ends. Feigning to be a confidante of Marie-Antoinette, Lamotte forged letters from the queen which fondly mentioned the cardinal and her increasing affection for him. Intent on extorting money from Rohan, Lamotte began including requests for the queen's favorite charities in the letters; these donations were, of course, retained by the countess. When Rohan expressed his desire to see the queen, Lamotte arranged for a rendezvous in the gardens at Versailles with a prostitute disguised as Marie-Antoinette. After a year of such meetings, the cardinal was completely convinced of his favor with Marie-Antoinette. Seizing the opportunity, Lamotte prevailed upon Rohan to act as intermediary for the queen's purchase of a lavish necklace

consisting of 540 diamonds, which, owing to its great expense, had to be purchased secretly from the jewelers Boëhmer and Bassange. Still believing himself to be a favorite of the queen, Rohan complied. The scandal was revealed when the jewelers failed to receive payment, and Boëhmer sent a note to Marie-Antoinette, who in turn denied having purchased the necklace. Further revelations of the intrigue followed, and Rohan and Lamotte were imprisoned.

A trial date was set for 22 May 1786. Rohan maintained that he had bought the necklace in the queen's name and that the Comtesse de Lamotte had been the link between Marie-Antoinette and himself. Lamotte claimed that the cardinal had dealt directly with the jewelers without the queen's knowledge and accused him of having stolen the necklace. Pamphleteers and caricaturists reveled in the details of gossip surrounding the trial: Rohan as the queen's lover, a cardinal having cuckolded the king, a prostitute disguised as the queen. Public opinion generally held that the queen was either guilty of having used Lamotte to trick Rohan or of having commissioned Rohan to buy the necklace for her. Rohan's subsequent acquittal was seen as a confirmation of the queen's guilt, and large cheering crowds greeted him upon his release from the Bastille. Lamotte was sentenced to imprisonment but escaped to England several months later, where the publication of her memoirs in 1788 helped keep the memory of the affair alive throughout the Revolution and the fall of the monarchy. The scandal was so infamous in the public's mind that a seemingly straightforward representation of the necklace was sufficient to act as a satire against the queen.

72. ANONYMOUS
French
La Boîte à Pandore (Pandora's Box), ca. 1791
Etching with hand coloring on blue paper
B 534
160 x 244, 204 x 274
Bibliothèque nationale, Qb1 25 juin 1791
[M100761]

Executed in a style reminiscent of contemporary caricatures by the English artist James Gillray, this print depicts a group of aristocrats looking on with a mixture of delight, horror, and curiosity as the Austrian ambassador presents them with a box from which a doll named "Antoinette" has popped.

72

Decorated with the imperial arms of Austria, the box reads, "Of all evils, this is the worst," and the ambassador exclaims, "Here is the only jewel in Austria on which one can put a price." This caricature derives its punch from the popular association of the queen with the mythological character Pandora, who was sent to earth by Jupiter and, despite warnings, opened a box from which emerged all the evils that beset mankind, thus bringing an end to the Golden Age. It was popularly held that the Austrians purposely sent Marie-Antoinette, disguised as a gift or peace offering, to become the bride of Louis XVI, cuckold him, and defeat the French in order to bring them under Austrian dominance.

THE FLIGHT TO VARENNES

73. ANONYMOUS
French
Emjambee de la Sainte Famille des Thuilleries a Montmidy (The Holy Family Strides from the Tuileries to Montmédy), ca. 1791
Etching with hand coloring on blue paper
DV 3929, B 274
311 x 476, 354 x 479
Bibliothèque nationale, Qb1 21 juin 1791
[M100673]

Holding a broken scepter, Marie-Antoinette strides from the Palais des Tuileries to "Montmidy" (Montmédy) on the northeastern frontier, which is represented by boulders forming a bridge and surmounted by a clock reading *midi* (noon). She carries the king and the dauphin on her back and pulls the princesse and Madame Elisabeth, the king's sister, behind her. Directly beneath the queen to the

right is the Duc de Coigny, a colonel and squire to the king (in numerous pamphlets, he was also alleged to be Marie-Antoinette's lover and the father of the princesse). Next to de Coigny stand Cardinal Rohan and the Comtesse de Lamotte, who raises the diamond necklace made infamous by the scandal of 1786 (cat. no. 71). Supporting the rock formation representing Montmédy from below are three émigrés implicated in counter-revolutionary plots: Jacques-Antoine-Marie de Cazalès, a noble deputy to the Estates General who emigrated after the flight; Abbé Jean Siffrein Maury, also a deputy to the Estates General, who emigrated in 1791 (cat. nos. 55–59); and the Vicomte de Mirabeau, leader of the Black Legion counter-revolutionary army (cat. nos. 98, 104). All three were famous orators and Noirs, or aristocrats on the extreme right of the Constituent Assembly. To the left of the print, past the French border are "Monsieur" and "Madame," the king's brother the Comte de Provence and his wife, who encourage the royal flight and offer sacks of money.

The implication that Marie-Antoinette is the primary force behind the flight is made clear by the words she utters, "I carry all." Following the royal family's move from Versailles to Paris, the queen became suspected of dealings with the Comité

73

autrichien, a counterrevolutionary group that advocated monarchical absolutism. Parisians were convinced that she was transmitting information to the Austrian enemy and the émigrés. This caricature associates the demise of the monarchy with scandals such as the Diamond Necklace Affair and the queen's numerous amorous liaisons. This is achieved by the presence of Rohan, a number of sexual innuendos contained within the printed dialogue, and the loosened bodice of the Comtesse de Lamotte, who suggestively holds the diamond necklace under the queen's skirt. Marie-Antoinette's more dangerous political relationships are suggested by the group of counterrevolutionary émigrés, whose dialogue indicates that their hopes rest with the queen successfully carrying the royal family.

As noted by de Vinck, this caricature was probably the first of a series of similar prints. The *Enjambée impériale* (DV 4357) represents Catherine II with one foot in Russia and the other in Constantinople, while beneath her various monarchs (including Louis XVI, who makes reference to his own *enjambée*) comment admiringly. Other *enjambée* prints show Napoleon striding from Elba to Paris and from Madrid to Moscow (DV 8981).

74. ANONYMOUS
French
Fuite du roi (The King's Flight), ca. 1791
Etching with hand coloring on blue paper
H 10988, B 277
231 x 330, 276 x 346
Bibliothèque nationale, Qb1 21 juin 1791
[M100674]

74

Disguised as a cook, Louis XVI advances toward a waiting coach, preceded by Marie-Antoinette, who, as the caption informs, crushes the tortured figure of Loyalty beneath her feet. The queen leans for support upon Count Hans Axel von Fersen, a Swedish diplomat presumed to be her lover, who is depicted with bizarre animal legs, evidence of his bestial nature. (Fersen was King Gustavus III's secret agent for French affairs and arranged for the royal family's flight to Varennes; he even drove

them on the first leg of their journey and, after the escape failed, took refuge in Brussels and organized counterrevolutionary actions on behalf of both his own monarch and the French royal family.)

The queen also receives the advice of the "imperial eagle," while the pope, as Fanaticism personified, flies above her, shrieking and gesticulating. The dauphin and princesse are put aboard the coach, while other nobles, waiting to accompany them, linger about and carouse with prostitutes ("des groupes de fille de joie"), enjoying one final assault upon the dignity of the French people.

This is a rich and bitter image, depicting the flight as a complicated affair of intrigue, debauchery, violence, and deception (Louis was actually disguised as a valet and Marie-Antoinette traveled under the passport of a Madame von Korff). Typical of many caricatures of the royal family, this lampoon places the queen at the center of the affair, directing its progress and humiliating her husband. The king is most often portrayed as a simpleton, deceived and cuckolded by the ambitious, greedy, and lascivious Marie-Antoinette.

75. ANONYMOUS
French
Trait de l'histoire de France du 21 au 25 juin 1791 / ou la Métamorphose (Feature of French History from 21 to 25 June 1791; / or, The Metamorphosis), ca. 1791
Etching with hand coloring on blue paper
DV 3932, B 286
338 x 458, 369 x 462
Bibliothèque nationale, Qb1 25 juin 1791
[M100729]

Combining the genres of allegory and caricature, this print depicts the flight to Varennes as a satiric Bacchanalian procession in which Louis XVI is portrayed as the Greek god Silenus. The portrayal of Silenus as a heroic nude figure is unusual, as standard representations depict the god as a fat old drunkard who is at the same time wise and possessed of the gift of prophecy. The king, like Silenus, is shown as having a dual nature; while alluding to the monarch's often caricatured fondness for drink, the print nonetheless portrays him as a hero, albeit one who is being led astray.

Louis sits astride André-Boniface-Louis de Riqueti, the vicomte de Mirabeau. The vicomte is encased in a wine keg; he was commonly referred to as Mirabeau-*tonneau* (Mirabeau the barrel), due to his corpulence and intemperance. Angered

75

by the king's declaration of support for the constitution on 4 February 1790, Mirabeau was one of the first ardent royalists to emigrate. Here he is defeated by Louis's enormous weight and is seen vomiting wine, his head becoming a sort of spigot.

As the legend indicates, Louis's evil genius betrays him and shows the route to Austria, the opposite from that which the king wishes to take. Marie-Antoinette, dressed as Folly, drives the chariot, holding the court jester's scepter in one hand and the reins of two crayfish in another. Crayfish are the symbol of the zodiac sign Cancer, which begins on 21 June, the date of the flight to Varennes. They are also traditionally associated with inconstancy or misfortune; together with the owls, who are symbolic of Satan and the powers of darkness, these crustaceans lead the misguided Louis on his ill-starred flight. Contributing to this chaos of misdirection is a guide mounted on horseback who gallops to no avail within a squirrel cage. Next to this device is a tocsin, which will eventually sound the alarm and reveal the king's attempted escape.

76. ANONYMOUS
French
J'en ferai un meilleur usage, et je sçaurai le conserver (I'll Make Better Use of It, and I'll Know How to Keep It), ca. 1791
Etching with hand coloring on blue paper
DV 5839, B 492
200 x 270, 233 x 300
Bibliothèque nationale, Qb1 25 juin 1791
[M100769]

77. ANONYMOUS
French
Hé hu! Da da! (Gee Gee! Haw Haw!), ca. 1791
Etching with hand coloring on blue paper
DV 3930, B 276
158 x 223 (sheet)
Bibliothèque nationale, Qb1 25 juin 1791
[M100771]

In the spirit of the preceding two caricatures — though not as dramatic and bitter as the first (cat. no. 74), nor as complex and allegorical as the second (cat. no. 75) — these two images portray Louis XVI as a simpleton led astray by the scheming and duplicitous Marie-Antoinette.

In the first print (cat. no. 76), Louis is portrayed as a child being pushed along in his walker by the queen. He has dropped his royal scepter and has picked up the dauphin's paper windmill, which he seems to prefer. Meanwhile, the dauphin has secured the fallen scepter, indicating his readiness to assume the throne, and he arrogantly asserts, "I'll make better use of it, and I'll know how to keep it." It is an image with a sharp barb, indeed; not only has the king been humiliated by the continued cuckolding he has suffered from his manipulating wife, his ignoble arrest, and his forced return to

76

77

Paris, he is now being ridiculed and dismissed by his own son and made to seem a child, stripped of his manliness.

The second caricature (cat. no. 77) depicts the flight itself, and the king is portrayed as a youngster riding a toy stag, again pushed along by the shrewish queen. They approach Montmédy (compare cat. no. 73), represented as a kind of rebus that combines a miniature mountain *(mont)* with a clock face labeled only with noon *(midi)*. As he spies the illusory goal and rides innocently to his humiliation and eventual demise, the king pronounces the childish sounds "Hé hu! Da da!"; these form a verbal sign for the infantilization Louis has suffered at the hands of Marie-Antoinette.

over a chamber pot. This is intended as a comment on Louis's reputed sexual impotence (the use of this visual configuration to suggest a phallus dates to the sixteenth century and the prints of Albrecht Dürer). The bottles littering the ground are labeled to imply that Louis has become a drunken pig as a result of swilling the wine of émigré aristocrats and of foreign governments in Spain and the Rhine. One broken bottle is labeled 21 June. The fact that bottles of wine from Alicante, Spain, and one attributed to the aristocrats are tied together at the right is perhaps intended to suggest that such a coalition existed.

78

78. ANONYMOUS
French
Ventre Saint Gris ou est mon fils? / Quoi! C'est un cochon? / C'est lui même, il noye sa honte (Gadzooks! Where Is My Son? / What! He's a Pig? / It's Himself, He Drowns His Shame), ca. 1791
Etching with hand coloring on blue paper
DV 4002, B 299
143 x 223, 169 x 238
Bibliothèque nationale, Qb1 25 juin 1791
[M100744]

Henry IV (1553–1610), the first Bourbon king of France, appears in this caricature bareheaded and wearing the cross of the Saint-Esprit. He is surprised to discover his descendant Louis XVI hiding in a barrel outside of Paris following the flight to Varennes. Henry's worthy successor has become a pig with the ears of an ass. The barrel in which the pig-king hides is equipped with a faucet standing

79. ANONYMOUS
French
Que faites vous / ma fille? / Quel désespoir? / J'etois alterée du sang des François / n'ayant pu éteindre ma soif / mon désespoir m'a plongé au fonds de ce / puits / Ah! Maudits Français pourquoi m'arretiez vous? (What Are You Doing / My Daughter? / What Despair? / I Was Thirsty for the Blood of the French / Unable to Quench My Thirst / My Despair Hurled Me to the Bottom of This / Well / Ah! Damned French Why Did You Stop Me?), ca. 1791
Etching with hand coloring on blue paper
DV 4004, B 291
215 x 155, 235 x 183
Bibliothèque nationale, Qb1 25 juin 1791
[M100746]

Empress Maria Theresa of Austria, mother of Marie-Antoinette, finds her daughter hiding in a well following the flight to Varennes. She points at

79

her own crown to remind her daughter of her royal ancestry. As the title of this print suggests, Marie-Antoinette, unable to quench her thirst for the blood of the French, despairs and curses the people for having prevented the fulfillment of her desire.

While Louis XVI is often portrayed in caricatures as a foolish drunkard (cat. no. 75), a pig (cat. no. 78), or a well-meaning but weak and misled fool (cat. nos. 76, 77), caricatures directed against Marie-Antoinette were more virulent, portraying her as a foreign invader intent on the destruction of France. The queen had long been referred to as *l'Autrichienne* (the Austrian) by the French people, but her foreign ancestry was considered particularly threatening during the period of the flight to Varennes. At that time it was widely believed that because of her Habsburg family connections, she was engaged in transmitting information to the Austrian enemy. Popular songs composed around 1790 warned that the queen "had promised to cut the throats of the whole of Paris" (Vovelle, 1984, p. 199).

80. VILLENEUVE (?)
French, active 1789–1799
Louis le parjure (Louis the Perjurer), ca. 1791
Etching with roulette, printed in colors
DV 3921, B 278
70 (diameter)
Bibliothèque nationale, Qb1 25 juin 1791
[M100748]

81. VILLENEUVE (?)
French, active 1789–1799
Son Excellence M. la Baronne de Korf parti furtivement de Paris dans la nuit du 20 au 21 juin 1791 (Her Excellency the Baroness de Korf Who Sneaked Out of Paris during the Night of 20–21 June 1791), ca. 1791
Etching with roulette, printed in colors
DV 3922, B 278
70 (diameter)
Bibliothèque nationale, Qb1 25 juin 1791
[M100751]

82. ANONYMOUS
French
Les Deux ne font qu'un (The Two Are But One), ca. 1791
Etching with hand coloring on blue paper
DV 3925
148 x 211, 204 x 258
Bibliothèque nationale, Qb1 25 juin 1791
[M100753]

80

81

Following the flight to Varennes, Louis XVI was frequently labeled "the perjurer" in *libelles*, songs, and caricatures. The manifesto he left behind at the Palais des Tuileries revealed his opposition to the Revolution and made clear that he had been lying to the Constituent Assembly, buying time until he could use foreign support to reinstate an absolute monarchy. In *Louis le parjure* (cat. no. 80), the king is portrayed as a pig, who, disguised as a servant, dutifully followed his mistress Marie-Antoinette traveling under the passport of the fictitious Russian lady "Madame von Korff." In the second print (cat. no. 81), the queen is caricatured as a strange female hyena, her head crowned with serpents. De Vinck attributed these pendant prints to Villeneuve as part of his *Collection général des caricatures de la Révolution française.*

The combination of the prints of the king and queen (cat. nos. 80, 81) results in a bizarre two-headed monster (cat. no. 82). Equally guilty, the

Les deux ne font qu'un

82

component figures find themselves immobilized as they pull against each other, unable to move in either direction. Of note, Louis has now acquired the horns of a cuckold.

83. ANONYMOUS
French
Retour de la famille royale, a Paris le 25 juin 1791 (Return of the Royal Family to Paris on 25 June 1791), ca. 1791
Etching with hand coloring on blue paper
DV 3979, H 11000
230 x 343, 263 x 361
Bibliothèque nationale, Qb1 25 juin 1791
[M100721]

83

Led by National Guardsmen, the royal family is escorted back to Paris following the ill-fated flight to Varennes. Also shown inside the carriage are Jérôme Pétion de Villeneuve, the mayor of Paris, and Antoine-Pierre-Joseph-Marie Barnave, a deputy of the National Constituent Assembly, who were sent to accompany the king and queen on their return.

The gravity of the situation is conveyed by the solemn faces of the royal family and the multitude of guards who march silently, visually overwhelming the tiny figures of the king and queen imprisoned in their carriage. The large crowds that lined the streets of Paris on this occasion are not visible in the print, which focuses instead on the military forces that captured the royal family and prevented their escape.

The sobriety of this image contrasts sharply with the succeeding caricature (cat. no. 84), which depicts the members of the returning royal family as pigs en route to market or, more to the point, to slaughter.

84. ANONYMOUS
French
La Famille des cochons ramenée dans l'étable (The Family of Pigs Brought Back to the Sty), ca. 1791
Etching with hand coloring
DV 3987, B 294
124 x 213, 145 x 227
Bibliothèque nationale, Qb1 25 juin 1791
[M100773]

Members of the once dignified royal family — Louis XVI, Marie-Antoinette, the dauphin, the princesse, and Madame Elisabeth, Louis's sister — are now caricatured as pigs brought back to Paris in a coach of straw by triumphant National Guardsmen following the ill-fated flight to Varennes. Blum has identified the male occupant sitting at the rear of the carriage as "Monsieur," the king's brother the Comte de Provence. The comte, however, managed to successfully escape to Brussels on the same night that the king and his family attempted to flee.

La famille Des Cochons ramenée Dans L'étable

84

THE FALL OF THE MONARCHY

85. ANONYMOUS
French
L'Idole renversée (The Idol Overturned), ca. 1791
Etching with hand coloring on blue paper
DV 4919, B 295
290 x 267 (sheet)
Bibliothèque nationale, Qb1 25 juin 1791
[M100738]

L'idole Renversée

85

France, personified as a beautiful woman, appears dressed in a robe adorned with fleurs-de-lis, the traditional emblem of the French kings. She uses a club similarly decorated to strike a bust of Louis XVI from its pedestal. Soldiers, a policeman, a grenadier of the National Guard, and a man of the people support the royal crown above her head with their bayonets and pikes. A child, dressed as a grenadier, raises his gun, attempting to contribute to this effort.

Though many revolutionaries called for Louis XVI's execution following the flight to Varennes, they continued to favor the idea of a constitutional monarchy. The Constitution of 1791, approved on 3 September by the Constituent Assembly and on 13 September by the king, retained limited powers for the monarch. While de Vinck dates this caricature to after 10 August 1792 and the fall of the monarchy, Blum maintains that it was created following the flight to Varennes in 1791. He argues that it represents the king as a useless idol and presents the people supporting the crown without him. The earlier date would seem more appropriate, for this is not a republican image. By 1793, however, this figure of a monarchical France wielding a club emblazoned with the fleurs-de-lis would become a club-wielding Hercules, the emblem of the radical republic (Hunt, 1983, p. 99).

86. VILLENEUVE

French, active 1789–1799
Louis le traître lis ta sentence (Louis the Traitor Read Your Sentence), 1793
Etching and aquatint with roulette
DV 5209, B 555
203 x 170, 309 x 229
Bibliothèque nationale, Qb1 17 janvier 1793
[M101811]

In this extraordinary image, a vigorous and muscular hand has broken through a brick wall and is shown writing upon it. The message thus inscribed warns Louis XVI that, "God has numbered thy king-

dom and finished it; thou art weighed in the balances, and art found wanting."

The warning is taken from Daniel 5:26–28 and is the writing on the wall by the divine hand of the Scriptures that appears at the banquet of Belshazzar. As Klaus Herding points out in his essay in the present catalogue, however, the representation of the revolutionary hand differs from the divine hand in three significant ways: first, it breaks through the wall from below, signifying that its legitimacy derives from the people, rather than from God on high; second, the dramatic breaking through the wall is evidence of the force used against the king and his palace; and third, the wall itself is full of cracks, indicating the inevitable collapse of the monarchy. The image thus represents violent insurrection as the means of accelerating the natural process of decay to which the monarchy had succumbed.

The text printed below the image — interrupted by the stark vignette of the guillotine and the stern warning, "She awaits the guilty" — is drawn from the *Réponse d'un sans-culotte aux réflexions de [Jacques] Necker sur le procès de Louis Capet*, written by C. Durocher and published as a pamphlet in 1792. It reads in part, "One hundred times guilty and one hundred times pardoned, Louis the Last has tried the goodwill and generosity of the people too much....The most sacred law, the security of twenty-four million men, demands that he be judged; and the glory of France, linked to the judgment of the present generation and of future generations, demands that he be punished." This excerpt refers to the debates in the National Convention as to whether the king should be tried. Numerous procedural issues were discussed — for example, should Louis XVI be judged by a regular court or a special tribunal — and the debate continued until the Convention decided on 3 December 1792 that it was competent to judge the monarch. The trial began on 11 December, and more than a month later, the king was found guilty of conspiracy against the nation and of criminal attempts against the security of the state. After a vote on the penalty and a second vote on the issue of a reprieve, Louis XVI was condemned to die on the guillotine on 21 January 1793 (Arasse, no. 41).

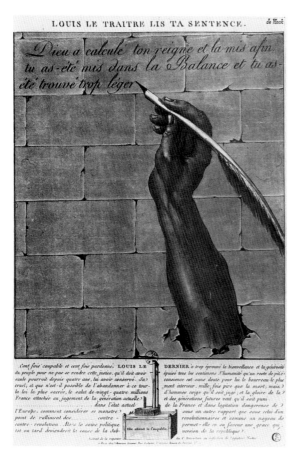

86

87. VILLENEUVE
French, active 1789–1799
Le Désarmement — de la bonne-noblesse (The Disarmament — of the Good Nobility), ca. 1791
Etching with roulette, printed in colors
DV 3880
128 x 100, 150 x 109
Bibliothèque nationale, Qb1 28 février 1791
[M100502]

88. ANONYMOUS
French
Copie exact des infames poignards / dont etoient armés ceux qui furent arrêtèe / par la-garde nationale le 28 fev. 1791 (An Exact Replica of the Infamous Daggers / with Which Those Were Armed Who Were Arrested / by the National Guard on 28 Feb. 1791), 1791
Etching
268 x 175, 275 x 183
Bibliothèque nationale, Qb1 28 février 1791
[M100501]

These prints are provocative representations of the "infamous daggers" used by a group of nobles who called themselves the Chevaliers du poignard and attempted to kidnap the king from the Palais des Tuileries in February 1791. This action was a

88

part of the increased counterrevolutionary activities that took place in early 1791; these also included the breaking up by force of a camp of some twenty thousand National Guardsmen in the south of the Vivarais and the armed uprising in the Vendée led by the Baron Lézardière. Refractory priests, who were allied to the nobles, increased their agitation and became active agents of the counterrevolution. Disorders grew more violent until a religious war broke out in France later in the spring of 1791.

The bold depiction of the dagger in Villeneuve's image (cat. no. 87) with the ruffled sleeve of the nobleman visible along the lower edge, suggests amputation or the literal "disarming" of the nobility, an act of dismemberment that prefigures the many decapitations that would occur during the Terror. By the same token, the shape of the dagger, the position of the hand, and the symbolic severing of the supporting arm imply a threatened castration of the nobility, a common conceit in revolutionary caricatures.

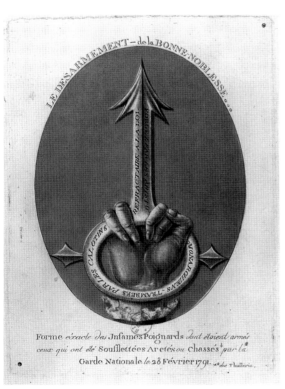

87

89. VILLENEUVE
French, active 1789–1799
Ecce Custine (Behold Custine), ca. 1793
Etching and aquatint with roulette
B 575
181 x 141, 285 x 205
Bibliothèque nationale, H 11601
[G162993]

90. VILLENEUVE
French, active 1789–1799
Matière à réflection pour les jongleurs couronnées / qu un sang impur abreuve nos sillons (Matter for Thought for Crowned Jugglers / May Our Fields Run with an Impure Blood), 1793
Etching with roulette
DV 5206, H 11460, B 559
160 x 140, 258 x 208
Bibliothèque nationale, Qb1 21 janvier 1793
[M101880]

These images, two of the most remarkable and repulsive produced during the Revolution, glorify the single most symbolic act of its official violence: the severing of a human head. In the first example (cat. no. 89), the subject is a popular hero who ran

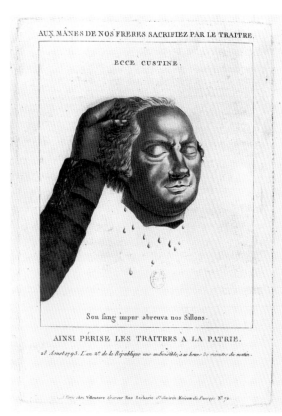

89

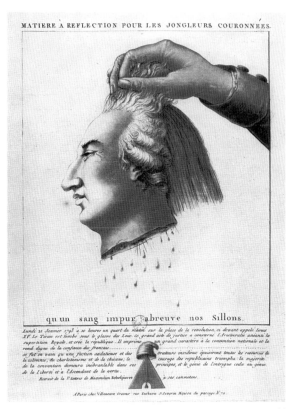

90

afoul of the government; in the second, it is Louis XVI (cat. no. 90). (For further discussion of the symbolic import of the act of beheading, refer to Ronald Paulson's essay in this catalogue.)

The Comte de Custine went to the Estates General in 1789 as a representative for the nobility of the Metz region. In the early years of the Revolution, however, this highly successful general resumed his military career and fought against foreign enemies, as well as counterrevolutionaries, in defense of the new France. On 21 October 1792 he seized Frankfurt and was given command of the revolutionary Army of the Rhine. His triumph was short-lived, however, for in March 1793 the enemy forced him to retreat and isolated twenty thousand of his men at Mainz, many of whom died. Nevertheless, two months later Custine was appointed to command the all-important Northern Army and continued to enjoy widespread popular support. He proved to be politically inept, however, expressing contempt for the Convention, quarreling with the Committee of Public Safety, and charging his fellow generals and the war ministry with incompetence. On 22 July 1793 he was arrested for having corresponded with the Duke of Brunswick (a failed attempt at opening negotiations) and for having aided the enemy to conquer French fortresses (referring to the abandoning of his troops at

Mainz). A month later he was found guilty and guillotined.

In this print, which like so many of the most striking and effective images of the Revolution was published by Villeneuve (compare cat. nos. 86, 87), Custine's severed head is held up "to the Manes [the venerated spirits of the ancient Roman dead] of our brothers [the revolutionary heroes who fell at Mainz] who were sacrificed by the traitor." The caption below reads, "His impure blood has watered our fields." The image is a powerful warning: no one, not even a popular hero like Custine, lies outside the reach of the law.

Under the republic's sacred law, Custine, a warrior for the Revolution, was the equal of Louis XVI, hated symbol of monarchical tyranny, and the king was liable to the same kind of judgment as any other citizen (cat. no. 90). Transgression of the law, as these prints make frighteningly clear, could mean death of the most gruesome kind for anyone (Arasse, no. 152).

91. ANONYMOUS
French
Mort de Louis Capet 16ᵉ du nom, le 21 janvier 1793 (Death of Louis Capet 16th of the Name, on 21 January 1793), ca. 1793
Etching with hand coloring on blue paper
DV 5169, H 303
300 x 455, 326 x 471
Bibliothèque nationale, Qb1 21 janvier 1793
[M101878]

91

Contemporary depictions of the execution of Louis range from royalist images featuring a heroic king facing death at the hands of bloodthirsty *sans-culottes* (Arasse, pp. 55, 57, 59) to ostensibly more documentary versions. This print tends toward the latter category but remains distinctly revolutionary in character.

Its title refers to the king as Louis Capet, giving his name as if he were a commoner; and its rather indifferent depiction of the anonymous figure of the monarch, diminished by the surrounding crowds, supports the view of his execution as simply that of another enemy of the Revolution who deserved no special recognition. The print's documentary tone is meant to portray this most compelling moment of the Revolution as simply a matter of course.

92. VILLENEUVE
French, active 1789–1799
Réception de Louis Capet aux enfers par grand nombres de brigands ci-devant couronnées (Reception of Louis Capet in Hell by a Large Number of Previously Crowned Bandits), 1793
Etching and aquatint with roulette
DV 5228, H 11480, B 560
266 x 364, 332 x 398
Bibliothèque nationale, Qb1 21 janvier 1793
[M101909]

Louis Capet, stripped of his royal title, has just been ferried across the mythical River Styx and is received in hell by deceased monarchs, ancestors, and friends. He is greeted first by King Charles IX (1550–1574), who is described in the legend as being, like Louis, an assassin of the French, and by King Charles I of England (1600–1649), who was executed for treason against the English people. Emperors Joseph II (1741–1790) and Leopold II (1747–1792) of Austria appear slightly to the right and in the legend are sarcastically referred to as the worthy brothers of Louis's chaste spouse.

Among the assembled are a number of former French kings: Louis IX (1214–1270); Henry IV (1553–1610), the first Bourbon king of France; and Louis XIV (1638–1715). Louis XVI's grandfather Louis XV (1710–1774) rushes toward his grandson but is restrained by women whose disordered clothing proclaims them to be prostitutes, a reference to this monarch's amorous exploits.

92

In the foreground are Louis's "faithful agents," all guillotined by the revolutionaries. They are identified in the legend as the counterrevolutionary Thomas de Mahy, the marquis de Favras; Laporte; Barnabé Farmian de Rosoi, known as Durosoi; Bacman; the Feuillant foreign minister Claude Antoine Valdec de Lessart; La Rivière; Brissac; the foreign minister and ambassador Armand-Marc Montmortin de Saint-Herem; and Marie-Thérèse Louise de Savoie-Carignan, the princesse de Lamballe, who was accused of being the lover and favorite of Marie-Antoinette.

To the left, another foreign-born French queen Maria de' Medici (1573–1642), wife of Henry IV, and the evil French queens Brunehaut (died 613) and Frédégonde (545–ca. 597) rush toward the Styx hoping to find "Messalina-Antoinette," their imitator; a hovering spirit shouts through a ram's horn,

informing them that Louis precedes her. (In pamphlets and caricatures, as well as during the proceedings of her trial, the queen was called a contemporary Messalina, referring to the profligate wife of the witless Roman emperor Claudius, who was also put to death.) Marie-Antoinette approaches from the Temple on the other side of the river, holding her head in her hands, while a winged guillotine flies through the sky above her. After having "handed to Fanaticism the hypocrite's declaration," that is, Louis's will, Charon, the boatman who ferries the souls of the dead across the Styx, returns to the earthly side of the river. There, as the text informs, he will pick up Paris, the assassin of Madame Pelletier. In the background to the right the Elysian Fields are visible where the victims of Louis's reign dance around the Tree of Liberty, which they have erected under the auspices of the Supreme Being.

Caricatures of the enemies of the Revolution being ferried across the Styx already existed by this period (Arasse, p. 53, nos. 48, 49), but none displays the elaborate detail of Villeneuve's representation. By comparing Louis XVI and Marie-Antoinette with the evil monarchs of the past and the enemies of the Revolution, the entire succession and the idea of the monarchy itself are rendered worthless. The execution of the king and the anticipated guillotining of the queen are then justified.

93. JACQUES MARCHAND
French, 1769–after 1810
Saule pleureur (Weeping Willow), ca. 1793,
after Jean-Baptiste Coste
Etching and stipple
366 x 486, 450 x 510
Bibliothèque nationale, Qb1 21 janvier 1793
[M101918]

94. PIERRE-JEAN-JOSEPH-DENIS CRUSSAIRE
French, 1749–after 1800
L'Urne mystérieuse (The Mysterious Urn), ca. 1793
Etching and stipple
H 11974
206 x 150, 227 x 166
Bibliothèque nationale, Qb1 21 janvier 1793
[M101904]
(Not in exhibition)

L'URNE MYSTÉRIEUSE

Une femme désolée, représentant la France assise près d'un monument funèbre élevé à l'auguste Famille de Louis XVI, sur lequel est placée l'urne mystérieuse dont les deux cotés et les dessus.)

94

93

Seeming at first to be a straightforward depiction of a weeping willow — perhaps a plate from a series of prints of various flora — catalogue number 93 actually contains the profiles of Louis XVI and Marie-Antoinette, which appear as silhouettes on either side of the tree's trunk. Unlike most silhouettes, however, these suggest likeness not by a positive presence, but rather by a negative one. Thus, in a very subtle and witty way — playing on both the reversal of the typical profile and the metaphorical implications of the "weeping" tree — this image gives the royal couple a presence in the form of memory and evokes feelings associated with mourning for and remaining loyal to them. To underscore this point, a distraught young girl appears draped upon a sarcophagus in the background.

In contrast to the simplicity of the *Saule pleureur, L'Urne mystérieuse* (cat. no. 94) represents the evocative absence of the king and queen through a multitude of symbolic references in addition to their "negative" profiles, which are evident on either side of a funerary urn (the profiles of their children can be seen among the branches of the weeping willow). A grieving woman representing France sits beside the urn, from which smoke emanates, symbolizing love that survives death. The urn's pedestal is decorated with an equilateral triangle representing the Christian Trinity, a winged hourglass suggesting fleeting time, sickles evoking Saturn who cuts time short, and a snake with its tail in its mouth symbolizing eternity. Beneath the tree the Hydra of evil is struck down by lightning, while the sun, representing hope, breaks through the clouds above.

Memorial images incorporating silhouettes of members of the royal family were often produced following their executions, and not only by royalists. They represent the public's reluctance to accept the demise of the king and queen and the assumption that monarchs were necessary to the establishment of a constitutional government. Significantly, the motif of a hidden or "negative" profile often appears in prints of deposed revolutionary figures following 9 thermidor, and it is found again in prints lamenting the first exile of Napoleon in 1814.

The fall of the Bastille on 14 July 1789 triggered the flight from France of the Comte d'Artois and other nobles, clergy, and members of the Third Estate. They constituted the first wave of the over 150,000 French citizens who emigrated during the revolutionary era. The Comte d'Artois, brother of Louis xvi, was the figure most prominently associated with the decadence and frivolity of the court and with the intransigence of the Notables during the meeting of the Estates General. On the night of 16–17 July 1789 the count left Versailles for the Austrian Netherlands where Marie-Christine, sister of Marie-Antoinette, was vice-regent. Later, he moved to Turin where he was soon joined by Charles Alexandre de Calonne, the former controller general of finances under Louis xvi.

Over the next two years, d'Artois pleaded with European sovereigns to restore Louis xvi to full power, arguing that the cause of the king of France was the cause of all sovereigns. In the summer of 1791, he settled in Coblenz, where he joined his brother the Comte de Provence, who had fled France in June 1791 to preside over a shadow government. There, thousands of émigrés had gathered and formed a small army. From this base d'Artois continued to seek support for the restoration of the French monarchy. When the French declared war against Austria in April 1792, he commanded a small corps of cavalry that followed behind the Austrian and Prussian forces invading France. Although defeated at Valmy in September, d'Artois continued to symbolize the forces that threatened to undermine the Revolution in France.

Numerous legislative acts were directed against the émigrés. On 12 February 1792 French citizens who corresponded with émigrés were declared traitors, and those caught fleeing France were arrested. In April 1792 those who had left France after 1 July 1789 and failed to return by 1 May 1792 were banished forever, and in October 1792 the National Convention decreed the death penalty for those who had returned to France after May of that year. Although such punitive legislation remained in effect after the Terror, the number of returning émigrés reached tidal proportions by 1797, with tens of thousands coming back under the Directory. Significantly, there were émigrés among all elements of French society, and as years passed, ideological differences weakened their unity, destroying attempts to coordinate counterrevolutionary activities.

95. Anonymous
French
Retour d'un émigré (Return of an Emigré), ca. 1791
Etching with hand coloring
DV 3717
234 x 158 (sheet)
Bibliothèque nationale, Qb1 12 novembre 1791 [M101029]

Retour d'un Emigré

95

In order to stem the tide of émigrés leaving France subsequent to the king's flight to Varennes, the Legislative Assembly issued a decree on 9 November 1791 ordering all émigrés to return within one month or face the appropriation of their goods and income for the benefit of the nation "without prejudice to the rights of wives, children..." (Stewart, p. 272). Though the decree was vetoed by the king, it marked the beginning of a series of laws directed against the émigrés that finally came to be enforced when war began the following April.

Perhaps as a warning, this caricature lampoons a pitiful and downtrodden émigré who has donned the liberty cap too late and without any real conviction. The windmill to the left and the wooden shoes worn by the dejected expatriate suggest the Austrian Netherlands, the destination of many of the wealthier nobles who left France during the first wave of emigration in 1789 (Godechot, 1971, p. 149).

96. ANONYMOUS
French
Le Conseil / électoral (The Electoral Council), ca. 1791
Etching with hand coloring on blue paper
DV 4378, H 11106, B 511
318 x 496, 383 x 521
Bibliothèque nationale, Qb1 11 septembre 1791 [M100888]

After their arrival at Coblenz, the Comte d'Artois and the Comte de Provence gathered together a council to continue the counterrevolutionary activities of the Turin Committee, which d'Artois had formed when he first emigrated in 1789. Louis XVI's former controller general of finances Charles Alexandre de Calonne acted as first minister in this shadow government, which had the support of émigrés, various German princes concerned about their seigneurial rights in Alsace, and agents at the courts of Austria and Russia.

In this print, Clement-Wenceslaus, the prince-bishop of Treves and uncle of the Comte de Provence and the Comte d'Artois (who appear enthroned to the right), presides over the council. Among those discussing plans for the invasion of France are various German bishops; princes; a deputy from Savoy; Spanish and Russian ministers; Baron de Bender, an Austrian general; and a number of émigrés including the Marquis de Bouillé, the Vicomte de Mirabeau (who, because of his rotund shape and intemperance, was often called Mirabeau-*tonneau*, *tonneau* meaning "barrel"); and the Prince de Condé. On the wall behind them are maps of the forts at Landau and Neuf-Brisach, while on the floor lie plans for attack on Alsace and Antibes.

96

This anonymous caricature ridicules the council members by giving them grotesque animal faces; most of them appear as bewhiskered cats who are barked at by the council's usher, the dog in the center. The futility of their military efforts is suggested by the "general's baton for rent," which, like the rifle and cannon loader to the left, lies neglected and untouched before those assembled.

97. ANONYMOUS
French
Grand Conseil / des émigrans (The Great Council / of the Emigrants), ca. 1791
Etching with hand coloring on blue paper
DV 4375, B 516
300 x 499, 370 x 524
Bibliothèque nationale, Qb1 décembre 1791
[M101079]

As in the preceding caricature, Clement-Wenceslaus, prince-bishop of Treves, enthroned in the center (1), presides over the council of émigrés at Coblenz. He reads correspondence from the King of Spain and the Holy Roman Emperor Leopold II. At his side are the Comte d'Artois and the Comte de Provence, "the sovereign Princes of the empire" (4). Also included in the council are the Bishop of Treves, the Bishop of Cologne, who gestures at a map of France, the Prince of Württemberg, and various other foreign monarchs interested in the projects of the émigrés. In the foreground, two monkeys wheel in the Bishop of Mainz in his bath; he holds papers referring to the affairs of the provinces of Brabant and Liège, areas which would be annexed by the French in 1793–1794. Mainz itself was captured by General Custine's Army of the Rhine in September 1792 (see cat. no. 89).

The artist of this caricature undoubtedly made the preceding one as well. The format and general composition are the same in each, as are the manner of etching and the script in the key. More important, however, each image exhibits a highly sophisticated sense of portrait caricature, apparent in the exaggeration of facial features and body types and the subtle representation of individuals

Grand Conseil des émigrans

97

in terms of animal characteristics (a cat's whiskers, a donkey's nose and jowls). This is a kind of pure caricature not often seen in France during the Revolution (pp. 15–16) and betrays a considerable knowledge of English examples, particularly the work of Thomas Rowlandson and James Gillray, and even the paintings of John Mortimer (Godefrey, no. 79).

98. ANONYMOUS
French
La Mascarade (The Masquerade), ca. 1791
Etching with hand coloring
DV 4360, B 503
292 x 470, 381 x 500
Bibliothèque nationale, Qb1 décembre 1791
[M101082]

In the summer of 1791, following his expulsion from the court at Turin, the Comte d'Artois arrived at Coblenz with his brother the Comte de Provence; there they joined forces with the Vicomte de Mirabeau and his Black Legion. At this time d'Artois sought aid from Prime Minister William Pitt of England, King Frederick William II of Prussia, and the Sultan of Turkey, and he renewed his efforts to obtain military assistance from the Holy Roman Emperor Leopold II. Catherine II of Russia was the monarch most consistently supportive of the émigré cause and the only one to recognize the Comte de Provence as regent and later king.

The Comte d'Artois, the Comte de Provence, and their supporters are depicted here as members of a masked circus traveling in search of royal alliances. The procession is led by the Comte d'Artois (2), who pays homage to Empress Catherine II (1), while the Comte de Provence (3) looks on. The Vicomte de Mirabeau (4), dressed as an Eastern potentate, stands alone in the right foreground. A chariot, labeled "four-wheeled confessional to Coblenz," is drawn by a bear representing a deputy from the city of Bern. On the chariot sit the Duc de Broglie, a member of the council of émigrés

98

1 *Vice Legat portant les Bulles et Indulgences*
2 *S. M. Allobroge ou le Roi des Ramoneurs*
3 *Charles Doyen de St Jacques de Compostelle*
4 *Député du Canton de Bâle*
5 *La Grosse Danseuse du Nord*
6 *Le Despote de Berlin*
7 *Riquetti la Houpe en habit du Matin*

8 *Vicaire Apostolique*
9 *L'Homme aux trois Couronnes ou le Geryon du Nord*
10 *Holenlove Commandant la Legion Mirabeau aux ...*
11 *Le Cardinal Rigaud portant le singe de Siste V*
12 *Le Ci-devant Patron des Liegeois*
13 *Le donneur de Benedictem Apostoliques*
14 *La Renommée publiant les exploits de cette belle Caravane*
15 *Cordon d'Echola. Grenadiers*

Les Pelerins de St Jacques

99

---

at Coblenz; the Marquis de Bouillé, whose garrisons were supposed to rendezvous with the royal family during the flight to Varennes; members of the "secret cabinet of the court of Vienna," among them the Sultan of Turkey; and other officers and advisors to the princes. Louis XVI, although referred to as a monkey, is depicted as a cat-catching rat who rides atop the chariot bearing the émigrés' banner. Escorting the strange vehicle is Pope Pius VI ridden by Holenlove and receiving a therapeutic enema from an apothecary described below as a "secret friend of the merchant of indulgences." Two mysterious and unidentified costumed figures to the left, at the rear of the procession, await the outcome of the ludicrous affair.

99. ANONYMOUS
French
Les Pelerins de St Jacques (The Pilgrims of Saint James), ca. 1791
Etching with hand coloring on blue paper
DV 4361, B 257
307 x 484, 385 x 504
Bibliothèque nationale, Qb1 décembre 1791
[M101080]

A motley group of Bosch-like figures is shown here making a pilgrimage to the famous Romanesque cathedral at Santiago de Compostela in northwestern Spain, which is represented generically in the right background. The cathedral is said to have been built on the site of the grave of Saint James and was one of the most celebrated pilgrimage destinations in medieval Europe. Here, however, the pilgrimage, traditionally a sacred journey made in penance for sins, becomes a satiric caravan of émigrés in search of foreign alliances. The procession is led by the "Vice Legat," probably the Comte de Provence (1), and his brother the Comte

1 *Le Compère Léopold faisant jouer le Mannequin Condé en Merettin .*

2 *Monseigneur en Pierrot faisant des Lazzis .*

3 *Son Frère faisant fonction d'aboyeur .*

4 *Le Tolpach Lambesc, ou l'Arracheur de Dents vendant le Baume - antirevolutionnaire .*

5 *Musicien faisant une Fanfarre .*

LA FOIRE DE COBLENTZ

OU

LES GRANDS FANTOCCINI FRANCAIS

6 *Le Cousin Bourbon en Scaramouche faisant Danser la bergère des Bosquets .*

7 *L'Abbesse de Rémiremont distribuant les billets .*

8 *Mirabeau Tonneau jouant du Pouce .*

9 *Mme de Balb . . .*

10 *Mr De Calonne .*

11 *Le Fameux Cust . . . faisant le Contre-poids .*

d'Artois, "Charles doyen of Saint James of Compostela" (3). The princes are joined by various European rulers: the King of Sardinia, referred to as "S. M. Allobroge or the king of the chimney sweeps" (2); the deputy of the canton of Bern, one of the principal émigré strongholds (4); Catherine II of Russia, "the fat dancer of the North" (5); and Frederick William II of Prussia, "the despot of Berlin" (6). Other émigré supporters and advisors in the caravan include the Vicomte de Mirabeau, known as "the Barrel," in his "morning outfit" (7); the Sultan of Turkey (8); the Holy Roman Emperor Leopold II of Austria (9); and Pope Pius VI (13). Overhead, flying just before the pope ("the dealer in papal benedictions"), Fame trumpets the exploits of the caravan and vomits papal briefs and various excommunications before him. The burlesque humor and grotesque depictions suggest that this caricature must be by the same artist as the previous print. He shares with the artist of catalogue numbers 96 and 97 a highly individualized style and a talent that place him among the most remarkable of the "anonymous" artists of the revolutionary period.

100. ANONYMOUS
La Foire de Coblentz / ou / les Grands Fantoccini / français (The Coblenz Fair; / or, / The Great French Puppeteers), ca. 1791
Etching with hand coloring on blue paper
DV 1961, H 11095, B 500
314 x 521, 393 x 545
Bibliothèque nationale, Qb1 27 août 1791
[M100868]

From the time of their arrival at Coblenz, the Comte de Provence, the Comte d'Artois, and the Prince de Condé persisted in calling on European monarchs to intervene and crush the French revolutionaries. Their appeals met with mixed results, however, as these leaders were more interested in annexing French territories than in supporting the émigrés.

The Declaration of Pillnitz, signed on 27 August 1791 by the Holy Roman Emperor Leopold II and Frederick William II, the king of Prussia, recognized the plight of Louis XVI as "a matter of concern to all the sovereigns of Europe" and called on the other powers to join in strengthening the "foundations of a monarchical government" in

France (Stewart, pp. 223–24). The declaration was purposely vague, however, and was intended only as a sign of support and encouragement for the French royal family. Its effect actually proved quite the opposite. The European powers failed to rally to Louis XVI's side, and the Declaration of Pillnitz provided justification for those revolutionary factions supporting the extension of the fight for liberty to neighboring powers. Thus, the French declared war on Austria and Prussia in April 1792.

In this caricature the émigrés are portrayed as the "great French puppeteers," actors in a circus sideshow farce conducted by Leopold II. The Prince de Condé is portrayed as a marionette manipulated by the emperor, while the Duc de Bourbon, the prince's son, is disguised as Scaramouche, the foolish boaster. The comtes de Provence and d'Artois are both disguised as Pierrot, the clown and buffoon. To the right, Madame de Balbi, mistress of the Comte de Provence, and Charles Alexandre de Calonne, the former controller general of finances, appear unwilling to participate in the show. The Vicomte de Mirabeau, approaching from the left, buys a ticket from Condé's daughter, the Abbesse de Remiremont (cat. no. 103). In the background at the right, the Prince de Lambesc hawks anti-revolutionary and anti-patriotic balm to no avail.

101. ANONYMOUS
French
Le Jeu de l'émigré / au premier coup! C'est bien jouer! (The Game of the Emigré / at the First Go! Well done!), ca. 1792
Etching and mezzotint with roulette
DV 4371, B 612
183 x 291, 241 x 329
Bibliothèque nationale, Qb1 février 1792
[M10116]

The émigrés' ambitions are given form in this counterrevolutionary caricature, and the European monarchs are shown at the castle of the comtes d'Artois and de Provence on the banks of the Rhine at Coblenz. The Comte d'Artois has thrown a ball (labeled "Bender" for the Austrian general Blaise-Colombeau, the baron de Bender) to knock down leading members of the Legislative Assembly, while Empress Catherine II of Russia, the Holy Roman Emperor Leopold II, King Gustavus III of Sweden, King Frederick William II of Prussia, and the Comte de Provence look on in

101

amusement. The pins represent Jacques Pierre Brissot de Warville, leader of the Girondins; Brissot's ally Marie Jean Antoine Nicolas de Caritat, the marquis de Condorcet; François Chabot, a Capuchin monk turned revolutionary; the Girondin leader Marguerite Elie Guadet; Pierre Victurnien Vergniaud; Maximin Isnard; Antoine-Louis Albitte; Claude Basire; and Philippe-Jacques Ruhl. Their heads, attached to the pins, resemble the severed heads that had been paraded through Paris atop pikes.

Interestingly, this image employs the same satirical conceit of ninepins, or skittles, used in an earlier prorevolutionary caricature entitled *Le Jeu de quilles*. There, the Third Estate is shown bowling in the background while an aristocrat and clergyman exchange remarks in the foreground. The aristocrat announces, "I am leaving, Monsieur l'Abbé, I have lost my turn" ("j'ai manqué mon coup," playing on the expression *coup manqué*, or "abortive attempt," as it applies to unity among the political orders). The clergyman responds, "It happened to me, too" (Vovelle, 1986, vol. 1, p. 225). The resemblance suggests that the open commerce in caricatures during this period led counterrevolutionaries to borrow and adapt revolutionary prototypes for their own purposes. In addition, the highly finished style of this etching and mezzotint, as well as its formal rendering of personages and diagonal composition, recalls Villeneuve's *Réception de Louis Capet aux enfers* (cat. no. 92) and suggests a further exchange of influence between prorevolutionary and counterrevolutionary caricaturists.

102. ANONYMOUS
French
Le Gazettier / de Coblentz (The Journalist / from Coblenz), ca. 1791
Etching with hand coloring on blue paper
DV 4411, B 529
327 x 507, 391 x 515
Bibliothèque nationale, Qb1 avril–mai 1791
[M100586]

With the announcement of war on 20 April 1792, the émigrés in the Coblenz circle of the Comte de Provence, Comte d'Artois, and Prince de Condé believed that the defeat of the revolutionaries was at hand and that their own return to noble status would soon follow. In this caricatured gathering of émigrés at a Coblenz café, a deputy from the court of Vienna announces the declaration of war between France and Austria. The Prince de Condé's daughter, Louise-Adelaïde de Bourbon, known as "Mademoiselle," faints at the news and is assisted by Cardinal de Rohan and the Comtesse de Lamotte, while her father rushes to her assistance. Behind them, "la petite Bibi," Madame de Balbi, mistress of the Comte de Provence, shows a newspaper to an ex-Jacobin, while to the right the Comte de Provence, Comte d'Artois, Duc d'Angoulême, Vicomte de Mirabeau, Charles Alexandre de Calonne, and other émigrés discuss the news. On the wall are newspapers purporting to be from the various counterrevolutionary allies: the *Courier of Europe*, the *Gazette of Utrecht*, the *Journal of Princes*, the *Prussian Courier*, and the *Journal of Saint Petersburg*.

103. ANONYMOUS
French
*Grande Armée / du cidev¹. prince de Condé
(The Great Army / of the Ci-Devant Prince de
Condé)*, ca. 1791
Etching with hand coloring on blue paper
DV 4409, B 494
297 x 504, 402 x 526
Bibliothèque nationale, Qb1 22 mars 1791
[M100537]

In his château at Worms, the Prince de Condé
reviews the troops recently sent to him by his supporters in Strasbourg. From his pipe emanates
smoke containing the arms destined to accomplish
his vast projects. Next to Condé, his aide the
Comte d'Autichamp meditates on the attack, while
Condé's daughter Louise-Adelaïde de Bourbon,
known as "Mademoiselle," and his grandson the
Duc d'Enghien arrange the regiments of toy soldiers. Condé's son the Duc de Bourbon reviews the
enrollment list, and next to him, Madame Monaco,
Condé's mistress, displays a group of books, including a copy of *Don Quixote*. The Vicomte de

Mirabeau enters from the left, as do a physician
and a menacing apothecary holding a clyster. Two
monkey-squires, just to the left of the prince, carry
his mask, an ass's head.

Condé's "formidable army" is thus revealed to
be no more threatening than a box of toy soldiers
that provides amusement for his daughter and her
nephew, both of whom emigrated with the Duc de
Bourbon in 1789. The prince's daughter features
frequently in caricatures as the Abbesse de Remiremont (cat. no. 100), a position of privilege conferred
upon her in 1786 by Louis XVI in recognition of her
great piety; the title is mocked here by her immod-
est dress.

The smoke of the prince's pipe dreams dissi-
pates into the battle painting behind him, which
links his fantasies with the destruction of Worms by
the French in 1689 (a destruction that they would
repeat in 1792). D'Autichamp's expression indicates his recognition of the ineffectiveness of Condé's forces, while the map of Clermont he holds
also mocks the prince's grand designs. In March
1791 the annulment of the Donation of Clermont
deprived the prince of an annual 600,000 *livres* of
rent; this loss forced him to pawn his jewels,

*Grande Armée
du cidev.ᵗ Prince de Condé*

103

which are seen in his pipe smoke, to support his army. A final insult is given by the dog at right whose collar indicates that he belongs to Père Duchesne (a similar incident was recounted in issue no. 56 of Hébert's *Le Père Duchesne*).

104. ANONYMOUS
French
Envoi d'un supplément d'armée / au ci devant prince de Condé par MM. les Noirs ou Du cul de sac...(Shipment of Extra Troops / to the Ci-Devant Prince de Condé by MM. the Noirs; or, The Dead End...), ca. 1791
Etching with hand coloring
DV 4415, B 495
300 x 487, 407 x 528
Bibliothèque nationale, Qb1 22 mars 1791
[M100539]

The smallest of the three émigré armies was that of the Vicomte de Mirabeau (often referred to as

Mirabeau-*tonneau*, "Mirabeau the Barrel"), who established his "Black Legion" at Yverdon in Switzerland following his emigration in 1790. In 1791 he left Switzerland and relocated at Colmar in the duchy of Baden, where another émigré, Cardinal de Rohan of the notorious Diamond Necklace Affair (cat. no. 71), now the bishop of Strasbourg, offered him hospitality. There, the viscount could remain close to other émigré armies led by the princes and to the Prince de Condé himself.

In this image Mirabeau-*tonneau*, wearing his characteristic barrel armor and sporting a turkey on his helmet and a skull emblazoned on his sleeve, leads his "dead-end" regiment toward Condé's army, seen in the background at right. As the key reveals, he is followed by "the first violin of the Bishop of Speyer" on stilts, who is accompanied by an abbé, a Savoyard gentleman, and a German prince. Behind them Cardinal de Rohan, wearing both the "infamous dagger" of the nobility (cat. nos. 87, 88) and the notorious diamond necklace, carries reinforcements for Condé's toy army. These are beginning to fall from the ass the cardinal is riding; one box is labeled "eighty thousand infantry"; and the one on the ground, "fifty thou-

104

sand cavaliers with arms and baggage." The nature of this equipment is implied by the bottle and wine-glass stamped on one box. Behind the cardinal are an almoner and a "pasquin" on an ass; additional ineffectual reinforcements can be seen making their way in the background. The entire misguided affair is preceded by an ironic figure of Fame, who announces the new arrivals, as a similar herald had done more grotesquely for the procession of pilgrims in *Les Pelerins de S' Jacques* (cat. no. 99).

105. ANONYMOUS
French
La Contre Révolution (The Counterrevolution), ca. 1791
Etching with hand coloring
DV 4419, B 496
286 x 521, 385 x 536
Bibliothèque nationale, Qb1 14 septembre 1791
[M100983]

At the left of this image, the Prince de Condé (1) is shown preparing his émigré army for an attack on the rock of the "French constitution," from which the tricolor flag of liberty flies over the Rhine. Surrounding Condé are his aides, General d'Autichamp (2), Antoine Séguier (3), and Charles Alexandre de Calonne (4), as well as Madame de Lamotte the "aide de lit de camp" (7). Included in Condé's army are the Cardinal de Rohan, the "Cardinal Collier," portrayed as a drum major (5); the Abbé d'Eymar, who carries the white royalist flag (labeled "the pastoral letter"); and the Vicomte de Mirabeau, who leads a battle corps of nobles, fugitives, Capuchin monks, and other clergy. Bringing up the rear are the revealingly clad "maid" of the counterrevolution, the Duchesse de Polignac, and various other generous women ("corps de bataille"). In the distance, General Bouillé, who commanded the garrison that was to meet the royal family at Varennes, can be seen riding in the opposite direction.

This is a humorous image depicting the émigrés' army as a motley and desperate group of pathetic aristocrats, clergy, and camp followers, blindly trailing after one another, like lemmings destined to drown in the Rhine. Actually, however, the émigrés were beginning to represent a mounting threat to the revolutionaries at the time this print was made. They gathered about the Comte d'Artois and the Comte de Provence by the thousands, and over a

period of twelve months, they aggressively sought the support of foreign governments and eventually followed behind the Austrian and Prussian forces in their battles against France. As the threat they posed became increasingly serious, innocent burlesques such as this one would give way to restrictive legislative acts aimed at depriving the émigrés of their rights, property, and ultimately their lives.

106. ANONYMOUS
    French
    L'Attaque de la constitution (The Attack on the Constitution), ca. 1791
    Etching with hand coloring on blue paper
    DV 4432, H 384, B 498
    289 x 490, 375 x 515
    Bibliothèque nationale, Qb1 14 septembre 1791
    [M100984]

The motley counterrevolutionary army, observed in catalogue number 105 has further

degenerated in this print, dissolving into mass confusion as the émigrés begin their assault on the rock of the "French constitution." Cardinal de Rohan (1) is represented as a human cannon fired by the "fury of pride and avarice"; from his mouth shoot fanatical counterrevolutionaries aimed at the constitution, but they crash against the rock and fall into the Rhine. Additional ammunition is delivered by the Abbé Maury who carries a basket of cannonballs heated by a mad Capuchin monk over red-hot coals. The Prince de Condé (4) complains of the failure of the attack to Madame de Lamotte, while the Abbé d'Eymar whispers his own plans into the ear of the "maid" of the army (5). In the background, the army corps uses cannonballs to play racket games, while the Vicomte de Mirabeau (6) commands another useless assault on the immovable rock of the constitution.

107. ANONYMOUS
French
Défaite des contre révolutionnaires (Defeat of the Counterrevolutionaries), ca. 1792
Etching with hand coloring on blue paper
DV 4433 [B 497]
290 x 490, 411 x 516
Bibliothèque nationale, Qb1 5 avril 1792
[M10144]

Defeated in their attempts to attack the rock of the constitution, the counterrevolutionaries tumble over one another madly trying to escape. (From the rock now flies a flag showing Liberty holding a scroll noting the twenty-three new French departments.) The Vicomte de Mirabeau, his barrel broken, falls by the Rhine clutching a broken bottle; next to him is Charles Alexandre de Calonne,

who has also fallen, dropping his gold into the river. The Prince de Condé wearing a papal tiara, his baton broken, receives advice from General d'Autichamp, while the Bishop of Speyer tries to revive Madame de Lamotte, who has "taken her last fall." The frustrated Abbé d'Eymar pulls the remains of the "oriflamme épiscopale" (the white royalist flag) from the Rhine, which has proven its downfall. By contrast, the Baron de Breteuil, riding with the "maid" of the counterrevolution, holds aloft the flag of the nobility and clergy, now topped with a liberty cap.

Undoubtedly published together, this image and catalogue numbers 105 and 106 were meant to portray, almost cinematically, a burlesque view of the folly of counterrevolutionary activities. Liberty, solid and immovable as the rocks of the Rhine, represents the inviolability of the revolutionary regime.

107

108. ANONYMOUS

French

La Contre Révolution / ratée ou les / Paniers percés (The Failure of the Counterrevolution; or, The / Spendthrifts), ca. 1792

Etching with hand coloring

DV 1962, H 11389, B 513

307 x 467, 345 x 473

Bibliothèque nationale, Qb1 2 mars 1792

[M101121]

Sophisticated in both conception and execution, this caricature lampoons the fate of the Prince de Condé, following the death of the Holy Roman Emperor Leopold II, who was the brother of Marie-Antoinette and the principal benefactor of Condé's émigré army.

The caption describes the action thus: Condé, the "panier percé" (spendthrift), who always follows the emperor, tries to amuse his mistress.

Leopold, frightened by the sound of a bee, trips, falls, and dies, causing "the great dummy" Condé, to stumble over him and break in half. Condé's mistress, whom, we are told, history will call "the counterrevolution," exclaims that she too is lost now that Leopold is dead. The "petit Charlot," or "the werewolf" (the Comte d'Artois), lifts Condé up by his strap, imploring him to have courage, while the Comte de Provence orders the army to halt. In the background grenadiers, priests, monks, and attorneys, as well as General d'Autichamp, the Marquis de Bouillé, and the Prince de Lambesc stand idly by observing the antics of Condé and his party.

109. ANONYMOUS
French
Grand Débandement de l'armée anti-constitutionelle (The Great Rout of the Anti-Constitutional Army), ca. 1792
Etching and mezzotint
DV 2964
172 x 226, 221 x 256
Bibliothèque nationale, Qb1 15 juin 1792
[M101205]

109

In this royalist lampoon a detachment of women, who are described as having played a role in the Revolution, reveal themselves to the emperor's troops, thus forcing them to disband. Leading the women is "la demoiselle Teroig" (Madame Théroigne), who frightens the troops with her "république"; while Madame de Sta[ël], Madame Condor[cet], Madame de Dondon, Madame Silles (de Genlis, the marquise de Sillery), Madame de Calo[nne], and Madame Talmouse (de Laval-Talmont)—all aristocratic women who openly supported revolutionary ideals—each present a "villette." (This is a reference to the Marquis de Villette, an ardent revolutionary.) Behind the women, *sans-culottes* and Jacobins gather, threatening the troops with pikes topped with hams and sausages.

This extraordinary image functions on the one hand as a form of self-criticism, depicting the counterrevolutionary army as cowardly and easily dispersed by a poorly armed troop of revolutionaries led by a few aristocratic women. On the other hand, and quite remarkably, it gives form to the royalist fears of the Revolution as emasculating: voracious aristocratic women shamelessly bare their sex and, in concert with the Jacobins, hold aloft the phallic spoils of war. In this respect the print is simi-

lar to Victor Hugo's report of an incident that would occur during the fighting of June 1848. At that time, a young woman, known to be a prostitute, appeared on the crest of a barricade, pulled up her dress, and dared the troops to fire on her (Hertz, p. 29). This caricature, like the many obscene images of Marie-Antoinette and the Abbé Maury, is indicative of a frequent turn of mind in revolutionary imagery: the representation of a political threat as a sexual one (Hertz, p. 27).

110. ANONYMOUS
French
Bombardement de tous les trônes de l'Europe, / et la chûte des tyrans pour le bonheur de l'univers (The Bombardment of All the Thrones of Europe, / and the Fall of the Tyrants for the Happiness of the Universe), ca. 1792
Etching with hand coloring
DV 4470, B 622
228 x 372, 261 x 400
Bibliothèque nationale, Qb1 octobre 1792
[M101657]

In a wonderfully scatological and richly irreverent caricature, Liberty stands atop three tiers of bare-bottomed deputies to the National Assembly and ignites a cannon which fires into the posterior of Louis XVI and forces him to vomit vetoes that rain upon the crowned heads of Europe, the pope, and William Pitt, the prime minister of England. Liberty's cannon bears the inscription "Violent emetic" and is transported on wheels bearing the words "Free arbitrator of the French people." From the bare bottoms (literal *sans-culottes*, as one figure calls them) "Liberty" streams forth, as does the "Ça ira" (the most notorious of revolutionary songs, a refrain of which called for the aristocrats to

110

be hung from lampposts). A gigantic Prussian eagle departs with a crown which might have shielded the monarchs from the stain of Liberty, but the bird apologizes, "Except for these dogs of *sans-culottes,* I would protect you."

This caricature focuses upon the failed attempts of Empress Catherine II of Russia to organize a royal crusade against revolutionary France. She rises above her fellow monarchs, powerful, angry, and monstrously bare-breasted, shouting at them, "Return you cowards, and I will make you all bite the dust...how I regret my poor rubles!" A year later, when the empress tried to arrange an invasion of France by an émigré army, which was to gather in the Channel Islands, she was frustrated by the lack of English support. Two later proposals to put Russian armies at the disposal of England were rejected because the British refused to subsidize Catherine's troops. Increasingly, from 1791 through 1794, Catherine II was alone in her strident denouncements of the revolutionaries and in her vigorous attempts to organize an invasion of France.

111. ANONYMOUS
French
Le Nouvel Astre français ou la Cocarde tricolore suivant le cour du zodiaque (The New French Star; or, The Tricolor Cockade Following the Course of the Zodiac), 1793
Etching and mezzotint
DV 1751, B 556
253 x 304, 283 x 332
Bibliothèque nationale, H 11338
[G162727]
(Not in exhibition)

Beneath the signs of the zodiac and the "new French star" represented by the tricolor cockade, Chronos, or Time, uses his scythe to extinguish the mortal flames of the European monarchs. Among those represented are: Louis XVI, "the traitor and the last," who has been replaced by an altar of the fatherland surmounted by the fire of patriotism; the Holy Roman Emperor Joseph II and his brother and successor, Leopold II, whose flames have been replaced with Phrygian caps; King Gustavus III of Sweden, who was assassinated in March 1792; King Frederick William II of Prussia; Pope Pius VI; Sultan Selim III of Turkey (incorrectly designated Selim II); Empress Catherine II of Russia; Catherine's former lover King Stanislaw II of Poland; Queen Maria I Francesca Elisabeth of Portugal; King Victor Ama-

111

deus III, the duke of Savoy and king of Sardinia; King George III of England; and King Charles IV of Spain.

As discussed in detail by Klaus Herding in his essay in the present catalogue, *Le Nouvel Astre français* is actually quite complex in that it advocates a new system of government established through violent action while continuing to refer to the older circular perception of revolution. Thus, the print supports its argument historically (the circle of kings), naturally (the rays of the sun), and astronomically (the zodiac). The new star is announced as Time brings the circular movement of royalty to an end. Inscriptions contained in the rays of light emanating from the star justify revolutionary violence by recalling the precepts of Enlightenment philosophy.

Of note, the traditional sequence of signs of the zodiac has been altered to underscore the meaning of the print. By beginning the zodiac with Virgo rather than Aries, Leo the lion, symbol of royal power, is made to fall directly above the tricolor cockade and the fallen head of Louis XVI (Arasse, p. 126). In addition, the first day of Virgo, 21 January, was the date of the Louis XVI's execution.

112. ANONYMOUS

French

*Congrés des rois coalisés, ou les Tyrans
(découronnés) (The Congress of the Allied
Kings; or, The [Uncrowned] Tyrants)*, ca. 1793

Etching

DV 4358, B 609

303 x 461, 422 x 558

Bibliothèque nationale, H 11854

[G163294]

This print may have been commissioned by the
Committee of Public Safety from (Charles-
Jacques?) Mailly (Archives nationales, AF II, 66, dossier 489, fol. 3, 2 nivôse an II). In it the European
monarchs of the First Coalition are gathered
together around a table in an arrangement suggestive of the Last Supper. Together, they consult a
map and plan the invasion of France. Over the map
appears a Phrygian cap, symbol of the indivisible
French Republic, and from it blinding rays of light
emanate. Above the door, the Gallic cock, emblem
of vigilance, clutches a triangle, the symbol of

equality. Bolts of lightning shoot from the triangle,
striking the crowns of the European monarchs.

At the far left peering from behind a curtain is
King Stanislaw II of Poland, who has been excluded
from the coalition as his country has been parti-
tioned by Prussia, Russia, and Austria. At the end
of the table on the left, Empress Catherine II of
Russia, the Polish monarch's former lover,
attempts an *enjambée* (cat. no. 73) but is stopped by
a bolt of lightning. Her "great" projects, indicated
by a ship that has run aground and a fire of straw, lie
at the foot of her throne. To the right of Catherine
are King Frederick William II of Prussia and Victor
Amadeus III, the duke of Savoy and king of Sardinia, who was known disparagingly as "King of the
Marmots." At the center of the table the Holy
Roman Emperor Francis II raises the map in a figurative attempt to "overthrow" the French Republic; his double-headed eagle is struck by lightning
and falls clutching the emperor's crown, inadver-
tently revealing a double-headed snake of malicious leadership which underlies the royal diadem.
To the right, King Charles IV of Spain tries to shield
his face from the radiant light. At the end of the

112

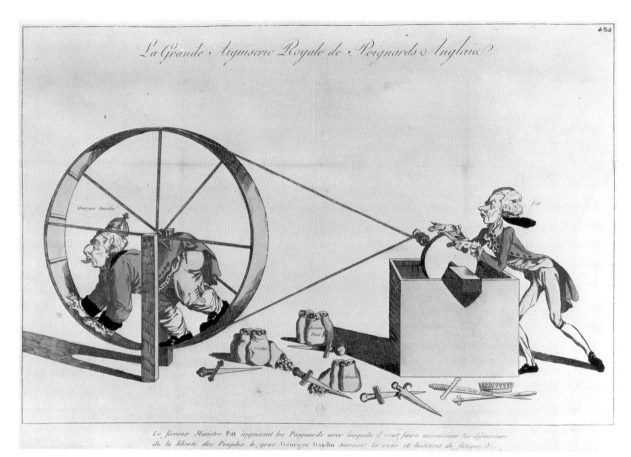

table on the right of the print, King George III of England throws down the "gold of corruption" at the urging of Prime Minister William Pitt, whose long nails reveal his diabolical character. Using a hook, Pitt also tries to steal the city of Toulon, the scene of Napoleon's victory of 1793 over the English, Spanish, and French royalists. Seated at the extreme right, Pope Pius VI holds a papal bull condemning the godless revolutionaries; the dove representing the Holy Spirit lies dead at his feet. King Ferdinand IV of Naples, referred to in the legend as the "Neopolitan Monkey," emerges from under the table to join the coalition. He sits on a shield emblazoned with the fleurs-de-lis of the French kings and offers the pope a wooden horse.

In contrast to the preceding print, which shows the European royalty literally being "snuffed out," the monarchs in this etching are felled by a more violent supernatural force. The triangle in the claws of the Gallic cock suggests the Christian Trinity; the Masons also used this device to represent the past, present, and future as embodied in the Deity. By 1794 it would come to symbolize the Supreme Being for the revolutionaries. The triangle as employed in this context may thus suggest the notion of revolutionary violence as a vehicle for the dispensation of divine justice.

113. Dubois

French, active 1790s
La Grande Aiguiserie royale de poignards anglais (The Great Royal Knife-Sharpening Establishment for English Daggers), 1793–1794
Etching with hand coloring on blue paper
DV 4386, B 594
321 x 510, 396 x 560
Bibliothèque nationale, Qb1 mai 1794
[M102821]

Although this print is often attributed to David, André Blum cites a decree issued by the Committee of Public Safety on 30 May 1794 (11 prairial an II) in which *citoyen* Dubois was ordered to produce one thousand copies of the caricature *La Grande Eguiserie [sic] royale de poignards anglais* (the decree is preserved in the Archives nationales, AF II, 66, dossier 489, fol. 24). We follow Blum, attributing this accomplished design to Dubois and not to David.

In his essay in this catalogue, Albert Boime suggests that Jacques René Hébert's frequent attacks in *Le Père Duchesne* on England's attempts to destroy French commerce and hire assassins to kill revolutionary leaders inspired this cartoon. Hébert regularly accused George III and his prime minister,

EXPLICATION.

N.° 1. *George Roi d'Angleterre commande en personne l'élite de son Armée Royal-Cruche N.° 2 il est conduit par son Ministre Pitt ou Milor Dindon N.° 3 qui le tient par le Nez pour mieux lui prouver son attachement. L'avant-Garde de la Royal Armée N.° 4 reçoit un échec à la porte de la Ville N.° 5 qui est occasionné par la colique de quelques Sans-Culottes placés au haut de la Porte N.° 6. L'avant-Garde dans sa défaite brise les cruches, dont il ne sort que toutes sortes de Bêtes venimeuses N.° 7 qui est l'esprit qui les anime. Fox ou Milord Oïe N.° 8 ferme la marche monté sur sa Trompette Anglaise et qui témoin de l'échec sonne un rappel en arrière par prudence Artillerie Anglaise nouvelle N.° 9 qui a la vertu d'éteindre les incendies et de éclairer les fortifications.*

4391

114

William Pitt, of sharpening their daggers to assassinate the French revolutionaries. This caricature depicts George III as a squirrel turning a wheel that drives the grinder's stone on which Pitt sharpens his knife. The caption is even more specific: "The famous minister Pitt sharpening the daggers with which he intends to murder the defenders of the people's liberty. The fat Georges Dandin turning the wheel and panting from exhaustion."

This is a lampoon of surgical precision: George III is made to look like a fat, dumb animal who can be made to run ceaselessly without direction; Pitt, drawn like the daggers he works on — thin, pointed, and sharp — is dressed like a vain and self-possessed fop. There is little else in this image, and nothing more is needed. Officially commissioned, it was meant to make its point instantly and without controversy. The enemy had to be immediately identifiable and the threat it posed, convincing. Dubois, about whom nothing is known, was clearly up to the task.

114. Jacques-Louis David
French, 1748–1825
L'Armée des cruches (The Army of Jugs),
1793–1794
Etching with hand coloring on blue paper
DV 4391, B 604
300 x 500, 390 x 533
Bibliothèque nationale, Qb1 juillet 1794
[M102902]

Between August and September 1793 the Committee of Public Safety requested the "Deputy David to employ his talents and all the means in his power to augment the number of caricatures which could arouse the public spirit and make it perceive precisely how atrocious and ridiculous are the enemies of Liberty and the Republic" (Blum, 1916, p. 195). By May 1794 David submitted two designs and a projected budget for printing them in black and white and in color. The Committee accepted the proposal and on 18 May 1794 (29 floréal an II) decreed that David produce the caricatures in editions of five hundred each (Archives nationales, AF II, 66 dossier 489, fol. 17, 29 floréal an II). This print and the next (cat. no. 115) were the result of that commission, and they stand as evidence of the Committee's belief in the efficacy of official satire in the campaign against external threats.

The Committee of Public Safety had been established in January 1793 in response to the emergencies brought about by the war that had been declared eight months prior. As the threat of foreign invasion and the effects of civil discord intensified, the Committee became more desperate and exercised greater control over revolutionary life. Acting independently of the Convention, it demanded that all citizens prove their patriotism and Jacobin spirit, and it summarily arrested and executed its opponents.

David's caricatures were therefore commissioned, produced, and distributed at a time when identifying and eradicating the enemies of the Revolution were of paramount concern. In this image King George III of England is depicted as a potbellied pot leading the British troops against the French and being led, in turn, by a turkey (identified in the caption as the prime minister, William Pitt). As Albert Boime points out in his essay in the present catalogue, numerous visual and verbal puns are at work in this image to attack the English. The word *cruche*, for example, can mean both a "jug" and a "blockhead" or "dolt." Similarly, the French word for turkey, *dindon* recalls the verb *dindonner*, literally "to dupe," as well as the word *dandin*, which has traditionally been used to designate a blockhead (cat. no. 113).

Thus, the advancing English army and its leaders are portrayed as dolts and blockheads. To add insult to injury, French *sans-culottes* squat overhead upon a gate, bare their buttocks, and defecate upon the army, reducing the English pots to *pots de chambre*. In the background stands a row of "cannons," which the caption calls, "the new English artillery which has the virtue of being able to extinguish fires and dissolve fortifications." These are, of course, giant syringes or clysters used for administering enemas.

William Hogarth's *The Political Clyster* (1757), in which lilliputian figures representing government ministers apply the clyster to John Bull, is an important precedent to consider here. In David's case, clysters are used as a means of assaulting the English but not in the direct manner that Hogarth had employed. Here, British attacks on the French literally backfire, causing the invading army to suffer humiliation of the grossest kind. The *sans-culottes* take obvious delight in the means by which they have defeated the rigid, prim, and proper English.

115. JACQUES-LOUIS DAVID
French, 1748–1825
Gouvernement anglois (The English Government), 1793–1794
Etching with hand coloring on blue paper
DV 4389, B 605
248 x 392
Bibliothèque nationale
(Not in exhibition)

David's second caricature commissioned by the Committee of Public Safety (Archives nationales, AF II 66, dossier 489, fol. 18, 29 floréal an II) is even more scatological than the first (cat. no. 114). The English government is depicted as a "flayed Devil," whose monstrous Medusa-like head is enveloped in snakes and whose bare buttocks assume the likeness of King George III. From the king's mouth (the devil's anus) spew the taxes imposed upon English citizens. The caption beneath the print describes the subject as the English government "personified by the figure of a Devil skinned alive....The portrait of the king is located at the rear end of the government which vomits on its people a myriad of taxes which overwhelm them." David is suggesting that despite their constitutional system of government, the English are enslaved by the economic policies of their king. It is an anti-English and an anti-monarchical image, one that refuses to compromise with anything other than a fully republican government.

Significantly, in his effort to make the English king appear grotesque, David relied upon one of the earliest European political prints, the *Papstesel (Pope-Ass)* designed by Wenzel von Olmütz for a pamphlet with texts by Luther and Melanchthon, published in 1523 (p. 21). There, the pope is represented by a monster with a donkey's head, a woman's naked torso, a scaled body, one human hand and one hoof-hand, one griffin's foot and a hoof, and an ass with a face from whose mouth emerges the head of a griffin or dragon. The compound image was meant to unmask the pope by revealing his true nature as similar to that of an ass, harlot, or dragon. The ass-face motif is of particular interest in considering David's print.

Octavio Paz has written of the occurrence of this motif in a woodcut by the nineteenth-century Mexican caricaturist José Guadalupe Posada:

> When we say that the ass is like another face, we deny the soul-body dualism; we laugh because we have resolved the discord that we are. But the victory of the pleasure principle does not last long; at the same time that our laughter celebrates the reconcilia-

N.º 1. Gouvernement Anglois

EXPLICATION.

N.º 2. l'Anglois né Libre.

Ce Gouvernement est représenté sous la figure d'un Diable écorché tout vif, accaparant le Commerce et revêtu de toutes les décorations Royal, le Portrait du Roi se trouve au derrière du Gouvernement lequel vomit sur son Peuple une multitude d'impôts avec lesquelles il le foudroye. Cette prérogative est attaché au Sceptre et à la Couronne.

115

tion of the soul and body, it dissolves it and makes it laughable. Once again…when we laugh at our ass — the caricature of our face — we affirm our separation and bring about the total defeat of the pleasure principle. Our face laughs at our ass and thus retraces the dividing line between the body and the spirit. (Paz, p. 5)

Paz interprets the ass-face metaphor as one that points up the vulnerability of human identity, the narrow line between repressed and explosive behavior, human and bestial nature. In the hands of the political caricaturist — either von Olmütz or David — it becomes a vehicle for exposing the weakness of its subject (the pope or George III), removing the cloak of venerability and exposing a naked figure replete with very human contradictions. Thus unmasked, the monarch or the head of the church must appear before adherents and opponents alike in the theater of religious or revolutionary politics. As in the original context of this motif — the Reformation — David uses this device to undermine the authority of his enemy and to subject him to a kind of anal counterattack.

Notorious for his calls for popular violence and advocacy of revolutionary dictatorship, Jean-Paul Marat was one of the foremost radicals of the Revolution. He was born into a lower middle-class Calvinist family in Switzerland in 1743 and settled in England in 1765. There, he received a medical degree and became a prosperous physician and writer of philosophical treatises. He moved to France in 1777, where, as a liberal and a democrat, he devoted himself to medicine and science and sought admission to the prestigious Academy of Sciences. He was never admitted, however, and, blaming a conspiracy of academicians, turned increasingly to political journalism.

In February 1789 Marat advocated a constitutional monarchy and a declaration of rights. In September he began publishing *L'Ami du peuple,* a journal in which he increasingly opposed the king and the Constituent Assembly. Pursued by police for inciting insurrection, he fled to England in October of 1789. From his place of exile, he called on the French people to accept a dictatorship of either a military tribunal or a single ruler. He ultimately returned to France and advocated a limited monarchy as late as February 1791, believing a republic to be impracticable. Following the flight to Varennes in June 1791, he called for the king's execution. As testimony to his increasing popularity among the people, Marat, who by this time had become a leading left-wing Montagnard, was elected to the Convention as a deputy from Paris.

Later he was accused of having instigated the massacre of prisoners in September 1792 and the Parisian food riots of 25 February 1793. On 13 April 1793, the National Convention voted to send him before the Revolutionary Tribunal where he was acquitted unanimously. Three months later, however, he was murdered by the royalist Charlotte Corday, as he lay in his medicinal bath dying of skin and lung diseases. Thus, he became the Revolution's first martyr to liberty and the subject of numerous popular images. Jacques-Louis David's dramatic portrait of the assassinated Marat, painted in 1793 (Brussels, Musées royaux des beaux-arts), remains an icon of the Revolution, a powerful image of sacrifice and political fanaticism.

116. JEAN FRANÇOIS TOURCATY
French, 1763–after 1793
Marat, ca. 1793, after Simon Petit
Etching, engraving, and stipple
DV 5255
363 x 270, 409 x 301
Bibliothèque nationale, H 11529
[G162920]

116

Marat was a powerful orator and the influential editor of the popular journal *L'Ami du peuple.* He frequently called for the troops to execute perfidious generals and for the people to assassinate all traitors; this led to his being accused of instigating numerous acts of popular violence, including the September Massacres of 1792 and the Parisian food riots of February 1793. On 13 April 1793 the National Convention voted to send him before the Revolutionary Tribunal. After an impassioned speech in his own defense, Marat was unanimously acquitted. In this dramatic portrait, after a painting by Simon Petit, Marat is shown at the tribune speaking out forcefully against the charges leveled at him. His words are visible on the sheets of paper before him: "Citizens, I come to this tribune to share with you my opinion of the great interests of the people. They have supported with courage the weight of the Revolution. At the sight of the dangers threatening the nation they left their homes for.... Yes, citizens, the welfare of the people is the supreme law. We cannot ignore this great principle."

The print's sophisticated and delicate use of diverse intaglio techniques made a celebrity of Tourcaty, its engraver, who, like Simon Petit, the author of its design, was active in the 1790s exhibiting in the infrequent salons (Musée Carnavalet, no. 99).

117. ANONYMOUS
French
La Grande Colère du diable (The Devil's Great Anger), ca. 1793
Etching with hand coloring on blue paper
DV 5287
209 x 289, 260 x 329
Bibliothèque nationale, Qb1 13 juillet 1793
[M102101]

118. ANONYMOUS
French
Souper du diable (The Devil's Supper), ca. 1793
Etching with hand coloring
DV 6473
170 x 222, 212 x 240
Bibliothèque nationale, Qb1 13 juillet 1793
[M102102]

119. ANONYMOUS
French
Indigestion du diable (The Devil's Indigestion), ca. 1793
Etching with hand coloring
DV 6474
168 x 220 (sheet)
Bibliothèque nationale, Qb1 10 août 1793
[M102189]

Marat made frequent and vociferous attacks, first against the monarchy, then against the moderate Constituent Assembly, and finally, as a Montagnard deputy to the National Convention, against the Girondins and Enragés, or radical deputies, with whom the Montagnards competed for the

LA GRANDE COLERE DU DIABLE

117

attention of the *sans-culottes*; these assaults made him in turn the subject of many equally vociferous counterattacks.

In the highly charged caricature, *La Grande Colère du diable* (cat. no. 117), Marat is accused of fathering *sans-culottes* with the devil's wife. A hideous, grimacing devil-woman gives birth to a ceaseless succession of *sans-culottes*, as she cries out to her devil-mate, "Alas my dear husband, it is the wretched Marat who raped me." The angry devil, restrained by two young demons (one of whom remarks, "Here we are no more exempt from it than in Paris"), cries back, "Oh rage, oh furor, I am made a cuckold by a Jacobin." At the same time, a recently delivered *sans-culotte* reaches out from the arms of an attendant and addresses the devil as "my dear little daddy," while in the lower left, two more *sans-culotte* babies begin to walk as one calls back to the other, "It will be very hard to pick ourselves up, our father has become an aristocrat."

In a related caricature, *Souper du diable* (cat. no. 118), a devil sits before a table preparing to cut up

SOUPER DU DIABLE.

118

INDIGESTION DU DIABLE.

119

and eat Marat, who roasts before him on a spit over an open fire, while other devils skewer a *sans-culotte*, who cries out to Marat to help her. In a third satire, *Indigestion du diable* (cat. no. 119), a miserable devil vomits and defecates *sans-culottes*. He sits on a closestool (*chaise percée*) attended by two ghoulish creatures who remark, "We told you so, nothing is more indigestible than all those scoundrels"; he is also served by an apothecary who carries "tea," which has given him "relief."

Such images are simple in composition, straightforward in execution, and unmistakable in meaning: Marat is a dangerous aberration whose repugnant actions and strident calls for popular violence have angered even the devil himself, and his deeds will come back to haunt and, ultimately, destroy him.

120. ANONYMOUS
French
La Mort du patriote Jean Paul Marat (Death of the Patriot Jean-Paul Marat), 1793
Etching and mezzotint
DV 5289, H 11520
168 x 270, 253 x 347
Bibliothèque nationale, Qb1 13 juillet 1793
[M102093]

On 13 July 1793 Charlotte Corday, a young royalist from Normandy, entered the private chamber of the radical revolutionary leader Marat and stabbed him to death as he lay in his medicinal bath. The murder occurred at a time when many thought that the fall of the revolutionary government was imminent. Foreign armies threatened France on its

eastern borders, while the counterrevolutionary forces within the country were gaining greater strength, particularly in the Vendée to the west where they were crushing the republican troops and rapidly approaching the important city of Angers. At the same time, food prices were soaring, encouraging city dwellers to suspect farmers of withholding food shipments and driving up prices. On 15 June a petition had been presented to the government calling for a law against hoarders. The murder of Marat further inflamed the populace at this time of political crises.

LA MORT DU PATRIOTE JEAN PAUL MARAT DÉPUTÉ A LA CONVENTION NATION.^LE EN 1793; &c. &c.

120

121. JACQUES MARCHAND
French, 1769–after 1810
Assassinat de J. P. Marat (Assassination of J.-P. Marat), 1793, after Claude-Louis Desrais
Etching and mezzotint with roulette
DV 5303, H 11524
215 x 326, 245 x 349
Bibliothèque nationale, Qb1 13 juillet 1793
[M102089]

At the time of Marat's assassination, a neighbor rushed into his room to see Charlotte Corday stabbing the revolutionary leader (cat. no. 120). This witness grabbed Corday and held her until the authorities could come to take her away. In this print, as soldiers accompany Corday out of the room, the man tells his story to Guellard du Mesnil, the police commissioner, who sits at a table collecting evidence. Standing to the right of the neighbor are Simonne Evrard, who is in tears, and either the surgeon Philippe-Jean Pelletan or the commissioner Laurent Bas.

News of the assassination soon spread throughout Paris. At the Convention on the following day, 14 July, delegations of citizens from all over the city

ASSASSINAT DE J.P. MARAT

121

rose to denounce Charlotte Corday and pay tribute to Marat. On 15 July the Convention commissioned David to make arrangements for the funeral. He responded by recalling that on the day following Marat's death, he had been asked by the doctor who had performed the embalming how the body was to be displayed to the public. "As you know," David reported, "parts of his body can't be shown because he had a kind of leprosy and his blood was inflamed." Thus, David decided to present Marat's body covered with a damp cloth that would be moistened from time to time to prevent putrefaction. The corpse was raised on a pedestal with the bathtub, woodblock, and inkwell arranged as they had been at the time of his death (Schnapper, pp. 154–56).

The moving funeral, the burial (which took place "under the trees where he so enjoyed dispensing advice to his fellow citizens"), and the subsequent translation to the Panthéon on 24 September 1794 contributed to the formation of a popular cult of Marat, who had been designated an official "martyr to liberty." Prints such as this one played an important role in the development and popularity of this cult.

Claude-Louis Desrais was a history painter, known especially for his military and battle paintings of the Revolution and Empire and for his drawings of charming genre scenes, fashion plates, and popular portraits (Carlson and Ittmann, no. 100). Jacques Marchand was a highly competent engraver, known for his reproductive mezzotints of historical subjects and his portraits of Napoleon.

122. ANONYMOUS
French
A la memoire de Marat, l'ami du peuple, assassiné le 13 juillet 1793 (In Memory of Marat, Friend of the People, Assassinated 13 July 1793),
1793
Etching and aquatint
241 x 341, 328 x 412
Bibliothèque nationale, Qb1 13 juillet 1793
[M102088]

A la memoire de MARAT, L'ami du Peuple, assassiné le 13 Juillet 1793.

122

This highly stylized allegory of the death of Marat stands in marked contrast to the more direct and prosaic depictions in the previous two prints. Here Marat's torso, highly muscled and idealized, is uncovered and his wound exposed; the blood drips down to stain the sheet draped over his left arm. His hand still grips the pen with which he has written his final words, and he gazes one last time at his muse, the figure of Liberty. She is dressed in an antique gown and holds a fasces crowned with a laurel wreath and topped by a Phrygian cap. The murderer, Charlotte Corday, the knife still clutched in her hand, has been caught while attempting to flee by two winged dragons who torment her. From the right, the personification of Vengeance flies at the assassin grabbing her hair and preparing to thrash her. Crowds of Marat's supporters who rush toward the room may be seen through the open door.

In its spare classical setting and planar composition, with the dying Marat set off against a simple architectural background and a large billowing drapery, the print is reminiscent of numerous Neoclassical death scenes, including Gavin Hamilton's *Andromache Bewailing the Death of Hector* of ca. 1761 (now lost, but known from an engraving by Domenico Cunego of 1764), Jean-Baptiste Greuze's *Septimius Severus and Caracalla* of 1769 (Paris, Musée du Louvre), and Jacques-Louis David's *Death of Socrates* of 1787 (New York, The Metropolitan Museum of Art). By reference to such antique prototypes, Marat's martyrdom attains monumental stature.

123. JACQUES-LOUIS COPIA
French, 1764–1799
Portrait de Marat assassiné (Portrait of the Assassinated Marat), 1793, after Jacques-Louis David
Engraving
DV 5313, H 11543
275 x 218, 297 x 220
Bibliothèque nationale, Ef 103 réserve

At the time of Marat's murder, David was the president of the radical Jacobin Club. The day before the assassination, he had sent a deputation from the club to visit Marat, who was also a member and the organization's leading theoretician. They found the ailing Marat in his bath writing his last thoughts to the people on a desk made of a simple board placed across his tub. Thus Charlotte

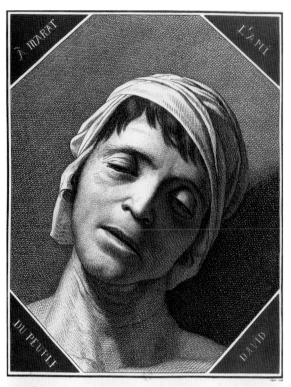

Ne pouvant me corrompre, ils m'ont assassiné.

123

Corday was to find and murder him on 13 July 1793 (cat. no. 120).

David responded to the assassination with his famous painting the *Death of Marat* (1793), now in the collection of the Musées royaux des beaux-arts, Brussels (p. 80). He depicted Marat alone in his bath, his pen still in one hand, the letter of introduction from Charlotte Corday in the other. The painting hung in the National Convention chambers with that of another assassinated revolutionary hero, Louis-Michel Lepelletier de Saint-Fargeau, also painted by David. At the request of the Convention, both pictures were engraved in order to disseminate the image of noble sacrifice throughout the republic. At the same time, David also executed a pen drawing of the assassinated Marat, which is now in the collection of the Château de Versailles (R.F. 1921). It is this image as engraved by Copia in 1793 that is reproduced here.

Copia was one of the most successful reproductive engravers of the revolutionary period. He was a close friend of the painter Pierre Paul Prud'hon, whose designs he often engraved (cat. no. 159), and he also reproduced the works of Alexandre-Evariste Fragonard (cat. no. 128) and Louis-Léopold Boilly, or Boyli (cat. nos. 154, 155). In the *Portrait of the Assassinated Marat*, Copia captured in vigorous and coarsely engraved lines the brutal quality of

David's drawing. It is an image of great power. The inscriptions in the engraving's four corners read: "To Marat / the friend / of the people / David." The inscription beneath reads: "Unable to corrupt me, they have assassinated me" (Musée Carnavalet, pp. 44–45).

124. JEAN JOSEPH FRANÇOIS TASSAERT
French, 1765–1835
M^{le}. A^{ne}. Cte. Corday (Mlle Anne Charlotte Corday), ca. 1793, after Jean-Jacques Hauer
Etching, aquatint, and stipple
DV 5379
318 x 229, 367 x 255
Bibliothèque nationale, H 11563
[G162954]
(Not in exhibition)

In April 1793, following the debate in the National Convention between the Girondins and the Montagnards over whether to try Louis XVI, the Central Revolutionary Committee of Paris called for the expulsion of twenty-two Girondin deputies. Two months later, twenty thousand armed *sans-culottes* surrounded the Convention and forced twenty-nine reluctant deputies from their positions of leadership, effectively eliminating the Girondins as a political force.

Many of these deputies fled to Caen in Normandy, where Marie-Anne Charlotte Corday d'Armans, the daughter of a minor noble, attended a convent school. Their presence became evidence to Charlotte Corday that the Montagnards were destroying the work of the Revolution. She held Marat to be chiefly responsible for these events and decided early in July to go to Paris and assassinate him. On 13 July she gained access to his private room by promising news of the recent Norman revolt. As they spoke, Corday pulled a knife and stabbed the Montagnard leader fatally. Four days later, following a brief trial, she was guillotined, becoming a martyr for the enemies of the Montagnards.

In this effective portrait, the simple beauty of Charlotte Corday is given an added dimension of fierce and principled political commitment. She is depicted as a modern Judith, the slayer of Holofernes, capable of the most violent of crimes. Her strong, immovable stance and relentless, confident stare give form to a recurrent fear in revolutionary images: the representation of a political threat as a sexual one (Hertz, p. 27).

124

125. ANONYMOUS
French
Marie Anne Charlotte Corday ci devant Darmans âgée de 25 ans assassin de Marat ecrivant sa derniere lettre à son pere (Marie-Anne Charlotte Corday Née Darmans Aged 25 Years Assassin of Marat Writing Her Last Letter to Her Father), ca. 1793
Etching and mezzotint
DV 5349
163 x 293, 248 x 347
Bibliothèque nationale, H 11552
[G162943]

Much like the current event prints representing the murder of Marat and subsequent arrest of Charlotte Corday, this image was meant to document an actual moment in the history of the Revolution.

Corday is shown in prison, writing her final letter to her father: "Pardon me, my dear father, for having

125

ended my life without your permission, I have revenged innocent victims, I have prevented other disasters. One day the people will know the truth and will rejoice for having been rid of a tyrant...I hope that you will not be tormented; in any case, I believe that you will have defenders in Caen... Goodbye, my dear father, please do not forget me or, worse, rejoice at my leaving: the cause is beautiful. I embrace my sister whom I love with all my heart, and my parents. Do not forget the verse of Corneille: 'The crime was the scandal, and not the scaffold.'"

It is a sentimental image, portraying Corday as a serious, thoughtful, and even courageous figure, not at all the mad assassin that the previous image would suggest.

126. VILLENEUVE

French, active 1789–1799

O Peuple! Marat ton plus fidele amis n'est plus (O People! Marat Your Most Faithful Friend Is No More), ca. 1793

Etching, aquatint, and mezzotint with roulette

230 x 169, 277 x 210

Bibliothèque nationale, Qb1 13 juillet 1793

[M102099]

In this heroic funerary image of Marat, the martyr's portrait is depicted on a simple but noble monument marking his burial place, which is described as "under the trees of the Cordeliers Gardens where he instructed the citizens." The Cordeliers Club was a Parisian political society whose influence over militant revolutionaries sometimes rivaled that of the Jacobins. It was founded in April 1790 as the Society of the Friends of the Rights of Man and of the Citizen and first met in the library of the former

Franciscan monastery on the street of the Cordeliers. The Club's first manifesto, printed in the *Moniteur* on 4 May 1790, stressed its role as a watchdog against the abuse of power by public authorities, and it soon adopted the eye of vigilance as its emblem. By September 1793 the Club had come under the influence of the ultrarevolutionary followers of Jacques René Hébert, publisher of *Le Père Duchesne* (pp. 76–78).

Marat had long been one of the group's most outspoken leaders, and following his funeral, the Cordeliers hung his embalmed heart from their ceiling and buried him in their garden. The club's political sympathies can be gleaned from the lengthy inscription below the image, which describes Marat as "the austere defender of rights and of the sovereignty of the people, the denouncer of all enemies, Marat, whose name alone will recall the services he rendered to the country." The caption continues, describing Charlotte Corday in a much different light than did the

126

previous image, "A Fury from Caen, Department of Calvados, from the house of the former Comte d'Orset, plunged a dagger into the breast of this apostle and martyr of the Revolution." It concludes with a charge to all citizens, "The hour of liberty has sounded," and Marat's blood is the "decree that thunders with the condemnation of all traitors...all patriots who go to the tomb of this great man, swear an oath anew, 'liberty or death.'"

With the abolition of the monarchy and the establishment of the republic on 21 September 1792, the revolutionary government began with earnestness to reconstitute French social and political life. To this end, language was ritualized and symbols were created; significantly, these symbols did not simply function as metaphors but, as Lynn Hunt has argued, served as a means to attain and confirm power (Hunt, 1984, p. 54). They legitimized the new regime and severed any remaining ties to the old order.

The formulation and acceptance of these new symbols, however, was not an easy process. At the inaugural meeting of the National Convention, deputies argued over the need for symbols of any kind. Should a sign or insignia be necessary to republican government? Do reason and nature, the foundations of the new regime, need representation? Some deputies argued that clear writing, clear speech, and clear argument were enough to convince the new citizens of the legitimacy of republicanism. Others, like Henri Grégoire, claimed that a sign was necessary to give a character of authenticity to all civic acts and to make authority public rather than individual.

The latter argument won the day, and in the case of the new calendar, for example, the government charged the Committee of Public Instruction to come up with both a suitable nomenclature and visual signs appropriate to the rational and natural bases of the new republic. Symbols were derived from classical and Egyptian sources, as well as Christian and Masonic repertoires. The carpenter's level (a Masonic sign) became the symbol of equality, the Roman fasces the symbol of union, the Roman laurel wreath the sign of civic virtue, and the Egyptian eye the emblem of vigilance; female figures, meanwhile, came to represent everything from liberty, nature, and France, to victory, philosophy, and charity.

As these symbols were officially determined, their graphic depiction was of the most sophisticated kind. It is on allegorical and emblematic images of this period that we most often find the names of designers, printmakers, and publishers, and it is here that we see evidence of the most determined Neoclassical draftsmanship. These official prints were meant to give form to the legitimate authority of the new revolutionary regime.

127. Philibert-Louis Debucourt
French, 1755–1832
Calendrier républicain (Republican Calendar), 1794
Etching and mezzotint
429 x 363, 439 x 369
Bibliothèque nationale, H 11952
[G163398]

127

This print represents the republican calendar of Year III (22 September 1794–22 September 1795) and shows the changes in the names of the months that reflect the agricultural emphasis decreed by the Law of 24 November 1793. The five complementary days at the end of the year are described at the bottom of the print as *sansculottides*, a name that had been abolished by the post-Thermidorian Convention on 24 August 1794, in favor of the term *jours complémentaires*. The artist, in all probability, had designed the calendar before this change in terminology occurred.

As the inscription relates, Philosophy, wearing the Phrygian cap, is seated on a marble throne decorated with the many-breasted Diana of the Ephesians, a symbol of fertility. Beneath her feet are the "Gothic monuments of error and superstition"— crumpled remnants of the Gregorian calendar and a papal insignia—which are held responsible for the developing of an "ignorant and ridiculous division of time." From the "great book of nature," Philosophy dictates the principles of the new calendar to her attentive genius. At her side are the book of morals and the triangle of equality resting on a base, the inscription of which proclaims the unity and indivisibility of the French Republic. Supported by the laws of nature, the new calendar is thus shown to be based upon rational principles and the civic virtues espoused by the revolutionary government.

This highly sophisticated print was designed and executed by Philibert-Louis Debucourt, a student of Joseph Marie Vien (who would later become David's teacher and, at the outbreak of the Revolution, had held the titles of first painter to the king and director of the French Academy). Trained as a painter, Debucourt was admitted to the Academy in 1781; five years later, however, he abandoned painting in favor of printmaking, becoming famous for his colored, multiple-plate intaglio prints depicting the elegant life of Parisian society. Bowing to the economic pressures of the revolutionary period, Debucourt executed single-plate prints in the English manner, of which this is a fine example (Carlson and Ittman, p. 287).

128. JACQUES-LOUIS COPIA
French, 1764–1799
Droits de l'homme et du citoyen (Rights of Man and of the Citizen), ca. 1793, after Alexandre-Evariste Fragonard
Etching
DV 4226
369 x 243, 444 x 291
Bibliothèque nationale, Qb1 3 septembre 1791
[M100879]

129. ANONYMOUS
French
Déclaration des droits de l'homme et du citoyen (Declaration of the Rights of Man and of the Citizen), 1793
Engraving
DV 4230
463 x 329
Bibliothèque nationale, Qb1 10 aout 1793
[M102149]

The Declaration of the Rights of Man and of the Citizen, which was made law on 26 August 1789, affirmed the sovereignty of the people as the basis

of the new order. It was incorporated, in various versions, into the constitutions of 1791, 1793, and 1795. Catalogue number 128 presents the original version of the Declaration as it appeared in the Constitution of 1791, while catalogue number 129 presents the expanded and more radical version that appeared in the Jacobin Constitution of 1793. In 1795 the Declaration was shortened and modified to conform to the more moderate constitution of a bourgeois republic (Stewart, p. 572).

Tablets engraved with the Declaration of the Rights of Man and of the Citizen were incorporated into numerous allegories and emblems throughout the Revolution (see cat. no. 133). In cata-

DROITS DE L'HOMME ET DU CITOYEN.

128

logue number 128 they are depicted as forming an antique stele and also recall the tablets given to Moses. Designed by Alexandre-Evariste Fragonard, the son of Jean-Honoré Fragonard, the print includes allegorical representations of the three civic virtues — Liberty, Equality, and Fraternity — and of the Republic, who is flanked by a Gallic cock and a sphere and is shown receiving pledges of allegiance from Roman warriors.

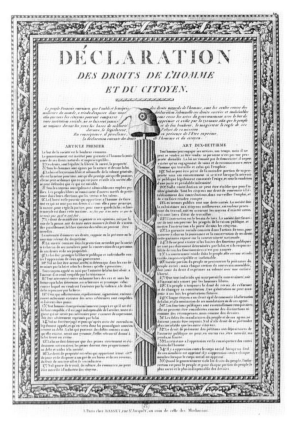

129

A student of David, Fragonard *fils* was a preco-
cious artist who had exhibited paintings in 1793 at
the Salon of the Palais national des arts when he
was only twelve years old (Renouvier, vol. 1, p. 197).
Yet there is no evidence to suggest that he would
have been capable of designing an image such as
this by 1791, the year in which the first constitution
was published. It is more likely that the print dates
from after 1793; this would suggest that versions of
the original Declaration were in circulation concur-
rent with those of the later document incorporated
into the Constitution of 1793.

In contrast to the ennobling antique imagery of
Fragonard's print, the anonymous engraving of the
1793 Declaration (cat. no. 129) employs a fasces
topped by a Phrygian cap, a Jacobin emblem of
unity highly appropriate to the character of the
more radical constitution of that year.

130. JEAN-FRANÇOIS JANINET
French, 1752–1814
Liberté (Liberty), 1792, after Jean Guillaume
Moitte
Etching and mezzotint
DV 6050, H 11793
368 x 262, 386 x 273
Bibliothèque nationale, Qb1 10 novembre 1793
[M102463]

Liberty became an increasingly dominant symbol in painting, prints, and sculpture after 1789.
Typically identified by the Phrygian cap, her other
attributes included the scepter of reason endowed
with a luminous eye, a lion on a leash, and a club.
After the overthrow of the monarchy in August
1792, the Constituent Assembly chose the symbol
of Liberty as the official seal of the republic (see
p. 38). Thereafter, the woman with the Phrygian
cap became a double allegory, representing both
Liberty and the French Republic (Agulhon, p. 18).

In this print, Liberty is presented as one of the
three principal civic virtues, the others being Fraternity and Equality (cat. no. 133). She is seated on a
throne, holding the Phrygian cap in one hand and a
club in the other. A traditional attribute of Hercules, the club was often associated with the killing of

130

229

the Hydra of despotism, which appears dead at Liberty's feet. The image is thus linked to prints of the taking of the Bastille that show the Third Estate triumphing over a similar many-headed beast (cat. nos. 25, 26).

Jean Guillaume Moitte was born in Paris in 1747, studied with the noted sculptor Jean-Baptiste Pigalle, and was accepted into the Academy in 1783. He was the son of the engraver Pierre Etienne Moitte and had two sisters who, before the Revolution, had engraved prints after designs by Jean-Baptiste Greuze and Philibert-Louis Debucourt (Renouvier, vol. 1, pp. 45–48). During the revolutionary period, he received important sculptural commissions for the Panthéon and the decoration of the triumphal arch erected on the Champ-de-Mars for the celebration of the National Federation in July 1790. He also designed numerous allegorical prints in the manner of his Neoclassical sculptural ensembles. These were often reproduced by Jean-François Janinet, the celebrated engraver of luxurious multiple-plate color prints after designs by François Boucher, Hubert Robert, and Nicolas Lavreince (Carlson and Ittman, pp. 90–91, 93–94). In the early years of the Revolution, Janinet executed numerous historical prints, including the fifty-six *Gravures historiques des principaux événements depuis l'ouverture des Etats-Généraux* published between 1789 and 1791.

131. BERNIER
French, active second half of the eighteenth century
La Liberté soutenue par la Raison, protège l'Innocence et couronne la Vertu (Liberty Supported by Reason, Protects Innocence and Crowns Virtue), ca. 1793, after Simon-Louis Boizot
Etching, mezzotint, and stipple
H 12177
360 x 537, 452 x 610
Bibliothèque nationale, Qb1 10 novembre 1793
[M102478]

132. JEAN-BAPTISTE CHAPUY
French, 1760–1802
La Liberté armée du sceptre de la Raison foudroye l'Ignorance et le Fanatisme (Liberty Armed with the Scepter of Reason Strikes Down Ignorance and Fanaticism), ca. 1793, after Simon-Louis Boizot
Engraving, mezzotint, and stipple
H 12178
352 x 516, 457 x 594
Bibliothèque nationale, Qb1 10 novembre 1793
[M102479]

Recalling images of the Annunciation wherein the Virgin receives a winged messenger, the first print (cat. no. 131) shows Liberty crowning Virtue and sheltering Innocence. Reason stands behind the group to the right, holding a scepter endowed with a luminous eye in her left hand. In the pendant print (cat. no. 132), Liberty strikes down Ignorance and Fanaticism with the scepter given to her

La Liberté soutenue par la Raison protège l'Innocence et couronne la Vertu

131

by Reason who stands at the left. Numerous allegorical prints such as these were produced and distributed in 1793 and 1794, during the height of the Cult of Reason.

As part of the larger movement to replace traditional Christianity with a civic religion, the Cult of Reason included dogmas (the Declaration of the Rights of Man and the republican constitution), rituals, symbols (carpenters' levels representing equality, fasces representing unity, and the Phrygian bonnet), and "sacred" architectural structures, such as civic altars. The cult's most dramatic presentation took place on 10 November 1793 in the Cathedral of Notre Dame, which had been con-

La Liberté armée du Sceptre de la Raison foudroye l'Ignorance et le fanatisme.

132

verted into a Temple of Reason. A symbolic mountain was surmounted by a Temple of Philosophy, and the flame of Truth burned from a rock while a choir of young girls sang a hymn to Reason and an actress in a tricolor robe played the role of Liberty. Members of the revolutionary government were suspicious of the Cult of Reason, however, because they considered its chief advocates to be atheists whose rejection of the belief in a Supreme Being and the immortality of the soul would undermine the moral foundation of the new republic.

These prints, which are typical of the highly stylized, Neoclassical compositions used in many revolutionary allegories, were designed by the sculptor Simon-Louis Boizot, an academician who had received the Prix de Rome in 1762. During the Revolution he contributed numerous designs for allegorical prints, described by Renouvier as "failing to distinguish themselves either by their grandeur or their originality of expression; they escape, by virtue of their banality, any classification as to school; but the type is serious, the draperies antique, the emblems easy to understand, and they fulfill their end as hieratic representations." This is a harsh criticism indeed, but one that aptly characterizes the radical Neoclassicism of revolutionary prints (Renouvier, vol. 1, p. 50).

133. JEAN-FRANÇOIS JANINET
French, 1752–1814
Egalité (Equality), ca. 1793–1794, after Jean Guillaume Moitte
Etching and mezzotint
DV 6053
368 x 262, 385 x 276
Bibliothèque nationale, Qb1 10 novembre 1793
[M102523]

Engraved by Jean-François Janinet after a design by the sculptor Jean Guillame Moitte (cat. no. 130), Equality is represented as an enthroned goddess, replete with emblems of fertility and nature. She holds a carpenter's level, the revolutionary symbol unique to her, and the Declaration of the Rights of Man and of the Citizen. Although not a right in itself, equality was considered the basis upon which all rights were distributed according to natural law (Scott and Rothaus, p. 301). As depicted here, Equality, seated firmly on her throne, embodies balance and permanence, qualities presumed to be inherent in the laws of nature guiding the Revolution.

The text of the Declaration of the Rights of Man here represented follows the original version of 1789, which was incorporated into the Constitu-

133

tion of 1791 (cat. nos. 128, 129). This would suggest a date of late 1794 for this print, following the fall of the Jacobins, and would indicate that it was intended to recall a less radical phase of the Revolution. If it was executed earlier, perhaps in 1793, it would have to have been intended for a conservative public aligned with the sentiments of 1791.

134. LOUIS-JEAN ALLAIS
French, 1762–1833
Egalité (Equality), ca. 1793, after Alexandre-Evariste Fragonard
Etching, mezzotint, and stipple
DV 6055
394 x 274, 462 x 330
Bibliothèque nationale, Qb1 10 novembre 1793
[M102503]

134

In contrast to the previous image, Fragonard's stark personification of Equality holds neither the carpenter's level nor the Declaration of the Rights of Man, the conventional attributes of this virtue. She appears instead as a figure of great strength, an emblem of force at the ready, confident in her power.

Equality's throne is decorated with prominent and highly abstract representations of the many-breasted Diana of the Ephesians, a symbol of fertility often used in this context (compare cat. no. 133) and on the throne of Philosophy as well (cat. no. 127). In other examples, however, fertility is only one of many attributes signifying the abundance and generative power of republican virtues founded on the laws of nature. Here, it is a sole attribute and gives Equality primacy among all the virtues as the natural basis for the new order.

Alexandre-Evariste Fragonard was an extraordinary designer whose images are considerably more abstract and iconic than those of the sculptors Jean Guillaume Moitte and Simon-Louis Boizot, for example (cat. nos. 130-33, 139). They are more in keeping the work of Louis-François Mariage (cat. no. 138) and represent at its most extreme the revolutionary period's fascination with antique sources. In this respect they resemble the highly geometrical architectural designs of Claude Nicolas Ledoux or Jean-Jacques Lequeu, which evidenced a purity, simplicity, and volumetric clarity that could at times border on the bizarre and fantastic. (For additional information on Fragonard *fils*, see cat. no. 128.)

Louis-Jean Allais was highly regarded as a designer whose portraits were frequently engraved or struck into medals. He also contributed designs for prints of the civic virtues, the revolutionary festivals, and the exhibition of the body of the martyr Louis-Michel Lepelletier de Saint-Fargeau. Much later, he was a principal artist for the collection of engravings entitled *Description de l'Egypte* (Renouvier, vol. 1, pp. 263-65).

135. LOUIS-JEAN ALLAIS
French, 1762–1833
Le Génie français adopte la Liberté et l'Egalité (The French Genius Adopts Liberty and Equality), ca. 1794, after Alexandre-Evariste Fragonard
Etching, mezzotint, and stipple
H 11978
393 x 508, 427 x 524
Bibliothèque nationale, Qb1 janvier 1794
[M102256]

In contrast to many other allegories and emblems of the Revolution, which concentrated on female figures, here the genius or spirit of France is represented as a colossus who dwarfs the female Liberty and Equality. As Lynn Hunt has noted, images of Hercules or a formidable colossus representing the French people became powerful symbols in 1793, replacing, at least during the Jacobin reign, the more typical female figures (Hunt, 1983, p. 105). Though he is not specifically depicted as Hercules, the spirit of France in this print is certainly portrayed as more powerful and aggressive than the moderate female virtues of Liberty and Equality who stand beneath his outstretched arms and depend upon his protection.

Fragonard *fils* derived his image of the French genius from the Olympian Zeus of Phidias, thus giving an ancient pedigree to this fatherly emblem of protection and the preservation of political freedom. (For additional information on Fragonard *fils*, see cat. nos. 128, 134; Allais is discussed in cat. no. 134.)

136

In contrast to more forceful images of revolutionary solidarity (cat. no. 135), Fraternity (cat. no. 136) and Unity (cat. no. 137) are represented here with children. Flanked by emblems of Liberty and Equality, Fraternity encourages Love and War to clasp their hands in friendship. In the second print, Unity distributes staves from the fasces of fraternity. Children and maternal figures were rarely represented in revolutionary allegories (p. 38). On the

LE GÉNIE FRANÇAIS ADOPTE LA LIBERTÉ ET L'ÉGALITÉ

135

136. PHILIBERT-LOUIS DEBUCOURT
French, 1755–1832
Fraternité (Fraternity), ca. 1793
Etching and mezzotint
187 x 153, 204 x 171
Bibliothèque nationale, H 11988
[G163436]

137. PHILIBERT-LOUIS DEBUCOURT
French, 1755–1832
Unité (Unity), 1793
Etching and mezzotint
188 x 152, 203 x 164
Bibliothèque nationale, Qb1 10 novembre 1793
[M102432]

137

1793 seal of the republic, for instance, Liberty and Equality were depicted as the younger female siblings of the republican Hercules. Lynn Hunt has described this as evidence of the revolutionaries' tendency to portray themselves as "young people without parents and without children…[imagining] themselves as part of no lineage" (p. 39). These prints prove an exception to the rule, however, and represent the civic virtues of Fraternity and Unity in terms of children who hold the promise of the future and hence require nurturing. (For information on Debucourt, see cat. no. 127.)

138. LOUIS-FRANÇOIS MARIAGE
French, active 1793–1814
Vérité (Truth), ca. 1793, after Alexandre-Evariste Fragonard
Etching and stipple
DV 6317
385 x 271, 450 x 310
Bibliothèque nationale, Qb1 10 novembre 1793
[M102541]

Engraved by Louis-François Mariage after a design by Fragonard *fils*, this extraordinary and

138

bizarre image depicts a seated figure of Truth throwing off the mantle of lies, hypocrisy, despotism, fanaticism, and other evils that threaten the purity of the new republic. Her blank eyes and iconic stare give Truth the look of an archaic statue, more abstract and removed than other allegorical figures of the Revolution. (For information on Fragonard *fils*, see cat. nos. 128, 134, 135.)

Mariage was known for his stipple-engraved portraits and vignettes executed to illustrate the works of Ovid and Racine. In 1792 he engraved the plates for P. Camper's *Dissertation sur les variétés naturelles qui caractérisent la physionomie des hommes des divers climats et des différents âges suivie de réflexion de la beauté…*, a treatise that developed upon Giovanni Battista della Porta's sixteenth-century analysis of physiognomy (Renouvier, vol. 2, p. 294; Wechsler, p. 181, n. 14). Mariage's career continued through the Empire, and during that time he produced numerous portraits and triumphant images of Napoleon.

139. ALEXANDRE CLÉMENT
French, active 1790–1800
La France républicaine / ouvrant son sein à tous les Français (Republican France / Opening Her Breast to All the French), 1792, after Simon-Louis Boizot
Etching and stipple
DV 6074
197 x 148 (oval), 291 x 228
Bibliothèque nationale, Qb1 21 septembre 1792
[M101511]

This robust and triumphant image of France, evoking emblematic representations of Charity and Fertility, suggests the bounty promised by the new regime. Radiant, France wears the liberty cap surmounted by a vigilant Gallic cock; around her neck, a carpenter's level, the revolutionary symbol of equality, hangs from a tricolor ribbon. As a representation of strength, France recalls Michelangelo's Delphic sibyl on the Sistine ceiling. Yet when compared to the many abstract female virtues represented during the Revolution — including others by Boizot (cat. nos. 131, 132) — she is more individualized and accessible, even maternal.

Alexandre Clément was a stipple engraver, and he was best known for his portraits after Louis-Léopold Boilly, which were published in the journal *Réunion d'artistes* in 1800 (Renouvier, vol. 1, p. 60).

LA FRANCE RÉPUBLICAINE.

Ouvrant son Sein à tous les Français.

139

president of the Committee, Charles-Gilbert Romme, who was heavily influenced by the Egyptian calendar and by Pierre-Sylvain Maréchal's earlier proposal for a revised calendar, the *Almanach des honnêtes gens* of 1788. The republican calendar was officially adopted on 5 October 1793, and the new system was declared to have begun retroactively on 22 September 1792.

The development of the new calendar had not been easy. Initially, it had been made to agree in some respects with the Gregorian calendar, and thus, Year II was to have commenced on 1 January 1793. This was changed in the fall of 1793, however, and the year was reordered to begin with the autumnal equinox, the date on which night and day are the same length, and hence an appropriate symbol of equality. Unfortunately, the equinox varied from year to year between 22 and 24 September, making the concordance between the old and new calendars more complex and the transition to the new system more difficult.

The poet Philippe François Fabre, known as Fabre d'Eglantine, was given the task of naming the months of the new revolutionary year. The Law of 24 November 1793 stipulated that the names be in keeping with natural phenomena consistent with the changing seasons and that the seasons should be indicated by distinct suffixes: *-aire* for autumn, *-ôse* for winter, *-al* for spring, and *-or* for summer. In

140. SALVATORE TRESCA
Italian, 1750–1815
Messidor (Messidor), 1793, after Louis Lafitte
Etching and stipple
265 x 203, 355 x 275
Bibliothèque nationale, Qb1 octobre 1793
[M102342]

141. SALVATORE TRESCA
Italian, 1750–1815
Ventôse (Ventôse), 1793, after Louis Lafitte
Etching and stipple, proof before letters
DV 6108
265 x 203, 351 x 272
Bibliothèque nationale, Qb1 25 octobre 1793
[M102338]

The monarchy was abolished and the republic declared on 21 September 1792. The following day, the National Convention charged its Committee of Public Instruction with the task of devising a Republican calendar that would be more rational, secular, and harmonious with nature than the Gregorian one (cat. no. 127). Its chief architect was the

140

141

order, the months were vendémiaire (vintage), brumaire (fog), frimaire (frost), nivôse (snow), pluviôse (rain), ventôse (wind), germinal (budding), floréal (flowering), prairial (meadows), messidor (harvest), thermidor (heat), and fructidor (fruit).

Richard Cobb has pointed out the unfortunate ironies that resulted when the natural and economic realities of a given year proved to be in sharp contrast to the promises implied by the names of the new months. For example, in messidor of Year II the harvest was disastrous, and in Year III it was even worse, only a third of the usual yield. The summers of 1794 and 1795 deserved the name thermidor, being the hottest on record for the century, but the abundance promised by fructidor and vendémiaire did not follow; instead, there were severe food shortages. Furthermore, there was a definite conflict between the official language and private discourse. As Cobb comments, "Can one imagine a watercarrier or a *savetier* [cobbler], a *décrotteur* [bootblack] or a horsedealer exclaiming: 'This is a warm day for *Frimaire*' or 'The leaves are turning late this *Fructidor*!'" (Cobb, 1981, p. 31). Certainly, the vocabulary of hope, innocence, and natural harmony proposed by the new calendar often ran counter to the reality of daily life during the Terror.

Taken from a calendar published in 1793, these prints are sophisticated responses to the task of representing the new months. Ventôse is portrayed as a river nymph, surrounded by emblems of the zodiac sign Pisces. Her hair and cape are blown by the wind that, as the caption of the published print describes, makes itself felt on the rivers, the earth, the fields and flowers, and lifts the birds in flight (the image reproduced here is a proof before the caption). It is an image of the life-giving force of the wind, which heralds the coming of spring and the promise of abundance and rebirth.

Messidor is an image of plenty and of a well-deserved rest after labors. She derives from the conventional emblem of Abundance, as described by Cesare Ripa in the 1603 edition of his *Iconologia*, but is more domestic (the same could be said of Ventôse, who derives, though more loosely, from the emblem of Air). Instead of conventional bags of money and containers of gold and jewels, Messidor has only a scythe and a bottle of wine. The caption below the published print describes her seductive charms and invokes Ceres, the Roman corn goddess, who offers the good life that will never fade or diminish, even upon waking.

Louis Lafitte, a history painter and student of Jean-Baptiste Regnault, won the Prix de Rome in 1791. He was widely known for his figure drawings and vignette designs for book illustrations, including an early edition of *Paul et Virginie* (Renouvier, vol. 1, pp. 128–30). Salvatore Tresca was a prominent reproductive printmaker who specialized in stipple engravings after the Old Masters. His prints after Lafitte for the republican calendar are considered among his finest works.

The Terror was both a policy and a set of institutions designed to intimidate enemies of the Revolution and thus assure their obedience. It is commonly divided into the First Terror (1792), the Terror as an instrument of government (September 1793 to spring of 1794), and the Great Terror (June and July 1794). The First Terror followed the fall of the monarchy and entailed the deportation or arrest of refractory priests and aristocrats who were accused of collaborating treasonably with the armies invading France. It was accompanied by riots and the lynching of suspected counterrevolutionaries and culminated in the September Massacres of 1792 when more than fourteen hundred inmates of Parisian prisons were murdered.

The governmental Terror began on 5 September 1793, when a large crowd of *sans-culottes* surrounded the National Convention and demanded more rigorous repression of counterrevolutionaries. The Revolutionary Tribunal was established to punish crimes against the Revolution, and legal status was granted to spontaneously formed revolutionary committees. Laws were passed authorizing execution within twenty-four hours of arrest in cases involving insurrection or civil war, and governmental authority was centralized in the Committee of Public Safety led by Robespierre. The Law of 22 Prairial (10 June 1794) initiated the period of the Great Terror by abolishing normal rules of evidence, depriving accused persons of any defense, and increasing enormously the potential body of suspects by redefining crimes against the Revolution. The effect of this law became apparent when more than thirteen hundred executions were carried out within six weeks. At the height of the violence, Robespierre was overthrown and the Terror's machinery dismantled. The Law of 22 Prairial was repealed on 1 August 1794, and the revolutionary committees were suppressed on 24 August.

The Terror was, on one hand, a dramatic response to attacks on the revolutionary government from within and without France. On the other, it was an instrument of class war, instigated by demonstrations of *sans-culottes* and culminating in Robespierre's Ventôse Decrees of 1794, which obligated the Convention to redistribute the property of suspects to indigent patriots in order to create a new social order. The emotions stirred by the Terror were fierce, making it a popular subject of propaganda prints and caricature.

142. ANONYMOUS
French
Sans culottes du 10 aoust de l'an 1er de la République française (Sans-Culotte of 10 August of the First Year of the French Republic), ca. 1792
Etching with hand coloring
250 x 170, 262 x 176
Bibliothèque nationale, Qb1 10 août 1792
[M101376]

142

In this print a typical *sans-culotte* appears armed for the *journée*, or demonstration, of 10 August 1792, when the combined forces of *sans-culottes* and *fédérés* marched on the Palais des Tuileries and were fired upon by the king's Swiss guards. This conflict resulted in the crowd's capture of the palace and the imprisonment of the royal family in the Temple, effectively marking the overthrow of the monarchy.

Sans-culottes could be recognized by their costumes, which distinguished them from other groups within the Third Estate. Robespierre used to differentiate between *golden breeches* and *sans-culottes*, and the *sans-culottes* themselves contrasted their dress with that of the better-dressed *muscadins* (or royalist sympathizers). Differences in dress were accompanied by distinct forms of social behavior, and the manners of the ancien régime were no longer acceptable after Year I. Determining a person's character by dress and manners was taken so seriously that *sans-culottes* found it difficult to accept any member of the former privileged classes. As one *sans-culotte* explained, "Such men are incapable of bringing themselves to the heights of our revolution; their hearts are always full of pride and we shall never forget their former grandeur and their domination over us" (Soboul, 1972, p. 3).

On 5 September 1793 a mass of *sans-culotte* demonstrators surrounded the middle-class National Convention and demanded more rigorous suppression of counterrevolutionaries. They also demanded imposition of price controls and food for the poor. The demands of the *sans-culottes* in effect forced the Convention to endorse the Terror. During Year II the *sans-culottes'* alliance with the Jacobins was central to the club's dominance of the Convention, while their subsequent indifference to Robespierre and his followers was in turn partially responsible for the Jacobin downfall on 9 thermidor.

143. ANONYMOUS
French
La Jolie Sans culotte armée en guerre (The Pretty Sans-Culotte Armed for War), ca. 1792
Etching with hand coloring
248 x 167, 260 x 174
Bibliothèque nationale, Qb1 10 août 1792
[M101377]

A militant *sans-culotte* woman stands armed and ready for a war that is to be waged on the home front, while her husband, sons, and brothers fight on foreign soil. *Sans-culotte* women played a prominent role in calling for a strong moral foundation for the new society. The Society of Republican Revolutionary Women, for instance, demanded that prostitutes be kept in national homes in healthy surroundings and have patriotic articles read to them twice a day (Soboul, 1972, p. 247). Numerous sketches of family life published in *Le Père Duchesne* emphasized the role of women who, as wives and mothers of revolutionaries, were felt to

La Jolie sans Culotte armée en Guerre .

143

be central to establishing the morality of family life through their tenderness and dignity.

Within the political structure, however, *sans-culotte* women played only a marginal role; they sat in specially reserved galleries in the meeting rooms of the popular societies but almost never actively participated in debates or discussions. In fact, while women were encouraged to attend such meetings in order to swell the audience, most of the members of these societies sought to discredit the Society of Republican Revolutionary Women (Soboul, 1972, p. 217). Women were able to play a more important political role in the *journées* and the bread riots when they joined with the masses of *sans-culottes* demanding equality and political reform (Hufton, p. 95).

144. VILLENEUVE
French, active 1789–1799
L'Amour sans culotte (Cupid Sans-Culotte), ca. 1793
Etching and mezzotint with hand coloring
65 (diameter), 80 (diameter)
Bibliothèque nationale, Qb1 10 novembre 1793
[M102374]

This charming emblem personifies the *sans-culotte* Love, a cupid who carries a pike adorned with trousers and crowns the symbol of equality with the laurel wreath of victory.

The *sans-culottes* wished to structure a system for revolutionary living that made personal virtue the model for public or patriotic virtue. They encouraged the acceptance of free unions between men and women, provided that such arrangements were founded on moral principles. Equal rights were demanded for children born of common-law marriages, and public oaths of love were considered just as legitimate as legal marriages. *Sans-culottes* sought a life of dignity without social prejudice, and a Love that worshiped equality was felt to be the appropriate basis of such a life.

145. ANONYMOUS
French
La Véritable Guillotine ordinaere, / ha, le bon soutien pour la liberté! (The True Ordinary Guillotine / Ha, the Good Foundation for Liberty!), ca. 1792
Etching
DV 4988, B 576
335 x 169
Bibliothèque nationale
(Not in exhibition)

This "true," as well as "ordinary," guillotine is presented as an ominous icon of the Terror. It stands like a monstrous beast with its mouth wide open waiting for the next victim to slip his head beneath the blade.

The concept for the machine was originated by Dr. J.-I. Guillotin, a professor of sciences at the University of Paris; he introduced it before the Con-

144

LA VERITABLE GUILLOTINE ORDINAERE,
HA LE BON SOUTIEN POUR LA LIBERTÉ!

145

stituent Assembly as a humanitarian means of executing criminals that would be quicker and less painful than other methods. In addition, as it would be used on offenders from every class, it represented a new kind of equality under the law (previously, decapitation had been reserved for the privileged).

Within the Constituent Assembly, Guillotin was a member of the Committee on Mendicancy and Public Health, and it was in this capacity that he introduced the idea of decollating all persons found guilty of a capital offense. Following his proposal, a machine was designed and carefully tested, first on animals, then on the corpses of paupers who had died in the hospital. It was first used in April 1792 to execute a thief. In January 1793 it would be used to execute the king, and during the Terror it would become an indelible symbol of revolutionary violence.

Although the machine became identified with the name of Dr. Guillotin, he merely proposed the concept; he never designed, and certainly did not invent, the guillotine. The new term was used mockingly by the royalist newspaper *Actes des apôtres* in a song ridiculing Dr. Guillotin for his ardent patriotism in proposing an egalitarian machine for executions (Arasse, p. 124).

146. ANONYMOUS
French
Robespierre, guillotinant le boureau après avoir fait guillot^r tous les Français (Robespierre, Guillotining the Executioner after Having Guillotined All the French), ca. 1793
Etching
DV 6539, B 577
140 x 84, 214 x 142
Bibliothèque nationale, H 11742
[G163137]

Resting on a tomb, Robespierre guillotines the executioner after having guillotined all the French. Behind him are the numerous guillotines with which he has exterminated not only his political allies and enemies (members of the Committee of Public Safety, Jacobins, Cordeliers, Brissotins, Girondins, Philipotins, Chabotins, and Hébertists, constitutional authorities, members of the National Convention, and participants in popular societies) but ordinary citizens as well (nobles, priests, *gens de talent*, the elderly, women, children, soldiers, and generals). De Vinck describes a later

state of this print, identifying the texts on the ground as the constitutions of 1791 and 1793 and also indicating that the guillotines are labeled with the names of groups for whom they were intended.

Maximilien Robespierre, a brilliant lawyer, was elected in 1789 to represent his native Arras at the meeting of the Estates General. He later served in the National and Constituent Assemblies, where

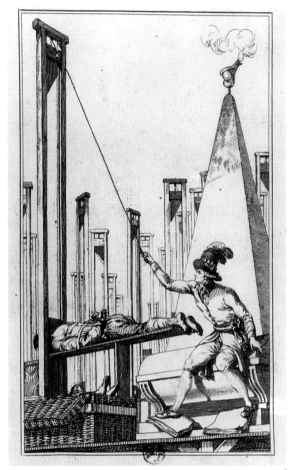

146

he distinguished himself as an orator of keen intelligence, if not great power. In April 1790 he was elected president of the Jacobin Club, having been a member since its founding. His increasingly strident attacks on the monarchy and, following the flight to Varennes, his consistent demands for the king's trial inspired slanders against him and threats upon his life. Over the next two years, in more than one hundred speeches delivered at the Jacobin Club and in his newspaper, *Le Défenseur de la constitution*, he vigorously denounced the secret plots of the court and its royalist supporters.

As threats to the new republic mounted both from within and without the country, Robespierre called for the collective dictatorship of the Convention and the administration of inflexible justice against everyone suspected of sympathizing with traitors to the Revolution. His forceful denunciations of opponents, including the Hébertists, created even more enemies. After the passage of the Law of 22 Prairial (10 June 1794), which he had endorsed, Robespierre was left with only a few ardent supporters. His declining health caused him to withdraw from public life until the final days of the Great Terror when he returned wishing to speak before the Convention and did so on 8 thermidor (26 July 1794). On the next day, however, he was refused permission to speak and a warrant was issued for his arrest. Declared an outlaw, he wounded himself with his pistol as his followers fell into total disarray and were arrested. On 10 thermidor (28 July 1794) Robespierre and twenty-two of his adherents were guillotined, and more than one hundred people would be killed over the next few days. The Great Terror was about to come to an end.

This bitter image criticizes what was perceived by some as Robespierre's fanaticism during the period of the Great Terror. He was viewed as working against the principles of the Constitution of 1791 and the Jacobin Constitution of 1793 and eliminating all opposing factions in order to maintain complete control.

Le Peuple Français,
Où le régime de Robespierre.

147

147. ANONYMOUS
French
Le Peuple français / où le Régime de Robespierre (The French People; / or, The Regime of Robespierre), ca. 1793
Etching
DV 6536, B 573
345 x 268, 491 x 333
Bibliothèque nationale, H 11915
[G163359]

Satirizing the plight of the French people during the regime of Robespierre, a young man, blindfolded and about to stumble over the rocks at his feet, searches in vain for Liberty, Equality, and Fraternity, who dance about him just out of reach. At the right, however, the figure of Death approaches and is about to touch the youth's hand. The game, the caption tells us, has turned against the player. He will be trapped by Death; such is the fate, the print suggests, of all citizens enduring Robespierre's Terror.

The Great Terror was originally justified by Robespierre and his followers as necessary to the war effort, but public opinion of its drastic measures began to turn after military successes in the spring of 1794 made them seem unnecessary. The Law of 22 Prairial (10 June 1794), which began the Great Terror, had abolished normal rules of evidence and had so greatly increased the potential body of suspects that virtually everyone was threatened. More than thirteen hundred persons were tried and executed in Paris within six weeks, arousing fears of Robespierre's dictatorial ambitions and greatly increasing the number of his enemies.

148. PIERRE LÉLU
French, 1741–1810
Le Triomphe de la Montagne (The Triumph of the Mountain), ca. 1793
Etching
445 x 335, 510 x 360
Bibliothèque nationale, H 11752
[G163348]

Here the Montagnards, supporters of the Terror, are represented in a triumphant Bacchanalian procession. Liberty and Equality ride on a chariot in

148

front of a Tree of Liberty hung with a banner reading, "Truth and reason." Liberty carries a mountainous form, the emblem of the Montagnards, which is inscribed with their motto, "Live free or die." Seated on the chariot in front of this couple is "Public Joy" (Virtue), who holds a cornucopia suggesting that abundance characterizes the reign of the Montagnards; this figure straddles the fasces representing unity. Mercury, "symbol of intelligence and activity," conducts the horses, while Hercules and Minerva exterminate various monsters (Girondins, Brissotins, and Rolandins) who threaten Liberty. A bright sun rises behind the tree and bathes an antique temple in the right background with light, thus signifying the new dawn of French prosperity under Montagnard rule.

From 1792 to 1795 the Montagnards held posts as left-wing deputies in the National Convention. They initially took their name from their seats, which were located in the highest rows of the Convention hall, but later they chose to emphasize the fact that Moses had brought the Commandments down from the mountain, "So too the Mountain of the Convention will give laws to France." The group's chief opponents were the Girondins, more moderate deputies who, for instance, were divided over whether to execute or exile Louis XVI in

December 1792. The Montagnards had called for the king's immediate execution.

Unable to stem the combined threat of foreign attack and civil war, the Montagnards, led by Robespierre, stepped up their campaign against the Girondin government in 1793. On 2 June the National Convention moved to arrest twenty-nine Girondin deputies, marking the triumph of the Montagnards. The victory of the Mountain is celebrated in this odd print. Half cartoon and half triumphal image, it recalls the great Hampton Court painting by Andrea Mantegna *The Triumph of Caesar*, although it is not so heroic.

149. VILLENEUVE
French, active 1789–1799
L'Egalité triomphante ou le Triumvirat puni (Equality Triumphant; or, The Triumvirate Punished), ca. 1793
Etching and mezzotint
DV 6545
276 x 205, 343 x 241
Bibliothèque nationale, H 11927
[G163372]

149

In this triumphant image, a winged figure of Equality carries the sword of justice in one hand and its scales in the other. She balances effortlessly on a carpenter's level, her revolutionary symbol, and in so doing smashes the heads of the tyrant Robespierre, the hypocrite Couthon, and the insolent Saint-Just.

Simply, but forcefully, this print celebrates 9 thermidor and the end of the Terror; it calls on all citizens to take up the cry "Long live the republic, liberty, and equality."

the base of the monument, a dog urinates on the king's death sentence and the Constitution of 1793, among other documents. A man squats and defecates on the tricolor flag, remarking sarcastically, "I have made the fourth color"; while a clown-like figure, who wears a sign on his back commemorating the National Convention's decree of the Constitution of 1793, responds coldly, "Traitor, the guillotine."

Atop the broken edifice, a small bird calls out "cras! cras! cras!" ("filth! filth! filth!"), commenting harshly on the events of 1793 that mark "the tragic end of the French Republic."

150. ANONYMOUS
French
Fin tragique de la République française (Tragic End of the French Republic), ca. 1793
Etching
B 583
220 x 270, 236 x 295
Bibliothèque nationale, H 11813
[G163212]

151. ANONYMOUS
French
Ramasse ton bonnet (Pick Up Your Cap), ca. 1793
Etching with hand coloring
266 x 218 (sheet)
Bibliothèque nationale, Qb1 décembre 1793
[M102660]

Far more subtle than the previous satire, this image cautions against the Terror and the departure from the original ideals that lay at the foundation of the Revolution.

Dressed in antique costume, Liberty carries the fasces of fraternity as she flees to the right. A young

Fin tragique de la République française

150

In a bitter commentary on the failures of the Revolution and the Terror, a pyramid—a conventional symbol of permanence—is shown broken in two; its top and the Phrygian cap that had crowned its summit lie in ruins.

Everywhere, the promises of the Revolution have gone awry. A second Phrygian cap hangs from a broken Tree of Liberty, as if from a scaffold. Gazing up at it, Voltaire queries, "When will you finish this foolishness?"; while, on the opposite side of the structure, a figure, who appears to be falling, cries out, "Ouf, ouf, what a lousy trick!" A medallion adorning the face of the pyramid represents a donkey braying to a cow, "We are all equal." Along

Ramasse ton bonnet ?

151

152

man in late eighteenth-century dress, who represents the "present," reaches down to retrieve the Phrygian cap that Liberty has either lost or left behind. As he bends down he admonishes, "Pick up your cap," attempting to make Liberty recall her duties.

152. JEAN-BAPTISTE-MARIE LOUVION
French, 1740–1804
Les Formes acerbes (Bitter Forms), 1795,
after M. Poirier de Dunkerque, avocat
Etching and stipple with hand coloring
DV 6143, B 586
278 x 359, 418 x 457
Bibliothèque nationale, H 12109
[G163627]

The central figure in this image is Joseph Le Bon, a member of the National Convention and the Committee of General Security, who implemented the policies of the Terror. He stands between the guillotines of Arras and Cambrai, cities where more than five hundred suspected enemies of the Revolution were executed on his order.

Drinking the victims' blood as it pours from the twin guillotines, this "cannibal" stands on piles of corpses, while two furies and assorted wild animals devour the headless bodies.

Above, under the watchful eye of Vigilance, Justice reveals Truth to the National Convention. According to the inscription, Truth holds two pamphlets entitled *The Anguishes of Death; or, Ideas of the Horrors of the Prisons at Arras Composed by Authors in Their Irons* and *Atrocities Committed against Women*. A winged figure heralds the good news that 9 thermidor has come and that henceforth humanity, justice, and virtue will be the order of the day. Below, to the left, freed prisoners cry, "War on all the agents of crime" as they rush from their jails. They clutch each other like the figures in David's drawings for the *Oath of the Tennis Court* and thus recall the origins of the Revolution. Le Bon's own fate is recorded along the lower edge of the print, "Condemned to die at Amiens. Executed 15 October 1795."

Published after the end of the Terror, prints such as this and the following example (cat. no. 153) are attempts to discredit the reign of Robespierre.

Anti-Jacobin factions also used the press for revelations about the "blood drinkers," attempting to sway public opinion away from a return to such extreme policies (Woronoff, p. 3).

153. JEAN-BAPTISTE-MARIE LOUVION
French, 1740–1804
Le Neuf Thermidor ou la Surprise angloise / aux honnêtes gens de tous les pays (The Ninth of Thermidor; or, The English Surprise / to Honest People of All Countries), ca. 1795, after M. Poirier de Dunkerque, avocat
Etching
DV 6550, B 606
234 x 348, 278 x 355
Bibliothèque nationale, H 12093
[G163611]

A young and simply dressed man personifying France stands before an ostrich, who, as the inscription explains has had the bad luck to bear monsters

LE NEUF THERMIDOR OÙ LA SURPRISE ANGLOISE
AUX HONNÊTES GENS DE TOUS LES PAYS.

153

such as Marat, Carrier, Robespierre, and Le Bon in her first egg laying. These offspring are shown being killed by the figure of Justice on the left. The print represents the events of 9 thermidor (27 July 1794) when, after his opponents prevented·him from speaking on the floor of the National Convention, Robespierre and many of his supporters were arrested and ultimately guillotined.

The inscription expresses the hope that Liberty will continue to "rid us of this breed of pest," as France offers one of the ostrich's second brood, comprised only of "friends of peace, universal happiness, and tranquillity of nations," to a stout Englishman. The Englishman contemplates France's promise of peace in disbelief and mutters "Goddem! Go on" between forkfuls of beef. This is an elegant caricature that turns the tables on the English, as the piggish John Bull is copied from a well-known caricature of 1792 by James Gillray, entitled *French Liberty—British Slavery*, which contrasts the free, but emaciated and bestial, *sans-culotte* to the plump, but enslaved, Englishman. Here it is England that appears bestial and France that holds forth the promise of civilization.

Dated fructidor an III (18 August–22 September 1795), the inscription states that the print was invented by the author of *Les Formes acerbes* (cat. no. 152). It shares with that print a detailed propagandistic inscription, complex allegorical meaning, and sophisticated style, and it was obviously intended for an educated audience. Both images must have been commissioned by some post-Thermidorian political faction intent on discrediting the government of the Terror, as well as encouraging a spirit of revenge against remaining Jacobins.

154. JACQUES-LOUIS COPIA
French, 1764–1799
Le Porte drapeau de la fête civique (The Color-Bearer of the Civic Holiday), ca. 1795, after Boyli [Louis-Léopold Boilly]
Etching, engraving, and stipple
341 x 259, 500 x 307
Bibliothèque nationale, Ef 108 réserve

155. JACQUES-LOUIS COPIA
French, 1764–1799
La Porte drapeau de la fête champêtre / au retour de Sa Majesté Louis XVIII dans sa capitale, le 3 mai 1814 (The Color-Bearer of the Country Fair / on the Return of His Majesty Louis XVIII to His Capital, on 3 May 1814), 1814, after Boyli [Louis-Léopold Boilly]
Etching, engraving, and stipple
341 x 259, 383 x 282
Bibliothèque nationale, Ef 103 réserve

As in earlier images of Louis XVI where the engraving plate was reworked (cat. nos. 64, 65), here the flag and the title of the print have been changed to instill new political meaning. This time, however, a revolutionary image (cat. no. 154) has been modified to become one that supports the Restoration of 1814 (cat. no. 155). In the earlier version, a

154

LE PORTE DRAPEAU DE LA FÊTE CHAMPÊTRE

155

156. ANONYMOUS
French
Unité, indivisibilité…du crime et de la misere / Le Miroir du passé pour sauvegarde de l'avenir (Unity, Indivisibility…of Crime and Misery / The Mirror of the Past as Safeguard for the Future), ca. 1797
Etching
420 x 350, 548 x 438
Bibliothèque nationale, Qb1 avril 1797
[M103694]

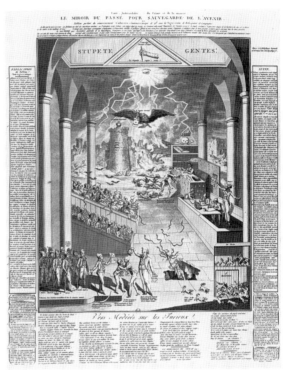

156

noble *sans-culotte* (whose costume came to be recognized as the "official" dress of his group) supports the tricolor flag of the Revolution, on which is written "Liberty or death." The strength of his arms, the rugged beauty of his face, and the way he dominates the landscape give a heroic quality to this figure and integrate the ambitions of the revolutionary government with those of rural France.

In the second print, the flag has been changed to the white banner of the Bourbons, which, significantly, had been the emblem of the counterrevolutionaries two decades before. The lasting appeal of this heroic image is obvious, and it stands as a testament to the power of Boilly's design. Very soon after its making, this print came to represent a highly significant source of any French government's legitimacy: the people and the strong emotional ties to the countryside. The transformation of the print, however, also suggests a kind of triumph over the Revolution in that the restored Bourbons have claimed one of its icons for their own.

In this extraordinarily complex allegory, a Revolutionary Tribunal (structured like a church service where death is the object of worship) is presided over by a monstrous figure labeled "energy" (3), who breathes fire and holds up a page from Marat's journal, *L'Ami du peuple*. The three princes of the church—the "triumtigres," Danton, Marat, and Robespierre—stand at the lower left. To the right, Danton has just removed a Phrygian cap from a skeleton ("the holy sister Equality") who is embracing the weakened Marat ("the Grand Master of the Order of the Cemetery"). To the left, and leading the holy fathers of the church of the Terror (Hébert, Chaumette, Fouquier-Tinville, Carrier, Le Bon, and Couthon), is Robespierre. He holds in his right hand a scythe, emblem of the Grim Reaper, and in his left hand, a sheet of paper bearing the words "the Law of 22 Prairial and of 17 September."

The first law accelerated the procedures of the Revolutionary Tribunal and effectively increased the number of those brought to trial. The second, also known as the Law of Suspects, defined categories of counterrevolutionaries: those who could not provide proof of their livelihood; those who had been refused certificates of civicism; former nobles and immediate relatives of émigrés, etc. Together, these laws represented the most important measures taken to legitimize the Terror. All of the men portrayed wear crossed bones of death under a carpenter's level as the emblem of their order, while the skeletal figures wear a badge with a guillotine.

An evil Medusa-headed fury breaks violently through the floor and unleashes serpents that dart out to join the revolutionaries. In the background, bats fly above the assembled, vultures pick at the remains of a male corpse, and a dying child lies across the body of her lifeless mother. From a tower in the distance, an owl, symbol of deceit, watches over the events, and behind him fires rage and lightning bursts forth under the legend "Providence or the justice of thermidor." Everything falls to ruin, and the crowned vulture of the Law of 22 Prairial hovers above this macabre scene of death and decay.

The borders of this print contain long and detailed explanations of the allegory, which mock the "cadavero-faminocratique" government of Robespierre. The purpose of this image, as the print's title makes clear, is to offer a vision of past horrors as a safeguard against any future recurrence of the Terror and its institutionalized violence.

X. The Directory

The Directory was a five-member executive committee established by the Thermidorian Constitution of 1795. Following the collapse of the Terror, it was intended to produce a stable, orderly, property-dominated society, erected, as Colin Lucas has noted, "on the unfettered disposition of oneself and of one's property, in which the victories of 1789 over privilege and despotism were protected by state apparatus firmly in the hands of property owners" (Scott and Rothaus, p. 965). Yet the Directory never succeeded in erasing the marked political divisions of the recent past or developing a strong "center" party to lend it support. It had inherited a desperate financial situation; the treasury was empty, paper currency was almost valueless, taxes were unpaid, and public institutions were without adequate funds. In addition, while treaties had been signed with Prussia, Holland, and Spain, France remained at war with Austria and England.

In May 1796 Babeuf's "Conspiracy of Equals," which was intent on suppressing individual property ownership and overthrowing the Directory, was discovered and put down. Babeuf and his followers were arrested, and the government swung further to the right. In September 1797, however, the moderate directors were replaced and right-wing deputies were purged from the legislative councils in a bloodless republican coup.

Although it failed to create a political consensus of moderate republican opinion, the Directory brought an end to the financial chaos and rampant inflation that had marked the Terror. It eventually fell victim, however, to the many political crises at home and to Bonaparte's military victories abroad. On 9 November 1799 (18 brumaire an VIII), the Directory was completely overthrown by a coup that resulted, the following day, in the election of Bonaparte, the Abbé Sieyès, and the Comte Ducos as provisional consuls empowered with the authority to revise the constitution.

The ironic combination of relaxed social tensions and continued political crises during the Directory produced a climate ripe for caricature. It was in this period that social caricature returned to France, having been overshadowed during the revolutionary years by political caricatures and propaganda prints.

157. Anonymous
French
Plaies de l'Egipte. / ou Etat de la France depuis 1789 jusqu'à l'établissement de la constitution actuelle (The Plagues of Egypt; / or, Conditions in France from 1789 to the Establishment of the Present Constitution), ca. 1795
Etching
DV 5334
246 x 294 (sheet)
Bibliothèque nationale, H 12268
[G163809]

Rather than legitimizing revolutionary events, this print compares eight moments from the Reign of Terror to the biblical ten plagues of Egypt. In the first plague at the upper left, the bodies of men, women, and children lie dead beside rivers which flow with blood from the massacres at Avignon, Jalès, Lyons, the Vendée, and Paris. The second, third, and fourth plagues — frogs, flies, and gnats — are interpreted within a revolutionary context as Jacobins, Jacobines, and Maratins, who are shown selling their radical newspapers in the second vignette. The fifth plague (the third vignette) is famine, which, the caption relates, resulted in the killing of dogs and other domestic animals for food. The sixth plague is described as ulcers, and these are attributed to worthless paper currency, a "source of misery." The seventh plague, at the lower left, is the thunder of the Revolutionary "Tribunal of blood," which, before it was abolished in May 1795, ordered the execution of the rich, noble, and learned. The eighth plague, the swarm of locusts, is epitomized by the commissioners of the various departments who so ruthlessly implemented the policies of the Terror (Jean-Baptiste Carrier, Jean-Marie Collot d'Herbois, Louis-Marie Stanislas Fréron, Joseph Le Bon, and others). The ninth plague is the "tenebrous cult of Marat," and the tenth (the death of the firstborn) is the bloody foreign and civil wars which unnecessarily deprived so many heroes of their lives in the name of *la patrie*.

157

158. DUBOIS
French, active 1790s
La Correction républicaine (The Republican Punishment), 1794
Etching with hand coloring
DV 4697, B 625
379 × 478, 434 × 510
Bibliothèque nationale, Qb1 juin 1794
[M102855]

158

Two victorious French generals administer a "republican punishment" to their military rivals. At right, General Jean-Baptiste Jourdan spanks the bare bottom of the Duke of Coburg, whom he defeated in the Battle of Wattignies on 15–16 October 1793. At left, General Jean-Charles Pichegru does the same to the Duke of York, represented as a young boy with the ears of an ass, whose forces were defeated in January 1794.

Blum cites an order issued by the Committee of Public Safety on 1 August 1794 (14 thermidor an II) commissioning the citizen Dubois to deliver a caricature entitled *Correction républicaine*. Following the defeat of Robespierre and his followers on 9 thermidor, the reorganized Committee of Public Safety concerned itself only with the conduct of war and diplomacy. Recalling these two famous victories, in addition to the others represented by the cities in the background (among them Jourdan's victory at Fleurus on 26 June), justified the Committee's continued support of the war effort.

159. JACQUES-LOUIS COPIA
French, 1764–1799
Constitution française (The French Constitution), ca. 1795, after Pierre Paul Prud'hon
Etching and stipple
405 x 504, 444 x 536
Bibliothèque nationale, Ef 103 réserve

Wearing the armor of Minerva, the Roman goddess of wisdom, the French Republic embraces the male figure of Liberty and the female figure of Fraternity. To the left of Fraternity are two children holding a lamb and a lion, signifying War and Peace. At the right Equality is represented as a bare-breasted woman who leads three more children bearing the symbols of the social ranks. Brought together by the Republic, Fraternity, Liberty, and Equality clasp hands, joining War, Peace, and the three orders in a harmonious union.

The Constitution of Year III, ratified on 22 August 1795, was the most extensive of the revolutionary constitutions. It was prefaced by a Declaration of Rights, which enumerated the duties of the citizen, as well as specifying that all people were entitled to liberty, equality, security, and property. In contrast to the radical Jacobin Constitution of 1793, the Constitution of 1795 sought to establish order and stabilize the government by giving power to the executive branch of the Directory. Its aim

159

was to avoid the ideological "errors" of earlier constitutions and establish a bourgeois republic.

Prud'hon's design is an image of this new harmony and stability. France, now represented in the guise of the goddess of wisdom, has joined together the three republican virtues, emphasizing peace and conciliation. Liberty is still vigilant, but not defiant; Equality is an elegant maternal figure with children; and Fraternity is concerned with reconciliation rather than revolutionary solidarity. Significantly, the inscription below stresses that the constitution is founded not only on rights but on responsibilities.

160. PHILIPPE-AUGUSTE HENNEQUIN
French, 1762–1833
Allégorie de la constitution (Allegory of the Constitution), 1795
Etching
326 x 478, 388 x 504
Bibliothèque nationale, H 12288
[G163836]

The French people, renewed by the Constitution of 1795, are here represented in the form of a young man, "ardent and full of vigor," who protects the woman personifying the Constitution from the daggers and arrows of "blind Fanaticism, Pride, and fierce Ignorance." The sun, marking a new day in the history of the French Revolution, rises behind the Constitution, just above the young man's shield, which bears the inscription, "Your arrows are blunt, my shield is the law"; its rays drive away the storm clouds of the Terror and the radical despotism of the Montagnards.

In its call for reformation and its strict Neoclassical delineation of figural form, the print brings to mind David's famous painting *Intervention of the Sabine Women* (1799). Indeed, Hennequin was a student of David, who, like his master, accepted the tenets of the Terror and, as a consequence, had been imprisoned for a time after 9 thermidor. He continued to paint sublime history pictures in the manner of this etching, exhibiting one in the Salon of 1799, entitled *The Triumph of the French People*, which depicted a figure armed with a club and holding the scales of justice, having just defeated the colossus of Royalty (Renouvier, vol. 1, p. 86). Hennequin enjoyed considerable success until he was exiled with David to Belgium following the fall of Napoleon and the restoration of the Bourbon monarchy in 1814.

161. BARTHÉLEMY JOSEPH FULCRAN ROGER
French, 1767–1841
Directoire exécutif (The Executive Directory),
ca. 1798, after Jean-Claude Naigeon
Etching and stipple
DV 6584
165 x 203 (sheet)
Bibliothèque nationale, H 12117
[G163635]
(Not in exhibition)

The figure of the French Republic leans on a stone which is inscribed "Constitution of Year III" and is adorned with the triangle of equality. A lengthy text published to accompany the print explains that the Republic holds a crown of oak and laurel, a symbol of "the rewards given by the government to those citizens who distinguish themselves"; she also grasps a rudder with five linchpins, a "symbol of the government." Below her feet lie "the monsters who represent sacerdotal, monarchical, and anarchical tyrannies." In the background the fasces of unity, supported by a shield, serves as a "symbol of the paternal solicitude of the magistrates"; the pomegranate surmounting the fasces is an "emblem of the people united and therefore the democratic regime." At the right the cock representing vigilance and courage holds a lightning bolt between its claws signifying the fate of the enemies of the Republic. Surrounding the figure of the Republic are the "attributes of sciences, arts, agriculture, and commerce that the government protects and a horn of plenty, symbol of the happiness of the French."

161

This print was commissioned by the decree of 20 September 1798 to serve as the official stamp of the Executive Directory beginning 22 September 1798 (1 vendémiaire an VII). It presents a peaceful, contemplative figure as the emblem of the republic, rather than the more aggressive and vigilant defender evident in earlier revolutionary prints (Hunt, 1984, p. 117). An appropriate image for the Directory, it is stable, secure, elegant, and refined, published for a highly educated public, which would be patient with the many symbols and capable of reading the long and complex prose explanation that was provided by the government.

Edmond de Goncourt suggested that Jean-Claude Naigeon designed this print after an original image by Prud'hon. There is, however, no documentary evidence to substantiate this claim. The engraver, Roger, was a student of Prud'hon, highly regarded for prints after his master's designs, and this may explain the stylistic similarity. Roger was also a student of Jacques-Louis Copia, who reproduced many of Prud'hon's designs (cat. no. 159).

162. ANONYMOUS
French
La Chiquenaude du peuple (The Finger-Flick of the People), ca. 1797
Etching and mezzotint
DV 6950
356 x 271, 384 x 284
Bibliothèque nationale, Qb1 4 septembre 1797
[M103768]

Represented by a colossal figure of Hercules, the unified French people brush away the annoying, parasitical figures of the clergy and the nobility. The strength and lasting power of revolutionary France is acknowledged by Victory who crowns the colossus with two laurel wreaths, each representing a significant moment of triumph over the counterrevolutionaries. According to de Vinck, the first of these incidents occurred on 5 October 1795 (13 vendémiaire an IV) with the suppression of a royalist insurrection that had been intent on preventing former National Convention members from maintaining control of the Directory. The second was the successful purge on 4 September 1797 (18 fructidor an V) of royalist members from the legislative councils of the Directory. The latter event occurred together with the driving of moderate deputies from the Directory, the reinstatement of harsh measures directed against refractory priests, and the expulsion of émigrés who had been provisionally readmitted to France.

Reviving the radical revolutionary figure of Hercules, this print represents the reversal of significant challenges made against the Directory. Ironically, however, the events of 18 fructidor isolated the Directory from both the conservative Notables and the lower classes, making it increasingly dependent on the military, which, in the person of Bonaparte, would bring about its end two years later.

La Chiquenaude du Peuple.

162

163. JACQUES MARCHAND
French, 1769–after 1810
*Les Dégraissés donnant la pelle au cul au
dégraisseur (The Unfattened Striking the Fat
Remover on the Bottom with a Shovel)*, 1797
Etching
DV 6955
249 x 364, 300 x 401
Bibliothèque nationale, Qb1 20 mai 1797
[M103707]

Deposited in the collection of the Bibliothèque
nationale on 31 March 1797, this caricature is
directed against Armand Gaston Camus, a member
of the Council of Five Hundred who is made readily

163

identifiable by his *camus*, or "snub nose." He is
being beaten with a shovel and a broom by two pen-
sioners, referred to in the caption as "the unfattened," while a figure to the left asks another why he
is so thin. The two attackers have presumably been
wounded in the foreign wars, and the meagerness of
their state pensions is blamed on Camus, referred to
in the caption as the "fat remover."

Even before the Revolution, Camus called for the
suppression of all privileges. He was elected to represent Paris at the Estates General and was appointed
archivist of the Constituent Assembly on 4 August
1789. He campaigned for an end to taxes paid to the
pope, the dissolution of the Order of Malta, and the
suppression of all orders of chivalry and all hereditary privileges. Upon election to the Council of Five
Hundred, Camus was offered positions with the
ministries of finance and police, but he refused
both. De Vinck suggests that it was at the time these
offers were made that this caricature was published,
and that it was inspired by accusations of impropri-
ety made against Camus in 1796. Although nothing
came of those charges, Camus left the Council of

Five Hundred on 20 May 1797 to become the director of the Archives of the Republic, a position he
retained until his death in 1804.

164. ANONYMOUS
French
*Le Traité de paix avec Rome / Baisez ça papa,
et faites patte de velours (The Peace Treaty
with Rome / Kiss That Papa, and Draw in
Your Claws)*, 1797
Etching, engraving, and stipple
DV 6902
232 x 298, 281 x 331
Bibliothèque nationale, Qb1 19 février 1797
[M103632]

In a satiric representation of the forced reconciliation of the church with the French government, an
infirm cat wearing a papal tiara receives the olive
branch of peace from the French cock and is advised
to accept the treaty and draw in his claws. As may be
observed in the similar representation of France in
Le Coq-à-l'âne (cat. no. 169), the vigilant Gallic cock
forcefully makes peace on his own terms.

Until Bonaparte's incursion into the Po Valley in
1796, which resulted in the creation of the Cispa-
dane Republic, France had not challenged the
authority of the increasingly ill and feeble Pope Pius
VI over the papal states of Italy. In June 1796, following the French occupation of the papal legations of
Bologna and Ferrara, the papacy assembled a ramshackle army to resist the French troops. Bonaparte
declared war on the papacy in January 1797 and, following the surrender of Mantua on 2 February 1797,
led an expedition into the papal states. On 19 February 1797 the Pope signed the Treaty of Tolentino,

LE TRAITÉ DE PAIX AVEC ROME

164

de Vinck

LE MEÂ CULPÂ DU PAPE.
Se vend a paris rue de La harpe n° 993.

165

agreeing to pay the Directory thirty million francs to avoid occupation of papal lands.

Ironically, Bonaparte's successful campaign contributed to his increasing independence from the Directory. Three months later, he would sign a preliminary peace treaty with the Habsburgs, organizing Italy into satellite governments of France and giving Venice to Austria. Although the Directory then wanted Bonaparte to move into Belgium and the Rhineland, he continued south, enjoying his greatest triumph fifteen months later as he defeated the British and gave France control of the lower Nile. In October 1799, he would return to France from Egypt and a month later would declare the end of the Directory.

165. Anonymous
French
Le Meâ culpâ du pape (The Pope's Mea Culpa), ca. 1797
Etching, aquatint, and stipple
DV 6899
163 x 262, 215 x 303
Bibliothèque nationale, Qb1 février 1797
[M103636]

"Culpable and ambitious," Pope Pius VI is ordered to make his mea culpa to France in the form of the Treaty of Tolentino of 19 February 1797. He kneels in his residence at the Castel Sant' Angelo in Rome, surrounded by boxes emptied of their treasures, and does penance for having previously refused the French offer of peace, a reference to his failure to adhere to the Armistice of Bologna on 23 June 1796. The Holy Spirit taunts him with his many wrongs: he has not followed the example of the apostles; he has refused the olive branch of peace; he has forfeited the treasury of the papacy; he no longer holds the keys of Saint Peter; and Bonaparte, the conqueror, now holds the sword of Saint Paul. For all of these failures, the grotesque and blindly ambitious pope is to blame.

The Treaty of Tolentino resulted in the confiscation of certain papal territories and the payment of thirty million francs to France. This emptied the papal treasury, virtually bringing the court of Rome under French control.

166

166. ANONYMOUS
French
Départ de l'état major du pape (Departure of the Pope's General Staff), ca. 1797
Etching on blue paper
DV 6890
230 x 359, 264 x 390
Bibliothèque nationale, Qb1 3 février 1797
[M103627]

167

167. ANONYMOUS
French
Avant garde du pape / ou l'Incroiable à Rome (The Advance Guard of the Pope; / or, The Incroyable in Rome), ca. 1797
Etching on blue paper
197 x 234, 232 x 354
DV 6891
Bibliothèque nationale, Qb1 3 février 1797
[M103625]

168

168. ANONYMOUS
French
Arrière garde du pape / ou la Frayeur du Reverend Père Caporal (The Pope's Rear Guard; / or, The Fright of the Reverend Father Caporal), ca. 1797
Etching
DV 6892
198 x 327, 258 x 379
Bibliothèque nationale, H 12298
[G163847]

Hideously grotesque and inept, a ramshackle regiment of the papal army is shown marching on (cat. no. 167) and retreating from (cat. no. 168) the superior and far more noble French armies as represented in the person of the dashing young general Napoleon Bonaparte.

Bonaparte's campaigns against the papacy and his ultimate victory, which forced the signing of the Treaty of Tolentino on 19 February 1797, were crucial to his later success in Egypt, his eventual return to France, his defeat of the Directory, and his election as first consul. Caricatures such as these played a crucial role in establishing and promoting his legend.

Ironically, Bonaparte, who was keenly aware of the subversive power of political caricature, would institute severe censorship laws under the Empire and would become the subject of some of the most biting English satires ever produced, those of James Gillray and George Cruikshank in the years from 1797 to 1815.

169. ANONYMOUS
French
Le Coq-à-l'âne / ou la Chasse au heros de
Kehll / Aller jeune présompteux, achever votre
apprentissage (The Nonsensical Tale; / or,
Kehll's Hero Hunting / Go, Presumptuous
Young Man, Complete Your Training), ca. 1797
Etching and stipple
282 x 236, 330 x 255
Bibliothèque nationale, Qb1 20 avril 1797
[M103683]

In this simple allegorical caricature, the cock of
the French Republic, perched in a Tree of Liberty,
appears to have just whipped a braying donkey,
who in fleeing has dropped an orb to the ground.
The orb, a traditional symbol of the Holy Roman
Emperor, identifies the donkey as Francis II of Austria, who lost his territories to the victorious French
armies. The "Kehll" mentioned in the inscription
may refer to the recapture of the German city of
Kehl by the Army of the Rhine and Moselle, which
established an important bridgehead for the
French army. In addition to suggesting that Francis
II is a braying fool, the riderless donkey, his face
twisted into a grotesque expression of fear, indicates that the Holy Roman Empire is now without
leadership and direction.

LE COQ-A-L'ANE.
ou la Chasse au 'heros de Kehll.
Allez jeune présompteux, achever votre apprentissage.

169

170. ANONYMOUS
French
Entre deux chaises le cul par terre (Falling
between Two Stools), 1797
Etching
DV 7399
412 x 319, 453 x 336
Bibliothèque nationale, Qb1 4 septembre 1797
[M103763]

Entre deux Chaises le Cul par Terre!

170

A hysterical three-headed man represents both
the three directors and the political tensions that
characterized the Directory period and forced the
government to look for challenges from all directions. This figure falls when the board he had been
sitting upon, which is labeled "political balance,"
caves in beneath him.

The balance had rested upon the proud and stylish royalist throne to the left of the print and the
revolutionary chair to the right. The wall that
upheld both chairs and was comprised of past
crimes and failures of the Directory (as various
labels in the foreground indicate) has crumbled,
sending the government crashing into the fires of
hell below.

Deposited at the Bibliothéque nationale on 30
June 1797, this pro-Jacobin satire precedes by two
months the bloodless coup of 18 fructidor (4 Sep-

tember) that resulted in the purging of both moderate and royalist deputies from the Directory. The new dawn prophesied by this image rises from behind the firm and lasting republican monument to the right and forces the clouds gathered above the royalist throne to disperse. It is a dramatic satire of the Directory, which was caught trying to please both the royalists and the revolutionaries and ultimately failed to satisfy either.

171. ANONYMOUS
Le Temt découvre la Vérité (Time Reveals Truth), ca. 1794
Etching and mezzotint
B 103
214 x 330, 270 x 360
Bibliothèque nationale, H 11926
[G163371]

171

As the "national sun" breaks through dark clouds and illuminates the action below, Time (1) reveals Truth (2) who crushes Feudality beneath her feet. She is supported by a composite figure representing Liberty, Equality, and Loyalty (4). Truth holds a mirror reflecting the sun's light onto Hercules (5), who represents the French people and destroys the tyrannical Hydra of the Triumvirate (Robespierre, Saint-Just, and Couthon). In the background, representatives of the four continents (or "reunited nations," as they are described in the caption) dance around a Tree of Liberty that is crowned by a tricolor flag and a Phrygian cap.

This is a post-Thermidorian image celebrating the triumph over the Terror. As the sun returns to dispel the darkness, Truth, sustained by the fundamental revolutionary principles, assists the people

in destroying the hideous monster representing Tyranny. The use of the Hydra links the abuses of power practiced by the privileged orders of the ancien régime (cat. nos. 25, 26) with those of the Terror and opposes both to the revolutionary goals of Liberty, Equality, and Loyalty.

The central role played by Loyalty in this image, as an equal of Liberty and Equality in support of Truth, indicates a concern that would characterize the Directory. This new government would stress fidelity to the nation and the fundamental principles of the Revolution as a means of preventing a recurrence of the fanatical rule of the few as practiced under the Terror. The four continents dancing together in the background are a reference to the increasing desire to restore peace and withdraw France from taxing foreign wars. (Between April and July 1795, France would sign peace treaties with Prussia, Holland, and Spain, leaving it at war only with Austria and England.)

This image is discussed in greater detail in Klaus Herding's essay in the present catalogue, p. 93.

172. ANTOINE MAXIME MONSALDY
French, 1768–1816
Le Triomphe des armées françaises (The Triumph of the French Armies), ca. 1797
Etching and stipple with hand coloring
DV 6928
278 x 440, 349 x 453
Bibliothèque nationale, Qb1 18 avril 1797
[M103669]

Ostensibly meant to glorify the combined triumphs of the French armies, this impressive image obviously celebrates the impressive victories of the young Bonaparte in contrast to the more modest conquests of his rival generals Jean-Charles Pichegru, Jean-Victor Moreau, and Louis-Lazare Hoche. On the far left, Hoche holds a small map of the Quiberon Peninsula in southern Brittany, the site of his defeat of the British Royal Navy in July 1795. Next to him, Pichegru and Moreau, commanders of the Northern Army and the Army of the Rhine and Moselle, hold a fragment of a map showing the territory conquered by those armies as well as Moreau's Army of the Sambre and Meuse.

However celebrated and significant these triumphs might have been, they appear meager when compared to those of Bonaparte and his army, represented by a much larger piece of the map. Indeed,

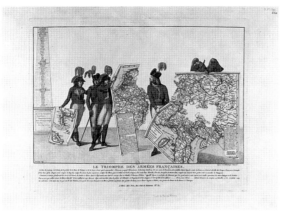

LE TRIOMPHE DES ARMÉES FRANÇAISES.

172

by March 1797 Bonaparte had taken his army within one hundred miles of Vienna and had forced the Austrians to sign the preliminary peace treaty of Leoben, an accord that would ultimately require them to cede to France the Austrian Netherlands (Belgium) and other significant territories. More to the point, however, Bonaparte signed the treaty without specific approval from the Directory, an indication of his growing independence from the ruling government in Paris. This independence and his fierce competitiveness are represented by the way he seems to have torn the map from the hands of Pichegru and Moreau, claiming for himself and his armies the lion's share of Europe and the gateway to further expansion in the Mediterranean and the Near East. As Bonaparte continued to increase the area of his triumphs, he exploited the propagandistic value of prints such as this one, commissioning artists to travel with his armies, document his victories, and glorify his leadership.

Monsaldy was a protégé of Charles-Nicolas Cochin, a fine etcher of the ancien régime, known for his prints of festival and funeral celebrations during the reign of Louis xv. Monsaldy exhibited prints at the salons of Year vi and Year x, and upon the coronation of Bonaparte as emperor in 1804, he would become a prominent court engraver, executing numerous portraits of the Empress Josephine and other important figures.

173. Antoine Maxime Monsaldy (?)
French, 1768–1816
Buonaparte couronné en Egypte par la Victoire (Bonaparte Crowned in Egypt by Victory), ca. 1798, after Philippe-Auguste Hennequin
Etching and mezzotint
DV 7371
450 x 329, 469 x 350
Bibliothèque nationale, H 12313
[G163862]

Another propagandistic image glorifying the triumphs of Bonaparte, this print shows the dashing young general being crowned by Victory as he embraces Minerva, the Roman goddess of wisdom, and Hercules, the revolutionary figure of triumphant France. On the ground rest the club of Hercules and the two-headed eagle of the Austrian Empire, defeated with the signing of the Treaty at Campoformio in October 1797.

Eight months later, Bonaparte would lead the French forces against the British in the Mediterranean, capturing the strategic island of Malta on 11–12 June and Alexandria on 30 June. Bonaparte then set out for Cairo, which he captured at the pivotal Battle of the Pyramids of 22 July. This dramatic victory gave the French control of the lower Nile and

173

gave revolutionary France an international military presence second only to that of England. Although the British navy, under the leadership of Admiral Nelson, attacked and destroyed the entire French fleet on 1–2 August 1798, Bonaparte consolidated his forces in Egypt and, a year later, attacked the Ottoman Empire, defeating the Turkish army at the Battle of Aboukir on 2 August 1799. The military situation secure, he returned to France a popular hero and emerged from the coup d'état of 18 brumaire a provisional consul, only to be made first consul on 25 December 1799.

Allegorical images such as this one played a critical role in Bonaparte's growing popularity. (For information on Hennequin, see cat. no. 160).

174. PHILIBERT-LOUIS DEBUCOURT
French, 1755–1832
La Promenade publique (The Public Promenade), 1792
Etching and aquatint, proof before letters
370 x 605, 498 x 697
Bibliothèque nationale, AA4 réserve

175. ANONYMOUS
French
Liberté de la presse, (Freedom of the Press), ca. 1797
Etching and stipple with hand coloring
205 x 306, 290 x 340
Bibliothèque nationale, Qb1 10 mars 1797
[M103642]

Even during the Revolution gay images of life in the capital continued to be produced, if only rarely. Debucourt's *La Promenade publique* (cat. no. 174) is one such image. It depicts well-to-do bourgeois gentlemen and women gathering in a public garden.

While such gatherings provided an opportunity to flirt, mingle, and scrutinize one's peers, they also provided a chance to discuss the political events of the day. Here, in the lower right, men gather about a table, caught up in animated conversation that is reminiscent of that engaged in by the newsmongers in catalogue number 11, an untitled print of ca. 1780.

The dissemination of opinions on the Revolution and of news concerning its progress was assisted by the publication of many journals representing diverse political positions. Catalogue number 175 depicts the excitement that resulted from

174

LIBERTÉ DE LA PRESSE

175

the reinstatement of freedom of the press under the Directory in October 1795. Men and women rush straight from the presses grasping newly published copies of *L'Ami des loix, L'Ami de la patrie,* and *Le Père Duchesne,* among other journals. Thrown to the ground in the frenzy that renewed freedom of the press has engendered is a pessimistic figure who drops papers bearing the words "ça va mal," an ironic twist on the notorious revolutionary song "Ça ira."

These two prints frame the Terror, as it were, portraying the informal public gatherings in 1792 and the excitement caused by the reemergence of political journals following the implementation of the Directory's new press laws.

As early as September 1797, Napoleon Bonaparte, the commander of the French army in Italy, had been approached to join the disaffected directors in overthrowing the Directory. Believing the time was not right for his return to Paris, Bonaparte had remained in Italy. Two years later, however, after an impressive campaign in Egypt, which was rendered useless by Admiral Nelson's defeat of the French fleet, he reconsidered. Accompanied by approximately four hundred of his most trusted men, he eluded British naval forces and reached the southern coast of France on 8 October 1799. He arrived in Paris approximately a week later and three weeks after participated in a coup that brought an end to the Directory.

On 10 November 1799 (19 brumaire an VIII), Bonaparte appeared before the legislative councils, the Ancients and the Five Hundred, and declared the end of the Directory. He sought and received authority, with the Abbé Sieyès and the Comte Ducos, to undertake constitutional revision. A month later, the Constitution of Year VIII was proclaimed with Bonaparte named as first consul. In this position, he had the power to directly choose and remove all high government officials.

Napoleon rejected a Bourbon plea for restoration of the monarchy and instead instituted new political agencies appropriate to a highly centralized state. Victorious at Marengo in northern Italy in June 1800, he forced Austria to sign the Treaty of Lunéville in February 1801, and a year later, England was made to sign the Treaty of Amiens, bringing peace to the Continent for the first time since 1792. Domestically, the Bank of France was created in January 1800, the first draft of the civil code was completed eleven months later, and a concordat with the papacy was achieved in July 1801, asserting Catholicism to be the religion of the majority of the French. The following year Bonaparte became sole consul for life, and in 1804 he was crowned emperor with succession decreed to be hereditary. The revolutionary era was over; it had been brought to a close in 1799 with the appointment of Bonaparte as first consul, and its end meant, effectively, the end of French caricature until Bonaparte's fall sixteen years later. For among his great achievements as consul, and later as emperor, was the institution of a rigorous and highly successful system of press censorship. Although he forbade caricature at home, Napoleon himself became the target of British caricature, among the most biting and vicious in the history of graphic satire.

176. Claude-François Fortier
French, 1775–1835
La Café politique (The Political Coffeehouse), ca. 1799
Etching
328 x 455, 384 x 470
Bibliothèque nationale, H 12682
[G164238]

Le Café Politique

176

This image, like others in the exhibition (cat. nos. 11, 174), portrays men gathered together, reading and discussing the latest news. The popularity of this subject was due not only to the rapidly changing political events of the period but also to the opportunity it provided for the caricaturist to represent diverse, and often animated, physiognomies. Here, men of various ages and appearances react to each other and to the news they are reading. Some gesture, cock their heads, and knit their brows; others display disgust or disbelief, leaning their heads on their hands, dropping their jaws, and looking away; still others seem more reserved, reading pensively and keeping to themselves. Representing the expression and posture of each figure is a difficult task, but one that lies at the heart of pure portrait caricature—a form that aims at revealing the subject's true character through the exaggeration of physical features.

This particular image is curious in one regard: the men are reading English newspapers, *The Morning Chronicle, The Morning Post,* and *The Times* can be discerned. During the First Consulate relations between France and England were particularly tense. By 1801 Britain would become increasingly isolated as Austria signed a peace treaty with France. The continuing possibility of a

French invasion, as well as the fall of Pitt's ministry on 4 March 1801, ultimately induced the British government to seek an accord with France; this resulted in the signing of the Peace of Amiens on 25 March 1802. Bonaparte, however, made preparations to invade England less than a year later, causing the English to again declare war on France on 16 May 1803.

177. ADRIEN-PIERRE-FRANÇOIS GODEFROY
French, 1777–1865
Le Thé parisien (Parisian Tea Party), ca. 1800,
after Fulchran-Jean Harriet
Etching with hand coloring
307 x 429, 409 x 493
Bibliothèque nationale, H 12757
[G164317]

178. ANONYMOUS
French
Untitled, ca. 1799
Etching
300 x 428, 322 x 436
Bibliothèque nationale, H 12686
[G164242]

As these two caricatures indicate, Parisian society under the Directory and Consulate, freed from the repressive climate of the Terror, cultivated refined pleasures and opulent dress, diversions that were often the subject of satire.

In each of these prints, well-to-do young men are entertained by prostitutes who wear costumes only slightly more revealing than the contemporary high-waisted gowns with plunging necklines worn by the fashionable young women of Paris. The men wear high-collared jackets, cravats, and either delicate slippers or soft boots that result in a ridiculous

Le Thé Parisien.
Suprême Bon Ton, au Commencement du 19.me Siècle.
A Paris, chez Martinet, Libraire, Rue du Coq St.Honoré.

177

178

profile which rises from narrow feet to broad shoulders and is further exaggerated by garments that seem to engulf the head.

The representation of fashionable men mingling with prostitutes was common not only in prints of the period but in paintings as well. Louis-Léopold Boilly's *Les Galeries du Palais-Royal*, exhibited in the Salon of 1804 (Paris, Musée Carnavalet), is only the most famous of these images (The Detroit Institute of Arts and The Metropolitan Museum of Art, New York, no. 8). It depicts men negotiating with prostitutes within the Galerie Montpensier of the Palais-Royal; the women are portrayed as an embellishment of the otherwise cold and uninviting gallery. Popular journalistic accounts described such women as "birds of paradise" who sang their siren songs from the dark, scented shadows of the gallery's stairways. Such portrayals, however, ignored the increasing threat prostitution posed to public health. Parent-Duchâtelet's seminal study of Parisian prostitution (1836) determined that the number of registered prostitutes more than doubled between 1812 and 1832 and that more than half of the city's prostitutes worked out of boutiques and *maisons de tolérance*

in the Palais-Royal. Prompted by the dramatic increase in prostitution that had already begun during the Directory, Parent-Duchâtelet warned that more and more diseased young girls would end up as vagrants and wards of the city's health system.

Caricatures such as these made fun of the allure of prostitutes, ridiculing young men as desperate and foolish in their vain pursuit of pleasure and fashion.

179. ANONYMOUS
French
Les Croyables / au tripot (The Croyables / in the Gambling Den), ca. 1800
Etching and stipple
277 x 332, 356 x 394
Bibliothèque nationale, H 12417
[G163967]

During the Directory and Consulate the elegant and richly dressed young men who populated the

LES CROYABLES
au tripot.

179

fashionable cafés and restaurants of Paris were referred to by the ironic title *croyables*; they also came to be called *incroyables, inconcevables,* or *payables.* Known for their long jackets with wide lapels and black velvet collars, tight breeches, walking sticks, and earrings, their vanity and extravagance made them the target of numerous caricatures. Their female counterparts, the *merveilleuses,* were known for their extravagant dress in the antique style, and satires directed against the fashionable excesses of these young women often had erotic overtones (cat. no. 180).

Weary of the austere dress of the early revolutionary period and freed from the repressive attitudes of the Terror, the affluent bourgeois society of the Directory and First Consulate sought a greater range of self-expression. As in the prerevolutionary period, caricature once again found a target in the peculiarities and extravagances of high fashion.

relaxed code of morality, and the bourgeoisie avidly sought out pleasure and entertainment. This was reflected in the opulence of women's fashions, particularly those worn by the *merveilleuses* who were known for their scanty greek-inspired dresses, constructed of transparent fabrics and often worn with sandals and rings on the toes. Women occupied a more dominant position in society at this time, and Madame Tallien and Josephine de Beauharnais, as well as others, could climb to the top ranks of society by becoming mistresses of influential men such as Paul-François-Nicolas Barras and Napoleon Bonaparte. In addition, prostitution flourished at all levels of society at this time (cat. nos. 177, 178).

Here, the new morality is satirized in a debauched harem scene where the *merveilleuses* are portrayed as prostitutes. A grotesque old procuress pushes a reluctant young woman before a wealthy and corpulent client, while other women line up behind. The tent-like interior of the room was fashionable among the nouveaux riches of the First Consulate, a reflection of Eastern influence on Neoclassical decoration.

LE SULTAN PARISIEN.
ou l'Embarras du Choix.

180

180. ANONYMOUS
French
*Le Sultan parisien / ou l'Embarras du choix
(The Parisian Sultan; / or, Too Many to
Choose From)*
Etching and stipple on blue paper
265 x 406, 279 x 504
Bibliothèque nationale, H 12470
[G164022]

Freed from the puritanical ideals that had characterized the Terror, Parisian society under the Directory and the First Consulate enjoyed a more

181. ANONYMOUS
French
*Le Premier et Incomparable Moulin a raser
toutes les têtes à barbe...(The First Incomparable Shaving Mill for All Bearded Heads...),*
ca. 1798
Etching on blue paper
280 x 425, 412 x 554
Bibliothèque nationale, H 12471
[G164023]

In the spirit of prerevolutionary satires of popular diversions such as mesmerism and hot-air bal-

LE PREMIER ET INCOMPARABLE MOULIN A RASER TOUTES LES TÊTES A BARBE et a Cheveux coupés à la Cherubin et à la Titus. &c.

181

looning (cat. nos. 6–10), this caricature pokes fun at a ridiculous scheme for the cutting of beards. Described in the caption as having been invented by one Bombardinelli of Florence, the contraption resembles a merry-go-round driven by camels; a musical accompaniment is provided by a band seated in a gallery above. As many as twenty men are able to stand before apertures in the interior wall of the machine and have their beards shaved by razor blades mounted on a disc. This ingenious, albeit foolish and dangerous, idea betrays the vanity of the fashionable young men of the Directory and First Consulate who prized their close-shaven appearance. To bring the point home, a fat, older, bewhiskered man, who has just arrived at this fictional locale by boat, is greeted by a young woman and advised, "Ah, shave yourself My Lord; you look like a Jew."

182. ANONYMOUS
French
Gargantua à son grand couvert (Gargantua at His Table), ca. 1805
Etching with hand coloring
198 x 298, 232 x 318
Bibliothèque nationale, Tf 18
[R079929]

183. ANONYMOUS
French
Après dinée de Gargantua (Gargantua after Dinner), ca. 1805
Etching with hand coloring
192 x 292, 237 x 315
Bibliothèque nationale, Tf 18
[R079931]

These highly sophisticated and accomplished caricatures lampoon the pleasure-seeking bourgeoisie of the late Revolution. As in the earlier

GARGANTUA A SON GRAND COUVERT.

182

APRÈS DINÉE DE GARGANTUA
Ou trafic du Bordeau

183

depiction of Louis XVI as Gargantua (cat. no. 68), emphasis here is placed on the subject's insatiable appetite. In catalogue number 182, the black-coated gentleman sits at a table beneath a grape arbor as legions of tradesmen and women deliver loads of food and drink. He cannot consume his food fast enough and is assisted by a young man who shovels more and more into his mouth. In catalogue number 183, the gentleman has finished his meal and relieves himself while awaiting yet more food and drink. These caricatures suggest that the bourgeoisie's appetite is boundless and that consumption and defecation have become an endless cycle of pleasure for members of this social class.

184. ANONYMOUS
    French
    Untitled, ca. 1799
    Etching
    208 x 315, 282 x 364
    Bibliothèque nationale, H 12492
    [G164045]

The Royal Academy's authority over artists, their education, and their participation in the official exhibitions or salons was severely challenged during the Revolution by a group led by David. Quarrels over these issues persisted, however, until the Constitution of 1791 outlawed the Academy along with other privileged bodies. The complete abolition of the Academy occurred two years later, and it was replaced by an Institute in 1795 with David among the initial forty-eight government-appointed members.

At the time that David was challenging the Academy's influence, his own artistic authority was under attack from a group of his students who were known as the Barbus (Bearded Ones) or the Primitifs (Primitives). Led by Maurice Quay, these young idealists called for a new kind of painting that would draw its inspiration not from the robust, muscular classicism of Roman art or the Italian Baroque (as had David's), but from the elegant purity and severity of Greek models (Levitine, pp. 54–72). Quay reportedly complained to a friend that, "David had actually begun the huge task of art reform, but…his indecisive character and limited ideas had diverted him into politics and he did not have the energy to complete the revolution needed in art" (Schnapper, p. 190).

In this caricature, a critic is seated in a gallery of the Louvre, attempting to write his guide to the

official exhibition. He is considering a sculpted copy of the Apollo Belvedere, a late fourth-century Greek work that the Neoclassical theorist Johann Winckelmann considered to be the perfect example of classical beauty. Its elegant nobility and refined linearity were very appealing to the Barbus, and its influence was felt even on David who, since

184

at least early 1796, had been working on the *Intervention of the Sabine Women* and had referred to the Apollo Belvedere in the male figure on the left of his painting (p. 75). The Barbus, nevertheless criticized David's painting for not being sufficiently primitive in style. David exhibited the *Intervention of the Sabine Women* privately in the Louvre beginning 21 December 1799 and published a catalogue in which he cited his antique sources and defended the nudity of the heroes he portrayed. This set off a lively controversy that contributed further to the debate begun by the Barbus.

The blindfolded fool in this caricature is dressed in a classical costume and holds a telescope to the critic's eye. The joke seems to be aimed at artists and critics who, like the Barbus and David himself, were meticulously following the models of the past at a time when revolutionary France was looking toward the future. (David had wanted to "paint ancient customs so accurately that any Greek or Roman seeing my works would have assumed I knew their ways" [Schnapper, p. 191].)

This is one of the earliest caricatures of artistic practice, a subject that would become increasingly popular over the next two decades; it is also evidence of the diversity of the caricatures that were produced under the Directory and First Consulate.

LES EMIGRES A ROME
A la lecture de la proclamation du Général Berthier le 16.ᵉ Février 1798. et le 28.ᵉ Pluviôse de l'an VI. de la République Française

185

185. ANONYMOUS
French
Les Emigrés à Rome (The Emigrés in Rome),
ca. 1798
Etching and stipple with hand coloring
208 x 308, 262 x 357
Bibliothèque nationale, Qb1 16 février 1798
[M103858]

With the signing of the Treaty of Tolentino in February 1797 (cat. nos. 164, 165), Pope Pius VI accepted the French Republic and ceded certain papal land holdings and thirty million francs to France. Following this defeat, the city of Rome fell into chaos, a situation that was exacerbated by the weakness of the papal government and the subversive activities of so-called Jacobins from the north. Several attempts were made to foment a revolution in Rome, and on 28 December 1797 a demonstration in front of the palace of the French ambassador, Joseph Bonaparte, led to the accidental shooting of a French general. Following this incident the French embassy was moved to Florence, but on 11 January 1798 the Directory secretly ordered Maréchal Louis-Alexandre Berthier, who had replaced Napoleon as commander of the Army of Italy, to march on Rome and establish a republic. This was accomplished on Februrary 1798.

In this print, a group of French émigrés despair upon reading Berthier's proclamation of the Roman Republic. The song inscribed beneath the image bemoans their fate and their failure to "save the ancient nobility and destroy this republic." The exaggeration of facial features is uncommon in French revolutionary caricatures, and in this instance it may reflect the bitterness with which the émigrés were viewed by the French. Until the invasion of Rome, the papal states had been the residence of such hated émigrés as the Abbé Maury, who was made a cardinal in 1794 by Pope Pius VI.

La derniere assemblée Papale

186

186. ANONYMOUS

French

La Derniere Assemblée papale (The Last Papal Assembly), ca. 1798

Etching with hand coloring

234 x 366, 272 x 410

Bibliothèque nationale, Qb1 16 février 1798

[M103857]

Reacting with the same despair demonstrated by the émigrés in the previous print (cat. no. 185), Pope Pius VI and his court "cry like fountains" at the news of the declaration of the Roman Republic in February 1798. Deprived of the contents of the papal treasury by the Treaty of Tolentino made with Napoleon the previous year (cat. nos. 164, 165), the pope and his cardinals, "the great penitents," must now leave Rome.

When the Roman Republic was proclaimed, Pius VI refused to leave the city on his own accord and was placed under house arrest and sent to Siena. While crowds turned out to honor the departing pontiff, there was no popular protest of his forced removal. The pope, ill and feeble, had maintained a determined resistance to the Revolution and had long been a target of its satire (cat. nos. 61–63).

187. PHILIBERT-LOUIS DEBUCOURT

French, 1755–1832

La Paix / à Bonaparte pacificateur / dix huit brumaire (Peace / to Bonaparte the Peace-maker / Eighteenth of Brumaire), 1801

Etching and aquatint

390 x 293, 513 x 410 (paper frame)

Bibliothèque nationale, H 12763

[G164323]

This image was published in 1801 on the occasion of the Festival of Peace that marked the second anniversary of Bonaparte's coup of 9 November 1799 (18 brumaire an VIII), which had ended the Directory. It depicts a young and innocent figure of Peace who holds a garland of flowers, an olive branch, and a cornucopia and is seated on a throne decorated with figures of Victory and Minerva, the Roman goddess of wisdom.

When published, this print was offered for sale with or without the decorative border. The border, which added four francs to the eight-franc price of the print, is replete with the profiles of Bonaparte as first consul (framed by a lion and a cock and supported by a base inscribed "Constitution"); Jean-Jacques-Regis de Cambacérès, the second consul; and Charles-François Lebrun, the third consul. It

187

also includes military emblems inscribed with Bonaparte's most famous battles, memorials to the men and women who died for the fatherland, and a dedication to Bonaparte "the peacemaker."

Luxuriously printed and elegant in design, *La Paix* celebrates the peace and prosperity of France following a decade of domestic and foreign wars.

188. SOPHIE JANINET
    French, active 1799–1815
    Napoleon, 1st consul (Napoleon 1st Consul),
    ca. 1799
    Etching and aquatint with roulette
    239 (diameter), 296 x 260
    Bibliothèque nationale, N2, Nap.I, t.3
    [R30174]

189. ANONYMOUS
    French
    L'Heureuse Etoile (The Lucky Star), 1802
    Engraving and stipple
    221 x 193, 263 x 210
    Bibliothèque nationale, N2, Nap.I, t.3
    [R30232]

The coup of 18 brumaire brought an end to the Directory and allowed Napoleon Bonaparte to

assume practically unlimited power over France. As first consul, he sought peace, political order, and financial stability. He revised the Constitution of 1795, made an agreement with the papacy that established Catholicism as the major French religion, instituted a new civil code, and made improvements in public education. He also implemented a police system and a rigorous, highly successful system of press censorship, which signaled an end to French political caricature until the advent of the July Monarchy in 1830. As a result, political satires of France became, for a time, the province of British caricaturists, such as James Gillray, Thomas Rowlandson, and Isaac and George Cruikshank, who developed extraordinarily violent and biting images directed against Bonaparte.

188

Recognizing the value of art as propaganda, Bonaparte commissioned highly idealized images of himself in various media, including formal portraits and historical paintings by Jacques-Louis David and Antoine-Jean Gros. In addition, portrait busts, such as these of Napoleon as first consul, were widely disseminated through prints, as well as on medallions and coins. The first print (cat. no. 188) is a simple representation of Bonaparte in the form of an antique medal. Engraved by Sophie Janinet, daughter and student of Jean-François Janinet (cat. nos. 130, 133), the first consul's Roman profile is characterized by the Latin inscription "vir," which denotes manhood, virility, and virtue. Sophie Janinet made her debut in the Salon of

189

1799, and in 1800 she exhibited a wash drawing of Bonaparte as first consul.

The second print (cat. no. 189) by an unknown artist commemorates Bonaparte's appointment in 1802 as first consul for life. This remarkable image transfigures the young, almost innocent, general into a mystical sign, a "lucky star" or apparition that has appeared in the heavens to guide the fate of the French.

190. Pierre-Nolasque Bergeret
     French, 1782–1863
     Les Musards de la rue du Coq (The Dawdlers of the rue du Coq), 1804
     Lithograph with hand coloring on blue paper
     219 x 376, 248 x 400
     Bibliothèque nationale, Tf 19
     [R079995]

When Pierre-Nolasque Bergeret drew this image of Aaron Martinet's retail establishment in 1804, the shop was both a *cabinet de lecture*, or public reading room, and a printshop specializing in caricatures. It comprised two buildings—each of five stories—which together housed some seven to eight thousand volumes and hundreds of prints

(Hautecoeur, pp. 205–340). Martinet's store was located on the Right Bank, near the Louvre and the Palais-Royal. Its location, its size, and its fashionable clientele all indicate the rise in status that French caricature had undergone. Formerly, caricatures had been largely anonymous and were produced and sold from shops on the Left Bank near the university and schools of law and medicine; by this time, however, they had become a profitable and highly respectable form of bourgeois entertainment, much like their mid-eighteenth-century English predecessors.

English caricature, especially social caricature, had been in advance of French caricature since 1736 when Arthur Pond published various prints after Italian caricatures, including some by Annibale Carracci and Pier Leone Ghezzi (Godefrey, no. 7). These contributed to the popular practice of collecting caricatures and of having one's own caricature drawn. Among the most successful London caricature shops were those of Matthew Darly on the Strand, William Humphrey on the Strand, and Hannah Humphrey on Bond Street. These businesses often appeared in caricatures depicting contemporary fashion and social intercourse. As in Bergeret's caricature, these prints showed fashionable men and women in exaggerated forms of elegant dress, craning their necks to look at one another and at the prints displayed in the windows. The joke in such images is that the caricatures within the shop are only reflections of the human comedy outside—a comedy involving the dress, manners, habits, and physiognomies of various social types.

Although it obviously refers to Debucourt's *La Promenade publique* of 1792 (cat. no. 174), Bergeret's print is more modern in character, depicting the crush of various types on the city's streets and using the new print medium of lithography. It thus marks the arrival of a true French social caricature and sets the stage for the eclipse of English caricature by Henry Monnier, Charles Joseph Traviès, Grandville, and Honoré Daumier during the late Restoration and the July Monarchy (Cuno, pp. 139–92).

A painter and engraver of history and genre subjects, Bergeret studied with David and exhibited for the first time in the Salon of 1806. He was one of the most important artists involved in the introduction of lithography to France and made lithographs after famous paintings by Poussin, Raphael, Bronzino, and others.

Les musards de la rue du Coq.

190

Selected Bibliography

Adhémar, Jean. *Graphic Art of the Eighteenth Century.* Translated by M. I. Martin. New York: McGraw-Hill, 1964.

Agulhon, Maurice. *Marianne into Battle: Republican Imagery and Symbolism in France, 1785–1880.* Translated by Janet Lloyd. Cambridge: Cambridge University Press, 1981.

Albert, Maurice. *Les Théâtres de la foire (1660–1789).* Paris: Hachette et Cie, 1900.

Alexandre, Arsène. *L'Art du rire et de la caricature.* Paris: Quatin Librairies-Imprimeries Réunies, 1892.

Arasse, Daniel. *La Guillotine dans la Révolution.* Exh. Cat. Vizille: Musée de la Révolution française, 1987.

Arnauldet, Thomas. "Estampes satiriques, bouffonnées ou singulières, relative à l'art et aux artistes français pendant les xviie et xviiie siècles." *Gazette des beaux-arts* 3 (September 1859), pp. 342–61.

Art Council of Great Britain. *French Popular Imagery: Five Centuries of Prints.* Exh. cat. London: Hayward Gallery, 1974.

Ashbee, C. R. *Caricature.* London: Chapman and Hall, Ltd., 1928.

Atherton, Herbert M. *Political Prints in the Age of Hogarth: A Study of the Ideographic Representation of Politics.* Oxford: Clarendon Press, 1974.

Babeu, Albert. *Les Bourgeois d'autrefois.* Paris: Firmin-Dodet et Cie, 1886.

Becq, Annie. "Expositions, peintres et critiques, vers l'image moderne de l'artiste." *Dix-Huitième Siècle* 14 (1982), pp. 131–50.

Belloc, Hilaire. *Marie-Antoinette.* New York and London: G. P. Putnam's Sons, 1924.

Bertaud, Jean-Paul. *Les Amis du roi: Journaux et journalistes royalistes en France de 1789 à 1782.* Paris: Perrin, 1984.

_____. *La Vie quotidienne en France au temps de la Révolution, 1789–1795.* Paris: Hachette et Cie, 1983.

Bluche, François. *La Vie quotidienne au temps de Louis xvi.* Paris: Hachette et Cie, 1980.

Blum, André. *La Caricature révolutionnaire.* Paris: Jouve et Cie, 1916.

_____. "L'Estampe satirique et la caricature en France au xviiie siècle." *Gazette des beaux-arts* (May–December 1910), pp. 379–92 (May), 69–87 (July), 108–20 (August), 243–54 (September), 275–92 (October), 403–20 (November), 447–67 (December).

Boime, Albert. *Art in an Age of Revolution.* Chicago: University of Chicago Press, 1987.

_____. "Marmontel's Bélisaire and the Pre-Revolutionary Progressivism of David." *Art History* 3 (1980), pp. 81-101.

Bordes, Philippe. *Le Serment du Jeu de paume de Jacques-Louis David: Le Peintre, son milieu et son temps de 1789 à 1792.* Paris: Editions de la Réunion des Musées nationaux, 1983.

Bornemann, Bernd. *La Caricature: Art et manifeste, du 16e siècle à nos jours.* Geneva: Skira, 1974.

Brookner, Anita. *Greuze: The Rise and Fall of an Eighteenth-Century Phenomenon.* Greenwich, Conn.: New York Graphic Society, 1972.

_____. *Jacques-Louis David.* London: Chatto and Windus, 1980.

Brown, Frederick. *Theater and Revolution: The Culture of the French Stage.* New York: Viking Press, 1980.

Bruel, François-Louis. *Collection de Vinck: Inventaire analytique.* 6 vols. Paris: Imprimerie nationale, 1914.

Bryson, Norman. *Word and Image: French Painting of the Ancien Régime.* Cambridge: Cambridge University Press, 1981.

Burke, Edmund. *Reflections on the Revolution in France.* Edited by Conor Cruise O'Brien. Harmondsworth: Penguin Books, 1968.

Burke, Peter. *Popular Culture in Early Modern Europe.* New York: New York University Press, 1978.

Carlson, Marvin. *The Theater of the French Revolution.* Ithaca: Cornell University Press, 1966.

Carlson, Victor I., and John W. Ittman. *Regency to Empire: French Printmaking, 1715–1814.* Exh. cat. The Baltimore Museum of Art and the Minneapolis Institute of Arts, 1984.

Carlyle, Thomas. *The French Revolution: A History.* New York: D. Appleton and Company, 1904.

Casselle, Pierre. "Sur le commerce de l'estampe à Paris dans la seconde moitié du xviiiᵉ siècle." Ph.D. diss., Ecole nationale des chartes, 1976.

Castelot, André. *Queen of France: A Biography of Marie-Antoinette.* Translated by Denise Folliot. New York: Harper and Brothers, 1957.

Champfleury [Jules-François-Félix Husson]. *Histoire de la caricature moderne.* Paris: Dentu, 1865.

_____ . *Histoire de la caricature sous la République, l'Empire, et la Restauration.* Paris: Dentu [1874].

Chastel, André. *The Sack of Rome, 1527.* Translated by Beth Archer. Princeton: Princeton University Press, 1983.

Chatelus, Jean. "Thèmes picturaux dans les appartements de marchands et artisans parisiens au xviiiᵉ siècle." *Dix-Huitième Siècle* 6 (1974), pp. 309–24.

Chaumié, Jacqueline. *Le Réseau d'Antraigues et la Contre-révolution, 1791–1793.* Paris: Librairie Plon, 1965.

Clement, Charles. *Prud'hon, sa vie, ses oeuvres et sa correspondance.* Paris: Didier et Cie, 1872.

Cobb, Richard. *Paris and Its Provinces, 1792–1802.* London: Oxford University Press, 1975.

_____ . *The Police and the People: French Popular Protest, 1785–1820.* Oxford: Clarendon Press, 1970.

_____ . "Thermidor or the Retreat from Fantasy." *Encounter* 57 (December 1981), pp. 30–42.

Conisbee, Philip. *Painting in Eighteenth-Century France.* Ithaca: Cornell University Press, 1981.

Crow, Thomas E. "'Gross David, with the Swoln Cheek': Review of *Jacques-Louis David,* by Anita Brookner." *Art History* 5 (1982), pp. 109–17.

_____ . "The Oath of the Horatii in 1785: Painting and Pre-Revolutionary Radicalism in France." *Art History* 1 (December 1978), pp. 424–71.

_____ . *Painters and Public Life in Eighteenth-Century Paris.* New Haven and London: Yale University Press, 1985.

Cuno, James. "Charles Philipon and La Maison Aubert: The Business, Politics, and Public of Caricature in Paris, 1820–1840." Ph.D. diss., Harvard University, 1985.

Dacier, Emile, Albert Vuaflart, and Jacques Herold. *Jean de Jullienne et les graveurs de Watteau au xviiiᵉ siècle Paris.* 4 vols. Paris: N.p., 1921–1929.

D'Almeras, Henri. *Marie-Antoinette et les pamphlets royalistes et révolutionnaires.* Paris: Albin Michel, Editeur, 1921.

Darnton, Robert. "The High Enlightenment and the Low-Life of Literature in Pre-Revolutionary France." *Past and Present* 51 (May 1971), pp. 79–103.

_____ . *The Literary Underground of the Old Regime.* Cambridge: Harvard University Press, 1982.

_____ . *Mesmerism and the End of Enlightenment in France.* Cambridge: Harvard University Press, 1968.

Daudet, Ernest. *Histoire de l'émigration pendant la Révolution française.* 3rd ed. Paris: Hachette et Cie, 1905–1907.

Davis, Natalie Zemon. *Society and Culture in Early Modern France.* Stanford: Stanford University Press, 1975.

Delécluze, E. J. *David, son école et son temps: Souvenirs.* 2nd ed. Paris: Didier et Cie, 1860.

Demuth, Norman. *French Opera: Its Development to the French Revolution.* Sussex: Artemis Press, 1963.

The Detroit Institute of Arts and the Metropolitan Museum of Art, New York. *French Painting 1774–1830: The Age of Revolution.* Exh. cat. The Detroit Institute of Arts, 1975.

Donakowski, Conrad. *A Muse for the Masses: Ritual and Music in an Age of Democratic Revolutions, 1770–1870.* Chicago: University of Chicago Press, 1977.

Dowd, David L. *Pageant-Master of the Republic: Jacques-Louis David and the French Revolution.* Lincoln: University of Nebraska Press, 1948. Reprint. Freeport, N.Y.: Books for Libraries Press, 1969.

Dull, Jonathan. *The French Navy and American Independence.* Princeton: Princeton University Press, 1975.

Duplessis, Georges. *Collection Michel Hennin.* 5 vols. Paris: H. Menu, 1877–1884.

Duverger, Erik. *Réflexions sur le commerce d'art au xviiiᵉ siècle.* Acts of the Twenty-First International Congress for Art History, vol. 3. Princeton: Princeton University Press, 1964.

Egret, Jean. *La Pré-Révolution française (1787–1788).* Paris: Presses universitaires de France, 1967.

Engerand, Fernand. *Inventaire des tableaux commandés et achetés par la direction des bâtiments du roi (1709–1792).* Paris: E. Leroux, 1901.

Ettlinger, L. D. "Jacques-Louis David and Roman Virtue." *Journal of the Royal Society of Arts* 115 (1967), pp. 105–23.

Faret, Nicolas. *L'Honnête Homme ou l'Art de plaire à la cour.* Edited by M. Magendie. Paris: N.p., 1925. Reprint. Geneva: Slatkine Reprints, 1970.

Fried, Michael. *Absorption and Theatricality: Painting and Beholder in the Age of Diderot.* Berkeley and Los Angeles: University of California Press, 1980.

Fryer, W. R. *Republic or Restoration in France? 1794–1797*. Manchester: University of Manchester Press, 1965.

Fuchs, Edward. *Die Karikatur der europäischen Völker: Vom Altertum bis zur Neuzeit*. Berlin: A. Hofmann, 1901.

Furet, François. *Interpreting the French Revolution*. Translated by Elborg Forster. Cambridge: Cambridge University Press, 1981.

Furet, François, and Jacques Ozouf. *Reading and Writing: Literacy in France from Calvin to Jules Ferry*. Cambridge: Cambridge University Press, 1982.

Gelbart, Nin R. "Frondeur Journalism in the 1770s: Theater Criticism and Radical Politics in the Prerevolutionary French Press." *Eighteenth-Century Studies* 17 (1984), pp. 493–514.

George, Mary Dorothy. *Catalogue of Political and Personal Satires Preserved in the Department of Prints and Drawings in the British Museum*. Vol. 5, *1771–1783*; vol. 6, *1784–1792*. London: British Museum Publications Limited, vol. 5, 1935; vol. 6, 1938. Reprint, 1978.

––––––––––– . *English Political Caricature to 1792: A Study of Opinion and Propaganda*. Oxford: Clarendon Press, 1959.

Gershoy, Leo. *The Era of the French Revolution, 1789–1799*. Princeton: Van Nostrand, 1957.

Godechot, Jacques. *The Counter-Revolution: Doctrine and Action, 1789–1804*. Translated by Salvator Attanasio. New York: Howard Fertig, 1971.

––––––––––– . *La Vie quotidienne en France sous le Directoire*. Paris: Hachette et Cie, 1977.

Godefrey, Richard. *English Caricature, 1620 to the Present*. Exh. cat. London: Victoria and Albert Museum, 1984.

Gombrich, E. H. *Art and Illusion*. New York: Pantheon Books, 1960.

––––––––––– . "The Dream of Reason: Symbolism in the French Revolution." *British Journal for Eighteenth-Century Studies* 2 (1979), pp. 187–205.

Gombrich, E. H., and Ernst Kris. *Caricature*. Harmondsworth: Penguin Books, 1940.

Goncourt, Edmond de, and Jules de Goncourt. *L'Art du XVIIIme siècle*. 2nd ed. 3 vols. Paris: G. Charpentier, 1881–1882.

Grand Carteret, John. *Les Moeurs et la caricature en France*. Paris: La Librairie illustrée, 1888.

Greenlaw, Ralph W., ed. *The Social Origins of the French Revolution: The Debate on the Role of the Middle Classes*. Lexington, Mass.: D. C. Heath and Company, 1975.

Greer, Donald. *The Incidence of the Emigration during the French Revolution*. Cambridge: Harvard University Press, 1951.

Grose, Francis. *Rules for Drawing Caricatures with an Essay on Comic Painting*. London: Samuel Bagster, 1791.

Hatin, Eugène. *Bibliographie historique et critique de la presse périodique française*. Paris: Firmin-Dodet et Cie, 1866.

Hautecoeur, Louis. *Louis David*. Paris: Editions de la Table ronde, 1954.

Henderson, Ernest F. *Symbol and Satire in the French Revolution*. New York and London: G. P. Putnam's Sons, 1912.

Herding, Klaus, and Gunter Ott, eds. *Karikaturen*. Giessen: Anabas-Verlag, 1980.

Hertz, Neil. "Medusa's Head: Male Hysteria under Political Pressure." *Representations* 4 (1983), pp. 25–55.

Hofmann, Werner. *Caricature from Leonardo to Picasso*. New York: Crown Publishers, 1957.

––––––––––– . *Goya: Das Zeitalter der Revolutionen, 1789–1830*. Munich: Prestel Verlag; Hamburger Kunsthalle, 1980.

Hollstein, F. W. H. *German Engravings, Etchings, and Woodcuts, 1400–1700*. 34 vols. to date. Amsterdam: Menno Hertzberger, 1959–.

Honour, Hugh. *Neo-Classicism*. Harmondsworth: Penguin Books, 1968.

Hourticq, Louis. "Les Parisiens aux salons de peinture." In *La Vie parisienne au XVIIIe siècle*. Conférences du Musée Carnavalet. Paris: Payot, 1928.

Hufton, Olwen. "Women in Revolution, 1789–1796." *Past and Present*, no. 53 (November 1971), pp. 90-108.

Hunt, Lynn. "Engraving the Republic: Prints and Propaganda in the French Revolution." *History Today* 30 (1980), pp. 11–17.

––––––––––– . "Hercules and the Radical Image in the French Revolution." *Representations* 2 (1983), pp. 95–117.

––––––––––– . *Politics, Culture, and Class in the French Revolution*. Berkeley and Los Angeles: University of California Press, 1984.

Isherwood, Robert M. *Farce and Fantasy: Popular Entertainment in Eighteenth-Century Paris*. Oxford: Oxford University Press, 1986.

Johnson, Douglas, ed. *French Society and the Revolution*. Cambridge: Cambridge University Press, 1976.

Johnson, W. McAllister. "Affiche, annonces et avis divers: The 'Estampe-Publicité' in Eighteenth-Century France." *Gazette des beaux-arts*, 6th ser., 102 (1983), pp. 121–28.

Koenig, Thilo, Robert Ohrt, and Christian Troster. "Die Stecher von London: Englische politische Karikatur unter dem Einfluss der französischen Revolution." In *Karikaturen*, edited by Klaus Herding and Gunter Ott. Giessen: Anabas-Verlag, 1980.

Kris, Ernst, and E. H. Gombrich. "The Principles of Caricature." *British Journal of Medical Psychology* 17 (1938), pp. 319–42.

Kunzle, David. *The Early Comic Strip*. Berkeley and Los Angeles: University of California Press, 1973.

Lambourne, Lionel. *An Introduction to Caricature*. Owings Mills, Md.: Stemmer House, 1983.

Landwehr, John. *Romeyn de Hooghe the Etcher*. Leiden: A. W. Sijthoff; Dobbs Ferry, N.Y.: Oceana, 1973.

Le Blanc, Charles. *Manuel de l'amateur d'estampes*. 4 vols. Paris: Emile Bouillon, 1854–1888.

Lefebvre, Georges. *The Coming of the French Revolution*. Translated by R. R. Palmer. Princeton: Princeton University Press, 1947.

_____. *The French Revolution*. Vol. 1, *From Its Origins to 1793*. Translated by Elizabeth Moss Evanson. N.Y.: Columbia University Press, 1964.

_____. *Napoleon: From 18 Brumaire to Tilsit, 1799–1807*. Translated by J. E. Anderson. New York: Columbia University Press, 1969.

Leith, James A. *The Idea of Art as Propaganda in France, 1750–1799: A Study in the History of Ideas*. Toronto: University of Toronto Press, 1965.

Levasseur, Emile. *La Population française*. 3 vols. Paris: Arthur Rousseau, 1889–1892.

Levitine, George. *The Dawn of Bohemianism: The Barbu Rebellion and Primitivism in Neoclassical France*. University Park, Penn., and London: The Pennsylvania State University Press, 1978.

Lewis, Gwynne, and Colin Lucas, eds. *Beyond the Terror: Essays in French Regional and Social History, 1794–1815*. Cambridge: Cambridge University Press, 1983.

Locquin, Jean. *La Peinture d'histoire en France de 1747 à 1785*. Paris: H. Laurens, 1912.

Lortel, J. "David caricaturiste." *L'Art et les artistes* 18 (March 1914), pp. 273–75.

Lough, John. *Writer and Public in France*. Oxford: Clarendon Press, 1978.

Lucas, Colin. "Nobles, Bourgeois, and the Origins of the French Revolution." *Past and Present* 60 (1973), pp. 84–126.

Lucie-Smith, Edward. *The Art of Caricature*. Ithaca: Cornell University Press, 1981.

Lynch, John Gilbert Bohun. *A History of Caricature*. Boston: Little, Brown and Company, 1927.

Mahon, Denis. *Studies in Seicento Art and Art Theory*. Westport, Conn.: Greenwood Press, 1971.

Malcolm, James Peller. *An Historical Sketch of the Art of Caricaturing*. London: Longman, Hurst, Rees, Orme, and Brown, 1813.

Malvano, Laura. "Le Sujet politique en peinture: Evénements et histoire pendant les années de la Révolution." *Histoire et critique des arts* 13–14 (Spring 1980), pp. 31–65.

Mariette, Pierre-Jean. *Histoire des plus célèbres amateurs français et de leurs liaisons avec les artistes*. Edited by M. J. Dumesnil. Vol. 1, *1694–1774*. Paris: Vve Jules Renouard, 1858. Reprint. Geneva: Minkoff Reprint, 1973.

Mazauric, Claude. *Jacobinisme et Révolution*. Paris: Messidor/Editions sociales, 1984.

Mellor, Alec. *Histoire de l'anticléricalisme français*. Paris: Editions Henri Veyrier, 1978.

Melot, Michel. "Social Comment and Criticism." In *Lithography: Two Hundred Years of Art, History, and Technique*, edited by Domenico Porzio. New York: H. N. Abrams, 1983.

Mercier, Louis-Sebastien. *The Waiting City Paris 1782–88: An Abridgement of "Le Tableau de Paris."* Translated and edited by Helen Simpson. London: George G. Harrap and Company Ltd., 1953.

Mitchell, Hannah. "Art and the French Revolution: An Exhibition at the Musée Carnavalet." *History Workshop* 5 (Spring 1978), pp. 123–45.

Murray, William James. *The Right Wing Press in the French Revolution, 1789–1792*. Suffolk: The Boydell Press for the Royal Historical Society, 1986.

Musée Carnavalet, Paris. *L'Art de l'estampe et la Révolution française*. Exh. Cat. Paris: Musée Carnavalet, 1977.

Olivier, Louis. "Amateurs and Connoisseurs: Laymen and the Fine Arts in the Ancien Régime." Ph.D. diss., Johns Hopkins University, 1976.

Parker, Harold Talbot. *The Cult of Antiquity and the French Revolutionaries*. Chicago: University of Chicago Press, 1937.

Parton, James. *Caricature and Other Comic Art in All Times and Many Lands*. New York: Harper and Brothers, 1878.

Paston, George [pseud.]. *Social Caricature in the Eighteenth Century*. London: Methuen and Company, 1906.

Paulson, Ronald. *Representations of Revolution (1789–1820)*. New Haven and London: Yale University Press, 1983.

Paz, Octavio. "Metaphor." In *Conjunctions and Distortions*. Translated by Helen R. Lane. New York: Seaver Books, 1982.

Perkins, David. "A Definition of Caricature and Caricature and Recognition." *Studies in the Anthropology of Visual Communication* 2 (1975), pp. 1–24.

Pomian, Krzysztof. "Marchands, connoisseurs et curieux à Paris au XVIIIᵉ siècle." *Revue de l'art* 43 (1979), pp. 23–36.

Popkin, Jeremy D. "The Newspaper Press in French Political Thought, 1785–95." *Studies in Eighteenth Century Culture* 10 (1981), pp. 124–45.

_____ . *The Right-Wing Press in France, 1792–1800*. Chapel Hill: The University of North Carolina Press, 1980.

Posner, Donald. *Annibale Carracci: A Study in the Reform of Italian Painting around 1590*. 2 vols. London: Phaidon Press, 1971.

Renouvier, Jules. *Histoire de l'art pendant la Révolution*. 2 vols. Paris: Vᵛᵉ Jules Renouard, 1863.

Réstif de La Bretonne, Nicolas-Anne-Edme. *Les Nuits de Paris, ou le Spectateur nocturne*. 8 vols. Paris: Merigot Jeune, 1791–1794.

_____ . *Le Palais-Royal*. Paris: Louis-Michaud, 1908.

Revel, Jean-François. "L'Invention de la caricature." *L'Oeil* 109 (January 1964), pp. 12–21.

Ribeiro, Aileen. *Dress in Eighteenth-Century Europe, 1715–1789*. London: Batsford, 1984.

Roche, Daniel. *Le Peuple de Paris: Essai sur la culture populaire au XVIIIᵉ siècle*. Paris: Editions Aubier-Montaigne, 1981.

Root-Bernstein, Michelle Marie. "Revolution on the Boulevard: Parisian Popular Theater in the Late Eighteenth Century." Ph.D. diss., Princeton University, 1981.

Rosenblum, Robert. *Transformations in Late Eighteenth-Century Art*. Princeton: Princeton University Press, 1967.

Rudé, George. *The Crowd in the French Revolution*. Oxford: Clarendon Press, 1959.

_____ . *Revolutionary Europe, 1783–1815*. New York: Harper and Row, 1964.

Saisselin, R. G. "Neo-Classicism: Images of Public Virtue and Realities of Private Luxury." *Art History* 4 (March 1981), pp. 14–36.

Schnapper, Antoine. *Jacques-Louis David, témoin de son temps*. Paris: Bibliothèque des arts; Fribourg: Office du livre, 1980.

Schultz, Juergen. "Introduction." In *Caricature and Its Role in Graphic Satire*. Exh. cat. Providence: Museum of Art, Rhode Island School of Design, 1971.

Scott, Samuel F., and Barry Rothaus. *Historical Dictionary of the French Revolution, 1789–1799*. Westport, Conn.: Greenwood Press, 1985.

Sewell, William H., Jr. *Work and Revolution in France: The Language of Labor from the Old Regime to 1848–*. Cambridge: Cambridge University Press, 1980.

Shikes, Ralph E. *The Indignant Eye: The Artist as Social Critic in Prints and Drawings from the Fifteenth Century to Picasso*. Boston: Beacon Press, 1969.

Soboul, Albert. *The French Revolution, 1789–1799*. Translated by Alan Forrest and Colin Jones. New York: Random House, 1975.

_____ . *The Sans-Culottes*. Translated by Remy Inglis Hall. Garden City, N.Y.: Anchor Books, 1972.

Sorel, Albert. *Europe and the French Revolution*. Translated and edited by Alfred Cobban and J. W. Hunt. London: Collins and the Fontana Library, 1969.

Stanton, Domna C. *The Aristocrat as Art*. New York: Columbia University Press, 1980.

Stewart, John Hall. *A Documentary Survey of the French Revolution*. Toronto and Ontario: The Macmillan Company, 1951.

Thiers, Adolphe. *The Mississippi Bubble*. Edited and translated by Frank S. Fiske. New York: W. A. Townsend and Company, 1859.

Thurner, Auguste. *Les Transformations de l'opéra-comique*. Paris: Castel, 1865.

Tiersot, Julien. *Histoire de la chanson populaire en France*. Paris: Plon-Nourrit, 1889.

Tocqueville, Alexis de. *The Old Regime and the French Revolution*. Translated by Stuart Gilbert. Garden City, N.Y.: Doubleday, 1955.

Verlet, Pierre. "Le Commerce des objets d'art et les marchands merciers à Paris au XVIIIᵉ siècle." *Annales, économies, sociétés, civilisations* 13 (1958), pp. 10–29.

Vigée-Lebrun, Elisabeth-Louise. *Souvenirs de Madame Vigée-Lebrun*. 3 vols. Paris: Bibliothèque Charpentier, 1867.

Vovelle, Michel. *The Fall of the French Monarchy, 1787–1792*. Translated by Susan Burke. Cambridge: Cambridge University Press, 1984.

_____ . *Religion et Révolution*. Paris: Hachette et Cie, 1976.

_____ . *La Révolution française: Images et récit, 1789–1799*. 5 vols. Paris: Editions Messidor, Livre Club Diderot, 1986.

Walter, Gérard. *Hébert et le Père Duchesne*. Paris: J. B. Janin, 1946.

Wechsler, Judith. *A Human Comedy*. Chicago: The University of Chicago Press, 1982.

Weiner, Margery. *The French Exiles, 1789–1815*. London: John Murray, 1960.

Wildenstein, G. "David, auteur de caricatures contre les Anglais commandées par la Convention." In *Omagiu lui George Oprescu cu prilejul împlinirii a 80 de ani*. Edited by T. Vianu and M. Popescu. Bucharest: Editura Academiei Republicii Populare Romine, 1961.

Woronoff, Denis. *The Thermidorean Regime and the Directory, 1794–1799*. Translated by Julian Jackson. Cambridge: Cambridge University Press, 1984.

Wright, Thomas. *A History of Caricature and Grotesque in Literature and Art*. London: Virtue Brothers and Company, 1865. Reprint. New York: F. Ungar Publishing Company, 1968.

Wrigley, Richard. "Censorship and Anonymity in Eighteenth-Century Art Criticism." *Oxford Art Journal* 6 (1983), pp. 17–28.

Zweig, Stefan. *Marie-Antoinette: The Portrait of an Average Woman*. New York: Viking Press, 1934.